Dulcedo Spiritus

THE SPIRITUAL TEACHING
OF THE NEW TESTAMENT

O God, grant me the strength to be gentle...
And enough calmness to be strong...
Grant me Thy love which will make
   me stronger than death —
So that with that love
I may possess that mildness
at whose touch difficulties
easily give way.

Dom Pie de Stemptinne

The Spiritual Teaching
of the New Testament

JULES LEBRETON, S.J.

translated by James E. Whalen   *Copy 3*

THE NEWMAN PRESS *Westminster, Maryland*
1960

Nihil obstat

EDWARD A. CERNY, S.S., S.T.D.

CENSOR LIBRORUM

Imprimatur

FRANCIS P. KEOUGH, D.D.

ARCHBISHOP OF BALTIMORE
April 5, 1960

The Nihil Obstat *and the* Imprimatur *are official declarations that a
book or pamphlet is free of doctrinal and moral error. No implication
is contained therein that those who have granted the* Nihil Obstat *and
the* Imprimatur *agree with the opinions expressed.*

The present translation was made from the fourteenth printing of
LUMEN CHRISTI, La doctrine spirituelle du Nouveau Testament,
published by Beauchesne et ses Fils, rue de Rennes, Paris, in 1948.

Library of Congress Catalog Card Number: 60–10725

Preface

The Apostolic Constitution *Deus Scientiarum Dominus* imposes on Faculties of theology the teaching of ascetical and mystical theology. This teaching should not be confused with spiritual conferences whose purpose is the students' ascetical and mystical formation. The professor does not aim directly at spiritual formation; he wishes to make known the Church's doctrine. This doctrine can be considered either in its present-day synthesis, or in the principal phases of its development, or in the different schools which transmit and interpret it.

As professor of the history of Christian origins, I have endeavored to grasp this ascetical and mystical theology in its origin, in the New Testament. I wanted to attempt, for spiritual doctrine, a historical study guided by the same method I had applied to the theology of the Trinity.[1] The difficulties of the task are great: we do not find in the New Testament a ready-made synthesis, but only fragments which must be compared with one another and assigned the importance they deserve in the constitution of the whole. But these passages, on the other hand, are stamped with a profundity

[1] Cf. the author's *Histoire du Dogme de la Trinité*, 2 vols., Paris, Beauchesne, 1910, and in tr., *History of the Dogma of the Trinity: from its origins to the Council of Nicaea; Vol. 1: The Origins,* tr. by Algar Thorold, London, Burns & Oates; N. Y., Benziger, 1939.

we shall find in no other document. Our Lord Himself has told us so: "The words that I have spoken to you are spirit and life" (Jn. 6:64). We shall try to grasp these words in all their force, directly, without gloss. Assuredly, we shall not isolate them from the Church's interpretation; but we shall not seek to give them the explicit development which, little by little, has been elaborated through the effort of theologians and the saints.

Our principal sources will be the Gospel and the letters of the apostles, especially those of St. Paul. In another work I have studied the life and teaching of our Lord.[2] I shall not resume that study under the same aspect, or with the same objective. Here I do not wish to recount Jesus' life, nor to expose in its entirety all His teaching, but to gather together from His life and words the ideal of Christian perfection and the rules of conduct He proposes to us. St. Paul and the other apostles will allow us to complete this study: in their lives we shall find models—ever so much less perfect, but purely human—whose slow and laborious formation provides us with many valuable lessons. Their teaching, moreover, posterior to the foundation of the Church, permits us to attain, in its living reality, that divinely instituted society, that Body of Christ, concerning which the Gospel furnished us only presages and promises. In this study of Christ and the nascent Church, we shall be guided by Mary, Mother of Jesus and our Mother. She will say to us again what she said to the people of Cana, "Do whatever he tells you" (Jn. 2:5). And she will secure the grace for us to do this.

[2] *La vie et l'enseignement de Jésus-Christ Notre Seigneur,* Paris, Beauchesne, 1931, and in tr., *The Life and Teaching of Jesus Christ Our Lord,* tr. by Francis Day, London, Burns & Oates, 1935; N. Y., Macmillan, 1949.

Translator's Note

For the original texts of the Latin and Greek Fathers of the Church, Father Lebreton has made frequent reference to the *Patrologia Latina* (*P.L.*) and *Patrologia Graeca* (*P.G.*) of J.-P. Migne, Paris, 1844 ff.

For the English translations of these texts, the reader may be referred to the following general collections:

Library of the Fathers, ed. by Pusey, Keble and Newman, Oxford, 1838–1888, 45 vols.

The Ante-Nicene Christian Library, ed. by A. Roberts and J. Donaldson, Edinburgh, 1866–1872, 24 vols. with a supplementary volume, ed. by A. Menzies, Edinburgh, 1897.

The Ante-Nicene Fathers. American reprint of the Edinburgh edition, revised by A. Cleveland Coxe, Buffalo, 1884–1886, 8 vols. with a supplement by A. Menzies (vol. 9) and A. Cleveland Coxe (vol. 10). The 10th vol. contains a bibliographical synopsis and a general index. Reprint edition by Eerdmans, Grand Rapids, Michigan, 1950–51.

A Select Library of Nicene and Post-Nicene Fathers of the Christian Church, ed. by Ph. Schaff and H. Wace, Buffalo and New York, 1886–1900, 28 vols.

Works of St. Augustine, a new trans. ed. by Marcus Dods, T.

Clark, Edinburgh; N.Y., Scribner's, 1872–1934, 15 vols.
Translations of Christian Literature, ed. by W. J. Sparrow-Simp-
son and W. K. Lowther Clarke. This collection, published
by the Society for Promoting Christian Knowledge (SPCK)
in London, comprises a series of *a*) Greek Texts, *b*) Latin
Texts, *c*) Liturgical Texts, *d*) Oriental Texts, London,
1917 ff.
Loeb Classical Library, N.Y., Macmillan and Harvard University
Press.

For more recent collections, the reader is referred to the cur-
rent series:
Ancient Christian Writers (ACW), Westminster (Md.), The
Newman Press, 1946 ff.
Fathers of the Church (FC), N.Y., Fathers of the Church, Inc.,
1948 ff.

In the present work by Lebreton, we refer only to these last
two collections. Other recent English translations, both of the
Fathers and of other religious literature referred to by Lebreton,
are mentioned whenever possible.

The translator wishes to take this opportunity to express his
gratitude for the valuable assistance of the editorial staff of The
Newman Press in the preparation of Father Lebreton's book for
the English speaking public.

James E. Whalen

Villanova University
Philadelphia, Pennsylvania
March 6, 1960

Contents

THE SPIRITUAL TEACHING
OF THE NEW TESTAMENT

chapter 1

❖❖❖❖❖❖❖❖❖

God, Our Creator and Father

A Scribe, having heard Jesus' discussion with the Sadducees and seeing that He had answered them well, asked Him this question, "What is the first commandment of all?" Jesus answered him, "The first commandment of all is, 'Hear, O Israel! The Lord our God is one God. And thou shalt love the Lord thy God with thy whole heart, and with thy whole soul, and with thy whole mind, and with thy whole strength' . . . And the second is like it, 'Thou shalt love thy neighbor as thyself.' There is no other commandment greater than these" (Mk. 12:28-31).[1]

This reply of Jesus enables us to touch the rock on which the whole Christian religion rests—faith in God alone. To formulate this faith, Jesus revived the daily prayer of every Israelite, the Shema; and the Scribe recognized it at once and echoed it back: "Well answered, Master, thou hast said truly that he is one and

[1] For the English translation of passages from the New Testament we employ the Confraternity edition (1945), and for passages from the Old, the Douay-Rheims version. (Trans. note.)

that there is no other besides him; and that he should be loved with the whole heart, and with the whole understanding, and with the whole soul, and with one's whole strength; and that to love one's neighbor as oneself is a greater thing than all holocausts and sacrifices." And Jesus, seeing that he had answered wisely, said to him, "Thou art not far from the kingdom of God" (Mk. 12:32–34).

It is the faith of Israel, then, that gives to Christian faith the basic formula on which the huge edifice will be erected. The Mosaic and prophetic revelation is not effaced, but fulfilled, by the Gospel. The affirmation of the one God, only Lord, loved above all things, will be sacred to the Christians as much as and even more than it was to the Jews; this is what the martyrs will confess unto death. To this intransigence of faith will be united, more ardent than ever before, the jealousy of love. The Son of God will have Christians understand, as no man had ever yet understood, what it is to love God above all things.

In this luminous revelation there will gradually appear the Envoy of God, His Christ and His Son, not only as revealer, but as object of the revelation: "This is everlasting life, that they may know thee, the only true God, and him whom thou hast sent, Jesus Christ" (Jn. 17:3). And close to Him, revealed by Him, given by Him, Christian faith will attain the other Advocate, the Holy Spirit. But this flowering of Christian faith, far from hurting the unity of the "one true God," will make Christians understand it more deeply as the ideal model of unity they should strive to realize among themselves, "that they may be one even as we are" (Jn. 17:11; cf. 17:22).

1. JUDAISM'S FAITH IN GOD

Faith in God's unity governs the whole Christian religion and stamps on its adoration the intransigence which opposes it to the whole of paganism. St. Paul ceases not to inculcate this in the Christians: "We know . . . that there is no God but one. For even if there are what are called gods, whether in heaven or on earth (for indeed there are many gods, and many lords), yet for us there is only one God, the Father from whom are all things, and we unto him; and one Lord, Jesus Christ, through whom are all things, and we through him" (1 Cor. 8:4–6).

It is in the doxologies, especially, that this affirmation is solemnly repeated:[2]

To him who is able to strengthen you in accordance with my gospel, and the preaching of Jesus Christ . . . to the only wise God, through Jesus Christ, be honor forever and ever. Amen (Rom. 16:25, 27).

To the King of the ages, who is immortal, invisible, the one only God, be honor and glory forever and ever. Amen (1 Tim. 1:17).

To the only God our Savior, through Jesus Christ our Lord, belong glory and majesty, dominion and authority, before all time, and now, and forever. Amen (Jude 25).

It is by no means only the properly divine names of "God" and "Lord" which are thus exclusively reserved to the heavenly Father and to Jesus Christ. Christian faith goes farther in its intransigence: it does not tolerate attributing with the same value both to God and men praises or titles. To the man who greeted Him, calling Him "Good Master," Jesus straightway replied, "Why dost thou call me good? No one is good but God only" (Mk. 10:18).[3] And elsewhere, addressing the Jews, He tells them:

Do not you be called "Rabbi"; for one is your Master, and all you are brothers. And call no one on earth your father; for one is your Father, who is in heaven. Neither be called masters; for one only is your Master, the Christ" (Mt. 23:8–10).

[2] On the use of these formulas in the Christian worship of the first centuries, one can consult E. Peterson, ΕΙΣ ΘΕΟΣ, *Epigraphische, Formgeschichtliche und Religionsgeschichtliche Untersuchungen,* Göttingen, Vandenhoeck, 1926, pp. 130–140.

[3] We shall not conclude from this that the Son of God cannot, Himself, be also called good with all the force of that term; but Jesus' questioner had not yet recognized Him as the Son of God; he saw in Him only a man. Jesus wants to teach him that all human goodness is nothing compared with the goodness of God. (Cf. our *Histoire du Dogme de la Trinité,* t. I, pp. 309–311.)

These statements have been inscribed deep in the Christian conscience. The disciple of Jesus Christ fails not to recognize either social distinctions or family relationships: he renders to Caesar the things that are Caesar's (Mt. 22:21); he obeys religiously the divine precept to honor his father and his mother (Mt. 15:4; 19:19). But neither this authority nor this love can prevail over the divine rights of God and His Christ; once opposed to them, they become self-condemnatory.

This jealous intransigence has consecrated the liberty of the Christian conscience: on the Jews, constrained by so many human traditions, it has bestowed the liberty of the children of God: "Every plant that my heavenly Father has not planted will be rooted up. Let them alone; blind guides they are of blind men" (Mt. 15:13–14). To the pagans, subjected to so much servitude, it has said, "You have been bought with a price; do not become the slaves of men" (1 Cor. 7:23). The model of this liberty will be the Apostle: "With me it is a very small matter to be judged by you or by man's tribunal. Nay I do not even judge my own self . . . he who judges me is the Lord" (1 Cor. 4:3–4).

God our only Father; Christ our only Master, Judge, Lord: the whole of human life is governed by an exclusive adoration, a jealous love, an uncompromising faith. The unity of life is ensured; can we say that, by the same token, there is ensured its nobility and fruitfulness? Here everything depends on the God to whom man gives himself. In the epoch of Christian origins we used to find in pagan religions many fanatics who kept repeating to their god, "Thou art all for me!" Peterson has cited many examples of this.[4] Here I shall recall only that passage of the rhetorician Aelius Aristides, contemporary of Marcus Aurelius, recounting one of his visions: at the sight of Asclepius appearing before him, he exclaims, " 'There is only thou!' cried I to the god; and he said to me, 'There is only thou!' " [5]

The god echoes the man. This god is, after all, only a play of

---

[4] ΕΙΣ ΘΕΟΣ. Particularly in the cult of Serapis: pp. 227-240.

[5] *Discours sacré*, publ. Dindorf, IV, pp. 517–518. This text is quoted more at length in *Histoire du Dogme de la Trinité*, t. II, p. 67.

the human imagination: man is not raised to God; God is degraded to the level of man.

The Jewish religion knew not these indignities; it received its faith from a divine revelation to which it remained submissive. Yet even there human weaknesses made themselves felt: dogmatic intransigence is colored too often by a national exclusiveness. We hear it in the commentary of Aqiba on *Exodus:* the nations ask Israel, "Where has thy beloved gone? We want to look for him with you." But the Israelites answer them, "You have no part with him at all; my beloved belongs to me and I to him."[6]

2. CHRISTIANITY'S FAITH IN GOD

In contrast with this exclusive Judaism, Christianity appears as a completely new and ever so rich flowering of the Mosaic revelation. The starting point for this new revelation is the Incarnation of the Son of God and His message. Jesus has told us, "No one knows the Son except the Father; nor does anyone know the Father except the Son, and him to whom the Son chooses to reveal him" (Mt. 11:27). St. John will recall this at the conclusion of the prologue to his Gospel: "No one has at any time seen God. The only-begotten Son, who is in the bosom of the Father, he has revealed him" (Jn. 1:18).[7]

---

[6] *Mekilta de-Rabbi Ishmael: a critical edition on the basis of the manuscripts and early editions,* with an English trans. by J. Lauterbach (The Schiff Library of Jewish Classics), Philadelphia, The Jewish Publication Society of America, 1933: on *Exodus,* XV, 2. On the religious state of the nations with regard to Palestinian Judaism, one can read J. Bonsirven, S.J., *Le Judaisme palestinien au temps de Jésus-Christ: sa théologie* (Biblio. de théologie historique), Paris, Beauchesne, 1934, t. I, pp. 99–107. He concludes: "These statements put us in close touch with the way Jewish thinking conceives every general view of the world as a function of Israel: its particularism governs and subjects to itself every possible universalism." We must admit, however, that it is only after the great upheavals and disasters of the years 70 and 133 that this particularism is closed to all proselytizing and becomes sectarian.

[7] These affirmations of Our Lord have illumined the whole theology of

Christian revelation fails not to acknowledge Israel's prerogatives: the God preached by Jesus is "the God of Abraham,
and the God of Isaac, and the God of Jacob" (Mt. 22:32). He
it is, also, whom the apostles preach: "The God of Abraham and
the God of Isaac and the God of Jacob, the God of our fathers,
has glorified his Son Jesus" (Acts 3:13). Heir to Israel's prerogatives, the Church will love to call herself "the Church of
God" (Acts 20:28), "the people of God" (Heb. 4:9; 1 Pt.
2:10). "Now I mean this: the Law which was made four hundred and thirty years later does not annul the covenant which
was ratified by God, so as to make the promise void. For if the
right to inherit be from the Law, it is no longer from the promise.
But God gave it to Abraham by promise" (Gal. 3:17–18).

This argumentation of the Apostle, going back beyond Moses
to Abraham, and elsewhere to creation,[8] we find already in our
Lord's preaching. It appears sometimes in order to rule out a
toleration;[9] more often than not, to give to the religion of Israel

---

the Church, especially in her struggle against Gnosticism; she has disengaged the essential themes which overthrow the whole of Gnosticism: the
mysteries of God naturally transcend every created intelligence; God, out
of love, has revealed them to us through His Son, and this knowledge has
become the patrimony, not of a privileged caste, but of the entire Church.
Here one may care to read again the fine texts of St. Irenaeus, especially
Adv. Haer., IV, 6, and in tr., *The Treatise of Irenaeus of Lugdunum against
the Heretics,* tr. by F. Hitchcock, London, SPCK, 1916.

[8] On this argumentation cf. Bonsirven, *Exégèse rabbinique et exégèse
paulinienne,* pp. 267–268: "It is in the Church that the divine prophecies
reach their perfect fulfillment. Indeed, the promise made to Abraham,
which is at the beginning of the historical intervention of the supernatural
in the world, is truly realized only in Jesus Christ and in the Christians
who compose His Body. Israel shares, no doubt, in the promise, and we
can call her in some measure its holder. Still, the Law appears as a re-
strainer of the promise, almost as its antagonist, because the Law compromises its complete and universal fulfillment. In the era of the promise,
then, the history of Israel takes the form of an intermediate and prepara-
tory period."

[9] Thus in the question of divorce: "They said to him, 'Why then did Moses
command to give a written notice of dismissal, and to put her away?' He
said to them, 'Because Moses, by reason of the hardness of your heart,

the broad perspectives which the legalism of the Scribes tended to narrow. Here the contemplation of the God-Creator plays a very efficacious role: the God of Israel is also the God who created heaven and earth. Israel knew that, but did not draw from it the religious consequences which Christian revelation made evident thereby: if everything in the world is the work of God, then there is nothing in the world essentially impure.[10] And, what is even more significant, we are to recognize in all men creatures of God and objects of His fatherly providence. If this providence watches over both the good and the wicked, our love must extend both to our friends and to our enemies: we must be perfect as our heavenly Father is perfect (Mt. 5:43–48). The legislation of the Sabbath itself will also have to be transformed in this light: God's rest, which men strive to venerate and to imitate, is not an idle repose: God works unceasingly; Jesus, like the Father, works unceasingly, and He heals men on the Sabbath (Jn. 5:16–17).

These few passages already foreshadow in what sense Israel's religion will be transformed in the light of the revelation brought by the Son of God. A better understanding of God's transcendence will give a better grasp of His immense sovereign domain: His kingdom, unlimited in space as in time, imposes itself on all men and summons them all. Up to the time of our Lord's passion, His Messianic activity and that of His apostles will be reserved to the house of Israel. But this reserve is only temporary, and as such it is presented by Jesus: "And I, if I be lifted up from the earth, will draw all things[11] to myself" (Jn. 12:32). After His resurrection, the last instructions He gives His apostles will sweep away all barriers: "All power in heaven and on earth has been given to me. Go, therefore, and make disciples of all nations, baptizing them in the name of the Father, and of the Son, and of the Holy Spirit, teaching them to observe all that I have

---

permitted you to put away your wives; but it was not so from the beginning' " (Mt. 19:7–8).

[10] Acts 10:10–16, 28.

[11] Father Lebreton's translation reads "all men," following the original Greek. (Trans. note.)

commanded you; and behold, I am with you all days, even unto the consummation of the world."[12]

At the same time that this domain is universal, it is interior and sovereign, and its requirements cannot be divided. God requires that He alone be adored, He alone served. To the devil who asked Him to prostrate Himself before him, Jesus replies, "Begone, Satan! for it is written, 'The Lord thy God shalt thou worship and him only shalt thou serve' " (Mt. 4:10).

This adoration imposes on the Christian a total submission: the whole will of God is sacred to him; there can be no question of disputing it, of asking the reason for it. Thus in the problem, insoluble for us, of predestination, the proper attitude for us is one of submission, full of faith and trust.

Thou sayest to me: "Why then does he still find fault? For who resists his will?" O man, who art thou to reply to God? Does the object moulded say to him who moulded it: "Why hast thou made me thus?" Or is not the potter master of his clay, to make from the same mass one vessel for honorable, another for ignoble use? (Rom 9:19–21).

Here we shall not see a predestination to final ends, heaven or hell; that is not the question. It is a matter concerning the present life: God has given each of us his lot, whether brilliant or commonplace, and no one has the right to ask Him to account for His choice. For everyone this existence, be it lofty or humble, is surrounded by graces which will make of it, if man so wishes, an upright and holy existence. But it will still remain true that the starting point of these lives, their setting, their circumstances, and their helps are chosen for each one by a sovereign will which we have no right to judge. This ever so powerful and wise will of the Father gives us a security which no other will could give us,

12 Mt. 28:18–20. On this question of the universality of the Gospel message, cf. M. Meinertz, *Jesus und die Heidenmission*, 2nd ed. (Münster, Aschendorff, 1925), and in the *Histoire générale comparée des Missions*, publ. Baron Descamps (Paris, Plon, 1932), the chapter we have devoted to the *Evangile de Jésus-Christ*, pp. 35–36.

much less our own;[13] but to accept this guarantee, we must believe in God.

The adoration of the will of God should not be, for the Christian, simple submission, but earnest love, tending to the accomplishment of this holy will. The Son of God has given us an example of this from the first moment of His life: "Behold, I come . . . to do thy will, O God" (Heb. 10:7). When man has kept up this service throughout his lifetime, he will await his reward only from the faithfulness and mercy of God: "When you have done everything that was commanded you, say, 'We are unprofitable servants; we have done what it was our duty to do' " (Lk. 17:10). In justice, we have a right to nothing; but God deigned to promise us that He Himself would be our reward.[14] In the Old Testament, He had given, beneath many a symbol, this assurance to the patriarchs and prophets; from the start of His ministry, in the Sermon on the Mount, the Son of God solemnly promulgated this promise: to the poor, the meek, the afflicted, the hungry, the merciful, the pure, the peacemakers, the persecuted, He has promised happiness, that is to say, the possession of the kingdom, the sight of God.[15]

He knows our nature, He who has created it and taken it up. He knows that it has been made for God and that only the possession of God can fully satisfy it. If human life has a meaning, if its efforts are not to go unrewarded, it is there that it must

---

[13] We can recall the Platonic myth of Er the Pamphylian [*Repub.* X, 15, p. 617E, and in tr. *The Dialogues of Plato*, tr. by B. Jowett (Oxford, 1892), p. 334.]: after their previous existences, men, on the threshold of a new life, are called to choose its condition. Their imprudent choices involve almost all of them in unhappiness. But they alone are responsible for it.

[14] On this gratuitous nature of the eternal reward, one may read again St. Francis de Sales, *Traité de l'amour de Dieu*, XI, 6, quoted below, pp. 150–151, and in tr. *Treatise on the Love of God*, Dublin, Duffy; London, Thomas Jones, 1852, pp. 449–450; new ed. tr. by H. B. Mackey, Westminster (Md.), Newman, 1942.

[15] Here I shall not take up again a commentary on the beatitudes. The reader can refer, if he so desires, to what I have said about them: *Vie et enseignement de Jésus-Christ*, t. I, pp. 171–197; and below, pp. 142–154.

tend. And Jesus opens for us the way we must follow to arrive at that unique and essential beatitude. In the course of His preaching, He will not weary of confirming this promise at the same time that He formulates anew the requirements of His service; thus, to the young man: "If thou wilt be perfect, go, sell what thou hast, and give to the poor, and thou shalt have treasure in heaven; and come, follow me" (Mt. 19:21). And, on this same occasion, when St. Peter reminds Him, in the name of the Twelve, that they have left all to follow Him, He replies, "Amen I say to you that you who have followed me, in the regeneration when the Son of Man shall sit on the throne of his glory, shall also sit on twelve thrones, judging the twelve tribes of Israel. And everyone who has left house, or brothers, or sisters, or father, or mother, or wife, or children, or lands, for my name's sake, shall receive a hundredfold, and shall possess life everlasting" (Mt. 19:27-29).

In comparison with this beatitude which fills all our desires, in comparison with this possession of an infinite good, no other good can be put in the balance. And if the option is imposed on man, he must sacrifice all for the kingdom. Thus the man who has found a treasure in a field, must sell all that he has and buy the field (Mt. 13:44); the merchant who has found a pearl of great price must sell all that he has and buy the pearl (*Ibid.,* 45-46). This is wisdom, and since it is a question of the kingdom of God, the unique goal of our lives, it is our duty.

It is in this light that we must read again the conditions for service, as Jesus proposes them to His disciples:

He who loves his father and his mother more than me is not worthy of me, and he who loves son or daughter more than me is not worthy of me. And he who does not take up his cross and follow me, is not worthy of me. He who finds his life will lose it, and he who loses his life for my sake, will find it (Mt. 10:37-39; cf. Mt. 16:24-26).

If anyone comes to me and does not hate his father and mother, and wife and children, and brothers and sisters, yes, and even his own life, he cannot be my disciple. And he who does not carry his cross and follow me, cannot be my disciple (Lk. 14:26-27).

He who loves his life, loses it; and he who hates his life in this world, keeps it unto life everlasting. If anyone serve me, let him follow me; and where I am there also shall my servant be. If anyone serve me, my Father will honor him (Jn. 12:25–26).

These requirements of Jesus, the Apostle St. Paul made the law of his life and imposes them, in turn, on his disciples:

The things that were gain to me, these, for the sake of Christ I have counted loss. Nay more, I count everything loss because of the excelling knowledge of Jesus Christ, my Lord. For his sake I have suffered the loss of all things, and I count them as dung that I may gain Christ and be found in him (Phil. 3:7–9).

It is this perspective of the kingdom of God that makes us understand the terrible condemnation of scandal:

If thy hand or thy foot is an occasion of sin to thee, cut it off and cast it from thee! It is better for thee to enter life maimed or lame, than, having two hands or two feet, to be cast into the everlasting fire. And if thy eye is an occasion of sin to thee, pluck it out and cast it from thee! It is better for thee to enter into life with one eye than, having two eyes, to be cast into the hell of fire (Mt. 18:8–9).

These texts we shall come across later on when we study the teachings given by Christ to His disciples. But we must consider them, on this first contact we are making with the Gospel, in order to grasp in them the nature of the new law: it is a law of love, but a law, nonetheless; and its exigencies are as pressing as the exigencies of love.

The omnipotence of God, moreover, better understood, lightens the burden of this law: if human frailty cannot raise itself to the height of God's requirements, God Himself will carry it there. For a rich man to be saved is a greater miracle than for a camel to pass through the eye of a needle; but God can do it, for "all things are possible with God" (Mk. 10:27). With the same assurance John the Baptist said, "God is able out of these stones to raise up children to Abraham" (Mt. 3:9). And St. Paul: "They also, if they do not continue in unbelief, will be grafted in; for God is able to graft them back" (Rom. 11:23). The angel Gabriel, announcing to Mary the great miracle of the virgin conception, will say to her, "Nothing shall be impossible with God" (Lk. 1:37).

This faith in the omnipotence of God gives to the Apostle his assurance amidst every calamity and every danger: "If God is for us, who is against us? . . . For I am sure that neither death, nor life, nor angels, nor principalities, nor things present, nor things to come, nor powers, nor height, nor depth, nor any other creature will be able to separate us from the love of God, which is in Christ Jesus our Lord" (Rom. 8:31, 38–39).

We see from all these passages the nature of this omnipotence: it is never conceived as an unconscious, irresistible dynamism which we can acquire by magic.[16] It is a force which God can, if He so wishes, communicate to men and which reveals its origin through its religious and moral efficacy.

His most exalted work is the communication of life; Israel used to sing of it: "The Lord killeth and maketh alive, he bringeth down to hell and bringeth back again."[17] This divine prerogative will appear more evident than ever in Jesus' resurrection: this great miracle is attributed either to the Father, who has resurrected His Son,[18] or to the Son, who is, Himself, the source of life.[19]

It is here, especially, that God is revealed as He Who "killeth and maketh alive . . . bringeth down to hell and bringeth back

[16] This superstition, so widely diffused in paganism, is encountered among the neo-Platonists, in Plotinus himself (for example, *Ennead* IV, 4, 10, publ. Bréhier, pp. 147–148 and in tr. by S. Mackenna, N. Y., Pantheon, 1957), in Porphyry (*Philosophie des Oracles;* cf. J. Bidez, *Vie de Porphyre,* Ghent, 1913, pp. 17 ff.), and still again in Jamblichus.

[17] 1 Kgs. 2:6; cf. Dt. 32:39; Tob. 13:2; Wis. 16:13.

[18] Acts 3:15,26; 4:10; 5:30; 10:40; 13:30 ff.; Rom. 4:24; 8:11; 10:9; 1 Cor. 6:14; 15:15; 2 Cor. 4:14; Gal. 1:1; Eph. 1:20; Col. 2:12; 1 Thes. 1:10; 1 Pt. 1:21.

[19] Jn. 2:19. These two attributions are not mutually opposed; we find them both in the same letter of St. Ignatius of Antioch: *Smyrn.* 2 and 7, and in tr. *The Epistles of St. Ignatius of Antioch,* tr. by J. Kleist, S.J. (ACW 1), Westminster (Md.), Newman, 1946, pp. 90 and 92. Cf. *Histoire du Dogme de la Trinité,* t. I, p. 344, n. 9, and p. 511.

again." Thereby the divine omnipotence is more firmly understood: it is no longer only a discretionary power which extends
as far as God wishes it to;[20] it is a sovereign power which knows
not the mortal limits that death imposes on our actions.

The life-giving power of God shines forth in the Resurrection;
but to discerning eyes it is revealed by its daily action. Jesus calls
our attention to this: "Which of you by being anxious about it
can add to his stature a single cubit? And as for clothing, why
are you anxious? See how the lilies of the field grow; they
neither toil nor spin, yet I say to you that not even Solomon in all
his glory was arrayed like one of these" (Mt. 6:27–29). St.
Paul, too, will recall to the Corinthians the life-giving action of
God: He alone can make the plants grow: "I have planted,
Apollo watered, but God has given the growth. So then neither he
who plants is anything, nor he who waters, but God who gives the
growth" (1 Cor. 3:6–7).

In this teaching given to the Corinthians, the Apostle makes
use of the daily spectacle of vegetable life to enable them to catch
a glimpse of the divine action of grace; and, indeed, it is God's
creative action that prepares us to understand better His intimate
and all-powerful action in our justification. Life will always be
for us an unfathomable mystery,[21] even in its most lowly manifestations. Jesus was wont to say to His disciples, "Thus is the
kingdom of God, as though a man should cast seed into the
earth, then sleep and rise, night and day, and the seed should
sprout and grow without his knowing it" (Mk. 4:26–27). The
God who makes the seed grow which is sown in the ground, is
also the God who sows in our souls the seed of the kingdom and
makes it germinate there.

From these mysteries of natural life, the disciples of Jesus will

[20] "Whatsoever the Lord pleased he hath done" (Ps. 134:6).
[21] The mother of the Machabees recalled this to her sons in order to sustain their hope in the vivifying action of God: "I know not how you were
formed in my womb: for I neither gave you breath, nor soul, nor life,
neither did I frame the limbs of every one of you. But the Creator of the
world, that formed the nativity of man, and that found out the origin of
all, he will restore to you again in his mercy, both breath and life . . ."
(2 Mach. 7:22–23).

be led to recognize the mysteries of the life of grace and to believe in them. They will recognize God's omnipotence in the salvation of the rich (Mk. 10:27), in the forgiveness of sins (Lk. 7:49), in the miraculous efficacy of faith (Mk. 9:22). St. Paul will say, "I can do all things in him who strengthens me" (Phil. 4:13). And the life-giving power of God which they adore in Jesus' resurrection, they will acknowledge it also in Jesus vivifying whom He will: "As the Father raises the dead and gives them life, even so the Son also gives life to whom he will" (Jn. 5:21).

3. GOD, OUR FATHER

All-powerful, intimate, life-giving, the action of God in us is not only the action of a Creator, but of a Father. The paternity of God was not unknown among the Jews;[22] but only the Son could fully bring this doctrine to light and give to it, in His teaching as in His life, its rightful place—the pre-eminence. From the time of the Sermon on the Mount, Jesus invites His disciples to a continual intimacy with the Father, who sees in secret and to whom they should offer their prayer, their alms, their fasts, all their justice (Mt. 6:1–18). They must strive to become children of the heavenly Father by imitating His perfect holiness and especially His love, which excludes no one (Mt. 5:48). They must have a filial trust in this Father, who cares for them and who will procure for them whatever is necessary (Mt. 6:25–34). Their prayer will be the *Pater* (Mt. 6:9–13; Lk. 11:2–4). The prayer of the children of God should rise up to their Father in all trust: "If you, evil as you are, know how to give good gifts to your children, how much more will your heavenly Father give the Good Spirit to those who ask him!" (Lk. 11:13). It is above all in forgiveness that this fatherly mercy bursts forth: here one should read again the whole parable of the prodigal son (Lk. 15:11–32). What moves us the most in this scene is the intimate character bestowed on it by Jesus. The whole religious drama of humanity is reflected in the humble story of the father and his

22 Cf. Bonsirven, *Le Judaisme palestinien*, t. I, pp. 138–139.

two children: one, wayward and penitent; the other, faithful to his duty, but lacking in pity for his brother. The father bends over both with the same solicitude: he celebrates the return of the prodigal; and as for the elder son, who considers himself poorly requited for his long fidelity, he makes him understand the value of his communal life with the father: "Son, thou art always with me, and all that is mine is thine." [23]

This family intimacy makes the offense appear more serious, but also the repentance more sorrowful, the pardon more moving, more full of love. The feast is not only the token of reconciliation accorded the prodigal: it is, first and foremost, the irresistible impulse of the father: "We were bound to make merry and rejoice" (Lk. 15:32). This wonderful trait is found again in the other parables of mercy, that of the drachma, that of the sheep (Lk. 15:1–10): all heaven rejoices over the conversion of the sinner. We recognize there the message of the Son of God revealing to us the Father's love.

In the talks at the Last Supper these revelations will be still more intimate and more touching:

In my Father's house there are many mansions. Were it not so, I should have told you, because I go to prepare a place for you. And if I go and prepare a place for you, I am coming again, and I will take you to myself; that where I am, there you also may be (Jn. 14: 2–3).

If anyone love me, he will keep my word, and my Father will love him, and we will come to him and make our abode with him (14:23).

No longer do I call you servants, because the servant does not know what his master does. But I have called you friends, because all things that I have heard from my Father I have made known to you (15:15).

Amen, amen, I say to you, if you ask the Father anything in my name, he will give it to you. Hitherto you have not asked anything in

[23] It is the share which the Son has received from the Father: "All things that are mine are thine, and thine are mine" (Jn. 17:10). Here one might read again the parable of the two sons: Mt. 21:28–32.

my name. Ask, and you shall receive, that your joy may be full. These things I have spoken to you in parables. The hour is coming when I will no longer speak to you in parables, but will speak to you plainly of the Father. In that day you shall ask in my name; and I do not say to you that I will ask the Father for you, for the Father himself loves you because you have loved me, and have believed that I came forth from God. I came forth from the Father and have come into the world. Again I leave the world and go to the Father (16:23–28).

I in them and thou in me; that they may be perfected in unity and that the world may know that thou hast sent me, and that thou hast loved them even as thou hast loved me. Father, I will that where I am, they also whom thou hast given me may be with me; in order that they may behold my glory, which thou hast given me, because thou hast loved me before the creation of the world. Just Father, the world has not known thee, but I have known thee, and these have known that thou hast sent me. And I have made known to them thy name, and will make it known, in order that the love with which thou hast loved me may be in them, and I in them (17:23–26).

We shall resume later on the study of these inexhaustible words. Here we only wish, by catching the accent, to recognize their origin and bearing. Only the Son of God could speak to us in this way: the Father whom He reveals to us is He who has loved his Son "before the creation of the world," and that eternal love is in us also; the Father loves us. This message is the Christian revelation: it is the adoption of sons. Only the Son could bring us this revelation and grant us this grace.

The revelation of the Father, which the Son communicates to us, transforms the dogma, already so touching in the Old Testament, of divine Providence. In the Psalms, especially, God has appeared not only as the Creator and sustainer of life, but as He who watches over and guides it:

Whither shall I go from thy spirit? or whither shall I flee from thy face? If I ascend into heaven, thou art there: if I descend into hell, thou art present. If I take my wings early in the morning, and dwell in the uttermost parts of the sea: even there also shall thy hand lead me: and thy right hand shall hold me. And I said: "Perhaps darkness shall cover me: and night shall be my light in my pleasure." But darkness shall not be dark to thee, and night shall be light as the day: the darkness thereof, and the light thereof are alike to thee. For thou hast possessed my reins: thou hast protected me from my mother's womb. I will praise thee, for thou art fearfully magnified: wonderful are thy works, and my soul knoweth right well. My bone is not hidden from thee, which thou hast made in secret: and my substance in the lower parts of the earth. Thy eyes did see my imperfect being, and in thy book all shall be written: days shall be formed, and no one in them. But to me thy friends, O God, are made exceedingly honourable: their principality is exceedingly strengthened. I will number them, and they shall be multiplied above the sand: I rose up and am still with thee (Ps. 138:7–18).

In the Sermon on the Mount, the Son of God gives us the same teaching under a still more persuasive form, with a more penetrating stress:

Do not be anxious for your life, what you shall eat; nor yet for your body, what you shall put on. Is not the life a greater thing than the food, and the body than the clothing? Look at the birds of the air: they do not sow, or reap, or gather into barns; yet your heavenly Father feeds them. Are not you of much more value than they? But which of you by being anxious about it can add to his stature a single cubit?

And as for clothing, why are you anxious? See how the lilies of the field grow; they neither toil nor spin, yet I say to you that not even Solomon in all his glory was arrayed like one of these. But if God so clothes the grass of the field, which today is alive and tomorrow is thrown into the oven, how much more you, O you of little faith! Therefore do not be anxious, saying, "What shall we eat?" or "What shall we drink?" or "What are we to put on?" (for after all these things the Gentiles seek); for your Father knows that you need all these things. But seek first the kingdom of God and his justice, and all these things shall be given you besides. Therefore do not be anxious about tomorrow; for tomorrow will have anxieties of its own. Sufficient for the day is its own trouble (Mt. 6:25–34).

This life program proposed by Jesus to His disciples has been engraved on the Christian conscience. In vain did Renan endeavor to reduce it to a dream born under the balmy sky of Palestine. Galilee's rough peasants were not dreamers spending their lives in a "total indifference to exterior things." To refute him it suffices to read again the parable of the unmerciful servant (Mt. 18:21–35) or that of the marriage feast (Mt. 22:1–14). Jesus' discourse is not an idyll; it is a religious exhortation. Christians are not deterred from applying themselves to work: Jesus will remind them that whosoever has put his hand to the plow should think, henceforth, only of the furrow without looking back; that whosoever sees himself entrusted with a talent, should not bury it in the ground, but turn it to good account. But He also teaches them that this work should be pursued in a spirit of filial trust towards the heavenly Father.

This trust assures to Christian life a peace it would search for in vain elsewhere; but it requires a discerning and constant faith. In the ordinary course of life, it seems that God pours out pell-mell good things and bad on every man. Did not our Lord speak to us in the discourse on the Mount of our "Father in heaven, who makes his sun to rise on the good and the evil, and sends rain on the just and the unjust" (Mt. 5:45)? He proposes to us this universal mercy as the model of our charity. But often we have trouble coming up to that ideal, and this fatherly goodness seems to us quite unconcerned. Faith finds a lesson in this apparently confused distribution of good and bad things: "God, says St. Augustine, wants us to know how to distinguish the goods which He pours out in the present life to serve as a consolation for captives, from those He reserves for the age to come to bring about the happiness of His children; or, to speak more emphatically, God wants us to know how to distinguish the truly despicable goods He gives so often to His enemies, from those He guards preciously in order to communicate them only to His servants. *Haec omnia tribuit etiam malis, ne magni pendantur a bonis.*" [24]

We must go further: these apparently fortuitous happenings, which give to human life such a confused aspect, are all ruled

[24] Bossuet, *Sermon sur la Providence,* Paris, Lebarq, IV, 229.

by a fatherly providence which ordains them to the good of the elect: "We know that for those who love God all things work together unto good, for those who, according to his purpose, are saints through his call." [25] Trials are proportioned to man's strength: "May no temptation take hold of you but such as man is equal to. God is faithful and will not permit you to be tempted beyond your strength, but with the temptation will also give you a way out that you may be able to bear it" (1 Cor. 10:13). It is for this divine protection that Jesus has us ask in the Lord's Prayer: "Lead us not into temptation," or, as many of the ancient Fathers translate: "Do not abandon us to a temptation we cannot bear." [26]

Quite often in his apostolic ministry the Apostle had experienced this fatherly providence involving him in very painful tribulations, but always proportioned to his strength:

We carry this treasure in vessels of clay, to show that the abundance of the power is God's and not ours. In all things we suffer tribulation, but we are not distressed; we are sore pressed, but we are not destitute; we endure persecution, but we are not forsaken; we are cast down, but we do not perish; always bearing about in our body the dying of Jesus, so that the life also of Jesus may be made manifest

[25] Rom. 8:28: ". . . in adding: '. . . according to his purpose,' he [Paul] does not intend either to limit or restrict his preceding assertion, but he is expressing only the motive of divine benevolence towards all those who love God; this motive is the call to faith with which they have been favoured." Cf. F. Prat, S.J., *Théologie de saint Paul* (Biblio. de théologie historique), Paris, Beauchesne, 1930, t. I, pp. 238–239, and in tr. *The Theology of Saint Paul,* tr. by J. Stoddard, Westminster, (Md.), Newman, 1946, I, p. 241.

[26] St. Hilary, *In Ps.,* CXVIII (*P.L.,* IX, 510); St. Jerome, *In Mt.,* XXVI, 41 (*P.L.,* XXVI, 199); Chromatius, *Tract., in Mt.,* XIV, 7 (*P.L.,* XX, 362); St. Ambrose, *De Sacramentis,* V, 4 (*P.L.,* XVI, 454) and in tr. *On the Sacraments,* tr. by T. Thompson (Trans. of Christian Lit.), N. Y. Macmillan, 1919; St. Augustine, *De Sermone Domini in Monte,* II, 9, 30–34 (*P.L.,* XXXIV, 1222–1234) and in tr. *The Lord's Sermon on the Mount* (ACW 5), tr. by J. Jepson, Westminster (Md.), Newman, 1948. Cf. P. Dobroslav Simovic, O.F.M., *Le commentaire du "Pater" chez les Pères latins de Tertullien à saint Augustin inclusivement,* unpubl. thesis in theology. *Vie et enseignement de Jésus-Christ,* t. II, p. 82, note.

in our bodily frame. For we the living are constantly being handed over to death for Jesus' sake, that the life also of Jesus may be made manifest in our mortal flesh. Thus death is at work in us, but life in you (2 Cor. 4:7–12).

What appears in the life of the Apostle, and in the life of each of the faithful, is even more manifest in the history of the Church, and quite particularly in its origins: in the course of the first centuries she came up against bloody persecutions which bruised her, without breaking her. Due to imperial legislation, adherence to Christianity created for every neophyte a danger of ruin and death. All his goods, his very life, no longer belonged to him except by a slender thread; he must give all, literally, to possess the kingdom of God. This total sacrifice, generously consented to, gives to his religion a depth, an impetus which Christians of peaceful times will envy.[27] There will be only an elite to pay so high a price for God's grace. But God does, indeed, want an elite: "Do not be afraid, little flock, for it has pleased your Father to give you the kingdom" (Lk. 12:32). And this Church, which nothing protects here below and which everything threatens, lives nonetheless. Around the year 249, Origen wrote:

He [God] always fought for them [Christians] and from time to time stopped the opponents of the Christians and the people who wanted to kill them. For a few, whose number could be easily enumerated, have died occasionally for the sake of the Christian religion by way of reminder to men that when they see a few striving for piety they may become more steadfast and despise death. But God prevented their whole race from being annihilated because He wanted it to be established and the whole world to be filled by this most pious teaching of salvation.[28]

---

[27] Cf. below, p. 231, n. 20, the regret expressed by Origen in the course of the years following the persecution of Severus.
[28] C. Cels., III, 8, and in tr. *Origen: Contra Celsus,* tr. by H. Chadwick, N. Y., Cambridge Univ. Press, 1953, p. 133.

At the same time that God covers His children with His vigilant protection, He sustains them interiorly with His grace, and by this, especially, is His providence revealed. The person who views events only from the outside perceives only a confused medley of good and bad things, falling haphazardly on the good and the wicked. But if we consider the grace which accompanies these showerings and the fruits which they produce, we recognize the fatherly will of God. The Book of Acts recounts to us that on the road to Damascus Saul was suddenly thrown down and surrounded by a light from heaven. He got up no longer able to see. They led him by the hand to Damascus, where he remained blind for three days, neither drinking nor eating (Acts 9:3–9). A little further on we find the story of the magician, Bar-Jesus: he tries to oppose the preaching of St. Paul: the Apostle "gazed at him and said, 'Behold, the hand of the Lord is upon thee, and thou shalt be blind, not seeing the sun for a time.' And instantly there fell upon him a mist of darkness, and he groped about for someone to lead him by the hand" (Acts 13:9, 10, 11).

Everywhere we see Christ's adversaries stricken with a temporary blindness; this is all that the witnesses of these prodigies perceive, and yet what a difference between that punishment and this conversion! The magician is nonplussed; no longer will he be able to oppose the Christian preaching or deceive the proconsul Sergius Paulus. For Saul, that terrifying unhorsing is the decisive grace of his life and the mainspring of his apostolate: he saw Jesus, he prays, and three days later he recovers his sight, receives baptism, and is filled with the Holy Spirit.

To help bring to light this profound aspect of the divine action, the Epistle to the Hebrews shows us in these trials marks of the providence of God, who corrects His children and raises them up:

You have forgotten the exhortation that is addressed to you as sons, saying, "My son, neglect not the discipline of the Lord, neither be thou weary when thou art rebuked by him. For whom the Lord loves, he chastises; and he scourges every son whom he receives." Continue under discipline. God deals with you as with sons; for what son is there whom his father does not correct? But if you are without discipline, in which all have had a share, then you are illegitimate children and not sons.[29]

Revealed to the Christian by these teachings of Christ and the apostles, the will of the heavenly Father appears to him as the light illuminating his life and the power sustaining it. He submits to it with docility. But the Son of God's example carries him higher: it breathes into him the filial spirit. The will of God is no longer simply welcomed with a loving submission; it is pursued enthusiastically: "Thy will be done on earth, as it is in heaven" (Mt. 6:10). Jesus has told us, "My food is to do the will of him who sent me" (Jn. 4:34). The disciple is urged on by that deep impulse which the Spirit of Christ communicates to him, and by this, especially, he resembles his Master: "Whoever does the will of God, he is my brother and sister and mother" (Mk. 3:35).

It is above all by the contemplation of the life of the Son of God that we can engrave in our hearts this filial love. But from now on we can understand that in this, indeed, lies all our nobility and happiness. In heaven, caught up by the irresistible love of the Father, we can no longer have any other will but His. Here below we do not see Him yet. But faith lets us recognize Him sufficiently to render Him lovable to us above all else. If man is faithful to this faith and to this love, his life is no more than a preparation for eternal life: caught up by the hand of the omnipotent Father, he breaks through the narrowness of his selfishness, he escapes the inconstancy of caprice. His action has but a single goal, the one which God proposes to him. No longer can anything shatter the unity of his life, for nothing can snatch him out of the hand of the Father (Jn. 10:29).

In exchange for all that, what is asked of the Christian? The gift of himself. The teaching of the Master will make us understand the length and depth of the effort He expects from us. What

[29] Heb. 12:5–8, quoting Prv. 3:11–12.

He seeks is a new creation.[30] Each one can discern the meaning of this effort in the humble setting of his personal life; he can follow it in the whole history of humanity. Creation, which is recounted in Genesis, is only a starting point, just as in the case of each man, his birth is. That is what St. Irenaeus was teaching, from the end of the second century:

It is by this upbringing that man, a product of creation, conforms himself, little by little, to the image and likeness of the unproduced God. The Father takes pleasure and ordains, the Son works and creates, the Spirit nourishes and gives growth, and man progresses and mounts towards perfection, that is to say, approaches the unproduced God. For he who is not produced is perfect, and that is God. And man had first to be created, then to grow, then to become an adult, then to multiply, then to get his strength, then to come to glory, and then, once arrived at glory, to see his Master. For it is God that he must see; and the sight of God renders us incorruptible, and incorruptibility brings us very close to God.[31]

Sin had disfigured the divine image which the hand of God had stamped on man; but, says St. Irenaeus again:

Adam could not flee from the hands of God, those hands which the Father addressed when He said, "Let us make man to our image and likeness." That is why, when the time was fulfilled, not by the will of the flesh, nor by the will of man, but by the good pleasure of the Father those hands made a living man, so that Adam might be made to the image and likeness of God.[32]

These fine texts recall the great vicissitudes of the religious drama being unfolded on earth: the Fall and the Redemption, man's sin and the merciful Incarnation of the Son of God. These

[30] 2 Cor. 5:17; Gal. 6:15. Cf. Eph. 2:10,15; 4:24; Col. 3:10; James 1:18. Cf. Kittel, *Theologisches Wörterbuch zum Neuen Testament,* Leipzig, 1932 ff; and in tr. *Bible Key Words,* tr. by J. Coates, N.Y., Harper, 1951.
[31] *Adv. Haer.,* IV, 38, 3. *P.G.,* VII, 1105. Cf. *Histoire du Dogme de la Trinité,* t. II, p. 585.
[32] *Ibid.,* V, I, 3. *P.G.,* VII, 1123.

two great events imprint on the spiritual teaching of the New Testament its character: it is not a religious philosophy; it is at once a history and a doctrine: man has fallen; God has ransomed him through the Incarnation and the death of His Son. By means of these two events the religious destiny of mankind finds itself completely transformed: by sin, it appears lost beyond repair, and even after the Redemption it carries the scars of a wound from which it will always suffer. And the filial adoption, which even for the innocent Adam was a grace of God, is for his guilty and redeemed children a boundless mercy. By the Incarnation, humanity is united to the divine nature in the Person of the Son of God; thereby was knit an intimacy between God and man which no one could dare dream of. The divine filiation, which belongs to the Head of humanity by right of nature, is communicated by Him to all those whom He has deigned to make His brothers. We are children of God; this priceless privilege is for us not only a title, but a reality (1 Jn. 3:1).

The rest of this study will bring out this twofold character of the Christian's religion: the deep humility belonging to the redeemed; the immense hope belonging to the children of God.

❖❖❖❖❖❖❖❖❖

Men, the Slaves of Sin

We have briefly outlined the teaching which the Son of God has given us about His Father and our Father, His God and our God. This revelation has illumined all those who have welcomed Him with a pure heart. But these latter, in the days of Christ, were few and far between: "The light shines in the darkness; and the darkness grasped it not" (Jn. 1:5).

1. ALL ARE SINNERS

On the day Isaias received his prophetic mission, he was warned of the blind obstinacy his message would encounter:

And I heard the voice of the Lord, saying: "Whom shall I send? and who shall go for us?" and I said: "Lo, here am I, send me." And he said: "Go, and thou shalt say to this people: Hearing, hear, and understand not: and see the vision, and know it not. Blind the heart of this people, and make their ears heavy, and shut their eyes: lest they see with their eyes, and hear with their ears, and understand with their heart, and be converted and I heal them" (Is. 6:8–10).

This text has been recalled by the Synoptics (Mt. 13:10–17; Mk. 4:10–12; Lk. 8:9–10), by St. John (12:37–40), and by St. Paul (Acts 28:25–27), in order to explain the blindness of the Jews in the face of Jesus' message. Our Lord Himself had cruel experience of this hardness of heart He could not overcome: "O unbelieving generation, how long shall I be with you? How long shall I put up with you?" (Mk. 9:18; cf. Mt. 17:16; Lk. 9:41); He had to curse the Lake cities (Mt. 11:21; Lk. 10:13); He wept over Jerusalem (Lk. 19:41). The cause of this blindness is obvious: it is sin: "The light has come into the world, yet men have loved the darkness rather than the light, for their works were evil" (Jn. 3:19). The bad conscience shuns the light and soon becomes incapable of perceiving it: "If thy eye be sound, thy whole body will be full of light. But if thy eye be evil, thy whole body will be full of darkness. Therefore if the light that is in thee is darkness, how great is the darkness itself!" [1]

And surrounding Him, indeed, Jesus sees only sinners. One day when they began to talk to Him of the Galileans massacred by Pilate, He replied, "Do you think that these Galileans were worse sinners than all the other Galileans, because they have suffered such things? I tell you, no; but unless you repent, you will all perish in the same manner. Or those eighteen upon whom the tower of Siloe fell and killed them; do you think that they were more guilty than all the other dwellers in Jerusalem? I tell you, no; but unless you repent, you will all perish in the same manner" (Lk. 13:2–5).

God alone is good (Mk. 10:18; Mt. 19:17; Lk. 18:19); men are bad (Mt. 7:11; 12:34). Jesus is the green wood; men are dead wood (Lk. 23:31). All men are God's debtors, insolvent debtors, who can acquit themselves in His regard only by imploring His mercy.[2]

All these texts emit the same sound: neither hardness, nor

---

[1] Mt. 6:22–23. At the end of his treatise on the Trinity, St. Augustine will say to his soul: "Why canst thou not see the light? Because of thy infirmity? And whence comes thy infirmity, if not from thy iniquity?" (*De Trinitate*, XV, 27, 50. *P.L.*, XLII, 1097.)

[2] Mt. 6:12; 18:25–27; Lk. 7:42.

scorn, nor bitterness, but the clear-sighted candor of one who "knew what was in man" (Jn. 2:25); better still, the compassion of the physician who wants to cure sickness, of the Savior who desires to lift the sinner up again.

In his severe condemnations, St. Paul will not go beyond these judgments of Jesus, except to give them a sharper form:

Scripture shut up all things under sin, that by the faith of Jesus Christ the promise might be given to those who believe (Gal. 3:22). We have argued that Jews and Greeks are all under sin, as it is written, "There is not one just man; there is none who understands; there is none who seeks after God. All have gone astray together; they have become worthless. There is none who does good, no, not even one . . ." All have sinned and have need of the glory of God. They are justified freely by his grace through the redemption which is in Christ Jesus (Rom. 3:9–12, 23–24).

The initial cause of this universal downfall St. Paul recognized in the sin of Adam: "As through one man sin entered into the world and through sin death, and thus death has passed into all men because all have sinned." [3]

In one of these texts (Rom. 3:12), the Apostle, repeating the words of the Psalmist (Ps. 13:3), rightly applies to sinners what in the Book of Wisdom the sinners said of the just: these are good for nothing (Wis. 2:11). And it is only too true: with the just and with sinners the conceptions of the world are entirely opposed. Both lose their life: the just love God above all things and attach themselves only to Him; sinners prefer the world to Him and are enslaved to the world.

There are, no doubt, among sinners great inequalities. Jews and pagans are all under sin; and yet the condition of the pagans is not the same as that of the Jews: the pagans have fallen into more shameful faults; the Jews, who have received the oracles of God, have a heavier responsibility.[4] But both have sinned

[3] Rom. 5:12. Cf. Prat, *Théologie de saint Paul*, t. I, pp. 253–261; t. II, pp. 209–211. Freundorfer, *Erbsunde und Erbtod beim Apostel Paulus*, Münster, 1927.

[4] Cf. Rom. 1:18–32; 2:17–29.

against the light: the pagans themselves, "although they knew
God, they did not glorify him as God or give thanks" (Rom.
1:21).

This infidelity is the great offense and the great unhappiness
of man, and it is Christianity alone which has made us understand that.[5]

[5] The lexicographic study of the word ἁμαρτία already enables us to grasp
the transcendence of Christian theology: in the language of Plato or Aristotle, ἁμαρτία is said of the awkward or feeble action of one who misses
the mark; in the LXX, the same word takes on a religious meaning and
signifies a violation of the law; in the Gospels and Epistles it will be,
above all, the infidelity of man turning away from God. Cf. Kittel, t. I,
pp. 295–320, and in tr. *Bible Key Words;* Kierkegaard, *Traité du Désespoir,*
tr. by Fenlov and Gateau (N.R.F., 1930), p. 183, and in tr. *The Sickness
Unto Death,* tr. by W. Lowrie, Princeton Univ. Press, 1941, p. 144: "Pre-
cisely the concept by which Christianity distinguishes itself qualitatively
and most decisively from paganism is the concept of sin, the doctrine of
sin; and therefore Christianity also assumes quite consistently that neither
paganism nor the natural man knows what sin is; yea, it assumes that
there must be a revelation from God to make manifest what sin is. For
it is not true, as a superficial view assumes, that the doctrine of the atonement is the qualitative difference between paganism and Christianity. No,
the beginning must be made far deeper, with sin, with the doctrine of sin,
as Christianity also does." P. 148: "O when one beholds a man who protests that he has entirely understood how Christ went about in the form
of a lowly servant, poor, despised, and, as the Scripture says, spat upon—
when I see the same man so careful to betake himself thither where in a
worldly sense it is good to be, and accommodate himself there in the
utmost security, when I see him apprehensive of every puff of wind from
right or left, as though his life depended upon it, and so blissful, so utterly
blissful, so awfully glad—yes, to make the thing complete, so awfully
glad that he is able to thank God for it—glad that he is held in honor by
all men—then I have often said to myself and by myself, 'Socrates, Socrates, Socrates, can it be possible that this man has understood what he
says he has understood?' " P. 150: "But where does the difficulty lie? It is
to be ascribed to a fact of which the Socratic view itself was aware (though
only to a certain degree) and sought to remedy, that it lacks a dialectical
determinant for the transition from having understood something to the
doing of it. In this transition Christianity makes its start; by proceeding
along this path it proves that sin lies in the will, thus attaining the concept
of defiance; and then, in order to make the end thoroughly fast, it adjoins
to this the dogma of original sin . . . In pure ideality, where there is no

Here was missing the light of Christ. The Incarnation of the Son of God, His lessons, and especially His example will pour forth this light on humanity. We shall endeavor to contemplate it. But first of all we must consider and, if possible, resolve, an agonizing problem: How did the human race happen thus to be led astray? The universe is by no means the work of a demiurge or of a bad God, as the Marcionites and Manichaeans imagined: it has been created for man by the very good God. The paternal home prepared for us by our Father has become for us a temptation and the occasion of our fall.

Man is not a pure spirit; he must grow, little by little, in strength, knowledge and virtue. This progress is sustained by the

---

question of the real individual man, the transition is accomplished by necessity (in the System indeed everything comes about by necessity), in other words, there is no difficulty at all connected with the transition from understanding to doing . . . In the world of reality, on the other hand, where it is a question of the individual man, there is this tiny transition from having understood to doing . . . On the contrary, here begins a very prolix story.

"In the life of spirit, on the other hand, there is no stopping . . . everything is actuality: in case then a man the very same second he has known what is right does not do it—well then, first of all, the knowledge stops boiling. And next comes the question how the will likes this thing that is known. If it does not like it, it does not follow that the will goes ahead and does the opposite of that which the intelligence understood, such strong contrasts occur doubtless rather seldom; but the will lets some time pass, there is an interim, that means, 'We'll see about that tomorrow.' All this while the intelligence becomes more and more obscured, and the lower nature triumphs more and more. For, alas, the good must be done at once—at once, the moment it is known (and hence the transition goes so easily in the pure ideality where everything is 'at once'), but the strength of the lower nature consists in dragging a thing out. The will has no particular objection to it—so it says with its fingers crossed. And then when the intelligence has become duly darkened, the intelligence and the will can understand one another better; at last they agree entirely, for now the intelligence has gone over to the side of the will and acknowledges that the thing is quite right as it would have it. And so there live perhaps a great multitude of men who labor off and on to obscure their ethical and religious understanding which would lead them out into decisions and consequences which the lower nature does not love, extending meanwhile their aesthetic and metaphysical understanding, which ethically is a distraction."

material world, indispensable condition of his life, knowledge, and moral formation. The universe is for man better than a sustainer of his life and an instrument of his progress. It is a revelation of God: "Since the creation of the world his invisible attributes are clearly seen—his everlasting power also and divinity—being understood through the things that are made" (Rom. 1:20). In His infinite goodness, God has poured forth on this whole material creation an attractiveness, a splendor, which should make known to men the liberality and the infinite power of their heavenly Father.[6]

Even more than the material universe, human society is valuable to man: in a fraternal collaboration, all, relying on one another, must be lifted up toward their Father. God has willed that their individual and social life be penetrated with an attraction which invites man to the humblest and highest offices: intimacy of the home and family life when, the doors being closed, he enjoys in common joys and troubles, bereavements and births, all those mysteries of life which penetrate, ennoble, and render attractive the love formed by God. And then, beyond the narrow family enclosure, there are the great human societies, cities and countries; there is the whole of humanity which gives to our so short lives the material, artistic and moral riches elaborated by so many men who have reached out, as we reach out ourselves, towards an ideal of goodness and justice. And all that under this fair sky, on this venerable and maternal earth, our crib, our family home, our tomb. "O Lord our Lord, how admirable is thy name in the whole earth! For thy magnificence is elevated above the heavens . . . What is man that thou art mindful of him? or the son of man that thou visitest him?" (Ps. 8:2,5.)

Inanimate creatures reveal God, for they are the work of God. But man makes Him even much better known, for he is His image. At the same time that God was manifesting Himself to

---

[6] Cf. St. John of the Cross, *Canticle,* strophe 5: "Scattering a thousand graces, He passed through these groves in haste, and, looking upon them as he went, left them, by his glance alone, clothed with beauty." In tr. *Complete Works,* tr. and ed. by E. Allison Peers from the critical ed. of P. Silverio de Santa Teresa, 3 vols., Westminster (Md.), Newman, 1953.

man in men, He invited him also to love Him in them. In our hearts our Father put the desire to possess Him and the concern to be worthy of this. This sovereign good, the most precious of all, had also to be the most common. If this desire remained pure, it would be free of all jealousy, and, as men multiplied, it would ensure the convergence of their efforts towards God and, as a consequence, the union of their souls. What a beautiful sight this might have been, a truly fraternal humanity, tending to God in a loving accord, and supported in its impetus by a docile and peaceful universe.

Today humanity is divided: each of us is a humanity unto himself. If man had remained faithful to God, each of us would have found in his moral life, from its first waking moments, that profound unity towards which now tend so many laborious efforts. In sinners, such as we are, the love of self is opposed to love for God as a rival, and shields itself from the love of neighbor with all the jealousy of its indigence. In the divine plan it was not meant to be so:

It is impossible for a man to love God and not love himself. Furthermore, he alone knows how to love himself, who loves God. Certainly that man loves himself sufficiently who is anxious in his actions to enjoy the sovereign and true good. If this good is nothing else but God, as our sermons have taught, who can doubt that he loves himself who loves God? What else? Between men themselves ought not there to exist some bond of love? Why, of course, there should, so much so that it is a matter of faith that no surer step can be taken for rising to the love of God than the charity of man for man.[7]

At the completion of the work of the Son of God, we shall contemplate the restoration of that unity, willed by God and shattered by sin: "I in them, and thou in me; that they may be perfected in unity" (Jn. 17:23). It was the image of God, stamped on man by the Creator, which was to have ensured the unity of mankind. Men have disfigured the image and broken the unity. But He has come, the perfect Image of the Father: He gathers to-

[7] St. Augustine, *De Moribus Ecclesiae*, XXVI, 48.

gether and raises up again the dispersed men; He lives in them, and makes of them the one holy Church.

But to raise up fallen mankind in this way, there was wanting the redemptive blood of the Son of God, the sufferings and laborious effort of all His faithful. Whence came so steep a fall? From the fact that man, instead of respecting in himself and in other men the image of God, turned away his gaze from this divine likeness, so as to see only those human beauties and powers, which he claimed to enjoy for their own sake and which he envied or coveted in others. And likewise, in the whole material universe surrounding him, man no longer contemplated the work of God; he thought only of exploiting and enjoying it. And thus man turned against God Himself such a beautiful universe as this—too beautiful, alas, since it has become a temptation for him. According to the intention of the Creator, this world was to be for man, not a temptation, but a support. But this paternal intention was frustrated by the selfishness of man who, having forgotten God, stopped to take greedy enjoyment in the gifts he received from Him, instead of using them chastely to mount up towards God. This is the lesson written on the first page of the Bible; the teaching of Jesus and His apostles has stamped it still more deeply on the Christian conscience.

If our study of sin was principally historical, if its primary purpose was to acquaint us with the moral environment in which the New Testament appeared, we shall have to dwell at first on the profound differences which distinguish, in this epoch, the Jewish world from the pagan world.

The Jewish world is, then, purified of all idolatry [8] and is strictly monotheistic; the Roman-Hellenistic world, on the contrary, is completely enslaved to polytheism and idolatry. Here it will suffice to recall the feeling of repulsion St. Paul experiences, on the occasion of his entrance into Athens, at the sight of that city encumbered with idols (Acts 17:16). The epistles of the Apostle, especially to the Romans (1:18–32) and to the Corinthians (I, 8:5–6; I, 10:7–32) express, when confronted with similar

[8] Cf. *Histoire du Dogme de la Trinité*, t. I, pp. 102 ff.; Bonsirven, *Le Judaisme palestinien*, t. I, pp. 149 ff.

disorders, the same reprobation. This religious degradation has its repercussions in the moral life: God has delivered the pagans over to the impure desires of their hearts, to their ignominious passions (Rom. *ibid.*). It is from this environment that the Corinthian converts have emerged, and St. Paul reminds them of this (1 Cor. 6:9–11). In the Jewish world which the Gospel makes known to us, these vices against nature would not appear.[9] Here we encounter cases of lewdness and adultery; but we feel weighing on these offenses a reprobation which we do not always note in the pagan world.[10] There is no need to teach the Jews that fornication is a sin; it must be taught to the converts come over from paganism (Acts 15:29).

This moral inequality of the two worlds, pagan and Jewish, is a historic fact of great significance: it helps the historian to grasp the misunderstandings and even the scandals which, in the primitive Church, sometimes oppose the converts from Judaism to those from the Gentile world. He has to marvel, also, at the immense power of the Church which knew how to unify these two worlds and to purify paganism. From the theological point of view, it was no less consequential: it causes the virulent poison to appear which idolatry is pouring into the moral life: it disintegrates that life, it degrades it; it dishonors at one and the same time God and man.

These considerations are very important, but they will not detain us. Here we do not have to describe the moral state either of the Jews or of the pagans; our aim is to disengage from the New Testament the spiritual doctrine it proposes to us. In this question of sin, the teaching we have to garner emphasizes much more the universality of the downfall than the unequal degrees we can distinguish: "Jews and Greeks are all under

---

[9] One might note that when Jesus recalls the offenses and chastisement of Sodom (Lk. 17:28–29), He is content to describe a wholly material life, which no longer finds room for God. He says nothing of the infamous vice of Sodom. We can find in this choice an indication of the moral state of the Jews whom our Lord was addressing (cf. below, pp. 36–39).

[10] One might read again, for example, the episode of the Penitent Woman of Galilee (Lk. 7:36–50) and that of the Adulteress (Jn. 8:1–11).

sin" (Rom. 3:9). What, then, is sin which humbles under its yoke the Pharisees of Jerusalem as well as the degenerates of Rome and of Corinth?

St. Paul makes it known when, speaking of the pagans, he writes that they "exchanged the truth of God for a lie, and worshipped and served the creature rather than the Creator" (Rom. 1:25). This text is applied in all its rigor only to idolators; but it condemns all sinners: all have "served the creature rather than the Creator." We shall understand this better by applying ourselves to the Gospel texts. There we shall find, not definitions, but descriptions of sin; and it will not be difficult to gather its teaching.

In the parable of the Great Supper (Lk. 14:16–24), Jesus portrays the appeals of God to man, and the refusals man opposes to them:

A certain man gave a great supper, and he invited many. And he sent his servant at supper time to tell those invited to come, for everything is now ready. And they all with one accord began to excuse themselves. The first said to him, "I have bought a farm, and I must go out and see it; I pray thee hold me excused." And another said, "I have bought five yoke of oxen, and I am on my way to try them; I pray thee hold me excused." And another said, "I have married a wife, and therefore I cannot come." And the servant returned, and reported these things to his master. Then the master of the house was angry and said to his servant, "Go out quickly into the streets and lanes of the city, and bring in here the poor, and the crippled, and the blind, and the lame . . . I tell you that none of those who were invited shall taste of my supper."

This parable is transparent, and the warning it gives us very serious. The guests steal away, not by inventing false pretexts nor by deliberately offending the administrator, but simply because they are more interested in their own affairs than in his feast. They feel no hostility towards him; their reply is courteous. And still his condemnation of them is definitive: never shall they enter. They violated the great law of the Gospel: seek first the kingdom of God and His justice. The banquet they despised is the heavenly banquet; the administrator, insulted by their refusal, is the King of heaven. All are condemned.

The same doctrine inspires a whole group of narratives which,
like this one, belong to the narrative of the Journeys (Lk. 9–18).
First there is the sketch of the rich man who knows not how to
store up his bountiful harvest but dreams only of constructing
new barns: ". . . 'I will say to my soul: "Soul, thou hast many
good things laid up for many years; take thy ease, eat, drink, be
merry." ' But God said to him, 'Thou fool, this night do they
demand thy soul of thee; and the things that thou hast provided,
whose will they be?' So is he who lays up treasure for himself,
and is not rich as regards God" (Lk. 12:16–21). There is the
parable of a rich man who used to dress in purple and fine linen,
and feasted each day sumptuously; and of a poor man, named
Lazarus, who remained lying by the door all covered with ulcers. "And it came to pass that the poor man died and was borne
away by the angels into Abraham's bosom; but the rich man also
died and was buried in hell. And lifting up his eyes, being in torments, he saw Abraham afar off and Lazarus in his bosom."
He beseeches Abraham, who responds to his supplications: "Son,
remember that thou in thy lifetime hast received good things,
and Lazarus in like manner evil things; but now here he is comforted whereas thou art tormented" (Lk. 16:19–25). Finally,
there is the eschatological discourse: "As it came to pass in
the days of Noe, even so will it be in the days of the Son of
Man. They were eating and drinking, they were marrying and
giving in marriage, until the day when Noe entered the ark,
and the flood came and destroyed them all. Or as it came to
pass in the days of Lot. They were eating and drinking, they
were buying and selling, they were planting and building; but
on the day that Lot went out from Sodom, it rained fire and brimstone from heaven and destroyed them all. In the same wise
will it be on the day that the Son of Man is revealed" (Lk.
17:26–30).

Parables, stories, prophecies of the last days—all repeat to
us the same lesson: the great sin of which humanity is guilty,
and which God chastises so severely, is to be concerned only

with the goods and joys of earth and to forget God. To make His
disciples understand this capital teaching, Jesus brings it out in
those little pictures of all the ôther grounds for complaint He
might have against men. The rich man who wants to enjoy his
bountiful harvest, the rich man who dresses in purple and every
day has a big feast—have they enriched themselves dishon-
estly? Nothing indicates it. And more surprising still, while recalling the times of Noah and Lot, Jesus says nothing of the
crimes these sinful generations were guilty of. What He retains
of their scandalous history is only the vulgarity of material enjoyments which are, alas, the sole concern of so many men: eating, drinking, planting, building, marrying. And all that is legitimate, no doubt, as long as it does not cause the kingdom of God
and His justice to be forgotten. But if earth causes heaven to be
forgotten, if it alone is loved and desired, earth becomes a hell
and leads to another hell. Illumined by faith, goods here
below enable us to recognize the love of the heavenly Father
and to desire His kingdom. If the light of faith is extinguished,
things "are no more than what they are"—vanities. This is the
whole theme of Ecclesiastes: "Vanity of vanities, and all is vanity. What hath a man more of all his labour, that he taketh under
the sun? . . . The eye is not filled with seeing, neither is the
ear filled with hearing" (Eccl. 1:2–3, 8). St. Paul, taking up the
same theme, interprets it more profoundly and discloses to
men the source of their illusions and deceptions: "Creation
was made subject to vanity—not by its own will but by reason
of him who made it subject—in hope, because creation itself
also will be delivered from its slavery to corruption into the
freedom of the glory of the sons of God" (Rom. 8:20–21).

These selfish enjoyments are judged by their fruits: poisonous
foods they are which contaminate human life. But we must
complete this moral teaching by the religious teaching on which
Jesus has often insisted and which governs this whole doctrine:
"No one can serve two masters; for either he will hate the one
and love the other, or else he will stand by the one and despise
the other. You cannot serve God and mammon" (Mt. 6:24;
cf. Lk. 16:13). Here again we find the great religious principle

which determines the whole of Christian asceticism: God alone served, alone adored. On this principle Jesus and His listeners were easily of one accord; but in its application, the Pharisees kept refusing to follow the Master. St. Luke tells us so: after recounting that maxim of Jesus on God and mammon, he adds, "The Pharisees, who were fond of money, were listening to all these things, and they began to sneer at him. And he said to them, 'You are they who declare yourselves just in the sight of men, but God knows your heart; for that which is exalted in the sight of men is an abomination before God.' " [11]

This attitude of the Pharisees and the severe condemnation of Christ enable us to grasp better the import of this whole doctrine. We are not quits with God when we have given Him the ritual worship which the Pharisees carried out exactly; we must love Him above all things. And this is impossible for one who lets himself be carried away by an anxious preoccupation with the goods of earth. Jesus warns of this in the very passage we are interpreting: "Do not lay up for yourselves treasures on earth . . . For where thy treasure is, there thy heart also will be." [12]

Anyone who lets his heart be flooded with the love of perishable goods, closes it to God, and that is his offense: it is the sin of adultery, which so often was the object of the Lord's reproach to His people, who betrayed Him to give themselves over to the gods of the nations. Each of the faithful, like the people as a whole, is united to our Lord as the bride to her spouse, and Christ is divinely jealous of that fidelity;[13] it is His first requirement: "He who loves father or mother more than me is not

[11] Lk. 16:14–15. This statement is found in St. Luke in the same chapter as the parable of the Unjust Steward and the story of the Rich Man and Lazarus.

[12] Mt. 6:19, 21; cf. Lk. 12:34. It is also the conclusion which Jesus draws from the story of the foolish rich man who thinks only of constructing new barns: "So is he who lays up treasures for himself, and is not rich as regards God" (Lk. 12:21). Cf. P. Joüon, *Recherches de Science religieuse,* 1928, pp. 353–354.

[13] Cf. 2 Cor. 11:2.

worthy of me" (Mt. 10:37). And if, in preference to Himself, we like not father and mother, but a treasure, the affront is even greater.

Some other statements of Jesus, and in particular the parable of the Prodigal Son, open up on sin a still wider perspective and reveal to us the intimate character of the Gospel religion: sin is the ingratitude of the child of God, seizing his goods for himself and renouncing his Father.

We do not have to take up in detail the narrative of the prodigal's departure and return, of his sin and pardon (Lk. 15:11–32); all our readers are familiar with it. The lesson we draw most often from it is an exhortation to repentance, to filial trust in the fatherly mercy of God—and nothing is more legitimate. But this remarkable narrative contains other teachings, no less valuable. It illumines powerfully the nature of sin. First of all, by the personages it puts on the stage: it is between a father and his son that this drama is acted out. The mistake of the child is in wanting to take without further delay his share of the inheritance, in order to go and enjoy it no matter where, far from the home of his father. With his father living, he has no right to his goods, not even to the share which later on will be owed to him upon his return home. To want henceforth to claim a reckoning of the tutelage and to have an account paid over to him, is an injustice and an insolence. What is all that if not, in the luminous transparency of the parable, the story of the sinner? Man is heir to all those goods he now uses; but it is only later, in another life, that he will enter into the possession of that inheritance (Mt. 5:4). To lay claim to them from God in order, henceforth, to take possession of them, is a folly and an insolence. But the most important element in this step is the rupture, the fleeing far away. And yet, is it not the pretension of all those who, while still here below, in spite of Jesus' warnings, fling themselves on all these goods, covet them and, if they can, possess themselves of them? In vain does Our Lord say to them: foolish is "he who lays up treasures for himself, and is not rich as regards God" (Lk. 12:21); in vain does He promise them "a treasure in heaven" (*ibid.*, 33). When they hear these promises, they do not have the strength to believe them. They will do as did the rich young man (Mt. 19:22), as did the prodigal—they will go away.

This departure, this flight far from the paternal home, is the great offense of the prodigal, and it is this especially which the story enables us to recognize in sin. For Hellenism, sin is an error of judgment or an awkwardness in understanding thoughts or things—a superficial view which fails to reach the depths of the moral life. Judaism saw in it above all a disobedience to the law of God, and thereby disengaged a distinctive element of sin, but without realizing its most inward aspect. Christianity discloses it: sin is the forsaking of God, the fleeing far from God. The sinner can make reparation for it only by returning to the home of his Father, by renewing with God the relations he had broken off. How can he do this? We shall see by studying the redemption of the sinner, his reconciliation with the heavenly Father. From now on, the story of the prodigal sets before our eyes the attitude of God with regard to the sinner.

This ingratitude of his child the father seeks not to oppose. He has had, no doubt, an inkling of this desertion and has endeavored to prevent it. But the child is obstinate and the father leaves him free in his decision. He even hands over to him that inheritance to which he has no right; and the young man goes away, far away. Thus it is that "God has given them up in the lustful desires of their heart to uncleanness, so that they dishonor their own bodies among themselves" (Rom. 1:24). God gives free rein to man's liberty; there is, here below, for the sinner, no more fearful punishment. Soon the inheritance is dissipated in debauchery; misery sets in and starvation; suffering, finally, awakens repentance. Here we recognize that educative role of suffering which Christian morality has put into sharp focus. The father corrects his child.[14]

---

[14] " 'He scourges every son whom he receives.' Continue under discipline. God deals with you as with sons; for what son is there whom his father does not correct? . . . All discipline seems for the present to be matter not for joy but for grief; but afterwards it yields the most peaceful fruit of justice to those who have been exercised by it. Therefore brace up the hands that hang down, and the tottering knees" (Heb. 12:6–7, 11–12).

The meeting of father and son is the most touching scene of the drama and the most revealing. From afar the father catches sight of his child: he runs to him, flings himself on his neck and embraces him. He gives him no time to finish his confession, but starts getting him ready for a feast; he orders a banquet, and they sit down to table. And presently, to the elder son who understands not and becomes indignant, the father will give this exalted reason for this joy: "We were bound to make merry and rejoice, for this thy brother was dead, and has come to life; he was lost and is found" (Lk. 15:32). And in the other parables of mercy, Jesus keeps coming back to dwell on that affirmation, so disconcerting to human selfishness: all heaven rejoices when a sinner does penance.[15] Here is one of the revelations of Jesus which provokes the greatest wonderment on the part of the Christian, the greatest scandal on the part of the unbeliever—if the unbeliever reflects on it.[16] Assuredly, it is one of those which make shine out most powerfully the Gospel's joyous newness.

So far in this parable we have considered only the prodigal son and his father. These are not the only actors in the drama: amidst the clamor of the banquet the elder son has appeared. Why this feast? he asks. "Thy brother has come, and thy father has killed the fatted calf, because he has him back safe and sound." The young man is indignant; the father comes out to entreat him to enter. But he answers his father, "Behold, these many years I have been serving thee, and have never

[15] This joy which the angels experience at the conversion of men will be one of the favorite themes of St. Gregory of Nyssa. Cf. J. Daniélou, in *Recherches de Science religieuse,* 1940, pp. 343–344, and 348 ff.

[16] Kierkegaard, in his *Sickness Unto Death,* has dwelt quite emphatically on the scandal of the unbeliever confronted with this affirmation of the Christian faith that God is concerned with the sin and with the salvation of each man: "It is for this man, for him also that God has come into the world, has let Himself be made flesh, suffered and died. And it is this God of suffering who almost begs and beseeches him to be willing to accept this help which is a gift! Truly, if there is any way at all of making one lose one's reason, is it not this?" [*Traité du Désespoir,* pp. 176–179.]

transgressed one of thy commands; and yet thou hast never given me a kid that I might make merry with my friends. But when this thy son comes, who has devoured his means with harlots, thou hast killed for him the fatted calf." The father said to him, "Son, thou art always with me, and all that is mine is thine; but we were bound to make merry and rejoice, for this thy brother was dead, and has come to life; he was lost, and is found" (Lk. 15:25–32).

This last scene of the parable is no less rich in instruction than the preceding ones, and for the study of sin we cannot neglect it. In this young man, so proudly conscious of his obedience to his father, there is, one feels, a resentment, a jealousy, which reveals the long-standing, repressed bitterness: his continually faithful services have gone unrecognized and unrewarded, and his brother, the vagabond gay blade, has been greeted, ever since his return, with an outburst of festivity! This indignant protest betrays the selfish preoccupations of this so well-behaved young man. He serves his father and does so willingly, but this service does not suffice for his joy: he must, at the very least, feast his friends from time to time and relax with them from the constraint of his service. What we catch a glimpse of here, under its most diminished and indulgent form, is the weakness of Pharisaism:[17] it claims to offer God a faithful service, and glories in this, in itself first of all, and before men, and before God (Lk. 18:11–12). This pride poisons his joy; he cannot taste the inward happiness which God gives to His children. He considers himself poorly paid by God; he recoups himself for it as best he can, greedy for money (Lk. 16:14), greedy for honor (Mt. 23: 5–7), greedy for domination (Mt. 23:13), and yet keeping in the depths of his heart a bitterness for his unrecognized services. And when he sees a sinner pardoned and tenderly received by

---

[17] This whole group of parables should be interpreted in the light of the short preamble which St. Luke gives to it: "The publicans and sinners were drawing near to him to listen to him. And the Pharisees and the Scribes murmured, saying, 'This man welcomes sinners and eats with them'" (Lk. 15:1–2). Cf. *Vie et enseignement de Jésus-Christ,* t. II, pp. 93–95.

the Master, he is exasperated (Lk. 7:36–50; Mk. 2:16; Lk. 19:7).

Frequently Jesus had to reprove these bad shepherds and protect His little flock against them. In this parable He advises these very ones with the tenderness of a father: "Son, thou art always with me, and all that is mine is thine" (Lk. 15:31). This happiness, is it not great enough to appease a human heart? It is the happiness of the Son of God. He will say to the Father in His supreme prayer, "All things that are mine are thine, and thine are mine" (Jn. 17:10). But to enjoy this happiness, we must renounce a narrow self-centeredness: we must lose ourselves, in order to find ourselves in God.

Had the elder son understood this paternal advice? The parable does not say; and the Gospel tells us elsewhere what Jesus said, in the last days of His life, while speaking to the high priests and to the Pharisees: "Amen I say to you, the publicans and harlots are entering the kingdom of God before you." [18] There is, indeed, in this perversion of the conscience, an even graver danger than in sins of the flesh: "The lamp of the body is the eye. If thy eye be sound, thy whole body will be full of light. But if thy eye be evil, thy whole body will be full of darkness. Therefore if the light that is in thee is darkness, how great is the darkness itself!" (Mt. 6:22–23).

2. THE STATE OF SIN

In going through the Gospel, we have gathered and meditated on Jesus' teachings: all men are sinners; captivated by the charm of perishable goods or by their own self-satisfaction, they have turned away from God. Avarice, lewdness, pride, every kind of sin has invaded mankind, the most dangerous being the most subtle, those which attack conscience itself, falsifying and blinding it. Henceforth man in his entirety is plunged into darkness. It is this state of sin which we must now consider.

[18] Mt. 21:31. These words belong to the parable of the Two Sons (ibid., 28–32); this parable, not so developed as that of the Prodigal Son, teaches the same lesson.

This state, we have said, is described by Jesus as a blindness. But we must note first of all, so as to have a good understanding of the Master's teaching, that not every blindness is a sin: there are some who are blind involuntarily, in whom blindness is not a sin, but an excuse. Man is not responsible for this; quite the contrary, his responsibility is found to be either suppressed or diminished. It is in this sense that Jesus says to the Pharisees, "If you were blind, you would not have sin. But now that you say, 'We see,' your sin remains" (Jn. 9:41). Sin supposes, then, that we see it clearly enough to recognize the signs by which God guarantees the authenticity of His message. Consequently, the more manifest these signs are, the greater is man's responsibility and his sin, if he refuses to believe: "If I had not come and spoken to them, they would have no sin. But now they have no excuse for their sin. He who hates me hates my Father also. If I had not done among them works such as no one else has done, they would have no sin. But now they have seen, and have hated both me and my Father" (Jn. 15:22–24).

The sinner refuses the light, his works are bad, and the light makes this malice apparent (Jn. 3:19–21). It is in this way, Jesus says, that men condemn themselves. This condemnation produces the punishment: the rejected light gradually grows dim until it disappears altogether. This progressive obscuring of the conscience is one of the most dramatic aspects of St. John's Gospel: we can follow it in the reactions of the Jews to the discourse at Capharnaum (6:67) and to the discourse at Jerusalem (7:11–36, 40–44; 8:31–59; 10:20, 22–39). Jesus had a painful experience of this refusal of the conscience which, won over for a moment by the attraction of the light, recovers itself afterwards and goes into hiding. Thus, after the triumphal entry into Jerusalem, He predicts to the Jews the greater triumph which He will win by the Cross: "And I, if I be lifted up from the earth, will draw all things to myself" (Jn. 12:32). The crowd protests, "We have heard from the Law that the Christ abides forever. And how canst thou say, 'The Son of Man must be lifted up'? Who is this Son of Man?" Jesus gives them this grave warning: "Yet a little while the light is among you.

Walk while you have the light, that darkness may not overtake you. He who walks in the darkness does not know where he goes. While you have the light, believe in the light, that you may become sons of light" (*ibid.*, 34–36).[19]

This light is Christ. Soon He is going to disappear, and the crowds of Jerusalem will see Him no longer. He is also the interior light which shines from His word and works and from which the gaze of man can turn away. And thus man becomes blind, but this blindness does not excuse him, for he blinded himself by turning away deliberately from the light.[20] As long as man persists in this refusal, nothing can lessen it; should he see a dead man rise, he would not give in (Lk. 16:31; Jn. 11:45–53). If the divine authority is too manifest, he turns his eyes away from it; questioned closely, he will answer: "I know not, I see not" (Mt. 21:27). Over such obstinate sinners the words of Our Lord have no hold (Jn. 8:37); they are from below, He is from above; they are of the world, He is not of the world (*ibid.*, 23); they are sons of the devil,[21] He is the Son of God (*ibid.*, 38, 44).

[19] St. Augustine, in Book X of the *Confessions,* has described at length these hesitations of the soul struggling between the attraction of the light and the seductiveness of the darkness. He comments on the text which we have just read, while transposing it from the historical sense to the psychological sense: "This life, which alone is happy, all men desire; the joy arising from truth all men desire . . . Why, then, do they not take their joy from it? Why are they not happy? Because they are more keenly concerned with other things which have greater power to make them unhappy than this one, which they faintly remember, to make them happy. 'Yet a little while the light is' in men; let them walk, walk, lest darkness overtake them" [*Confessions,* X, 23 (FC 21), tr. by V. Bourke, N. Y., Fathers of the Church, 1953, pp. 293, 294].

[20] This voluntary blindness has been described well by Kierkegaard, *Traité du Désespoir,* pp. 189–190, and in tr. *Sickness Unto Death* (cf. above, footnote, p. 31).

[21] It is understood that there cannot be any question here of a true filiation: but of an imitation and, more still, of a dependency. [Cf. Bonsirven, *Epîtres de saint Jean* (*Verbum Salutis,* 9), Paris, Beauchesne, 1954, p. 179.]

Thus this blindness is a servitude: the sinner is the slave of sin (Jn. 8:34; Rom. 6:16 ff.) and he belongs to the devil: he is under his domination or even in his possession. Thus Judas, of whom they said that, when he had received the morsel Jesus held out to him, "Satan entered into him" (Jn. 13:27; cf. 6:72; 13:2).

The sinner it is who has cast himself into this blindness, into this captivity; but it is not within his power to pull himself out. He has blinded himself, he cannot restore his own sight; he has sold himself as a slave, he cannot set himself free. Our Lord has clearly taught sinners that the debt they have contracted with God surpasses infinitely all their resources (Mt. 18:23–35); before Him they will never be but insolvent debtors (Lk. 7:42). Their only hope will be the mercy of their Father, who will forgive them all their debts if they themselves are merciful, and that is what Jesus teaches us to ask for: "Forgive us our debts, as we also forgive our debtors" (Mt. 6:12; Lk. 11:4).

After the death of Jesus, the foundation of the Church, and the gift of the Spirit, the Christians understand better the immensity of their obligations and, consequently, of their responsibility. The Epistle to the Hebrews recalls it to them with a forcefulness that makes us tremble:

It is impossible for those who were once enlightened, who have both tasted the heavenly gift and become partakers of the Holy Spirit, who have moreover tasted the good word of God and the powers of the world to come, and then have fallen away, to be renewed again to repentance; since they crucify again for themselves the Son of God and make him a mockery . . .

If we sin wilfully after receiving the knowledge of the truth, there remains no longer a sacrifice for sins, but a certain dreadful expectation of judgment, and "the fury of a fire which will consume the adversaries." A man making void the Law of Moses dies without any mercy on the word of two or three witnesses; how much worse punishments do you think he deserves who has trodden underfoot the Son of God, and has regarded as unclean the blood of the covenant through which he was sanctified, and has insulted the Spirit of grace? For we know him who has said, "Vengeance is mine, I will repay."

And again, "The Lord will judge his people." It is a fearful thing to fall into the hands of the living God.[22]

When we read over these frightening texts, we tremble, and instinctively would we say with St. Peter upon hearing the stern words of Jesus concerning the salvation of the rich: "Who then can be saved?" Our Lord answered him, "With men this is impossible, but with God all things are possible" (Mt. 19:26). He who has justified us at baptism can reconcile us by penance, but He alone can do it.[23]

Sin, then, is a terrible evil, and the ravages it causes are humanly irreparable. After reflecting on them, we understand better the infinite mercy and wisdom of the Father; it is to those unfortunates, to those vineyard murderers, that He has sent His Son. And indeed only the Son of God could raise them from so steep a fall: Light of the world, only He could give sight to the blind (Jn. 8:12); Son of God, only He could give filial liberty to the slaves of sin (ibid., 35–36): "The slave does not abide in the house forever; the son abides there forever. If therefore the Son makes you free, you will be free indeed."

3. SINNERS IN SOCIETY

So far we have considered sinners pursuing here below their individual existences. But, in reality, they do not live isolated;

22 Heb. 6:4–6; 10:26–31.
23 We can clarify these texts by those of St. John, in his first Epistle: he thinks that a Christian cannot sin: "No one who abides in him commits sin; and no one who sins has seen him, or has known him . . . Whoever is born of God does not commit sin; because his seed abides in him and he cannot sin, because he is born of God" (1 Jn. 3:6, 9). Nevertheless, he had said previously, "My dear children, these things I write to you in order that you may not sin. But if anyone sins, we have an advocate with the Father, Jesus Christ the just; and he is a propitiation for our sins, not for ours only but also for those of the whole world" (ibid., 2:1–2). We are aware in these texts, on the one hand, of the ardent faith of the apostle in the efficacy of baptism and in the grace of filial adoption; and, on the other hand, of his confidence in the mercy which still intercedes for fallen Christians.

sin reigns not only over individuals but over entire societies, whose members, like convicts riveted to the same chain, paralyze and bruise one another. Such appear to have been, in the story of Jesus, the Pharisees: one and the same pride, one and the same hate unite them; no one of them has the courage to break free from the group. They send some police to arrest Jesus; these men return, not having dared to touch Him: "Why have you not brought him?" "Never has man spoken as this man." "Have you also been led astray? Has any one of the rulers believed in him, or any of the Pharisees? But this crowd, which does not know the Law, is accursed." Nicodemus makes a timid attempt to intervene: "Does our Law judge a man unless it first give him a hearing, and know what he does?" "Art thou also a Galilean? Search the Scriptures and see that out of Galilee arises no prophet" (Jn. 7:45–52).

If a "master in Israel" is thus terrorized, how will the poor people fare? The parents of the man born blind dare not even give testimony on his blindness: "For already the Jews had agreed that if anyone were to confess him to be the Christ, he should be put out of the synagogue" (Jn. 9:22). We begin to feel that terrible power of religious society or of civil society closing every avenue to a person claiming release from them.[24]

What appears thus in the Gospel story, at the heart of a Jewish society governed still by respect for the Law, will be accentuated in a still more violent contrast among the pagans. This opposition of pagan society is already described in the Book of Wisdom, 2:11–20, where the sacred author has the pagans speak as follows:

That which is feeble, is found to be nothing worth. Let us therefore lie in wait for the just, because he is not for our turn, and he is contrary to our doings, and upbraideth us with transgressions of the law,

---

[24] Sometimes the obstacle will appear more tenuous without being less effective: simple worldly expediency, which can suffice to drive a man to crime. Thus Herod Antipas surrenders the head of John the Baptist at the whim of a dancing girl; he was very sorry to have to do it, but because of the oath he had given, because of all the guests surrounding him, he was reluctant to oppose the daughter of Herodias (Mk. 6:26).

and divulgeth against us the sins of our way of life. He boasteth that he hath the knowledge of God, and calleth himself the son of God. He is become a censurer of our thoughts. He is grievous unto us, even to behold: for his life is not like other men's, and his ways are very different. We are esteemed by him as triflers, and he abstaineth from our ways as from filthiness, and he preferreth the latter end of the just, and glorieth that he hath God for his father. Let us see then if his words be true, and let us prove what shall happen to him, and we shall know what his end shall be. For if he be the true son of God, he will defend him, and will deliver him from the hands of his enemies. Let us examine him by outrages and tortures, that we may know his meekness and try his patience. Let us condemn him to a most shameful death: for there shall be respect had unto him by his words.

This text has often been regarded as prophetic; we cannot see in it properly speaking a prophecy of the Passion of our Lord, but we should recognize in it one of the most accurate and profound expressions of the antagonism which opposes infidelity to faith. It is not a question of legislating persecution, and, indeed, this legislation is not necessary. The antagonism is more profound: it is in life: the just man, the pagans say, is contrary to our manner of acting; he is the living reproach of our thoughts; his sight alone is for us intolerable. Between pagans and the faithful, the conflict is inevitable.

We should note also the violent hate which bursts forth on this page. In the beginning it might seem that the faithful man is being reproached only for being a good-for-nothing in the city. But it is much worse: the chief complaint which they lodge against him is that of relying on God for his support: he calls himself the child of God, he boasts having God for his father. This claim is answered with an outburst of hate and a defiance of God Himself. We think we already hear the blasphemies of Calvary: "He trusted in God; let him deliver him now if he wants him; for he said, 'I am the Son of God' " (Mt. 27:43).[25]

---

[25] A similar remark could be made in reading, in Mt. 22:6–7, the second part of the parable of the marriage feast, which we have quoted above, following St. Luke: "The rest laid hold of his servants, treated them

4. THE HATRED OF GOD

As the revelation becomes more luminous, it provokes from sinners a more conscious and more violent opposition. Behind the
moral law, there appears the legislator; if one sets His prohibi-
tion at naught, there is no longer only transgression of His will,
there is scorn and hatred of His Person: "The wisdom of the
flesh is hostile to God" (Rom. 8:7).

This hatred is explained by the commandment which God
imposes on man and against which, in the full light of his conscience, man revolts; but it betrays also the influence of the
tempter. Ever since the first sin, Satan does his utmost to captivate
man and oppose him to God; by sinning, man makes himself
the slave of the demon and subjects to him this sensible world
which God had made the domain of men.

The Gospel story and the apostolic teaching clearly manifest
to us this tyranny of the demon over man and the world. We
see it in the temptations of Christ, particularly the last: "The
devil led him up, and showed him all the kingdoms of the world
in a moment of time. And he said to him, 'To thee will I give
all this power and their glory; for to me they have been delivered, and to whomever I will I give them. Therefore if thou
wilt worship before me, the whole shall be thine' " (Lk. 4:5–7).

Throughout the course of Our Lord's life the conflict is continued, especially in the exorcisms which from beginning to
end mark Jesus' ministry: "What have we to do with thee, Son
of God? Hast thou come here to torment us before the time?"
(Mt. 8:29; Mk. 5:7, 3:11; Lk. 4:41). These deliverances of
possessed persons are works of mercy, performed to relieve men,
but they are also a battle against Satan, and it is thus that
Jesus Himself presents them: "If I cast out devils by the Spirit
of God, then the kingdom of God has come upon you. Or, how
can anyone enter the strong man's house and plunder his goods,

---

shamefully, and killed them. But when the king heard of it, he was angry;
and he sent his armies and destroyed those murderers, and burnt their
city." Whenever sin becomes exasperated, it reveals its true nature: revolt against God.

unless he first binds the strong man? Then he will plunder his house" (Mt. 12:28–29).

The paroxysm of this conflict breaks out in Our Lord's passion and in His death: at the Last Supper Jesus warned His apostles that Satan desired to have them, that he might sift them as wheat (Lk. 22:31); a little later on, a more urgent warning is given: "The prince of the world is coming" (Jn. 14:30); and indeed throughout the course of the drama we feel the Jews being swept against the Son of God by a truly diabolic hatred. They think to triumph by causing Jesus to die; but this triumph of Satan is his downfall:

You, when you were dead by reason of your sins and the uncircumcision of your flesh, he brought to life along with him, forgiving you all your sins, cancelling the decree against us, which was hostile to us. Indeed, he has taken it completely away, nailing it to the cross. Disarming the Principalities and the Powers, he displayed them openly, leading them away in triumph by force of it (Col. 2:13–15).[26]

From then on, the conflict is continued:

Our wrestling is not against flesh and blood, but against the Principalities and the Powers, against the world-rulers of this darkness, against the spiritual forces of wickedness on high (Eph. 6:12).

The whole pagan religious world, which the apostles find opposed to them and which they must convert, is enslaved to demons. Not that the idol amounts to anything, for it is nothing;

---

[26] On this text one may read F. Prat, "Le triomphe du Christ sur les Principautés et les Puissances," *Recherches de Science religieuse,* 1912, pp. 201–229; Huby, *Saint Paul, Les épîtres de la captivité (Verbum Salutis),* 7th ed., Paris, Beauchesne, 1935, pp. 73–76. It is certain that St. Paul affirms the abolition of the debt contracted by sinful man; as for the Principalities and the Powers, whom Christ has "displayed openly," many exegetes consider them good angels; thus Prat and Huby. I hesitate to follow them, and I would be more ready to consider them as angels hostile to Christ and to the Christians, like those of whom mention is made in Eph. 6:12, quoted below.

but the sacrifices offered to it are in reality offered to demons.[27] Also when Paul comes into Athens, he sees, not without indignation, the whole city enslaved to idols (Acts 17:16). There is, then, behind this artistic, sceptical, brilliant façade a whole background which is rarely unveiled, but which leads the battle against Christ.

Through baptism Our Lord rescues from Satan the men He would conquer; Satan will revenge himself for this by his violent or treacherous attacks. The persecutions which shake the Christian structure from without, the heresies which attempt to damage it from within, are both maneuvers of Satan, and do not deceive the Christians. The martyrs regarded as their enemy neither the crowd nor the judge nor the executioner, but only Satan, against whom they opposed the might of Christ.[28] Similarly, St. Polycarp recognizes in the heresiarchs sons of Satan.[29]

At the end of this preliminary study, we are aware of the misery, incurable from the viewpoint of nature, of sinful humanity: having revolted against God, it has become the slave of sin and, through sin, the slave of the demon. Linked together by the complicity of their offenses, men oppose one another by their covetous desires: a man can lay hold of the goods he pursues only by snatching them from the hands of others; this precarious possession, forever in dispute, is the source of the continual revival of conflicts among brothers, families, and nations. Men can be united only in obedience to the one Shepherd; once the shepherd is driven away, the flock is dispersed and the sheep lose their way. It is in this way that mankind is viewed by Jesus:

[27] 1 Cor. 10:19–20. This conflict between Christianity and the demons will be affirmed, in the history of the apostles as in the Gospels, by exorcisms: (Acts 16:18; 19:13–17).
[28] Letter of the confessors of Lyons, in Eusebius, *Ecclesiastical History* (FC 19, N. Y., Fathers of the Church, 1954), V. 1, pp. 273, 278, 282–283. *Actes de sainte Perpétue*, 4, 10; cf. *The Passion of SS. Perpetua and Felicity, MM.*, tr. by W. Shewring, London, Sheed & Ward, 1931.
[29] Epistles to the Philippians 7, and in tr. *The Epistles and the Martyrdom of St. Polycarp* (ACW 6), tr. by J. Kleist, S.J., Westminster (Md.), Newman, 1948, p. 79. Cf. Irenaeus, *Adv. Haer.*, III, 3, 4.

He "had compassion on them, because they were like sheep without a shepherd" (Mk. 6:34). Assuredly, men are not lacking who claim the role of shepherds; but they are only "thieves and robbers"; their only concern is "to steal, and slay, and destroy" (Jn. 10:8, 10). And those who succeed in this wretched business are the most unfortunate of all: we have only to recall the lot of Herod, guilty of murdering his family.

All these discords, all these hatreds, all these sterile pains are the fruits of sin. To all these unfortunates Jesus will say, "Come to me, all you who labor and are burdened, and I will give you rest. Take my yoke upon you, and learn from me, for I am meek and humble of heart; and you will find rest for your souls. For my yoke is easy, and my burden light" (Mt. 11:28–30).

chapter 3

❖❖❖❖❖❖❖❖❖❖

The Coming of the Kingdom
of God

All was lost: forgotten, unrecognized or hated, God seemed driven from the world. The demon reigned over the land: "Jews and Greeks are all under sin, as it is written, 'There is not one just man; there is none who understands; there is none who seeks after God' " (Rom. 3:9–11).

It is then that God appears: "I was found by those who did not seek me; I appeared openly to those who made no inquiry of me" (Rom. 10:20, quoting Is. 65:1). He appears, not to punish the world, but to save it (Jn. 3:17).

The Incarnation of the Son of God, the work of a wholly gratuitous and all-powerful mercy, is the great mystery which will transform the universe, and especially the destiny of men. It is the supreme gift of God, an inkling of which, from the start of His ministry, Jesus gives to a few of His disciples whom He judges capable of rising that far: to Nicodemus: "God so loved the world that he gave his only-begotten Son, that those who believe in him may not perish, but may have life everlasting" (Jn. 3:16); to the Samaritan woman: "If thou didst know the gift of God, and who it is who says to thee, 'Give me to drink,' thou, perhaps, wouldst have asked of him, and he would have given thee living water" (Jn. 4:10).

This supreme gift of God reveals to us His love and, at the same time, the value and the purpose of our lives. Already creation had made us marvel at the divine liberality: God creates in order to have someone on whom to bestow His benefits.[1] Here the same love is manifested and with a splendor we could never have imagined: God gives us His Son, and to save us from our sins, He sends Him to die.

At the end of His life Jesus wanted to show to the leaders and the people of Israel this will of the Father in the parable of the Vine-dressers.[2] The master of the vineyard had sent one messenger after another to claim the rents; the disloyal vine-dressers had insulted, beaten, and finally killed all these envoys. The master had but one left—his beloved son. He sent him, after all the others, saying, "They will respect my son." This parable was spoken by Jesus four or five days before His death, against the Pharisees, in that city of Jerusalem "who killest the prophets" (Lk. 13:34). We cannot hear, without feeling a pang, these last words, "They will respect my son." Alas, has God, then, been mistaken? No, and thereby this divine gift appears so touching: God sent His Son to die, and His Son gave His life for those very ones who were to kill Him.

But before contemplating this sacrifice, we must consider that long series of God's endeavors crowned, at last, by the Incarnation: "God, who at sundry times and in divers manners spoke in times past to the fathers by the prophets, last of all in these days has spoken to us by his Son" (Heb. 1:1–2).

All tended thereto: the prophets heralded the Messias by their oracles; they foretold Him by their mission, their lives, their death. From that summit to which God at last has raised us, the

[1] Irenaeus, *Adv. Haer.*, IV, 14, 1, and in tr. *Treatise of Irenaeus of Lugdunum Against the Heresies,* London, 1916.
[2] Mk. 12:1–12; Mt. 21:33–46; Lk. 20:9–19.

sacred writer contemplates this long continuous line of witnesses to the faith: they "had experience of mockery and stripes, yes, even of chains and prisons. They were stoned, they were sawed asunder, they were tempted, they were put to death by the sword. They went about in sheepskins and goatskins, destitute, distressed, afflicted—of whom the world was not worthy" (Heb. 11:36–38).

There were, then, even in this world of sin, witnesses to the faith. Jesus will recall them as early as His Sermon on the Mount; these prophets, persecuted and put to death, are the forerunners of the Christians: to them belongs already the promised beatitude (Mt. 5:12; Lk. 6:23). They have maintained the hope and the desire of the faithful Israelites; they have testified to the love of God for His people; but they themselves were not saviors.[3]

This long waiting for the Messias, sustained by so many of the prophets, but also thwarted by so many persecutions, and put to the test by such long delays, by such painful silences on the part of God—this is for all Christians a great lesson: we cannot read again unfeelingly the plaints of the Psalmist:

How long, O Lord, turnest thou away unto the end? Shall thy anger burn like fire? Remember what my substance is: for hast thou made all the children of men in vain? Who is the man that shall live, and not see death: that shall deliver his soul from the hand of hell? Lord, where are thy ancient mercies, according to what thou didst swear to David in thy truth? Be mindful, O Lord, of the reproach of thy serv-

[3] "They have been sent, like the staff of Eliseus to the dead child . . . The staff was laid on the child; neither her voice nor her life came back: it was only a staff. He came down finally, He who had sent the staff, and He saved His people. Death has found once more its voice and its life" (St. Bernard, *In Cant. Hom.*, XV, 8. *P.L.*, CLXXXIII, col. 848, and in tr. Cf. *On the Song of Songs: Sermons In Cantica Canticorum*, tr. by a Religious of C.S.M.V., N. Y., Morehouse, 1952).

"Let God Himself follow His envoys, just as they have often promised, because without Him they can do nothing. [Eliseus] sent his servant and handed him his staff; and the deceased recovered neither his voice nor his life. I neither get up, nor shake off my dust, nor breathe, unless the prophet himself comes down and gives me a kiss with his mouth" (*ibid., Hom.* 2, 5, col. 791).

ants (which I have held in my bosom) of many nations: Wherewith thy enemies have reproached, O Lord; wherewith they have reproached, the change of thy anointed (Ps. 88:47–52).

It is from this protracted and painful waiting that we feel the deliverance at the dawn of the Gospel: in the *Nunc dimittis* of Simeon, in the gladness of Anna, in the joyful eagerness of the first disciples (Jn. 1:41).

Mankind had to implore this gift of God for a long time; a long desire had to plough those superficial souls and open them to grace. The same law is imposed again on us: the waiting seems long to our impatient selves; but when God has been given, we see clearly that there is no proportion between the waiting— though it last for centuries—and this gift of limitless value. It is this sovereignly precious Gift that we must study first of all.

1. THE AWAITED MESSIAS

In the first months of our Lord's ministry, after His first miracles, John the Baptist, prisoner in the fortress of Machaerus, sent to Jesus two of his disciples to ask Him: "Art thou he who is to come, or shall we look for another?" (Lk. 7:18–19; cf. Mt. 11: 2–3).

In the person of the Precursor, the whole of Judaism was interrogating Jesus, and the question he asked Him was the decisive question. The prophets had foretold the Messias by their oracles; they had presaged Him by their missions. This waiting for the Messias, sustained by so many divine promises, but also thwarted by so many persecutions, tested by such long delays and by so many painful silences on God's part, this expectation, was it finally fulfilled?

If, indeed, He who was to come had come, it was the coming of the kingdom of God; His faithful had nothing more to wait for here below; they could, like the old Simeon, sing their *Nunc dimittis.*

Throughout Jesus' ministry, we feel around Him the feverish impatience of the Israelites; we recognize it already in the case of John the Baptist's hearers when they ask him anxiously, "Who art thou? Art thou Elias? Art thou the Prophet?" (Jn. 1:19–21). The Samaritan woman asks Jesus, "I know that Messias is coming (who is called Christ), and when he comes he will tell us all things" (Jn. 4:25). And later the crowds of Jerusalem, drawn by the attraction of Jesus, but disconcerted by the opposition of their leaders: "Is not this the man they seek to kill? And behold, he speaks openly and they say nothing to him. Can it be that the rulers have really come to know that this is the Christ? Yet we know where this man is from; but when the Christ comes, no one will know where he is from" (Jn. 7:25–27); and others take up again: "When the Christ comes, will he work more signs than this man works?" (*ibid.,* 31); and a little while afterwards: "How long dost thou keep us in suspense? If thou art the Christ, tell us openly" (Jn. 10:24). In Galilee, the excitement is at an even higher pitch and breaks out sometimes in the enthusiastic adherence of a whole crowd; thus after the multiplication of the loaves: "When the people, therefore, had seen the sign which Jesus had worked, they said, 'This is indeed the Prophet who is to come into the world' " (Jn. 6:14).

We do not have to dwell here on the obscurity and the frailty of this faith: "The light shines in the darkness; and the darkness grasped it not" (Jn. 1:5). What is evident, at least, is the expectation of the Messias. This great hope, awakened by the prophets, has been diverted, no doubt, by bad teachers, obscured by human ambitions; but through all these clouds there pierces a little light still, and this light comes from Scripture: "You search the Scriptures, because in them you think that you have life everlasting. And it is they that bear witness to me, yet you are not willing to come to me that you may have life" (Jn. 5:39–40). Right there is one of the most moving aspects of the Gospel: before a people racked by an anxious yearning for the Messias, predicted and awaited for so long a time, the Messias makes His appearance and, more often than not, goes unrecognized. He is too divine, and transcends too much the expectation of the Jews. The little ones and the simple would recognize Him; the wise and the prudent see Him not:

"I praise thee, Father, Lord of heaven and earth, that thou didst hide these things from the wise and prudent, and didst reveal them to little ones. Yes, Father, for such was thy good pleasure. All things have been delivered to me by my Father; and no one knows who the Son is except the Father, and who the Father is except the Son, and him to whom the Son chooses to reveal him." And turning to his disciples he said, "Blessed are the eyes that see what you see! For I say to you, many prophets and kings have desired to see what you see, and they have not seen it; and to hear what you hear, and they have not heard it" (Lk. 10:21–24).

If the prophets did not have the happiness to see and hear Jesus, at least they hailed Him from afar in their prophetic vision and were glad: "Abraham your father rejoiced that he was to see my day. He saw it and was glad" (Jn. 8:56).[4]

In the second century, the Marcionites will think that Christ is wronged by being linked with the Old Testament and the prophets: this whole past belongs to the just God; Christ is the Son of the good God; He has come, sent by an unknown God into a world which was not expecting Him; if we hail Him as the Messias foretold by the prophets, we reduce Him to their level and fail to recognize His transcendence. St. Irenaeus, in refuting these attacks, has sketched in bold relief the close union of the prophets and Christ and, with the same stroke, the grandeur of this so long awaited King. What has Christ brought us that is new, the Marcionites say, if He has been thus foretold? Irenaeus answers them:

Know that He has announced to us all that is new by giving Himself, He who had been announced. A new principle had to come, which would renovate and vivify humanity. The servants who are before the king announce his coming, so that his subjects can make preparations to receive their Lord. But when the King has come, when his subjects have been filled with that joy which had been foretold to them, when they have received from him their liberty, when they have contemplated his countenance, when they have heard his words, when they

4 The Evangelist will speak in the same way, after quoting the words of Isaias at the time of his great vision in the Temple (Is. 6:10): "Isaias said these things when he saw his glory and spoke of him" (Jn. 12:40–41).

have enjoyed his gifts—no one with sense inquires what more the King has given, over and above the contribution of the forerunners who had announced Him. He has given Himself; He has given to men those gifts which had been promised and which the angels themselves are eager for.[5]

In the history of spiritual doctrine, as in the history of dogmatic theology, nothing is more important than that unity of the two Testaments in the Person of Jesus Christ foretold by the prophets, founder and Head of the Church. Just as the Gospel is not opposed to the Law, but consummates it, so Jesus is not opposed to the prophets; by His coming He fulfills their promises. His presence among us, the gift of the Spirit which He confers on us, the foundation of holy Church—these are the divine goods which the prophets had us hope for.

This is the One who was to come; and we do not have to await another. This second affirmation is no less important than the first: Jesus Christ consummates the whole past; He governs the whole future. It is towards Him that the entire Old Testament tends; it is upon Him that the whole New Testament depends. Just as the prophets are understood only in the light of Christ, who illumines and confirms their testimony,[6] so the Church is understood only by the life of Christ, who is its source and who, by His Spirit, continually fructifies and rejuvenates it. No Christian, then, will be so foolish as to expect another Christ, another revelation, another Gospel.[7] But neither will anyone ever claim to exhaust "the unfathomable riches of Christ" (Eph. 3:8). Thus we shall be on our guard against both fickleness and satiety; we

---

[5] *Adv. Haer.*, IV, 34, 1. *P.G.*, VII, 1083–1084.

[6] That is why St. Justin calls Jesus Christ "the interpreter of the misunderstood prophecies" (*Apology*, I, 32, 2); cf. *Dialogue*, 100, 2: "He has disclosed to us, by His grace, all that we understand of the Scriptures." Cf. *The Apologies of Justin Martyr*, Cambridge (Eng.), 1911, and *Justin Martyr, the Dialogue with Trypho*, tr. by A. Williams, N. Y., Macmillan, 1930.

[7] Cf. Tertullian, *De Praescriptione*, VII, 12–13: "After Christ, we have no need of curiosity, and after the Gospel, no need of searching. Once we believe, we have nothing else to believe. For the first article of our faith is that there is nothing else to be believed."

shall ever have but one Master, Christ (Mt. 23:10), but we must ponder the teachings of this Master and never tire of contemplating His life. No one but the Father can penetrate thoroughly its unfathomable depths.

Here one might read again the magisterial commentary which St. John of the Cross has given on the words of the heavenly Father at the time of the Transfiguration: "This is my beloved Son in whom I am well pleased; hear him" (Mt. 17:5).[8]

This jealous fidelity to Christ, the sole Master, will always be, for the Church, a fundamental dogma. In A.D. 155, at the time of the martyrdom of St. Polycarp, the Jews demanded of the governor that the Christians be refused the body of their bishop: "They will abandon the Crucified," they said, "and worship this man in good earnest." The Smyrnites replied:

They [the Jews] did not realize that we shall never bring ourselves either to abandon Christ, who suffered for the salvation of all those that are saved in the whole world—the Innocent for sinners!—or to worship any other. Him we worship as being the Son of God, the martyrs we love as being disciples and imitators of the Lord; and deservedly so, because of their unsurpassable devotion to their King and Teacher.[9]

Twenty years later, Montanism broke out in Phrygia, appealing to a new prophecy: Jesus, they said, had announced the coming of the Paraclete; this promise is realized: Montanus is the Paraclete, and his message surpasses all previous revelations, even those of Christ and the apostles.[10]

These sacrilegious claims shocked the conscience of the ortho-

---

[8] This commentary is quoted below, pp. 232–233.

[9] *Martyrdom of St. Polycarp,* 17, in *The Epistles and Martyrdom of St. Polycarp* (ACW 6), pp. 98–99.

[10] Cf. J. Lebreton and J. Zeiller, *Histoire de l'Eglise* (Fliche-Martin), II, *De la fin du 2ᵉ siècle à la paix constantinienne* (Paris, Bloud, 1938), p. 38, and the texts quoted there, and in tr. *The History of the Primitive Church,* tr. by E. Messenger, N.Y., Macmillan, 1953. Cf. P. de Labriolle, *La Crise montaniste,* Paris, Leroux, 1913, pp. 131 ff.

dox and were immediately condemned; but they found some adherents among the restless Christians eager for new revelations.[11]

In the following century, Mani will accept the responsibility for the affirmations of Montanus: he has received from the Paraclete the sovereign, definitive revelation.[12]

For a long time Montanism and Manichaeism have been defunct heresies, of interest only to historians. But this history lesson is valuable: it shows us, in contrast to the pride and restlessness of the human spirit, the humble fidelity of the Church: she has but one Master, Christ, and she will gladly repeat with St. Paul: "Even if we or an angel from heaven should preach a gospel to you other than that which we have preached to you, let him be anathema!" (Gal. 1:8).

At the beginning of this study, we ought to emphasize this affirmation, which gives to the Christian message its full significance. We shall strive, then, to set forth the mysteries of Jesus' life, the revelations He has made to us, the Church He founded, the treasures of grace He put into her hands. But, above all things, what is important for us to know is Christ Himself and His unfathomable riches: our whole spiritual life depends thereon.

Taking our inspiration from the New Testament, and especially from the Gospel, we shall study the Son of Man, the Gift of God, the Image of God, the Son of God, the Savior.

[11] It is remarkable that the most valuable conquest which Montanism made was that of the great African apologist who but lately had proven so strict with regard to every innovation and curiosity. Tertullian will write in *De Virginibus Velandis,* 1: "In its rudiments, justice relies on the natural fear of God. By the Law and the Prophets, it came to infancy. By the Gospel, it knew the ardor of youth. And now, by the Paraclete, it takes on a more settled maturity." Cf. de Labriolle, *La Crise montaniste,* p. 328, and his *Les Sources de l'histoire du Montanisme,* p. 14.

[12] Thus in the text: "The Paraclete has revealed to me all that has happened and that will happen, all that the eye sees, all that the ear hears, all that the intelligence understands. Through Him I have learned to know all; through Him I have seen all; I have become (with Him) one single body and one single spirit"—quoted by C. Schmidt, *Neue Originalquellen des Manichoeismus aus Aegypten* (Stuttgart, 1933), p. 35, and *Histoire de l'Eglise,* p. 316.

Little by little, in the humble, gentle Teacher, there will appear to us the beloved Son in whom the Father was well pleased
and to whom He urges us to listen.

2. THE SON OF MAN

If this Messias, foretold by the prophets, if this founder of the
Church, governs the history of mankind and even the entire history of the world, it is because He is the Son of God. Henceforth
and for eternity, the Son of God is one of us; He is Emmanuel,
God with us. But for a proper understanding of this presence, we
must bear in mind that this God comes among us, not as a
stranger, but as one of us: He was made man: "The Word was
made flesh" (Jn. 1:14). We read in the Book of Tobias a remarkable story: the angel Raphael, one of the seven who stand before the throne of God, has been sent by the Lord to Tobias, in
order to guide the young Tobias on his journey, cure the blind
father and deliver Sara. He carries out his mission faithfully and,
before returning to God, reveals his identity: "I am the angel
Raphael, one of the seven who stand before the Lord." Frightened, the father and the son fall down, face to the ground.
The angel reassures them and says to them: "When I was with
you, I was there by the will of God: bless ye him, and sing praises
to him. I seemed indeed to eat and to drink with you: but I use
an invisible meat and drink, which cannot be seen by men" (Tob.
12:15–19).

The Son of God did not come to us like the angel Raphael.
He did not disguise Himself in human form; He was made flesh.
When He ate and drank, it was not simply a guise: His body, like
ours, had need of food and drink; He was hungry in the desert
(Mt. 4:2); He was thirsty on the Cross (Jn. 19:28); near
Jacob's well He sat down, wearied from the journey (Jn. 4:6);
after a day of preaching, He fell asleep on the cushion of the
boat (Mk. 4:38). He took upon Himself all our miseries, save
sin and the ignorance which is its consequence. There will be,
no doubt, some proud, timid souls who will be ashamed of the
Incarnation of the Son of God and want to delete it from the

Gospel;[13] but this Docetism will be rejected by the Church as a heresy which imperils, along with the reality of the Incarnation, the reality of man's salvation. The apostle St. John combatted this error most strenuously[14] and after him, St. Ignatius of Antioch[15] and St. Polycarp.[16]

The vigor of this orthodox reaction makes more evident the importance of the dogma in question here: the flesh is not a principle of evil, incapable of salvation. The Son of God is united to it by His Incarnation; He purifies and nourishes it by His Eucharist, and He will raise it up on the last day.[17]

---

[13] Thus the author of the apocryphal *Acts* of John, ch. XCIII: "Sometimes I wanted to grasp Him and I would encounter a material, solid body; another day, when I touched Him, I felt an immaterial, incorporeal, a sort of non-existing substance. When He was invited by some Pharisee, we made our way there with Him. Our hosts gave some bread to each of us. He Himself took a piece, blessed it and shared it with us; a small piece satisfied us and our pieces of bread remained intact, and those who had invited Him were amazed. Often, when I walked with Him, I endeavored to see the imprint of His footsteps on the ground; for I saw Him raise Himself from the ground; but never have I been able to see the imprint." Cf. *Apocryphal New Testament,* tr. by M. R. James, Oxford, Clarendon, 1924 and 1950.

[14] "What was from the beginning, what we have heard, what we have seen with our eyes, what we have looked upon and our hands have handled: of the Word of Life . . . we announce to you" (1 Jn. 1 ff.). Cf. Jn. 19:34–35.

[15] He was "really born and ate and drank, really persecuted by Pontius Pilate, really crucified and died . . . really rose from the dead" (*Trall.,* 9 & 10; *Smyrn.,* 2; *Ephes.,* 7). Cf. in *The Epistles of St. Clement of Rome and St. Ignatius of Antioch* (ACW 1).

[16] *To the Philippians,* 7. Cf. *The Epistles and the Martyrdom of St. Polycarp* (ACW 6), p. 79.

[17] In connection with this one might read again the vigorous remonstrance of St. Irenaeus: "Those people are foolish to despise all of God's creation, to deny that the flesh is saved, to disdain its regeneration, to claim that it is incapable of incorruptibility . . . If the flesh is not saved, then the Savior has not redeemed us with His Blood, the chalice of the Eucharist is not the communion of His Blood, the bread we break is not the communion of His Body . . . How can one maintain that the flesh, nourished by the Body and Blood of Christ, and His member, is not open to God's grace, which is eternal life?" (*Adv. Haer.,* V, 2, 2.)

This dogma is of supreme importance in spiritual doctrine. It concerns, moreover, not only the flesh, but the whole of human nature. The Son of God has taken on not only flesh but also a soul and a body like our own, save for sin and its defects. We like to find in Him the spontaneity and freshness of human emotions, the love which the purity of a young man awakens in Him,[18] the joy He felt when the little children came running up to Him.[19] We are touched at His tears near the tomb of His friend,[20] at His pained surprise before the incredulity of His fellow citizens,[21] at His tears over unfaithful Jerusalem,[22] at His dread and anguish in the Agony.[23]

Such a real humanity is not an inaccessible ideal for us, but a model whose perfection, no doubt, we shall never equal, but which we can understand and strive to imitate. Here is one of the great benefits of the Incarnation.

3. THE IMITATION OF CHRIST

To the disciples who give themselves to Him, Jesus proposes, in a word, the rule of their life: "Follow me" (Mk. 1:17). He understands by that not only the type of fidelity which dogs His footsteps but, above all, the careful concern to imitate Him. He wants His disciples to be worthy of Him. It is an ideal whose perfection would be inaccessible to us, had not the incarnation of Our Lord brought it quite close to us. He takes hold of us, not only by His divine grace, but by the radiance of His human life. Surely He can ask us to follow Him:

He who loves father or mother more than me is not worthy of me; and he who loves son or daughter more than me is not worthy of me. And he who does not take up his cross and follow me, is not worthy

[18] Mk. 10:21: "and Jesus, looking upon him, loved him."
[19] Mt. 19:14.
[20] Jn. 11:35.
[21] Mk. 6:6.
[22] Lk. 19:41.
[23] Mk. 14:33 ff.; Mt. 26:37 ff.; Lk. 22:42–43.

of me. He who finds his life will lose it, and he who loses his life for my sake, will find it (Mt. 10:37–39; cf. 16:24–26).

If anyone comes to me and does not hate his father and mother, and wife and children, and brothers and sisters, yes, and even his own life, he cannot be my disciple. And he who does not carry his cross and follow me, cannot be my disciple. For which of you, wishing to build a tower, does not sit down first and calculate the outlays that are necessary, whether he has the means to complete it? Lest, after he has laid the foundation and is not able to finish, all who behold begin to mock him . . . So therefore, every one of you who does not renounce all that he possesses, cannot be my disciple (Lk. 14:26–29, 33).

If anyone serve me, let him follow me; and where I am there also shall my servant be (Jn. 12:26).

In the first months of His ministry, these appeals of Our Lord seemed stern in their demands. But as He becomes more intimately known to His disciples, this communal life with Him is presented more and more to them as the power and the joy of their lives. It remains a pressing duty for them, but already they find in it an inkling of a more intimate love attracting them.

Thus to the request of the sons of Zebedee asking for the first two places in the kingdom, Jesus replies: "You do not know what you are asking for. Can you drink of the cup of which I drink, or be baptized with the baptism with which I am to be baptized?" And they said to Him, "We can." "Of the cup that I drink, you shall drink; and with the baptism with which I am to be baptized, you shall be baptized . . ." And, giving this instruction a more general bearing, He continues, "Whoever wishes to become great shall be your servant; and whoever wishes to be first among you shall be the slave of all; for the Son of Man also has not come to be served but to serve, and to give His life as a ransom for many" (Mk. 10:38–39, 43–45).

To stamp this teaching even more deeply in the memory of His apostles, Jesus took it up again on the evening of the Last Supper while washing the feet of His disciples. And right afterwards He explained this lesson as follows:

Do you know what I have done to you? You call me Master and Lord, and you say well, for so I am. If, therefore, I the Lord and Master have washed your feet, you also ought to wash the feet of one another. For I have given you an example, that as I have done to you, so you also should do. Amen, amen, I say to you, no servant is greater than his master, nor is one who is sent greater than he who sent him. (Jn. 13:12–16).

And again, in the same talk: "Remember the word that I have spoken to you: No servant is greater than his master. If they have persecuted me, they will persecute you also; if they have kept my word, they will keep yours also" (Jn. 15:20).

Gradually the destiny which Jesus reserves to His apostles appears to them on the model of His own, and they themselves will have to bring to it the sentiments an example of which has been given them by their Master: humble service, dedication which yields to death for the ransom of all. All this will be the fruit of love, and it is above all by love that they will resemble their Master. Jesus tells them so again with emphasis in His farewell discourse: "A new commandment I give you, that you love one another; that as I have loved you, you also love one another" (Jn. 13:34). And again: "This is my commandment, that you love one another as I have loved you. Greater love than this no one has, that one lay down his life for his friends. You are my friends if you do the things I command you" (Jn. 15:12–14).

The death of Jesus, far from effacing these reminders, throws them into more striking relief. The Holy Spirit, according to the promise of the Master (Jn. 14:26), revealed to His disciples their full significance and carved them on their souls. The imitation of Jesus Christ will be, henceforth, the law of the Christian. St. Paul will say to his disciples, "Be imitators of me as I am of Christ" (1 Cor. 11:1; cf. 4:16; Phil. 3:17), and to the Philippians:

Have this mind in you which was also in Christ Jesus, who, though he was by nature God, did not consider being equal to God a thing to be clung to, but emptied himself, taking the nature of a slave and being made like unto men. And appearing in the form of man, he humbled himself, becoming obedient to death, even to death on a cross (Phil. 2:5–8).

We behold in this text the light which habitually illuminates the spiritual life of St. Paul and his preaching: to encourage his disciples to practise Christian virtues, he proposes to them the example of the Son of God and, by preference, he contemplates Him in the decisive choice of the Incarnation.[24]

It is less the daily detail of Jesus' words and actions which will captivate the Christians, than it is that incomparable splendor, that shining, gentle clarity of the Son of God, He who has lowered Himself to us, has lived among us, and who now lives in us.[25]

In the measure that the Christian habituates himself to behold and to imitate this model so close to him and yet divine, his eyes open up, his heart becomes purified, his soul elevated; he finds himself introduced into the intimacy of the Father, and invited to imitate Him.

4. THE KNOWLEDGE AND IMITATION OF THE FATHER

The whole effort of Jesus has been to raise His disciples to this summit of the spiritual life: ever since the start of His preaching, in the Sermon on the Mount, He has told them, "You therefore are to be perfect, even as your heavenly Father is perfect" (Mt. 5:48). It is above all on the last day at the Last Supper that He proposes to them, quite nearby, this divine Model they had thought inaccessible:

"I am the way, and the truth, and the life. No one comes to the Father but through me. If you had known me, you would also have

[24] Thus again, to exhort the Corinthians to give alms to the poor of Jerusalem, the Apostle says to them, "You know the graciousness of our Lord Jesus Christ—how, being rich, he became poor for your sakes, that by his poverty you might become rich" (2 Cor. 8:9).

[25] Cf. H. Pinard de la Boullaye, S.J., "L'imitation de J.-C. dans le Nouveau Testament," *Revue d'Ascétique et de Mystique,* 1934, p. 339.

known my Father. And henceforth you do know him, and you have seen him." Philip said to him, "Lord, show us the Father and it is enough for us." Jesus said to him, "Have I been so long a time with you, and you have not known me? Philip, he who sees me sees also the Father. How canst thou say, 'Show us the Father'? Dost thou not believe that I am in the Father and the Father in me?" (Jn. 14:6–10). "Yet a little while and the world no longer sees me. But you see me, for I live and you shall live. In that day you will know that I am in my Father, and you in me, and I in you" (*ibid.*, 19–20).

The discourse after the Last Supper is the loftiest revelation the Gospel has transmitted to us. It would have been unintelligible to the disciples at the time of their first contact with Jesus; if they can understand it in the Cenacle, it is because two years of life in common, of instruction, of example and graces, have gradually introduced them into the intimacy of Jesus.

Whoever, with the eyes of faith enlightened by the Holy Spirit, has seen the Son of God, such a one has seen the Father. This model of holiness which the apostles had constantly before them, they do not have to go beyond it, but only to penetrate and reproduce it. For more than two years they have lived continually in its light, without that splendor ever blinding them. The flesh is capable, then, of supporting this divine radiance; better still, in this light it discovers life.

Thus it is that, by the Incarnation of His Son, God has restored His original plan which sin had upset.

God had created man to His own "image and likeness" (Gn. 1:26), and man could have no more noble ambition than to resemble his Creator. But he could not, by his own efforts, raise himself to that superhuman perfection. In the earthly paradise, the demon had told him, in order to lead him into sin, "You will be like gods" (Gn. 3:5). Adam had let himself be led astray; since that fall, the ambitioned likeness seemed lost forever. And yet God's plan need not have been frustrated: by his sin, man had disfigured the divine imprint and fled far from God; God recovered him through the Incarnation:

Adam could not flee from the hands of God (the Son and the Holy Spirit), for to him the Father had once said, "Let us make man to our image and likeness." That is why, at the end of time, not by the will of the flesh, nor by the will of man, but by the good pleasure of the Father, his own hands have made living man, so that Adam might reproduce the image and likeness of God.[26]

Through the Incarnation of the Son of God, men have had quite nearby, before their eyes, a model whose perfection infinitely surpasses God's first sketch and, above all, their dreams. But for this wonderful restoration of the divine plan, they have had to wait a long time. During these centuries, men have commonly lost sight of their pristine grandeur and have renounced their spiritual ambitions. Occasionally, however, but very rarely, we encounter, even in philosophy, some aspiration to the likeness of God:

We ought to fly away from earth to heaven as quickly as we can; and to fly away is to become like God, as far as this is possible; and to become like him, is to become holy, just, and wise.[27]

These are noble words which do great honor to the philosophy which inspired them. But, if they reveal a deep-seated desire, we hesitate to say they open a way: are we sure of discerning the supreme justice, and can we hope to be elevated that high? We must recognize, furthermore, that this text is an isolated one in Plato. Elsewhere, moreover, the philosopher speaks of imitation of gods, not of imitation of God, and he himself gives the reason for this: "God mingles not with man; but through Love all the intercourse and converse of God with man, whether awake or asleep, is carried on." [28] Yet Platonism, of all Hellenistic philosophies, is the most spiritual, the most religious. The God of Aristotle, the One of Plotinus, are conceived of as supremely powerful forces, but unconscious of their action; they raise up,

---

[26] Irenaeus, *Adv. Haer.*, V, 8, 3. *P.G.*, VII, 1133.

[27] Plato, *The Dialogues: Theaetetus* (75 a-c), tr. by Jowett, v. 4, Oxford, 1892, p. 235. Cf. reissue of *Works*, tr. by Jowett, N. Y., Tudor, 1937.

[28] *Dialogues: Symposium*, v. 1, p. 573 (203 a). The devotees of a god are likened to him by love (*Phaedrus*, 252c–253ab; *Repub.*, X, 613b. Cf. *Dialogues*, v. 1, pp. 458–460 and v. 3, p. 329).

by attracting them, men whom they do not know. Here, much more even than in Platonism, we must repeat, "God mingles not with man."

For the Jews, God is not a stranger as He is for the pagans: He knows His people and His faithful, and He is known by them. "As a father hath compassion on his children, so hath the Lord compassion on them that fear him: for he knoweth our frame. He remembereth that we are dust." [29] To guide those blinded and to sustain those moulded from clay, God has given them His commandments; He has, through the prophets, made known to them His word; He instructs them by His Spirit, by His Wisdom. He even bids them be holy because He is holy.[30] Let us note, however, that here we understand above all that He is exempt from all Levitical impurity: the worship of Jahweh is holy, and requires stainless ministers.[31]

We are aware, moreover, in the whole of the Old Testament, of the concern to ensure God's transcendence, to remind the Israelites that God is infinitely above man, that His thoughts are above the thoughts of men, as much as heaven is above earth. This constant preoccupation is motivated only too rightly by the

[29] Ps. 102:13–14.

[30] Lv. 19:2.

[31] Cf. Bonsirven, *Le Judaisme palestinien,* t. I, p. 161: "If we try to penetrate further, we note that the conceptions [of holiness] are rather of a negative type: 'Be ye holy (that is, separated), because I the Lord your God am holy.' Separated, that is, avoiding all impurity, all evil and all injustice; thereby, the notion of holiness approximates those of purity and justice." On the conceptions of the imitation of Jahweh, cf. *ibid.,* t. II, p. 43; I. Abrahams, *Studies in Pharisaism and the Gospels,* N. Y. Macmillan, 1917, v. I, pp. 166–167; v. II (1924), pp. 138–182; S. Schechter, *Some Aspects of Rabbinical Theology,* N. Y., Macmillan, 1909, v. II, pp. 199–217. On the imitation of God in the religious philosophy of Philo, cf. Abrahams, *ibid.,* v. II, pp. 156–159. Philo's thought is clearly expressed in a text of his commentary on Genesis quoted by Eusebius (*Prep. Evang.,* VII, 13): "Nothing mortal would know how to be assimilated to the supreme Being, to the Father of the universe, but only to the second god who is his logos . . . It was impossible for anything produced to be assimilated to him who is above the logos, and who has an excellent and singular essence." We have quoted this text in the *Histoire du Dogme de la Trinité,* t. I, p. 228.

idolatry which surrounds and menaces Israel; but it is hardly favorable to the religious conception of the imitation of God.

It will be quite otherwise in the New Testament: it is the Son of God who reveals His Father, and this revelation enables us to penetrate into a divine intimacy which we could neither have ambitioned nor even have had an inkling of: "No one has at any time seen God. The only-begotten Son, who is in the bosom of the Father, he has revealed him" (Jn. 1:18). "No one knows the Son, except the Father; nor does anyone know the Father except the Son, and him to whom the Son chooses to reveal him" (Mt. 11:27).

Indeed, ever since the Sermon on the Mount, Jesus tells us, "You therefore are to be perfect as your heavenly Father is perfect" (Mt. 5:48).[32] This maxim has for its immediate object the love of enemies, and the form that it takes in St. Luke indeed specifies it: "Be ye merciful, therefore, even as your Father is merciful" (6:36). It is possible, nevertheless, that St. Matthew has preserved Jesus' expression more faithfully, as happens more often than not. This nuance, however, is of little importance to our study. What does interest us is the divine model which Jesus proposes to His hearers: "Love your enemies, do good to those who hate you, and pray for those who persecute and calumniate you, so that you may be children of your Father in heaven, who makes his sun to rise on the good and the evil, and sends rain on the just and the unjust" (Mt. 5:44–45).

---

[32] Abrahams, p. 151. After recalling Lv. 19:2, he continues: "With this idea of holiness went the other idea expressed by the term *tamim,* perfect, without blemish, whole-hearted, Godwards. It is at first sight tempting to hold that this is why Matthew expresses the Imitation formula in the terms: Be ye perfect, even as your heavenly Father is perfect. Such a formula would be a not unnatural derivative from: Be ye holy, for I the Lord am holy. Yet there is no verbal parallel in the Rabbinical literature to Matthew's form, it is original to him and unique in the Synoptics. Luke's version (VI, 36) 'Be ye merciful as your Father is merciful' has, on the other hand, many Pharisaic parallels, as we have seen."

5. THE DIVINE ADOPTION

To become "children of the heavenly Father" is the goal of Christian hope. If Jesus proposes it to us, it is because He Himself is God's Son, and because He makes us His brothers. This grace of the divine adoption is the supreme benefit of the Incarnation; it ought to transform our whole lives:

To as many as received him he gave the power of becoming sons of God; to those who believe in his name: who were born not of blood, nor of the will of the flesh, nor of the will of man, but of God (Jn. 1:12–13).

God had made of Adam a living soul; now He gives to men who believe in Him a "life-giving spirit" (1 Cor. 15:45). It is a "new creation" (Gal. 6:15); without it, no one can see the kingdom of God (Jn. 3:3). Jesus, in face of Nicodemus' astonishment, replies emphatically, "Amen, amen, I say to thee, unless a man be born again of water and the Spirit, he cannot enter into the kingdom of God. That which is born of the flesh is flesh; and that which is born of the Spirit is spirit" (Jn. 3:5–6).

This promise of God, which to Nicodemus seems so mysterious and even so incomprehensible, is illumined by the gift which God has made to us: "God so loved the world that he gave his only-begotten Son, that those who believe in him may not perish, but may have life everlasting" (Jn. 3:16). This life, which God gives to those who believe in His Son, makes of them children of God; and it is not simply a title, it is a life: "Behold what manner of love the Father has bestowed upon us, that we should be called children of God; and such we are" (1 Jn. 3:1).

To understand where this filial life is tending, let us gaze on Him who is by nature the Son of God. From all eternity, He is entirely orientated towards the Father, receiving from Him unceasingly all that He is, and bearing it back to Him in an infinite love, which is the Holy Spirit. In that Holy Trinity, the Persons are referred in their entirety one to the other; we would not know how to make room there for anything which isolates human persons, for anything of that life which they pursue in themselves and for themselves. In God, in that unity of nature, of will, of knowledge and action, whatever is personal is this movement of complaisance by which the Father embraces the Son, and the Son the Father. "All things that are mine are thine, and thine are mine" (Jn. 17:10). "This is my beloved Son, in whom I am well pleased" (Mt. 3:17; 17:5).[33]

The humanity of Jesus is not its own master; it is the humanity of the Son of God. From the first moment of His conception, it was taken up by an ever so powerful movement of the divine life which bears the Son towards the Father; and, from that first moment, the intuitive vision gave to this human nature of the Son of God the perfect contemplation both of the will of the Father and of the infinite complaisance which the Son takes thereby in His divine nature. And, in an irresistible movement of admiration and love, Jesus was given, never more to be taken back: "Sacrifice and oblation thou wouldst not, but a body thou hast fitted to me. In holocausts and sin-offerings thou hast had no pleasure. Then said I, 'Behold, I come—in the head of the book it is written of me—to do thy will, O God' " (Heb. 10:5–7).

This is the meaning of Jesus' entire life; it is the law of our own. But how can poor, sensual, selfish beings be elevated to so pure, so disinterested, so spiritual a life, to a life consisting entirely of an homage of filial love? This is impossible for man; it is possible for God: even from stones He can raise up children of Abraham (Mt. 3:9). There is still wanting that docility which He will not snatch from us, and which He would like to ask of us: "True worshippers will worship the Father in spirit and in truth. For the Father also seeks such to worship him" (Jn. 4:23).

How will the Father bring us round to this gift of ourselves? By presenting to us His Son, by laying hold of us through the attractiveness of this filial life, so divine and so human, the ideal model, and if we so wish, the source of our life. The Father, who

[33] We might note that the only words of the Father which are made to be heard in the Gospel are the words of love for the Son: at the baptism, at the Transfiguration; likewise at the entry into Jerusalem: "Father, glorify thy name!" "I have both glorified it, and I will glorify it again" (Jn. 12:28).

takes infinite pleasure in His Son, communicates to whom He will this complaisance. The whole heart of man is aware of it, but the whole heart of man can still refuse.

Men are classified by their docility or resistance. Some there are who, in preference to this filial docility which the Father asks of them, will choose the servitude of sin; they will remain sons of the devil (Jn. 8:44). But there are others who, won over by the attractiveness of Christ, will be rescued from their servitude and become children of God.

At Capharnaum, Jesus says to the wavering crowd surrounding Him, "Do not murmur among yourselves. No one can come to me unless the Father who sent me draw him" (Jn. 6:43–44); and He adds, "It is written in the Prophets, 'And they all shall be taught of God' " (*ibid.*, 45). We are reminded of these great promises of the Lord in Jeremias, for example: "I will give my law in their bowels, and I will write it in their heart: and I will be their God, and they shall be my people. And they shall teach no more every man his neighbor, and every man his brother, saying: Know the Lord: for all shall know me from the least of them even to the greatest, saith the Lord." [34]

This intimate knowledge of God will be communicated to the children of God, at the same time as they are given the spirit of adoption. This will be the principle of a new life, the pledge of beatitude: "This is everlasting life, that they may know thee, the only true God, and him whom thou has sent, Jesus Christ" (Jn. 17:3).

NOTE: *The Divine Filiation of Jesus and the Adoptive Filiation of the Christian*

The adoptive filiation which God bestows on us can be fully understood only as a participation in the filiation of the Son of God. Also the revelation of this signal grace was reserved to Jesus Christ; it is in making Himself known that He has prepared Christians to understand the sublime dignity to which the Father deigns to call them. This doctrine, expounded chiefly by St.

[34] Jer. 31:33–34; cf. Is. 54:13; Jl. 2:27.

Paul and St. John,[35] has been contemplated in their light by many Greek and Latin Fathers and by St. Thomas. Father Mersch has expounded in great detail this traditional doctrine, supporting it with the richest documentation.[36] Here it will suffice for us to recall some texts where the bond which joins our adoptive filiation with the natural filiation of Jesus Christ is more clearly indicated:

ST. IRENAEUS: How could we have participated in the adoption of sons, if we had not received from the Son the grace of being united to Him? (*Adv. Haer.*, III, 18, 7. *P.G.*, VII, 932). That is why the Son of God was made man; that is why He who is the Son of God willed as man to become the Son of man, so that, in receiving the adoption, he [man] might become a son of God (*ibid.*, III, 19, 1. *P.G.*, VII, 939; cf. *ibid.*, V, preface. *P.G.*, VII, 1120).

ST. CYPRIAN: *Filius missus esse et hominis filius fieri voluit, ut nos Dei filios faceret* (*De Opere et Eleemosynis*, 1. ed. Hartel, p. 373. Cf. *Saint Cyprian: Treatises: Works and Almsgiving* [FC 36], tr. by R. Deferrari, N.Y., Fathers of the Church, 1958, p. 227).

ORIGEN: The Savior is ever begotten by the Father; likewise, if you have the Spirit of adoption, God always begets you in Himself in each work, in each thought, and thus you become a son of God ever begotten in Christ Jesus (*In Jerem. Hom.*, IX, 4, ed. Klostermann, pp. 70, 24–27; cf. *In Joann.*, V, fr. XIC, ed. Preuscken, 563).

This theology blossoms forth especially in St. Athanasius, St. Hilary and St. Cyril of Alexandria. Here are a few texts among many others:

---

[35] In the expression of this adoptive filiation, we can distinguish a slight difference between St. Paul and St. John: St. Paul calls Christians "sons of God," υἱοί: Rom. 8:14, 19; Gal. 3:26; 4:5–7; Heb. 2:10; cf. Rom. 9:26; 2 Cor. 6:18. St. John reserves this term to the only-begotten Son, and calls Christians "children of God," τέκνα: Jn. 1:12; 11:52; 1 Jn. 3:1, 2, 10; 5:2.

[36] "Filii in Filio," *Nouvelle Revue théologique*, 1938, pp. 551–582, 681–702, 809–830. Cf. E. Mersch, S.J., *The Whole Christ: the Historical Development of the Doctrine of the Mystical Body in Scripture and Tradition*, tr. by J. Kelly, Milwaukee, Bruce, 1938, and his *Theology of the Mystical Body*, tr. by C. Vollert, S.J., St. Louis, Herder, 1951.

ATHANASIUS: There can be no adoption outside the true Son, since He Himself said, "No one knows the Father except the Son, and him to whom the Son chooses to reveal him . . ." Since, then, all those who are called sons and gods, on earth or in heaven, have received through the Word adoption and divinization, and since the Word is the Son, it is clear that all receive from Him, that He is before all, and even that He alone is true Son and true God of true God (*C. Arian.*, I, 39. *P.G.*, XXVI, 93). Men could not become sons, since they are by themselves creatures, had they not received in themselves the very Son of God. Also the Word made Himself flesh, to render man capable of divinity . . . We ourselves are not sons by ourselves, but He is who is within us; and God is not our Father by nature, but He is Father of the Word who is within us, in whom and by whom we cry out, "Abba, Father!" And the Father, on His part, says to those in whom He sees His own Son, "I have begotten you," and He calls them His sons (*C. Arian.*, II, 59. *P.G.*, XXVI, 273; cf. *C. Arian.*, I, 43. *P.G.*, XXVI, 100).

HILARY: *Natus enim ex Virgine Dei Filius, non tum primum Dei Filius cum filius hominis, sed in Filio Dei etiam filius hominis, ut et filius hominis esset filius Dei, naturam in se universae carnis assumpsit, per quam effectus vera vitis, genus in se universae propaginis tenet (In Ps., LI, 16. P.L., IX, 317).*

CYRIL OF ALEXANDRIA: He has dwelt amongst us: this is the profound mystery. All of us, indeed, were in Christ, and it is the common person of humanity which is rectified in Him . . . The Word has dwelt in all through a single One: One alone having been constituted Son of God in power according to the spirit of holiness, this dignity is communicated to the whole human race. So much so that, through One of us, this word affects us also: "I have spoken, you are all gods and sons of the Most High" (*In Joann.*, I, 9. *P.G.*, LXXIII, 161).

Just as all paternity in heaven and on earth comes from God the Father, because He alone is supremely and truly Father, so every filiation comes through the Son, because He alone is supremely and truly Son (*In Joann.*, II, I. *P.G.*, LXXIII, 213).

The Son of God became man, so that, in Him and through Him, men might be adopted as sons (*In Joann.*, XII, I. *P.G.*, LXXIV, 70).

Christ is at one and the same time the only Son and the first-born Son: He is only Son as God; He is first-born Son through the salutary union which He had contracted between Himself and us by becoming man. The purpose was, that we, in Him and by Him, might be made sons of God, both by nature and by grace: by nature, in Him and in Him alone; by participation and by grace, because of Him, in the Spirit (*De Recta Fide ad Theodosium*, 30. *P.G.*, LXXVI, 1177).

This theology—so dear to the Greek Fathers and to St. Hilary, who belongs to their group—is less familiar to the Latin Fathers, with the one exception, however, of the greatest among them, St. Augustine:

Unicus natura Dei Filius propter nos misericordia factus filius hominis, ut nos natura filii hominis, filii Dei per illius gratiam fieremus (*De Civ. Dei*, XXI, 15, and in tr. *The City of God*, tr. by G. Walsh, S.J., and D. Honan [FC 24], N.Y., 1954, p. 375).

Dicitur Filius Dei, sed ille aliter Filius Dei. Ille unicus, nos multi; ille unus, nos in illo unum; ille natus, nos adoptati; ille ab aeterno genitus per naturam, nos a tempore facti per gratiam (*In Ps.*, LXXXVIII, 7. *P.L.*, XXXVII, 1124).

Jam ergo in Domino, redempti sanguine ipsius, loti lavacro ipsius, filii sumus; quia sic multi sumus, ut in illo unus simus (*In Ps.*, CXXII. *P.L.*, XXXVII, 1634).

Quia filii Dei corpus sunt unici Filii Dei; et cum ille caput, nos membra, unus est filius Dei (*In Epist. ad Parth.*, 10. *P.L.*, XXXV, 2055).

Unicum eumdem ipsum, quem genuerat, et per quem cuncta creaverat, misit in hunc mundum, ut non esset unus, sed fratres haberet adoptatos (*In Joann.*, II, p. 9a).

St. Thomas has developed this theology at length in his commentaries on the Epistle to the Galatians and on the Epistle to the Romans; he has recalled it repeatedly in the *Summa Theologiae*.[37]

[37] *In Rom.*, expos. c. 8, lect. 6. *In Gal.*, expos. c. 3, lect. 9; c. 4, lect. 2; cf. lect. 3 *S. Theol.*, III, q. 39, a. 8, ad 3; q. 45, a. 4; q. 23, a. 1, ad 2, 3 and a. 5, ad 2; *Comp. Theol., ad Regin.*, 2, 5.

The theologians of the Vatican Council have proposed this doctrine in the schema of the *Doctrina Christiana:* Mansi, LIII, 292; cf. *ibid.,* 173, 234 (quoted by Mersch, *"Filii in Filio,"* p. 581).

6. THE GOD-MAN

The studies which we have just completed have enabled us to contemplate the "unfathomable riches of Christ" (Eph. 3:8), riches human and divine; but what we have to marvel at, especially, is that these divine and human gifts sustain and animate the life and action of a single Person: the Son of man is the Son of God. This unity of Christ is of supreme importance for the Christian: his whole spiritual life is governed by this dogma of faith.

The God-Man reveals to us, first of all, in the unity of His Person, the indissoluble union which, henceforth, will unite God and man. Never would we have dared to dream of one so close. As a result of their sin, men were separated from God by a chasm which was, for them, incapable of being bridged: they were without hope and without God. God comes to them, not as He had done up to then, through His servants, the prophets, but through His Son. Henceforth mankind will be united to God not only by those ties of adoration which men had severed, but by the indissoluble union of the two natures, divine and human, in Jesus Christ. And this Son of God, who deigns to become the Head of humanity, gives close access to the Father to all His members, that is to say, to every man who will be united to Him.

You were at that time without Christ, excluded as aliens from the community of Israel, and strangers to the covenants of the promise; having no hope, and without God in the world. But now in Christ Jesus you, who were once afar off, have been brought near through the blood of Christ. For he himself is our peace, he it is who has made both one . . . that of the two he might create in himself one new man, and make peace and reconcile both in one body to God by the cross . . . because through him we both have access in one Spirit to the Father (Eph. 2:12–16, 18).

Addressing himself to the Christians come over from paganism, the Apostle causes them to marvel at the divine peace, fruit of the blood of Christ: pagans and Jews see the wall crumble which for so long a time was a cause of their mutual separation. Mankind now forms but one people of the faithful, and this people at last find close access to God, by the blood of Christ, in the Holy Spirit. Thus are verified the prophecies which extolled the Messias as the cornerstone of the new building[38]: He unites the two walls up to then disjoined, and of the whole edifice finally completed, He makes the Temple of God.

Thus it is that Jesus is "our peace": He unites all of us to His Father, and all among ourselves. If we live united to Him as members are to the head, we are sure that nothing will separate us from the love of God:

I am sure that neither death, nor life, nor angels, nor principalities, nor things present, nor things to come, nor powers, nor height, nor depth, nor any other creature will be able to separate us from the love of God, which is in Christ Jesus our Lord (Rom. 8:38–39).

But if we are inseparably united to the heavenly Father, we cannot help but be united to all His children and love them, when we love Christ our Head and when we love God our Father.[39]

[38] In the parable of the Vine-dressers (Mt. 21:42; Mk. 12:10; Lk. 20:17), Jesus recalled the text of the Psalm (117:22) where it is said that the stone which the builders had rejected has become the cornerstone. Jesus compares with this text Is. 8:14; same comparison in 1 Pt. 2:6–8.

[39] St. Augustine, commenting on the first Epistle of St. John, writes: "The sons of God are the body of the only Son of God. Consequently, he who loves the sons of God, loves the Son of God; and he who loves the Son of God, loves the Father; and no one can love the Father, if he does not love the Son, and he who loves the Son, loves also the sons of God. What sons of God? The members of the Son of God. And by his love he, in turn, becomes a member, and love introduces him into the organism of the body of Christ; and thus it is Christ who loves Himself. Let no one give another love as the excuse for the exclusiveness of His love! This love maintains its own tight unity: just as He composes only a single organism, so of all those who constitute Him He makes a single whole and He melts them together as does fire. Thus in the case of gold, whose fusion makes a

Thus the unity of men in God is assured by the bond which attaches all of us to the heavenly Father, and this living bond is the Incarnate Son of God. Jesus Christ, living and dying for us, will consummate the union of all men among themselves and with God. This will be the fruit of His death[40] and of His Eucharist.[41] But the decisive step, which inaugurates and consecrates this union, is the Incarnation, uniting in the Son of God, by an indissoluble bond, humanity and divinity.[42]

He has dwelt amongst us: this is the profound mystery. All of us, indeed, were in Christ and it is the common person of humanity which is rectified in Him . . . The Word has dwelt in all through a single One: One alone having been constituted Son of God in power according to the spirit of holiness, this dignity is communicated to the whole human race. So much so that, through One of us, this word affects us also: "I have spoken, you are all gods and sons of the Most High." [43]

This union of divinity and humanity in the single Person of the Son of God has as a consequence not only the union of the human race with God; it also gives to the revelation made by the Son of God a unique value, which we must emphasize.

The message which He brings us has for its essential and primary object the divine mystery, and it is addressed to men. And its uniqueness lies in the fact that the bearer of the message is, at one and the same time, God and man; He is at home in both of these infinitely distant worlds. His knowledge of God "does not have its principle in a more or less confused experience, but in the same vision with which the Son of God sees His

---

single whole. But, unless the ardor of charity inflame them, it is impossible to melt the fragments into a single whole" (St. Augustine, *In Epistolam ad Parthos,* 10. *P.L.,* t. XXXV, 2055).

[40] Jn. 12:32; 11:52.

[41] Jn. 17:23.

[42] This aspect of the redemptive work, beheld especially in the Incarnation, has been brought out in particular by the Greek Fathers; one may read on this subject J. Rivière, *Le Dogme de la Rédemption,* 4th ed., Paris, Vrin, 1934, pp. 101–210 and in tr. *Doctrine of the Atonement: a Historical Essay,* tr. by L. Cappadelta, St. Louis, Herder (before 1928).

[43] St. Cyril of Alexandria, *In Joannem,* I, 9. *P.G.,* LXXIII, 161, quoted by Father Mersch, *"Filii in Filio," Nouvelle Revue théologique,* 1938, p. 573.

Father, with which God sees God; and the man who communicates it to men is the same God, made flesh." [44]

When Jesus says to His apostles, "The Father himself loves you" (Jn. 16:27), such ordinary words as these are of an inexhaustible plenitude: not only the men who have heard them, but all of Christ's disciples, right up to the last day, will rest their faith and hope on that filial assurance. "God speaks well of God"; He speaks of Him as a son speaks of his father, with a trust which nothing can shake. We do not experience in His voice ecstatic sighs, but the luminous peace of a knowledge which is natural to Him, in which He lives from all eternity, and which He communicates to us with the authority of a son. Heaven is the house of His Father; He goes there to prepare a place for us.

He has come from the Father and even now, living on earth, He can say to His disciples, "He who sees me sees also the Father . . . I am in the Father and the Father in me" (Jn. 14:9, 10). What He reveals to us is not, then, a message received of old and faithfully preserved in His memory; it is this inalienable and eternal divine life in which His humanity lives ever since the day it was created and taken up by the Son of God into the unity of His Person. From that moment, His soul has enjoyed the intuitive vision which it possesses by virtue of its union with the Word, and whose splendor will never be veiled.

Let us add that the object of His revelation is not only the heavenly Father, but also Christ Himself: "Now this is everlasting life, that they may know thee, the true God, and him whom thou hast sent, Jesus Christ" (Jn. 17:3). Here especially appear the exceptional terms of this revelation: He whom we must know is Jesus Christ; and He it is who reveals Himself to us. We understand Him so much the better because He who in the Gospel lives, teaches, and dies is truly a man. His humanity moves us, not only by the mystery of humility and love which it causes us to admire in the God-made-man, but also by the emphasis of this simple but sovereign human speech, which penetrates our souls without jarring them and illumines without dazzling.

[44] P. Rousselot, art. *"Intellectualisme," Dictionnaire Apologétique*, t. II, col. 1076–1077.

The children of Moses said of old to Moses: "Speak you to us, and we will hear. Let not the Lord speak to us lest we die" (Exod. 20:19). I do not pray thus, O Lord, I do not pray thus; but with the prophet Samuel, I humbly say: "Speak, Lord, for Your servant hears." And let not Moses speak to me nor any of the prophets; but do You speak to me, Lord God, You Who inspire and enlighten all the prophets. For You alone can fully instruct me without them; but they can accomplish nothing without You.[45]

Whence comes this assurance for Christians? It comes from the fact that this voice of Christ is a human voice at the same time that it is a divine voice; it has the sovereign authority of the word of God but, at the same time, the familiar accent of a human voice. The revelations of Jesus and, even more, His precepts and requirements, penetrate to the depths of our hearts without jarring them. Love opens our souls to them, it dilates and pacifies them. Let us recall, for example, Jesus' final pronouncements to His apostles:

Amen, amen, I say to you, that you shall weep and lament, but the world shall rejoice; and you shall be sorrowful, but your sorrow shall be turned into joy. A woman about to give birth has sorrow, because her hour has come. But when she has brought forth the child, she no longer remembers the anguish for her joy that a man is born into the world. And you therefore have sorrow now; but I will see you again, and your heart shall rejoice, and your joy no one shall take from you (Jn. 16:20–22).[46]

[45] *The Imitation of Christ*, III, 2. Cf. *Following of Christ, the Spiritual Diary of Gerard Groote* (attributed also to Thomas a Kempis) 1340–1384, founder of the Brethren and the Sisters of the Common Life, tr. from original Netherlandish texts (as ed. by J. Van Ginneken, S.J.) by J. Malaise, S.J., 2nd ed. (N. Y., America Press, 1939), pp. 138–139.

[46] Here we may read again that text of St. Maximus of Turin: "Our Savior owes us a particular affection; in Him is our God, but in Him is also our blood . . . Our Lord cannot be so stern as to forget His flesh, His members. For the Apostle says, 'No one ever hated his own flesh; on the contrary, he nourishes and cherishes it, as Christ also does the Church' (Eph. 5:29). Let us not despair of pardon, nor fear the hate . . . for in Christ is our flesh who loves us; we are His members and His flesh, as the Apostle says" (*Sermo* XXX. *P.L.*, LVII, 593–594).

chapter 4

❖❖❖❖❖❖❖❖❖

The Dawn of Salvation—
The Virgin Mary

1. THE VIRGIN MOTHER

"When the goodness and kindness of God our Savior appeared, then not by reason of good works that we did ourselves, but according to his mercy, he saved us" (Titus 3:4–5). These words of St. Paul are dear to the Church; she has us repeat them at Christmas time. And here, indeed, we behold the great revelation which the coming of the Lord brings us: it is His goodness and His love for men: He has given us His Son, who, out of love for us, was made man.

And that came to pass "in the days of King Herod," whose name alone evokes the remembrance of a bloody and infamous tyranny. The Jewish writer J. Klausner estimates two hundred thousand men, at least, to be the number of those massacred by order of Herod and his procurators during this terrible century;[1] this was a fifth of Palestine's population.

---

[1] *Jésus de Nazareth, son temps, sa vie, sa doctrine,* Paris, Payot, 1933, p. 242, and in tr. *Jesus of Nazareth: His Life, Times and Teaching,* tr. from the original Hebrew by H. Danby, N. Y., Macmillan, 1925.

The death of Herod, on the day after Jesus' birth, opens up, not an era of peace, but one of new crises: Archelaus, to whom his father had bequeathed the government of Judea, has to curb the Jews' wrath. The soldiers whom he sends are stoned or driven away; he has to dispatch his whole army and, in the very temple, massacre three thousand Jews. Soon afterwards, a new revolt is cruelly repressed by Sabinus and Varus; it springs up again and extends over the whole country. Galilee is stirred up by Judas, son of Ejechias, former adversary of Herod; Varus, legate of Syria, has to return with two legions. The town of Sephoris, quite close to Nazareth and capital of the province, is at first seized and devastated by the insurgents; recaptured by the Romans, it is burned; two thousand men are crucified by Varus; all the other inhabitants are sold as slaves.

Six miles away, at Nazareth, Jesus was growing up; He was not yet ten years old. Already, however, He Himself had been affected by the turmoil of imperial or local politics: before His birth, the census obliges Joseph and Mary to abandon the humble peace of their home; at Bethlehem they will be able to find only a cave for shelter, and a manger for a crib. After this extreme indigence, there is the hurried flight to Egypt, under the menace of Herod, who massacres all of Bethlehem's children.

And thus is opened the Christian era and, at the same time, the era of persecutions. And piercing through these darknesses and threats of death, the divine light appears. It is not at all that flashing brightness, those prodigies in the skies, which the Pharisees awaited; it is a quiet revelation to Mary, to John the Baptist and Elizabeth, to Joseph, to the shepherds, to Simeon and Anna, to the Magi. Instinctively, we would ask Jesus, as did St. Jude at the Last Supper: "How is it that thou art about to manifest thyself to us, and not to the world?" (Jn. 14:22). This timid question is from a disciple, who, nevertheless, was faithful; some unbelievers will be more insistent: "If thou dost these things, manifest thyself to the world" (Jn. 7:4). Neither understands the great law of the Son of God's revelation: "No one can come to me unless the Father who sent me draw him" (Jn. 6:44). These few witnesses of the mysteries of the childhood have been given by the Father to Jesus; Jesus has been revealed to them in a supremely beneficial apparition, but a brief one and, for the most part, one not to be repeated. The shepherds have returned to their flocks; the Magi have left for the Orient; Simeon has sung his *Nunc dimittis*. The Precursor himself will say later of Jesus, "I did not know him" (Jn. 1:33). And yet, with that first grace received by John, with that thrill of joy when Jesus, borne by Mary, drew near him, the whole life of the Baptist has been illumined.

Of all these witnesses there is one, the most intimate of all, whom we know better than the shepherds and the Magi, better even than Jesus' Precursor: that is His Mother.

We know her better; and yet we are aware how fragmentary and imperfect is the knowledge we have of her! Origen, in his preface to the commentary on St. John's Gospel wrote: "No one can understand this book, if he has not reclined on the heart of Jesus, and had Mary for his mother." [2] To penetrate Jesus' words and mysteries, we must know Mary as a child knows its mother. On two occasions (2:19, 51), St. Luke tells us that the mother of Jesus was wont to keep in her heart all the words of Jesus. The Evangelist knew the inestimable value of these recollections, and he was bent on echoing them to us. We shall strive to hear that deep voice; through Mary and in Mary we shall strive to understand the childhood of Our Lord.

It is at the Annunciation that we should first pause. The angel's greeting is stamped with a reverence we shall find again in no other angelic message;[3] Gabriel announces to Mary the conception and birth of her Son: "He shall be great, and shall be called the Son of the Most High; and the Lord God will give him the throne of David his father, and he shall be king over the house of Jacob forever; and of his kingdom there shall be no end." Con-

---

[2] *In Joannem,* I, 4, 23, ed. Koetschau, p. 8.
[3] To grasp the stress, it suffices to compare the apparition to Mary with the apparition to Zachary: to the priest the angel presents himself thus: "I am Gabriel, who stand in the presence of God; and I have been sent to speak to thee and to bring thee this good news" (Lk. 1:19). To Mary: "Hail, full of grace, the Lord is with thee" (*ibid.,* 28).

fronted with these sublime promises, infinitely surpassing all human hopes, Mary is neither troubled nor exalted; she asks only for the explanation to which she is entitled: "How shall this happen, since I do not know man?" This question indicates clearly her resolution to remain a virgin. God, who has inspired her with this resolution, consecrates it: "The Holy Spirit shall come upon thee and the power of the Most High shall overshadow thee; and therefore the Holy One to be born shall be called the Son of God." And Mary says, "Behold the handmaid of the Lord; be it done to me according to thy word" (Lk. 1:35, 38).

In this scene the role of Mary is decisive; it governs the whole history of mankind. The message which God sends her is not an order; it is a vocation, the highest one of all. Mary accepts it freely. She is associated thereby with the work of our redemption and united to our Savior as no other creature has ever been. The whole Christian tradition, since St. Irenaeus,[4] has recognized the fact that in the mystery of salvation Mary has the same share which Eve had formerly in our downfall.

Mary is united to her Son in the redemptive work and, first and foremost, in the gift which she makes of herself. "The Son of Man has not come to be served but to serve, and to give his life as a ransom for many" (Mt. 20:28). Mary wants only to be "the handmaid of the Lord"; and from this day on, she understands just what this service involves. At the time of St. Paul's conversion, Our Lord will say to Ananias, "I will show him how much he must suffer for my name" (Acts 9:16). What He will reveal to His Apostle, He hides not from His Mother; He loves and respects her ever so much; He does not involve her, without her knowledge, in the way of Calvary. One year later, Simeon will predict to her that a sword will pierce her soul; he only makes her recall, no doubt, more intimate revelations.

On the last day of the octave of Christmas, the Church celebrates in her liturgy the mystery of the Virgin Mother of

[4] Neubert, *Marie dans l'Eglise anténicéenne,* Paris, Gabalda, 1908, pp. 19–23. Cf. his *Marie dans le dogme,* 3rd ed., Paris, Spes, 1953.

God,[5] she has us repeat at Vespers and Lauds: "O wonderful exchange! The Creator of the human race, taking a body endowed with life, has deigned to be born of the Virgin. He is born a man, without human seed, and He communicates to us His divinity."

This "wonderful exchange" is one of the traits which enable us to penetrate more deeply into the mystery of the Incarnation and into the role of the Mother of God.[6]

God wants this exchange, of an incomprehensible liberality, to be accepted freely by man. And the message of the angel has for its sole object the securing of this consent. The Virgin Mary represents the whole of humanity; by agreeing to be the Mother of God, she gives to God this mortal flesh which allows Him to expiate our sins on the Cross and to ransom us.

This is what constitutes the wonderful grandeur of her role, but also the sorrow of her life. She will have the glory of bringing to man's redemption an indispensable cooperation, and of giving to God, consequently, a glory which no other creature will ever give Him, and to man, a hope of salvation which God willed

---

[5] This day is now consecrated to the Circumcision of our Lord; but for a long time the Church celebrated on this day the mystery of the Virgin Mary. And even today its liturgy is, in its main lines, that of a feast of our Lady.

[6] St. Augustine has brought out in a forceful way this *caeleste mercimonium:* "Christ, God and man, in order to communicate His life to us, has willed to share in our death. There was not in His nature a principle of death; nor in ours, a principle of life. . . . He could not find, then, in Himself the means to die; nor we, in ourselves, the means to live. But we could find in Him our life; and He could find in us His death. What exchanges! What He has given, and what He has received! . . . To be able to die for us, the Word was made flesh and dwelt amongst us." Then he recalls all the graces which have come to us from that death: "He has given them to us, He who has been nailed to the Cross . . . He was, on the Cross, covered with insults, in order to give us, from His heavenly throne, the Holy Spirit" (*Sermo, LXXX, 5. P.L., XXXVIII,* pp. 496–497). One might read on the same theme Father Przywara, S.J. *Deus Semper Maior, Theologie der Exerzitien,* Friburg im Breisgau, Herder, 1938–40, III, p. 378.

to make dependent on her consent. But her entire life, on the other hand, will carry the imprint, stamped deeply in her soul and in her flesh, of her redemptive vocation. Jesus came to give His life in redemption. He will tell this later to His apostles. He does not have to tell it to His Mother: she knows it; she understood it on the day of her virginal conception; she contemplated it throughout the life of her Son. This life, not only humble and poor but persecuted by all the tyrants from Herod the Great to Pilate, this life, inaugurated by the flight into Egypt and later to be consummated on the Cross—this is the life which the Son of God has chosen and which on the day of the Annunciation He came to ask of the one He has made His Mother. To have given it to Him is Mary's glory, but it is also her sorrow.[7] The only relief that sorrow had here below, Mary owes to the divine mercy, which allowed her to share with her Son in His sorrowful destiny. Jesus will say to His apostles, "Where I am there also

[7] Chardon has dwelt with great insistence on this sorrow of Mary: "No pure creature could ever attain a higher grace than to be the Mother of God; on the other hand, there is no affliction more cruel than for one close to God to be a cross for God. Mary realized that her exaltation was caused by God's abasement; that her glorious privileges were due to the union, within her holy womb, of uncreated beauty with the ugliness of our nature, of divine glory with the pain and ignominy necessary to satisfy for our crimes. . . . Mary would doubtless have been consoled if, after having clothed her Son in the habiliments of a sinner, she could herself have suffered whatever God in His eternal decree had resolved that Christ should suffer in time. Who can comprehend the greatness of her agony when she realized that her role as Mother required her to give her Son those borrowed garments of flesh which would draw down upon Him the malediction of His heavenly Father? She saw herself to be the cause, in the nature which she had given Him, of all the sufferings which our crimes deserved. It was she who subjected Him to the laws of providence, manifested in His regard by the most severe exactions of divine justice." (*La Croix de Jésus,* Paris, Cerf, 1937, pp. 187–188, and in tr. *The Cross of Christ,* I, St. Louis, Herder, 1957.)

In this text, as often elsewhere, Chardon pushes to an extreme the thesis he wants to defend; by isolating it from all other considerations, he falsifies it. In her motherhood our Lady undoubtedly found great sorrows, but also ineffable happiness; the canticle which, in those blessed days, reveals to us her feelings, is the *Magnificat.*

shall my servant be" (Jn. 12:26). This requirement is more pressing still for His Mother, and Mary yielded to it with all her love.

Nothing draws more intimately together the bonds of maternal and filial love than a common suffering. In this light let us recall the thirty years which Jesus spent with Mary and, first of all, the first impressions of the Child carried away in the dead of night, far from that Bethlehem which Herod is going to stain with blood, towards distant Egypt, the pagan land where the refugees will have to make their way laboriously; and during these years of struggle, of solitude and misery, let us gaze at the Child in the arms of His Mother as He fixes on her His deep, peaceful look; it is good to suffer with Him and for Him.

In contact with these first sufferings, Mary is beset with the bruisings and conflicts which await Him when He will begin to speak and to act; she is moved painfully by them, she looks at Him, and she sees in His eyes and in His heart so much love that sorrow is swallowed up in wonderment like a drop of water in a furnace: "God so loved the world that he gave his only-begotten Son . . . that the world might be saved through him" (Jn. 3:16–17).

And even more than at His patience, she marvels at His humility. At the Last Supper, at the sight of Jesus drawing near to wash his feet, Peter will exclaim, "Lord, dost thou wash my feet?" (Jn. 13:6). Already at the Jordan, John the Baptist, at the sight of Jesus asking him for baptism, had exclaimed, "It is I who ought to be baptized by thee, and dost thou come to me?" (Mt. 3:14). The agitation of the Precursor and of the apostle is quite understandable; we do not find it in Mary. Jesus is subject to her, and she commands Him. There is no failure, surely, to recognize His majesty, but there is respect for His will; He wants to be humiliated. She bows, she commands Him, and she adores Him. She is aware in that redemptive will of a wisdom and of a love so divine that she does not stop to think of the role which has devolved upon her; she gazes on these humblings of the divine majesty, she adores and she loves.

We have anticipated these events in order to discern the

strength and closeness of the bonds which, henceforth, forever unite Jesus and Mary. In this light we shall understand better the childhood of Our Lord and, first and foremost, the ineffable union which, from the Incarnation to the Nativity, unites Him to His Mother. Bérulle has fondly contemplated this mystery:

Jesus, then, is living in Mary, and forms a sort of part of her; and the heart of Jesus is quite close to the heart of Mary. Mary, then, is living in Jesus, and Jesus is her all. And the heart of Mary is quite close to the heart of Jesus and pours life into Him. Jesus and Mary, then, seem but one living being on earth. The heart of the one neither lives nor breathes except by the other. These two hearts, so close and so divine, and living together so lofty a life, how do they not affect each other? Only love can think of it, and only a divine and heavenly love. But only Jesus' own love can understand it.[8]

On the last day of His life Jesus will say to the apostles, "Abide in me and I in you . . . Without me you can do nothing" (Jn. 15:4–5). This dwelling of Jesus in the Christian is already ensured by the state of grace; it is ensured in a still more efficacious and close manner by Holy Communion. But the sacramental presence lasts only so long as the sacred species. Occasionally, in the case of favored ones of Our Lord, the Eucharistic presence is miraculously prolonged; likewise the presence of grace can be perceived habitually by the mind and can communicate to the Christian in a tangible way Christ's impetus and life. Thereby Our Lord reveals to us the goal to which His action tends: He is the Head, we are the members; we must be able to say, "It is now no longer I that live, but Christ lives in me" (Gal. 2:20).

In the light of these great examples, let us return to the life of the Son of God in Mary: from the first day of her Child's conception, Mary has been borne along to that ideal goal which is the aim of the singular favors bestowed on the saints: in Him she lives and He in her. To catch some glimpse of this divine

[8] *Oeuvres de piété,* 45, 9, 3rd ed., Paris, Bourgoing, 1665, p. 550 b. Cf. new edit., Paris, Montaigne, 1944.

intimacy, we can take for a term of comparison the highest mystical states. In the *Living Flame of Love,* St. John of the Cross describes the awakening of God in the soul to whom He is united and where He dwells, as follows:

"How gently and lovingly thou awakenest in my bosom . . ."
This awakening of the Son of God which the soul here desires to describe, is, as I believe, one of the loftiest and one which brings the most good to the soul. For this awakening is a movement of the Word in the substance of the soul, of such greatness and dominion and glory, and of such intimate sweetness, that it seems to the soul that all the balms and perfumed spices and flowers in the world are mingled and shaken and revolved together to give that sweetness; and that all the kingdoms and dominions of the world and all the powers and virtues of Heaven are moved. And not only so, but all the virtues and substances and perfections and graces of all created things shine forth and make the same movement together and in unison. For as Saint John says, all things in Him are life, and in Him they live and move, as the Apostle says likewise. Hence it comes to pass that, when this great Emperor moves in the soul, Whose kingdom, as Isaias says, is borne upon His shoulders (namely, the three spheres, the celestial, the terrestrial and the infernal, and the things that are in them; and He sustains them all, as Saint Paul says, in the Word of His power), then all the spheres seem to move together . . . Just as, when the earth moves, all material things that are upon it move likewise . . . And this is the great delight of this awakening: to know the creatures through God and not God through the creatures . . . Though the soul is substantially in God, as is every creature, He draws back from before it some of the veils and curtains which are in front of it, so that it may see of what nature He is, and then there is revealed to it, and it is able to see (though somewhat darkly, since not all the veils are drawn back) that face of His that is full of all graces . . . That which the soul knows and feels in this awakening concerning the excellence of God is wholly indescribable, for, since there is a communication of the excellence of God in the substance of the soul, which is that breast of the soul whereof the lines here speak, there is heard in the soul the immense power of the voice of a multitude of excellences, of thousands upon thousands of virtues. In these the soul is entrenched and remains terribly and firmly arrayed among them

like ranks of armies and made sweet and gracious in all the sweet-nesses and graces of the creatures.[9]

He whom Mary carries within her and nourishes with her blood, is He who is the "brightness of his glory and the image of his substance," and upholds all things "by the word of his power" (Heb. 1:3). He is silent but alive, and His Mother feels the quickening of His life and is united to it. On coming into the world, He said, "Sacrifice and oblation thou wouldst not, but a body thou hast fitted to me: in holocausts and sin-offerings thou hast had no pleasure. Then said I, 'Behold, I come . . . to do thy will, O God'" (Heb. 10:5–7). The immaculate Victim is still enclosed in the virgin tabernacle;[10] soon it will emerge from there to inaugurate its sacrifice. But henceforth the Son is offered to His Father, and united to His offering is Mary, moved with sadness and happiness. Her sacrifice is a cruel one, but it is ever so glorious to God and to her Son.

After a few days' journey, Mary arrives at the home of Eliza-beth and greets her. Now when Elizabeth heard Mary's greet-ing, the child quickened in her womb, and she was filled with the Holy Spirit. "Blessed art thou among women," she exclaims, "and blessed is the fruit of thy womb!" (Lk. 1:42). And Mary answers with the *Magnificat*.

The stress, one of humility and gratitude, is the same as in the answer to the angel; but it is no longer a word, it is a canticle. Prompted by Elizabeth's greeting, it is the first expression of the sentiments which, since the angel's visit and the Incarnation of the Son of God, filled His Mother's heart. This mystery is God's se-cret: Mary has spoken of it to no one, not even to Joseph. But the revelation made by the Holy Spirit to Elizabeth permits Mary to express before men the adoration and the gratitude which fill her soul.

This canticle "presupposes the knowledge of Anna's theme and of the sentiments expressed by the Psalms, all being cast in an

[9] *Vive Flamme,* str. 4, n. 4, ed. de Burgos, pp. 951–953, and in tr. *Complete Works.*
[10] *E virginis sacrario intacta prodis victima.*

original composition." [11] We note in Mary what will be so manifest in her divine Son: the Bible is the religious treasure of her
soul; spontaneously there rise to her lips reminiscences of the
Holy Books. Thus it will be with Jesus in His agony and at His
death: "My God, my God, why hast thou forsaken me?" (Mt.
27:46); "Father, into thy hands I commend my spirit" (Lk.
23:46). With both Son and Mother, the greatest happiness and
the most terrible suffering will find no other expressions than
those with which the Holy Books inspire them.

Elizabeth had extolled, above all, Mary's faith; Mary sees only
the omnipotent mercy of God: "My soul magnifies the Lord, and
my spirit rejoices in God my Savior." Assuredly, she recognizes
the grandeur of God's gift; she marvels at it, she praises Him for
it: "He has regarded the lowliness of his handmaid; for, behold,
henceforth all generations shall call me blessed." But she adores
above all in this divine work the omnipotence, the holiness, the
mercy of God: "Because he who is mighty has done great
things for me and holy is his name; and for generation upon
generation is his mercy, to those who fear him. He has shown
might with his arm, he has scattered the proud in the conceit of
their heart. He has put down the mighty from their thrones and
has exalted the lowly. He has filled the hungry with good things,
and the rich he has sent away empty. He has given help to Israel,
His servant, mindful of His mercy—even as he spoke to our
fathers—to Abraham and to his posterity forever" (Lk. 1:46-55).

In proportion as this canticle unfolds, we see only the power,
the holiness, the mercy of God. Mary adores Him and takes her
pleasure in Him. She herself disappears; God is all, she is nothing. This confession is the foundation of all sanctity. Let us not
suppose that she is unworthy of being the Mother of God. Quite
the contrary, we need only recall her Immaculate Conception,
her exemption from all concupiscence and all fault. Before God,
will her humility be less profound than that of other men? Certainly not, but more luminous and peaceful. In this soul, whose
gaze no deviation mars, whom no passion disturbs, the com-

[11] Lagrange, *Evangile selon saint Luc,* 7th ed., Paris, Gabalda, 1948, p. 53.

parison of herself to God is made in full clarity: God is the Lord, she the servant; God is the Omnipotent, the Holy, the Merciful; she is nothing, she has nothing, except the grace God bestows on her. She says, like Marie of the Incarnation, but with more penetrating insight and deeper adoration: "It is my glory that You are all and I am nothing. Blessed art Thou, O Lord!" [12]

After a stay of three months at Elizabeth's, Mary returns to Nazareth. There she finds Joseph distraught; he is still unaware of the mystery which has just been revealed to John the Baptist and to Elizabeth. God alone can make it known to him; Mary does not anticipate the divine message. For herself and for her spouse, these days of silence were full of anguish: "Joseph her husband, being a just man, and not wishing to expose her to reproach, was minded to put her away privately" (Mt. 1:19). Here we are aware of what a price God puts on His highest graces, what heroic fidelity He requires, and what secrecy. Later on, Jesus will ask His apostles to tell no one that He is the Christ (Mt. 16:20), to speak to no one of His transfiguration (Mt. 17:9). His mother has no need of these recommendations: she knows the respect she owes her God and she keeps silent. Finally an angel of the Lord appears to Joseph and reveals the mystery to him.

This anguish of the holy betrothed couple is going to be followed by the ineffable joys of the Nativity: Our Lord, so ardently desired by so many patriarchs and prophets, is going to appear at last in their arms. Yet for this happiness God wishes to prepare them by still another trial: the edict of Caesar Augustus forces them to leave the little home of Nazareth to go to be enrolled in Bethlehem, the city of David. God is bent on attesting in this way to the Davidic lineage of Christ. But He wishes also that the Savior He sends us appear to men in extreme destitution: He will have only a cave for shelter, only a manger for a crib. But the angels will form His court and will summon the shepherds thereto. In this union of human misery and divine

[12] Cf. Marie de l'Incarnation, *Ecrits spirituels et historiques,* publ. by Claude Martin, re-edited by Albert Jamet (4 vols.), Paris, Desclée de Brouwer and Quebec, à l'Action Sociale, 1929–39, t. II, p. 266.

glory, are sketched already the great traits of the God-Man and of His message: He will detach men from earth in order to raise them to God in glory. "Glory to God in the highest, and peace on earth among men of good will" (Lk. 2:14).

But what we should reflect on here especially is the mystery of Jesus' virgin birth. If we want to understand its lesson, let us recall St. Paul's teaching (1 Cor. 7:32 ff.): a married woman must please her spouse; a virgin thinks only of pleasing God; her heart is not divided. This liberty of an undivided love is the privilege of virgins; it is the glory of Mary. Assuredly, she loves Joseph; she loves the other members of her family: Elizabeth, Zachary, the little John, and later, those brethren of the Lord, so slow to believe and yet out of whom she will make faithful and devoted Christians. But all these loves do not divert her from the love she bears her Son; they all derive from this maternal and virgin source. It is the Child who leads His Mother to Elizabeth and to John; it is He who, through an angel, enlightens Joseph on the mystery of the Incarnation. He is, within the Holy Family, the source of all light and of all life. The Virgin Mary pours out His graces with open arms; from that time on, she is what she will always be—the dispenser of all Jesus' graces. She receives only to give. From the time she has conceived her Child, she by no means shuts herself up in her room to enjoy her happiness; she hastens to Judea, to inform those who unconsciously await and call for her. She will present Him for the homage of the shepherds, the Magi, Simeon, Anna—all those whom God sends to her. This virgin maternity suffers no division, nor any reserve; she possesses her treasure only in giving it, and she is eager to give it.

2. JESUS AND MARY

But in this virgin maternity, it is not only the mother we must consider, it is also her Child; His virgin birth is for us both a lesson and a promise. Born of the flesh, we feel its burden and its defilement: "I was conceived in iniquities; and in sins did my mother conceive me" (Ps. 50:7); "Who can make him clean that

is conceived of unclean seed?" (Jb. 14:4). Jesus will say to Nicodemus, "Unless a man be born again of water and the Spirit, he
cannot enter into the kingdom of God. That which is born of the
flesh is flesh; and that which is born of the Spirit is spirit" (Jn.
3:5–6); and St. John, "To as many as received him he gave the
power of becoming sons of God; to those who believe in his
name: who were born not of blood, nor of the will of the flesh,
nor of the will of man, but of God" (Jn. 1:12–13).

It is baptism that gives us this new birth, this purity vivified by
the Holy Spirit; the virgin birth of Jesus lets us hope for it.
Holy Church, too, at the second Mass of Christmas, has us ask
for the grace of this new birth: *"Hujus nos, Domine, sacramenti
semper novitas natalis instauret cujus Nativitas singularis hu-
manam repulit vetustatem"* (Postcommunion).

We owe this regeneration to a Virgin Mother, the holy Church.
St. Augustine likes to compare the Church to Mary, and to have
us venerate in the one as in the other the virgin fecundity which
gives the Savior to us and children to God.

Owing to this new birth, everything in the world is renewed:
"If then any man is in Christ, he is a new creature: the former
things have passed away; behold, they are made new!" (2 Cor.
5:17). Christians are transformed by the grace of baptism, and
the whole world is revealed to them in quite a different light, because now they go beyond its appearances to grasp its true nature
and profound orientation. Whence comes this transformation?
From the new birth when the Spirit has opened our eyes and revealed to us God and the world.[13]

Christians come over from paganism are keenly aware of this
transformation; St. Justin thus describes it:

Christ has said: "Unless you are born again, you will not enter the
kingdom of heaven" . . . In our first birth, we are born ignorant
and, according to the law of necessity, of a moist seed, in a mutual
union of our parents, and we come into the world with bad habits
and perverse inclinations. In order that we might not remain like this,

[13] Cf. the note of Father Allo on this text of St. Paul, pp. 167–168 in *Saint
Paul, première épître aux Corinthiens,* 2nd ed., Paris, Gabalda, 1956.

children of necessity and of ignorance, and in order that we might obtain the remission of our past offenses, they invoke in water the name of God the Father over him who wishes to be regenerated . . . (*Apol.*, 1, 61; cf. *The Apologies of Justin Martyr,* Cambridge [Eng.], 1911).

Our eyes have been opened and our fetters loosened: this world is the domain of God; we are His children; all of this is our paternal home and our heritage. "Where the Spirit of the Lord is, there is freedom." [14]

St. Augustine, in his *Confessions,* VII, 19 (FC 21, 1953, pp. 188–189), avers that, at the time of his adherence to Manichaeism, he could not conceive of the divinity of Christ; at least he admitted His virgin birth: "I thought of my Lord Christ only as a man of excellent wisdom, whom no one else could equal. Particularly, since He was born miraculously of a virgin, as an example of holding temporal things in contempt in comparison with the attainment of divine immortality, our real concern, He seemed to have merited very great authority as a teacher." Thus, even in this night of heresy, Augustine still perceived some rays of Christ's glory and recognized in Him some privileges of His virgin birth. This helps us to understand the fact that ordinary men, in the measure that they are faithful to the grace of their baptism, are found invested by the action of the Holy Spirit with a divine light, and that they taste, from the time of their mortal life, the liberty of the children of God.

Is not this the teaching of the Gospel? "To as many as received him he gave the power of becoming sons of God; to those who believe in his name: who were born not of blood, nor of the will of the flesh, nor of the will of man, but of God" (Jn. 1:12–13). "That which is born of the flesh is flesh; and that which is born of the Spirit is spirit. Do not wonder that I said to thee, 'You must be born again.' The wind blows where it will, and thou hearest its sound but dost not know where it comes from or where it goes. So

[14] 2 Cor. 3:17; cf. Gal. 2:4; 3:28; 4:22–31; 5:13; Rom. 6:13, 20, 22; 7:3–6; 8:2, 21; 1 Cor. 9:1, 19; 10:29; Harnack, *Wiedergeburt, Texte und Untersuchungen,* 42, 3, p. 104.

is everyone who is born of the Spirit" (Jn. 3:6–8). These words of Jesus enable us to catch a glimpse into the mystery of the action of the Spirit: He guides, He bears along, He raises up those whom He loves. The sensual man is disconcerted by this; the spiritual man recognizes in it a divine action and is full of admiration: "Whoever are led by the Spirit of God, they are the sons of God. Now you have not received a spirit of bondage so as to be again in fear, but you have received a spirit of adoption as sons, by virtue of which we cry, 'Abba! Father!' " (Rom. 8:14–15).

This transformation which makes spiritual men out of sensual men will be the endeavor of the whole Christian life. We are born of the Spirit, it is true, but after being born of the flesh. Our Lord can say to us what He said to the Jews: "You are from below, I am from above" (Jn. 8:23). Our whole endeavor, as long as we are on earth, is to unite ourselves more and more to Him who is from above, lifting up to Him those who are from below. There is only one human creature here below who has been exempted from these struggles: this is the Virgin Mary. Her conception was not, like that of her Son, a virgin conception; but, by a singular privilege, an immaculate conception. From the awakening of her conscience, she has been anticipated and seized by a grace to which she has surrendered wholeheartedly forever. This is a mere human creature, but the only one who can say, like her Son (Jn. 14:30), "The prince of the world is coming, and in me he has nothing." In the vast deluge which covers the world, the heavenly dove, the Holy Spirit, has found this virgin land where it has alighted and where, beneath its divine action, the Son of God has germinated. She alone will know this immaculate purity, but she has received it from God only to praise Him for it and to offer it to her divine Son: *Ave verum corpus natum de Maria virgine.*

After the ineffable happiness of Jesus' birth, there is the adoration of the shepherds, then the presentation in the Temple, when the Child is recognized and adored by Simeon and Anna: "Now thou dost dismiss thy servant, O Lord, according to thy word, in peace; because my eyes have seen thy salvation, which thou hast prepared before the face of all peoples: a light of revelation to the Gentiles, and a glory for thy people Israel" (Lk. 2:29–32). Mary and Joseph hear and marvel at this divine revelation. But these first rays of light reach only a few chosen souls; the others are still plunged in darkness. And for Mary herself this divine dawn is clouded over by the prophetic warning: "This child is destined for the fall and for the rise of many in Israel, and for a sign that shall be contradicted. And thy own soul a sword shall pierce, that the thoughts of many hearts may be revealed" (*ibid.*, 34–35).

Mary was prepared to hear these words; but, at the impact of them, all her painful premonitions confirmed by this prophecy are stamped on her soul, never more to be effaced. "The predicted sword already pierces her heart. The wound it makes will never close again. The shadow of Calvary is cast henceforth over her whole life, and, if the author of the *Imitation* could rightly say that Christ's whole life was a cross and a martyrdom, we must say the same thing, due allowance being made, of Mary. May there not be, then, any more joy for her? The years at Nazareth were happy years, in the sweet intimacy of Jesus. But, together with that deep joy, there existed in her soul—without, however, disquieting her—the pain caused by the ever-present prospect of the sword prophesied by Simeon . . . Happy to possess her divine Son, she could not stop to relish this joy; for the thought soon came to her that in raising this Child, she was preparing the Victim for the sacrifice. Thus joy and pain dwelt side by side in the heart of Mary, so that she might be our model in both . . . God probably did not judge it good to let her know in detail what sufferings were to plunge the sword into her heart. But even this obscurity had, too, its sorrowful side: all was to be feared, the evil in view being certain, though undetermined." [15]

[15] J.-V. Bainvel, S.J., *Le saint coeur de Marie*, Paris, Beauchesne, 1918, pp. 225–227. With this prophecy made to Mary we can compare the one Agabus will make later on to St. Paul: "The man whose girdle this is the Jews will bind like this at Jerusalem, and they will deliver him into the hands of the Gentiles" (Acts 21:11). Here again, a great friend of God is warned by a humble prophet of a great trial, which is certain, but which

From the day of the Annunciation, Mary is involved in a mystery which goes ever so far beyond her. She adores it and yields in all trust and peace to a divine action whose requirements are infinite and details unknown. She is the Mother of God; the Child she bears in her womb is a King whose reign will never end. But He is, at the same time, a Savior who will ransom us with His bloody death. This glory and death will be continually present to her mind. These visions would have overwhelmed any other creature; not for a moment do they disturb her peace. These sublime splendors do not illumine in advance the detail of her life, even in what she cherishes most. She seeks not to pierce its obscurity, but commits all to God: her honor, Joseph's conduct towards her and, above all, her enormous responsibility: the beloved Son of the Father, the Savior of men, is put entirely into her hands; she is His Mother. Events unfold, fraught often with threats. God intervenes only at the last moment, and Mary awaits this intervention in all docility and trust. The mysteries which follow upon one another are thus out of proportion to human experiences; it is the fate of a God which is at stake, and it is His own Mother who experiences them, and they trouble her not. This faith, detached from all disquiet, as from all human complacency, stems from the incomparable purity of her love.

To understand this love of Mary, let us glance at the other servants of God, and the greatest: the holy apostles. Assuredly, they loved Jesus with a sincere, generous, and very deep love. All can say with St. Peter, "Behold, we have left all and followed thee"; but they add with him, "What then shall we have?" (Mt. 19:27). This concern for rewards is legitimate. But the question thus put shows up the imperfection of their faith; had they known their Master better, they would have understood that He Himself was their infinite reward. Mary did not pose a similar question to the angel of the Annunciation; she said to him, "Behold the handmaid of the Lord" (Lk. 1:38).

The imperfection of the apostles is still more evident in other

---

remains little known. In both cases the divine warning does not allow the person receiving it to avoid the danger, but only to prepare himself for it in a spirit of faith and of submission to Our Lord's will.

incidents: the imperfection of St. Peter at Caesarea Philippi, when he tries to divert Jesus from the prospect of His Passion (Mt. 16:22); the imperfection of the sons of Zebedee, when they ask for the first two places in the kingdom (Mk. 10:37). And yet, just before that instance of weakness, Jesus had said to Peter, "Flesh and blood has not revealed this to thee, but my Father in heaven" (Mt. 16:17); and yet one of the sons of Zebedee was the apostle whom Jesus loved. These weaknesses of these great saints show how difficult it is for men, even when anticipated by God's greatest graces, to defend the purity of their love and to remain worthy of their Master's watchful love. And we understand that this zeal, though so sincere, was weak; in the masterpiece of God, mankind mingled its clay and, at the shock of the Cross, love wavered.

Jesus never loved anyone as He did His Mother; never was His love as watchful or as zealous. He takes pleasure in the abnegation of this virgin love which is borne towards God with no return to self, no disquiet, no ambition, no self-satisfaction, no concern for its own interests. This, truly, is the ideal model of the love which St. Paul will recommend to his disciples: "Even though we have known Christ according to the flesh, yet now we know him so no longer" (2 Cor. 5:16). Also, when some human praise risks casting a shadow on this immaculate love, Jesus thrusts it aside: " 'Blessed is the womb that bore thee, and the breasts that nursed thee.' 'Rather, blessed are they who hear the word of God and keep it' " (Lk. 11:27–28).

Hence also, in His relations with His Mother, His extreme reserve in all that concerns His Messianic ministry, and that from the age of twelve. Mary, finding her child in the Temple, is moved to say to Him, " 'Son, why hast thou done so to us? Behold, thy father and I have been seeking thee sorrowing.' 'How is it that you sought me? Did you not know that I must be about my Father's business?' And they did not understand the word that he spoke to them. And he went down with them and came to Nazareth, and was subject to them; and his mother kept all these things carefully in her heart" (Lk. 2:48–51). These last words of the Evangelist advise us of the deep meaning which Mary discovers in these words of her Son; she has to transmit it to us and point out its full significance. We notice also that Jesus resumes forthwith His obedient life at Nazareth. For an instant, the scene in the Temple has opened His parents' eyes and our own to a profound insight into the divine mystery; then the humble human life resumes its course.

We gather the same lesson from the scene at Cana, exactly parallel to the one in the Temple. After an answer which seemed like a lesson, the Child had at once followed Mary and Joseph in complete submission. At Cana, likewise, He asserts His independence in the exercise of His mission; then He works the requested miracle—discreetly, the hour for a more striking manifestation not having arrived as yet (Jn. 2:3–11).

A little while afterwards, at Capharnaum, they came to tell Jesus that His Mother and His brethren were looking for Him: "Who are my mother," He said, "and brethren? . . . Whoever does the will of God, he is my brother and sister and mother" (Mk. 3:32–35).

In these four circumstances, Jesus is addressing not only His mother, but at the same time all those surrounding Him, the Scribes in the Temple, the guests at the marriage feast of Cana, the crowd who throng Him in the house of Capharnaum or on the road. To all of them He recalls that the most sacred ties are not blood-ties, but all those which attach to the heavenly Father His beloved Son and, in Him, all the children of God. He told all His disciples, "He who loves his father or mother more than me is not worthy of me" (Mt. 10:37). He wanted also to shield against every human contagion Mary's immaculate love; and the Virgin was so pleased with this lesson that she had to bequeath to us its remembrance.

By no means, then, will we see in these words of Our Lord a disavowal of the praises offered to Mary, but the safeguard indeed of His hidden life. The Virgin stands aside; Jesus loves this effacement and protects it. Thus it is that Our Lord protects Himself from the ambitious dreams of His apostles. To St. Peter, who brushes aside the prospect of his Master's Passion, He will say, "Get behind me, satan, thou art a scandal to me; for thou dost not mind the things of God, but those of men" (Mt. 16:23). We feel in the severity of the reprimand that Jesus has been hurt to a very painful degree. He cannot allow anyone to turn Him aside from His Passion; nor does He allow anyone to tear His Mother away from her hidden life and from her silence. Only at the foot of the Cross will she have, during Jesus' lifetime, a privileged place, there to hear her Son's last sigh, and to receive from Him John, whose mother she is going to become.

This destiny seems stern. But the more we meditate on it, the more we marvel at it; and the whole life of our Lady shines with this pure light. We were recalling above the instructions given to the apostles to be silent, and we stated that never had Mary any need of them. We must make the same remark, with greater reason, about the seeking of the first places, when the holy apostles allowed themselves to be carried away during Our Lord's lifetime, which always remained foreign to Mary. The friends of Christ, even the greatest and the holiest, have to be put on their guard against an ever-greedy ambition. His Mother has no such effort to make; at the message of the Annunciation her spontaneous reaction was: "Behold the handmaid of the Lord" (Lk. 1:38). The conception and birth of Jesus have rendered this instinct still more imperative: the Son of God by becoming incarnate was made the servant of God—even more, the servant of every man He comes to save: "I am in the midst of you as he who serves" (Lk. 22:27). Mary, better than anyone else, has beheld this example and has marvelled at it; with all her faith she adores it, with all her love she loves it, and she is enthralled by it.

One of Our Lord's servants who put into practice most faithfully and most heroically the teachings of the Gospel and the example of Jesus, describes the fruits which she drew from them, as follows:

This loving approach of the sacred Incarnate Word produces in the soul an inexpressible unction and in her actions a sincerity, a rectitude, a candor and flight from every deviousness; it imprints on the heart the love of the cross and of those who have harassed it . . .

All these happy effects and many others which I do not mention come from the unction and continual attraction with which the Spirit of Jesus carries along the soul. This Spirit persuades, convinces and attracts so gently, that it is impossible to refuse Him anything, and furthermore He acts in the soul as in a home which is completely His own. This gentle persuasion is His language, and the response of the soul is to let herself be carried along by a loving yielding. The soul, without hurting its nature, which it draws easily after itself, is seen at peace amidst the most troublesome and difficult things . . . The soul is humbly courageous and free from human respect on occasions when justice and equity are in question, yet with an entire submission of judgment to those directing her.[16]

In this admirable description, I have left aside certain traits which, in other individuals, show up more the stubbornness of nature. In the Immaculate Virgin, this stubbornness is non-existent; of her especially we can say, "The Spirit of Jesus acts in the soul as in a home which is completely His own . . . the soul is seen at peace amidst the most troublesome and difficult things."

This sovereign peace gives to the virginal soul of Mary its peerless transparency; here is the most wonderful thing about it. But it is also what is most difficult for us, not only to imitate, but to imagine. St. Francis de Sales thus describes this love of Mary:

Like the dawn of day, which increases in brightness, not at different intervals, or by frequently interrupted efforts, but in one continued uniform manner . . . divine love increased in the heart of the Blessed Virgin, without interruption, violence or agitation. It is evident that no impetuous motion ever disturbed the heart of the Blessed Virgin; because love is in itself calm, agreeable, and peaceable; it only becomes impetuous, and has recourse to violent attacks, when it meets with opposition and resistance. But when it finds no obstacle to its entrance into a soul, when nothing opposes its progress, it always acts calmly, and conquers without violence . . . As everything in the Blessed Virgin favoured and seconded the attractions of grace,

[16] Marie de l'Incarnation, Letter to her son, *Ecrits spirituels,* t. IV, pp. 258–260.

the progress of divine love in her soul, though incomparably greater than in any other, was perfectly calm and tranquil.[17]

This clarity, this peace, this luminous transparency must be contemplated with great respect and great hope: it is a mystery which transcends our powers, but not our desires. Humanity, such as God had conceived and realized it at first, was really a virginal nature, summoned mercifully to an intimate union with God, which was to receive the grace of this union with a humble, docile, and peaceful fidelity. This masterpiece of God we behold in our Lady, and it is for us more than a souvenir, it is a promise: the Son of God, who by His death has ensured His Mother this immaculate purity, will be able by the same sacrifice to raise up our fallen nature again. It is a pity our lives will not know that purity which no stain sullies, that peace which no storm troubles. But, purified and pacified by the blood of Christ, they will be seized by a very gentle, maternal, and virile hand. It will be sufficient for Jesus, from the summit of the Cross, to say to His Mother, "Woman, behold thy son" (Jn. 19:26); the apostle St. John, carried away by that motherly love as by a powerful and peaceful stream, was, with no shock, raised up to God.

3. THE HOLY FAMILY

We have contemplated the Child Jesus and the Virgin Mary. They are, indeed, the ones who must especially hold our attention in the course of Our Lord's hidden life. But we should not forget that Jesus and Mary are not isolated here below; with Joseph they form the Holy Family. This family life is worthy of the most attentive study: it is the model of all human families, and it projects on the human formation of Jesus a strong, penetrating light.

With the *Magnificat* of Mary we have compared the canticle of Anna; we can compare also the conceptions of the two children:

---

[17] *Traité de l'Amour de Dieu,* VII, 14, and in tr. *Treatise on the Love of God,* Westminster (Md.), Newman, 1942, p. 308.

Samuel born of a sterile woman, Jesus born of a virgin. But the rearing of the two children is quite different: Samuel, as soon as he is weaned, is carried by his mother to the Temple, that he "may abide always there" (1 Kgs. 1:22); Jesus will be carried to the Temple, but only to be presented to the Lord; He will grow up with His parents at Bethlehem, in Egypt, and at Nazareth.

The heavenly Father willed that the human life of His Son be formed and developed in the ordinary setting of every human life, in a family. By this trait, too, He wished to indicate the reality of His Incarnation: in everything He will be like all men, "one tried as we are in all things except sin" (Heb. 4:15).

This slow human formation will be for us an ever so valuable example, but for those to whom God entrusts Him, it is an honor and a responsibility, transcending infinitely what men can bear. There will be needed very great graces from God and a continual assistance. No child will be precious like Jesus; none will be exposed to more dangers. The heavenly Father protects Him, but He wants men themselves to protect their Savior, and He confides Him to His parents.

Herod pursues Him to the death; God does not deliver Him by a miracle. He warns Joseph, who leaves for Egypt with the Child and His Mother. Submissive to a second message, Joseph, at the death of Herod, leads the Holy Family back to the land of Israel; but, learning that Archelaus reigns in Judea, he proceeds to Galilee, where the Child will be safer. Jesus keeps silent, like the child that He is. The heavenly Father gives only the essential warnings; for the rest He entrusts Himself to Joseph's prudence. He inspires him, He directs him, but through the web of human events, seemingly independent of Himself, He arranges things.

There is question of the most valuable life that has ever appeared in this world; God entrusts it to the protection of men. He watches over it with a zealous care, but this vigilance is exercised only through the humble ministry of Joseph and Mary. No mystery can better reveal to us the Providence of God, His apparent reserve, and the trust with which He honors those who represent Him here below. If He gives us signs, we ought to be submissive to them; if He postpones the decision, we know that His hand guides us and that, if we are united to Him, it ensures our step. These thoughts of faith are always meritorious; they are especially so here, where the interests at stake are of infinite worth. Nothing is more beautiful than this simplicity of human prudence knowing that it is guided by God, and fearlessly protecting a treasure whose infinite value it recognizes and for whom it is responsible to God and to the world.

The return to Nazareth will give to the Holy Family only a precarious assurance: the violent revolts of the Galileans and the ruthless repression light up the Sephoris with fires one can see from Nazareth; they cause to pass, across the hills and fields where the Child Jesus grew up, long lines of prisoners laden with the crosses they are to die on. The Mother of Jesus shudders at all these perils. But she sees clearly that flight is impossible; she must stay there, in that blood-soaked land: God will watch over His Son.

As for the Child, He seems unconscious of the danger; He entrusts Himself to His parents and grows up peacefully under their protection. This protection shields Him from the perils menacing Him; it is still more valuable in sheltering Him from the contacts which would be too hurtful to Him. Here especially the maternal vigilance of Mary is valuable to Him.

Addressing a woman religious, Jesus said to her: "How very much at home I was with My Mother; and how much I would like to be right at home with My spouses, a complete Master, doing there as I please!" Let us understand well this sentiment of Our Lord, its delicacy and depth. A God-Child in a human family! Where will enough purity, self-abnegation and simplicity be found, so that He might be able to say, "In this house I am right at home"? Let us rule out, obviously, the stains of sin. But how rule out the everyday preoccupations, the commonplace things, which bog men down and which are intolerable to the Son of God? Savior and Physician, He will have to come in contact with these things later on. He will submit to them, but not without suffering from them: "O unbelieving and perverse generation, how long shall I be with you? How long shall I put up with you?" (Mt. 17:16). What a man can put up with would be unbearable for a child; later He will say, "You are from below; I am from above" (Jn. 8:23). In His apostles themselves He will encounter the scorn which will render His thought unintelligible to them. "He says to them, 'Beware of the leaven of the Pharisees and Sadducees!' But they began to reflect, saying, 'We have brought no bread.' He said to them, 'Why do you not understand that it was not of bread I said to you, "Beware of the leaven of the Pharisees and Sadducees"?' Then they understood that he bade them beware not of the leaven of bread, but of the teaching of the Pharisees and Sadducees" (Mt. 16:6–12). Likewise at Jacob's well: " 'I have food to eat of which you do not know.' The disciples therefore said to one another, 'Has someone brought him something to eat?' 'My food is to do the will of him who sent me' " (Jn. 4:32–34). At Caesarea Philippi, it is worse: not only scorn, but rejection: at the prediction of the Passion, "Peter, taking him aside, began to chide him, saying, 'Far be it from thee, O Lord; this will never happen to thee.' He turned and said to Peter, 'Get behind me, satan, thou art a scandal to me; for thou dost not mind the things of God, but those of men' " (Mt. 16:22 –23).

We recognize in all these passages that, up to the death of Jesus and the gift of the Holy Spirit, the apostles could not usually rise up to the divine plane; their thoughts are human. This powerlessness was for the Son of God a great disappointment; but what might it have been for the Child Jesus? His Mother preserved Him from it: she lived in the light of God: "Blessed are they who . . . have believed" (Jn. 20:29). Also, between her Son and herself we are aware of no misunderstanding. Surely, there was a great inequality of light: Mary sometimes understood only imperfectly the words of Jesus; but she clung to them with all her love, in all docility and trust.

Around her the obscurity is profound. The people of Nazareth will later oppose to Jesus' preaching an incredible obstinacy: "Jesus said to them, 'A prophet is not without honor except in his own country, and among his own kindred, and in his own house.' And he could not work any miracle there, beyond curing a few sick people by laying his hands upon them. And he marvelled at their unbelief" (Mk. 6:4–6). As for the brethren of Our Lord, we see them still incredulous in the last year of His life: "Not even his brethren believed in him" (Jn. 7:5).

Mary and Joseph alone would give to their Child the support and joy of their faith. This faith was all the more necessary for them as they had to initiate Jesus into the religious traditions of His people. The dying Moses said to Israel, "Keep thyself, therefore, and thy soul carefully. Forget not the words that thy eyes have seen, and let them not to go out of thy heart all the days of thy life. Thou shalt teach them to thy sons and to thy grandsons" (Dt. 4:9). And again: "Is not he thy father, that hath possessed thee, and made thee, and created thee? Remember the days of old, think upon every generation: ask thy father, and he will declare to thee: thy elders and they will tell thee" (Dt. 32:6–7). These precepts of Moses were not forgotten: the heads of the family were witnesses of Israel's traditions, and they passed them on to their children.[18] Jesus, too, listened to these domestic teachings and was initiated by Joseph and Mary into the religious traditions of His people.

St. Luke, relating to us the visit of Jesus to the Temple, tells us of the doctors' amazement at the wisdom which was revealed in the questions and answers of this twelve-year-old child. It was for them only a dazzling experience, one which was quickly forgotten, no doubt; for Mary it was a radiant experience, and she rejoiced in it for thirty years. She herself was wont to live in the light of the Bible and, far better than the Scribes, she penetrated its transparency. Her *Magnificat* shows her to us nourished entirely by the Holy Books, even before the birth of Jesus. Now she must initiate her Son into this treasure of the religion of her fathers, and relate to Him the promises of God, the predictions of the prophets, the prayers of the Psalmist. In His preaching Jesus will rely constantly on this sacred tradition: "If you believed Moses," He will say to the Scribes, "you would believe me also, for he wrote of me" (Jn. 5:46); "Abraham your

---

[18] Thus every year, at the time of the celebration of the Pasch, a child was wont to ask the father of the family the meaning of the Paschal Supper, and the father would explain it to him.

father rejoiced that he was to see my day. He saw it and was glad" (Jn. 8:56). To the disciples of Emmaus, along the road, He recalls all the Scripture texts which speak of Himself; they do not recognize Him yet, but already their hearts are on fire (Lk. 24:27–32). Who will tell of the ardor within the heart of Mary when she teaches her Son all these prophecies which speak of Him. This text of the psalm, which Jesus will oppose to the Pharisees: "Out of the mouth of infants and sucklings thou hast perfected praise" (Mt. 21:16)—what force it takes on at Nazareth! And the text of Isaias which Jesus will comment on in the synagogue: "The Spirit of the Lord is upon me; because he has anointed me; to bring good news to the poor he has sent me . . ." (Lk. 4:18). Jesus had to say then: "Today this Scripture has been fulfilled in your hearing." What must Mary have thought while teaching Christ this oracle of the prophet? No doubt she did not add anything; but these words, radiant with a divine light and warmth, were carved on her soul. It is not seldom that a teacher or a mother, in contact with a very pure child being instructed in the first elements of religion, feels her own faith elevated, strengthened, and illumined. The faith of Mary was incomparably greater than any other human faith, and from herself to her Son the distance was infinite, and the intimacy, at the same time, perfect. What shall we say of the union which this slow upbringing formed day by day between these two souls?

Here we get an inkling of what an infinite source of graces for the Holy Family was the presence of the Child Jesus. This mystery merits our whole attention. Looked at superficially, it would seem that the birth of the Son of God brought to Mary and Joseph only persecution and destitution: there is, first of all, the distress at Bethlehem; there is soon the still more painful distress of the flight into Egypt and of the sojourn there. At Nazareth they were, no doubt, poor; but they had their home, and the workshop of Joseph assured them a living. Suddenly they are lacking everything: at Bethlehem, their shelter is a cave which the shepherds had made into a stable; in Egypt they are in still greater deprivation, indigent refugees wandering the roads in search of a resting place. When they returned to Nazareth, what would they find there? Amidst so many misfortunes, the Child keeps silent and seems helpless. He seems to be for His parents only a subject of deepest concern and a crushing responsibility for human weakness. His enemies will say on Calvary: "He saved others, himself he cannot save!" (Mt. 27:42). From His very first days, it is thus that the Savior appears: incapable of saving Himself.

And yet this silent and helpless infancy radiates with a glory we shall no longer behold until the Resurrection. This glory shines out, no doubt, only for privileged witnesses; it will be the same with the risen life of Our Lord. But these two mysteries are enveloped in a divine light which will illumine to the same degree neither the adolescence of Jesus, nor even His public life. The shepherds are summoned by an angel; Simeon and Anna are led by the Holy Spirit; the Magi, by a miraculous star; similarly, not only the Israelites, but the Gentiles who are drawn by God towards this Child.

This effulgence of glory is engraved in the heart of Mary, who reflects on it, in wonderment, and will make it known to us. She takes pleasure in this Providence of the Father. Does she not find therein, shining brightly, what she was wont to sing in her *Magnificat:* "He has regarded the lowliness of his handmaid . . . He who is mighty has done great things for me . . . He has put down the mighty from their thrones, and has exalted the lowly. He has filled the hungry with good things, and the rich he has sent away empty" (Lk. 1:48 ff.)? This grandeur escapes the human gaze: the humble, the poor, remain humble and poor. But their humility is elevated to heaven; their poverty is rich with ever so precious a treasure.

More truly even than Simeon, she can sing, "My eyes have seen thy salvation, which thou hast prepared before the face of all peoples: a light of revelation to the Gentiles, and a glory for thy people Israel" (Lk. 2:30–32). This effulgence is still a small thing compared to the hidden Light which faith beholds in this Child; He is the Light. In the morning we recognize the first glimmers of the dawn on the walls lit up by them; but it is only a very pale reflection, compared with the splendor of the sun soon to appear.

This divine light henceforth will transfigure the life of the Virgin. When parents see at last in their arms a child they have been long desiring, their lives are transformed. This little helpless baby, capable neither of defending nor of supporting itself nor of speaking, seems to bring to its parents only burdens and anxiety. And yet it brings them joy and hope; it unites them together, it draws them towards a better future, it gives to their lives the goal they will henceforth tend towards and the impetus to raise them there.

This is true of every child: how much more so of this one? Mary and Joseph seem uprooted, exiles in a pagan land, without resources, without help. They have the Hope of Israel, the Rock on which their faith rests. In this desert of Egypt, which they have to cross, they will recall their fathers led by the luminous cloud covering the Ark of the Covenant; they have better than the cloud, better than the Ark. St. Paul tells us that in the desert Israel drank from the water of the rock which used to follow her from one stopover to the next, and this Rock was Christ. For them it is no longer a symbol, it is the divine reality; it is the Rock, the Source of living water, the Son of God. He keeps silent, and He shines out; His silence will be for only a while; His shining forth will be extinguished no more.

In proportion as the Child will grow, in proportion, above all, as God will expand the virgin souls of Mary and Joseph, this divine light will flood them, penetrating them with its peaceful transparency and its glory. At twelve years of age, the Child will strike with astonishment and admiration the Scribes of Jerusalem, as yet very ill-prepared to hear Him. What will it be with Mary in the course of these thirty years? Some pious authors like to portray between the Mother and the Child long evenings of confidences, Jesus expounding to Mary all He will do and create—His Church, His apostles, His sacraments. I do not in any way care to contradict them; but what seems to me much more valuable than the detail of these predictions is the source of these graces, Christ Himself, each day more deeply known and adored. That is what St. Paul will desire for the Ephesians, that they "may be able to comprehend with all the saints what is the breadth and length and height and depth, and to know Christ's love which surpasses knowledge, in order that you may be filled unto all the fullness of God" (Eph. 3:18–19). That is what the disciples of Emmaus experienced: "Was not our heart burning within us while he was speaking on the road and explaining to us the Scriptures?" (Lk. 24:32). What is priceless for them is not the interpretations of Scripture, but the presence of Him who is their author and object. This is the meaning of the words of Jesus to the people of Nazareth: in the synagogue He has just read the prophecy of Isaias: "The Spirit of the Lord is upon me; because he has anointed me; to bring good news to the poor he has sent me." He gives the holy book back to the attendant, sits down and says, "Today this Scripture has been fulfilled in your hearing" (Lk. 4:17–21). The people of Nazareth shut their eyes to this attestation of the Messias. Words do not suffice to reveal Him; there is needed an inner illumination. Neither flesh nor blood make Him known, but the heavenly Father. The Mother of God, from the first day, perceived this divine revelation and yielded to it wholly and entirely, and the light filled her with the glory and happiness of this divine presence. Today the Scriptures are fulfilled; the promised Messias has been given to us, He is the Son of God and my Son!

Eusebius recounts in wonderment the remembrances of the childhood of Origen. His father Leonides, who was soon to die a martyr, used to teach his children the elements of Christianity. The precociousness of his son soon struck him with amazement:

The simple and superficial readings of the sacred words did not satisfy him, but he sought for something more, and already at that age busied himself with deeper speculations, so that he even caused his father annoyance, as he inquired what the intent of the inspired Scripture really was. His father seemingly rebuked him to his face, urging him not to seek anything beyond his age nor anything beyond the manifest meaning; but privately by himself he rejoiced greatly, and gave most profound thanks to God, the Author of all blessings, for having

deemed him worthy to become the father of such a boy. And it is
reported that he often stood near his boy as he slept and uncovered
his breast as if the Holy Spirit were enshrined within it, and rever-
ently kissed it, and counted himself blessed in his goodly offspring.[19]

There can be no question of comparing Origen's childhood
with that of Jesus. But the reverence, the veneration, the wonderment tendered by Leonides can help us to understand the happiness and adoration of the Mother of God. Her *Magnificat*
enables us to catch a glimpse of her religious life, illumined in
its entirety by the Bible. On contact with Jesus all these revelations catch fire: the God foretold by the prophets, she has carried in her womb, she holds in her arms! Up to now He has been
her hope; henceforth He is her life.

[19] *Ecclesiastical History*, VI, 2, 10–11. Cf. FC 29, pp. 6–7.

chapter 5

❖❖❖❖❖❖❖❖❖

The Mysteries of the Life of Jesus

The Son of God willed to live amongst us. He was not satisfied with passing through or with ransoming us by an act of love, by a drop of blood. He willed to go laboriously through the stages of our existence so as to sanctify them all:

He must save all men, all those who are reborn to God—babies, children, boys, youngsters, men, oldsters. That is why He went through all ages: among the babies a babe Himself, to sanctify them; among the small children, a small child, sanctifying those who live their first years, offering them a model of piety, justice and obedience; young man among young people, He became the model of young folk and sanctified them for the Lord . . . It is thus that He attained death, in order to be the first-born among the dead, holding in all things the first place, the prince of life, the first of all, the chief who marches at the head of all.[1]

[1] *Adv. Haer.*, II, 22, 4. *P. G.*, VII, 784. Carried away by his theme, St. Irenaeus has prolonged Jesus' life into old age. This is a stage we can overlook.

So profound a view as this has remained dear to Christian piety. The mysteries of Jesus' life appear to us as models towards which the imitation of all men must tend and, at one and the same time, as sources of the merits which sanctify them all.

God wanted us "conformed to the image of his Son"; [2] here what is said of the total perfection of Christ is applied to the various mysteries of His life, revealing to us diverse aspects of His infinite holiness. And because this unique model is inexhaustible, God, who takes a singular pleasure in Him, desires that men reproduce, with a particular application according to their vocation and state of life, its various perfections: the humility of His Incarnation, the charming candor of His childhood, the zeal of His apostolic life, and, above all, the sacrifice of His Passion and the glory of His Resurrection.

Exemplary cause of our perfection, the life of Our Lord is also its meritorious cause.[3] It is this thought we find recurring often in liturgical prayers, for example, in the Litanies: *"per incarnationem tuam, per nativitatem tuam, per baptismum et sanctum jejunium tuum . . . libera nos, Domine."*

These merits are applied to us by an intimate union with Our Lord which the Holy Spirit accords to us in each of His mysteries. In the course of the liturgical cycle, the celebration of feasts not only evokes remembrances, but engraves them in our souls. This grace will be so much the more fruitful as this union is deeper. A devout soul, meditating on the Nativity, relishes the freshness and simplicity of the divine Child; but how much better St. Francis, caught up by this mystery and by Our Lord's at-

---

[2] Rom. 8:29. Cf. St. Thomas, IIIª, q. 8, a. 1, on Christ, Head of the Church; Christ is the "first-born"; He is sovereign perfection (Jn. 1:14); "of his fullness we have all received" (*ibid.*, 16); He is Head, *secundum ordinem, perfectionem et virtutem.*

[3] We must note, however, that "the mysteries prior to the Passion are not by themselves operative with regard to our justification; they become so only in consequence of, and in virtue of, the sacrifice by which Christ redeems us and acquires the right to incorporate us in Himself and, thereby, to appropriate all His merits to us" (Anger, *Le Corps mystique*, Paris, Beauchesne, 1935. Cf. *The Doctrine of the Mystical Body according to the Principles of the Theology of St. Thomas*, N. Y., Benziger, 1931).

tractiveness! Likewise, Marie of the Incarnation is carried away by the irresistible force of Christ's words, at first in the religious life, then in that Canadian mission where she had to suffer so much and work so hard to establish the kingdom of Christ:

At the time of my religious vocation, the passages which treated of the counsels of the Gospel were for me so many suns which let my mind see their eminent holiness, and at the same time inflamed my whole soul with the love of their possession, and effectively brought about what God wanted of me, according to my state, concerning the practice of the divine maxims of the superadorable Incarnate Word . . . At the time of my vocation in the Canadian mission, all the maxims and passages which treat of the domain and spread of the kingdom of Jesus Christ and of the importance of the salvation of souls, for whom He had poured out His blood, were for me like so many arrows which kept piercing my heart with a bitter anguish for what the eternal Father was meting out in justice to this, His own beloved Son, against the demons who were robbing Him of what had cost Him so dearly.[4]

Quite as well as any text, a Gospel scene will be capable, under the action of the Holy spirit, of etching itself so deeply in the soul that nothing can efface it: the scene, for example, of Jesus in the arms of His Mother or on the Cross. Then there will begin to be realized the wish of the Spouse: *Pone me ut signaculum super cor tuum, ut signaculum super brachium tuum* (Ct. 8:6).

Such great and desirable graces as these are rarely granted by God; but does not the fault lie in the imperfect dispositions of those who pray for them? These mysteries have been willed by God for man's salvation only; is it ambitioning too much to implore from God this intimate union which transforms us into Him who has lived only for us? Is it not true that "whether we live or die, we are the Lord's" (Rom. 14:8), and that our whole life, consequently, should be entirely united with His?

To prayer ought to be joined, as much as lies within us, imitation. It is good and sanctifying to contemplate the Passion; it is

[4] *Relation of 1654* in *Ecrits*, t. II, pp. 426–427.

better to be able to say with St. Ignatius of Antioch, "Permit me to be an imitator of my suffering God." [5]

Martyrdom is undoubtedly an exceptional grace; but each Christian can and should apply to himself the words of St. Paul: "The love of Christ impels us, because we have come to the conclusion that, since one died for all, therefore all died; and that Christ died for all, in order that they who are alive may live no longer for themselves, but for him who died for them and rose again" (2 Cor. 5:14–15).

We can repeat, here, that lofty prayer of Bérulle:

Be in me, O Jesus, live in me, work in me, form and fashion in me Your states and Your mysteries, Your actions and Your sufferings . . . You are God's image; may I be the living image of Yourself. May I be made like unto You: immersing myself in Your mysteries, just as You wanted to make Yourself like unto me, immersing Yourself in my miseries. And may I bear the effects and marks of Your grace and glory, of Your power and life on earth. May Your birth make me born anew; may Your childhood establish me in innocence, may Your flight into Egypt make me flee the world and sin. May Your servitude make me Your slave; may Your bonds loose me and deliver me from my sins, from my passions, and from myself. May Your hidden and unknown life hide me from the world and from vanity; may Your solitude support me. May Your temptations strengthen me, may Your agonies comfort me, may Your languishment console me, and may Your death make me live and be born again into eternity.[6]

1. CHILDHOOD

Towards the end of the Galilean ministry, after the Transfiguration, Jesus came down again to Capharnaum. His disciples followed Him. They became engaged in a conversation which soon grew very lively. When all had rejoined Him in the house, Jesus asked them, "What were you arguing about on the way?" They keep silent, for on the way they had discussed with one another

[5] *To the Romans* (6). Cf. ACW 1, p. 83.
[6] *Elévation à Jésus,* Paris, Bourgoing, I, 12, p. 353.

which of them was the greatest (Mk. 9:32–33). Jesus then sits down, takes a child, embraces it, and says to them, "Unless you turn and become like little children, you will not enter into the kingdom of heaven. Whoever, therefore, humbles himself as this little child, he is the greatest in the kingdom of heaven" (Mt. 18:3–4).

A little later on, one day that some children were pressing around Jesus, they began to annoy the apostles, who thrust them aside. Jesus was displeased at this, and said to them, "Let the little children come to me, and do not hinder them, for of such is the kingdom of God. Amen I say to you, whoever does not accept the kingdom of God as a little child will not enter into it" (Mk. 10:13–15; cf. Mt. 19:13–14).[7]

Upon the return of the disciples sent out on a mission, Jesus rejoiced in the Holy Spirit and said, "I praise thee, Father, Lord of heaven and earth, that thou didst hide these things from the wise and prudent, and didst reveal them to little ones. Yes, Father, for such was thy good pleasure" (Lk. 10:21; Mt. 11: 25–26).

When Jesus enters the Temple, on the day of the palms, the children acclaim Him: "Hosanna to the Son of David!" The chief priests are indignant: "Dost thou hear what these are saying?" And he answers, "Have you never read, 'Out of the mouth of infants and sucklings thou hast perfected praise'?" (Mt. 21: 14–16).

All these texts take note of Jesus' fondness for children: these enter into the kingdom of heaven, they hear God's revelations, they chant His praises. The greatest in the kingdom of heaven is he who makes himself like a little child.

Many of these passages are understood without difficulty: to become like a child is a very meritorious and necessary humility: without it one lets oneself be poisoned by that ambition which Our Lord reproves so severely in the apostles.

But all these privileges of childhood stem from a still deeper source: the filial spirit towards God. The Christian ought to be

[7] See *Vie et enseignement de Jésus-Christ*, II, pp. 127–128.

in His hands like a child, in all docility, abandon, and trust. Henceforth, God will be able to bend over it, to reveal to it His secrets and to relish its praises. It is in this sense that St. John will write to his disciples, "I am writing to you, little ones, because you know the Father" (1 Jn. 2:14).

This filial abandon Jesus will teach to us in the discourse on the Mount: "Do not be anxious, saying, 'What shall we eat?' or 'What shall we drink?' or 'What are we to put on?' (for after all these things the Gentiles seek); for your Father knows that you need all these things. But seek first the kingdom of God and his justice, and all these things shall be given you besides" (Mt. 6:31–33).

He has given us the example of this in His childhood, letting Himself be carried by His holy Mother where and how she wishes, and relying on her for all.[8] Jesus in the arms of His Mother: this is a mystery full of instruction. In Jesus, this surrender is not a weakness which the infirmity of His childhood imposes on Him and which His maturity will reject; it is a filial disposition He will never renounce. He will not be borne forever in the arms of His Mother; but He will always be as closely dependent on the will of His Father; "I do always the things that

---

[8] Cf. St. Francis de Sales, *Amour de Dieu,* IX, 14, and in tr. *The Love of God,* p. 383: "If anyone had asked the divine infant Jesus, where he was going when in the arms of his blessed mother, he might have replied: 'I do not go; it is my mother who goes for me. Though I go where I am led, it is not by my own exertions, but by those of my mother. I do not desire to be carried by my mother; she who walks for me, also wills for me; as I only walk in her steps, I only will by her will.

" 'When I am in the arms of my blessed mother, I abandon every wish to her, except that of reposing on her bosom—of feeding on her sacred substance, of embracing her affectionately and caressing her tenderly. While thus occupied, I consider my mother as a tree of life, and I look on myself as the fruit of this tree, as her heart, or the soul which animates her. In this situation, I am indifferent about all things; my mother walks for me, in walking for herself; I need not will anything, because her will suffices for me. I do not notice whether she moves quickly or slowly— whether she goes on one side rather than another. I care not what she does, provided I remain in her arms and repose on her bosom, where I find more happiness than amidst the most beautiful lilies.' "

are pleasing to him" (Jn. 8:29); "My food is to do the will of him who sent me" (Jn. 4:34). On the Cross His last words will be, "My Father, into thy hands I commend my spirit" (Lk. 23:46).

We must not forget that in the moral and religious life of Jesus there was never any imperfection or weakness. St. Paul had to say, "When I was a child, I spoke as a child, I felt as a child, I thought as a child. Now that I have become a man, I have put away the things of a child" (1 Cor. 13:11). Jesus never had any childishness; He never had anything to reject from His past.

Moreover, the mysteries of His childhood are stamped with an eternal imprint, and they convey to all of us some unforgettable lessons. Even today, in heaven, the Son of God bears in his heart that same filial surrender which He showed forth in the arms of His holy Mother. By living under our gaze, this divine Child is for us not only the source of our joy, but the model of our life.[9]

In his discourse, pronounced May 17, 1925, at the canonization of St. Thérèse of the Child Jesus, Pius XI explains the way of spiritual childhood as follows:

It consists in feeling and acting under the control of virtue, as a child feels and acts naturally. Just as small children, blinded by no shadow of sin and attracted by no covetous desire of the passions, rejoice in the tranquil possession of their innocence, and ignorant of all malice and dissimulation speak and act as they think, and are revealed exteriorly as they really are—in this way Thérèse appeared more angelic than human and endowed with a simplicity of a child in the practice

---

[9] "Thus should we also act; our will should be as easily moulded by the will of God as soft wax is shaped by the hand. We should not amuse ourselves in forming desires and projects; we should have no views or pretensions, but leave the disposal of everything belonging to us in the hands of God. Let us cast all our 'care upon Him, for He hath care of us' (1 Pet. 5:7). Let us deposit in His sacred heart all our anxiety and solicitude, as well with regard to events which do not depend on us, as with respect to the selection between different objects; God will watch over the success of our affairs and decide on what will conduce most to our advantage" (St. Francis de Sales, *ibid.*, p. 384).

of virtue and justice . . . Conscious of her weakness, she surrendered and committed herself to divine Providence . . .[10]

The fundamental disposition, then, is innocence, and it is on this that all depends. Therefore, Our Lord, wishing to lead us along in this way, has raised up as a model a very pure soul, who could say, "I am not conscious of having refused God anything since I was three years old."

From this purity there springs simplicity: having nothing to hide, we hide nothing. We abhor pretense, the façades which screen empty spaces, the whited sepulchers which shroud corruption. We take literally Our Lord's injunction: "Let your speech be 'Yes, yes'; 'No, no'; and whatever is beyond these comes from the evil one" (Mt. 5:37; cf. Jas. 5:12). We parade nothing, we make a mystery of nothing. Towards those who command, our simplicity is filial and guileless, not concealing our miseries nor our failures nor our troubles nor our desires. A man who thinks himself prudent judges that all this is rather naïve; that one must be a dove but also a serpent, and that playing always with one's cards on the table makes one lose our trumps. And it may be, as a matter of fact, that on a particular occasion cleverness is more profitable. But all things considered, it is the simplicity of a child which will have the last word, with men most of the time, and always with God Our Father, whose judgment alone matters to His child.

Formed by Our Lord's teaching, the child of God pursues its life "in the secret of his face" (Ps. 30:21) and for His love: its prayer, its fasts, its alms—all are offered to the Father in secret, and the Father, who sees in secret, will take them into account for His Child. This is sufficient.

But it is here that there appears again this requirement of purity without which the spirit of childhood is only a dream.

[10] A.A.S., t. XVII, pp. 211–214. L'histoire d'une âme, éd. complète, pp. 586, 587. Cf. Autobiography, the complete and authentic text of L'histoire d'une âme, tr. by Ronald Knox, N. Y., Kenedy, 1958. —J. de Guibert, S.J., Documenta Ecclesiastica (Rome, Ed. Pont. Univ. Greg., 1931), p. 456.

How to pursue this life face to face with the Father, if we refuse Him anything? It may be that we still have to repulse persistent temptations and to combat stubborn faults. All this God pardons us, if our will resists them: "He sees the clay with which He shaped us, and He has pity on His poor children." But what He cannot tolerate from His children is a deliberate failing in His service, a conscious resistance to His will: for example, a feeling of spite which we do not wish to renounce, an ambitious design we entertain, or the irritation we nourish on the occasion of an order or a reprimand. Whoever has tasted God's fatherly love, knows also its zealous concern; and if he is tempted to resist Him, he hears in the depths of his heart the words of Jesus to Peter: " 'If I do not wash thee, thou shalt have no part with me.' 'Lord, not my feet only, but also my hands and my head!' " (Jn. 13:8–9).

But this purity, laboriously recovered, will it find once more the freshness of the first innocence? One cannot help asking with Nicodemus: "How can a man be born when he is old? Can he enter a second time into his mother's womb and be born again?" (Jn. 3:4). Here again, what is impossible for man is possible for God. "Do not wonder that I said to thee, 'You must be born again.' The wind blows where it will, and thou hearest its sound but dost not know where it comes from or where it goes. So is everyone who is born of the Spirit" (*ibid.,* 7–8).

This liberty, this freshness of a new life—all the baptized will know it. They will hear the exhortation which St. Peter addresses to them:

Lay aside therefore all malice, and all deceit, and pretense, and envy, and all slander. Crave, as newborn babes, pure spiritual milk, that by it you may grow to salvation; if, indeed, you have tasted that the Lord is sweet (1 Pt. 2:1–3).

Here is one of the attractions of Christianity: this appearance, in a world grown old, of this really young life, like that of a newborn.

This grace is the fruit of baptism. Occasionally we encounter it also in saints purified by an inner transformation in Jesus

Christ. St. Catherine of Siena, who had received this valuable charism, thus described it to her confessor:

My interior ardor is so great that, next to it, material exterior fire seems rather to cool than to burn. This ardor produced in my soul such a renewal of purity and humility, that I thought I had gone back to the age of four or five years.[11]

Without claiming this exceptional grace, every Christian can and ought to tend towards that ideal of candid purity which he adores in the Child Jesus.

We were admiring in St. Thérèse of Lisieux her innocence; that is what gives to her whole life its joyous assurance and impetus. In spite of all, in that life, one of the purest there are, the source has been sullied by original sin. To find a soul entirely pure, we must gaze on the Immaculate Virgin. Here, from the beginning, is the limpidity which others will find only in the waters of baptism; from it there comes to the virgin beauty of Mary that candor which no creature has equaled.

What more do we find in the soul of her divine Son? The grace of the hypostatic union and the gifts which flow from it, in particular the beatific vision which, from the first moment, illumined Him. In His Gospel, Jesus, wishing to give us a great respect for children, told us, "Their angels in heaven always behold the face of my Father in heaven" (Mt. 18:10). Of Jesus we must say, "This little Child always beholds the face of the Father in heaven."

To understand fully the significance of this grace, we must understand what the vision of God is; we can, at least, try to grasp some reflection of it. Let us see the soul of this child continually fixed in this contemplation of God. Around Him pass the shepherds, the Magi, Simeon, and Anna; nearer Him stand Mary and Joseph; and to Him He repeats silently, "Behold I come . . . to do thy will, O God" (Heb. 10:7). There is in this acqui-

11 Cf. the *Life of Saint Catherine of Siena by the Blessed Raymond of Capua, her confessor,* II, ch. 6, tr. from the French by the Ladies of the Sacred Heart, N. Y., Kenedy.

escence in the good pleasure of the Father a joy, an assurance, a peace, of whose infinite power we can get only an inkling. And if, having considered this filial love, we return to the innocence of this little Child, how ineffable it appears to us! There is not only purity, candor, and exemption from all imperfection and weakness, but there is, from the first moment, an infinite, irresistible love which bears the Son towards the Father. *Ita, Pater, quia sic fuit placitum ante te* (Lk. 10:21).

And right there is the starting point for this moral and religious life: this love of the Father, contemplated face to face, has preceded every other love, illumined every other knowledge. There never was in Jesus' life that dualism which so often divides our own: a religious life which illumines all, but by intervals and, in the ordinary course of things, with earthly horizons which limit the outlook to the precarious and changing point of view of God's creatures. To Jesus, on the contrary, all these things appear such as they are, sustained by the heavenly Father, and receiving from Him continually all they have of being, beauty, and life. The gaze of the Son of God penetrates, to the depths, the work of His Father. Better than any man has ever done, He marvels at it and loves it, as did God on the day of Creation: *Vidit Deus quod esset bonum* (Gn. 1:18).

At times we are surprised at the extreme simplicity with which Jesus sets forth the most heroic duties: man must have one sole concern, the kingdom of God; if some obstacle gets in his way, he must remove it at all costs, even if he has to cut off his hand or pluck out his eye. All that is spoken quite simply, as going without saying, and undoubtedly the evidence suffices to explain the simplicity of the words. But we understand it even better when we recall the continuity of this view: from the first awakening of conscience: the soul of Jesus not only never knew any shadow of sin, but it has been seized, since its creation, by the beatific vision. He can have in His will no failing, in His intelligence no obscuring.

This constant limpidity of gaze gives to His words their transparency, which no other human word can imitate. If you want to understand better these words of Our Lord, you must strive to listen to them with a simple, fresh soul, like that of a child. Without that you will be disconcerted, or will ascribe to them some kind of Stoic rigidity. Truly, God has hidden all that from the wise and prudent of this world; He has revealed it to the little children. If, by the grace of Christ, we become like them, we make a ready entrance into the kingdom. Instead of clenching our fists and stiffening up in a great effort, we say simply: To serve God, to do His will—we have nothing else to do here below; that is obvious.

To those souls transformed into the image of the divine Child, God communicates Himself with a truly fatherly intimacy. After describing these divine communications, St. Alphonsus Rodriguez adds:

Right there is what God communicates to His humble children, when both are alone by themselves. The child does not raise himself up for the great things it receives, but it gives glory to whom it belongs: to God. But what shall we say of the visits by which God consoles His children in prayer? "Let the little children come to me." O Sovereign and Eternal God! If the servants of God knew, if they knew the marvels, the divine secrets, which God communicates in prayer to these little ones, who know not how to search by themselves, but abandon themselves to God, placing their whole trust in Him, continually with Him, letting themselves be conducted and carried by their God! What a visit He pays them! He raises the soul, and in a great light He shows Himself to her and immerses her in His infinite perfections. There she faints with love for her Lord; she lets herself be carried by her God where He wants her to go, like a child.[12]

2. THE HIDDEN LIFE

After the first mysteries of Our Lord's childhood, there is His adolescence in Nazareth. He grew in wisdom and age and grace before God and men. During all this time, what is His life? That of the son of poor parents, in a village; He obeys and He works. The Church rightly applies to Him the words of St. Paul: "He differs in no way from a slave, though he is the master of

12 *Obras,* t. III, p. 434.

all" (Gal. 4:1). Truly He is the Master of all things, and still *nihil differt a servo*. And this, not only in the little house of Nazareth, but in this world, where He could enter as king and where He appears as a servant. St. Clement of Rome, echoing St. Paul, wrote: "The Sceptre of the Divine Majesty, the Lord Jesus Christ, did not, for all His power, come clothed in boastful pomp and overweening pride, but in a humble frame of mind, as the Holy Spirit has told concerning Him; for He says (Is. 53: 1–12): 'Lord, who has believed our teaching?' " [13] Is not this the humility of the Son, Heir and Lord of all, who makes Himself the servant of all?

When men are subjected to this long minority, they endure it poorly. Let us recall the elder son in the parable of the Prodigal: "Behold, these many years I have been serving thee, and have never transgressed one of thy commands; and yet thou hast never given me a kid that I might make merry with thy friends." But the father answered him, "Son, thou art always with me, and all that is mine is thine" (Lk. 15:29, 31).

These words on the lips of Jesus are particularly touching: they are those He addresses to the Father in His last prayer: *Et mea omnia tua sunt, et tua mea sunt.*[14] There is no finer share; but to appreciate its worth one must love the Father and live gladly in this filial dependency: everything between us is undivided, and everything is in His hands.

The prodigal son is impatient with this subjection and snatches from his living father his heritage; the elder son submits to it, but grudgingly. The Son of God takes His pleasure therein. He is the Heir; it is to Him that the Father has said, "Ask of me, and I will give thee the Gentiles for thy inheritance, and the utmost parts of the earth for thy possession" (Ps. 2:8). He is truly *heres omnium* (Heb. 1:2), but He wants only to be the servant of His Father; He executes His orders but transgresses none of them; He is not His own master, and yet He owns all.

Children of God, we behold in Jesus our Model: we learn from Him to use this world as a child uses its father's possessions,

[13] *Epistle to the Corinthians,* 16. Cf. ACW 1, p. 18.
[14] Jn. 17:10; cf. 16:15: *Omnia quaecumque habet Pater mea sunt.*

in all gratitude and dependence. St. Clement said in his epistle to the Corinthians who had to leave their country: "Every place will give you a glad welcome, for the land belongs to the Lord with all that it contains" (54, 3). In no wise is a Christian in exile; everywhere he is in the domain of his Father. His Father assures him the use of everything he needs. To those who wish to imitate Him right to the end in His poverty, Jesus will soon say, "If thou wilt be perfect, go, sell what thou hast, and give to the poor, and thou shalt have treasure in heaven; and come, follow me" (Mt. 19:21). This is the life of Nazareth: to have nothing which belongs to us as our own; not even to be able to dispose of ourselves, ever to be a minor. This is a fact, and it is the life which the Son of God has chosen on earth. *Omnia tua sunt, et tua mea sunt.* The first words seem stern; but the latter ones radiate happiness: it is good to be able to say to God: "What is Thine, is mine."

Here we rejoin the beautiful text of St. Paul, "All things are yours . . . and you are Christ's, and Christ is God's" (1 Cor. 3:22–23).[15]

Filial obedience will be the constant law for Jesus; it will govern His last years as it does His adolescence. But at Nazareth it appears even more manifest. Bread of life come down to earth, the Son of God is hidden like the seed; treasure of infinite value, He is hidden like the treasure in the field, like the pearl which only the connoisseur will be able to discover. These Gospel parables reveal to us a providential disposition, which will command the lives of the saints, and to which Our Lord has willed to be the first to subject Himself.

He knows what is in man. He sees the distress of souls—all those Jews lying helpless on the ground like a flock without a shepherd; and He, the Good Shepherd, comes not to them.

[15] Nothing has been dearer to the saints; cf. St. John of the Cross: "Mine are the heavens and mine is the earth; mine are the people, the righteous are mine and mine are the sinners; the angels are mine and the Mother of God, and all things are mine; and God Himself is mine and for me, for Christ is mine and all for me." [*Avis,* pp. 190–192, and in tr. *Complete Works.*]

Is this indifference? Certainly not, but obedience to His Father and mercy to men. He might have illumined, by His word, ten years sooner than He did, thousands of His contemporaries; but He might not have left to His countless disciples the example of His silent preparation.

And this example was for us indispensable. We are impatient to show off, to push ourselves into the first place, and as soon as possible: thus the prodigal son saying to his father, "Give me the share of the property that falls to me" (Lk. 15:12); thus the guest at the banquet who hurried up to take the place of honor (Lk. 14:8); thus Our Lord's brethren who will say to Him, "Go into Judea that thy disciples also may see the words that thou dost; for no one does a thing in secret if he wants to be publicly known. If thou dost these things, manifest thyself to the world" (Jn. 7:3–4).

These fits of impatience betray the avidity of our desires and the frailty of our lives. Nothing at all of that in the Son of God: the glory that belongs to Him is the eternal glory He had before the creation of the world, with the Father; it is the only one He ambitions (Jn. 17:5). It is one, too, that He gives to His own (*ibid.*, 22). The glory which comes from men, He does not want (Jn. 5:41); and He enjoins us to renounce it. He will say to the Pharisees, "How can you believe who receive glory from one another, and do not seek the glory which is from the only God?" (*ibid.*, 44).

Here again there appears the infinite distance which separates earth from heaven, those here below from Him who is from above (Jn. 8:23). In this Judea, so hard hit and which Jesus knows to be condemned to death, having before His very eyes the Cross whose shadow already falls upon Him, He works peacefully at His carpenter's bench. He knows that His days are numbered. He will say later on, "Are there not twelve hours in the day? If a man walks in the day, he does not stumble, because he sees the light of this world" (Jn. 11:9). These twelve daylight hours will already be waning when Jesus leaves Nazareth two or three years hence, and the light of the world will be veiled. "I must do the works of him who sent me while it is day; night is coming, when no one can work. As long as I am in the world I am the light of the world" (Jn. 9:4–5). The night is coming on, and He stays at Nazareth in His workshop, and it is there that He does the work of His Father.

He does not have to resign Himself, to do violence to Himself; He loves the will of the Father and takes pleasure in it. Soon He will say to His disciples, "When thou prayest, go into thy room, and closing thy door, pray to thy Father in secret; and thy Father, who sees in secret, will reward thee" (Mt. 6:6). Jesus, at Nazareth, has tasted the attractiveness of this life, hidden away in the secrecy of the Father; when He involves us in it, He speaks from experience. But if we wish to hear His lesson, we must bring to it the preparation it requires, especially faith: our life, if it is ruled by love for the Father, is wholly and entirely a filial homage; it may be obscure in the eyes of men, it is luminous before God.

3. THE PRECURSOR

While Jesus was growing up at Nazareth, His Precursor was living in the desert. The only thing we know of these thirty years is what St. Luke tells us of them (1:80): "The child grew and became strong in spirit; and was in the deserts until the day of his manifestation to Israel." Once more there appears the close union which attaches John the Baptist to Jesus: the same silent, hidden growth; soon, also, a similar martyrdom; the bloody death of John will presage that of Jesus. He whom Our Lord will extol as "a prophet, yes, and more than a prophet" (Mt. 11:9) will not have a year of active life: after a few months of preaching, He will have the signal honor of baptizing Jesus; then the Precursor will efface himself before the Messias; soon afterwards he will vanish in the dungeon of Machaerus and finally in death. And to prepare for so brief a career as this, he will have to spend thirty years in the desert, in the rigors of a severe penance, having for clothes only a hairshirt tightened with a cincture, for nourishment only what he could find in the desert—locusts and wild honey (Mt. 3:4).

The austerity seems to us even less rigorous than the solitude. John had been greeted by his parents as a miraculous child, the consolation of their old age; Zachary had extolled him as a prophet; he was the joy and the glory not only of his father and mother but of the whole countryside. He disappears into the desert as soon as he can support himself; they will never see him again. From our human point of view, it seems even more surprising to see him entirely separated from Nazareth, from Mary and Jesus; even in the womb of his mother, he had been sanctified by Jesus, at the time of the Visitation. He seems never to have seen Mary; as for Our Lord, he will see Him only on the day of the baptism and will know Him only by a heavenly revelation (Jn. 1:33).

And yet everything in him tends towards Jesus; he is only a voice which cries out, "Make ready the way of the Lord" (Mt. 3:3; Mk. 1:3; Lk. 3:4; Jn. 1:23). As for himself, he baptizes with water; He whom he heralds will baptize with the Holy Spirit and fire (Lk. 3:16). He is not worthy to loose the straps of His sandals (Mk. 1:7). And this long preparation for his ministry, this whole life of penance, prayer, and desire, will be carried on in the desert, far from Jesus.

He will baptize Christ, and he will have again the supreme joy of sending Him his best disciples; he will see, little by little, his ministry being extinguished. To his jealous disciples he will then say, "You yourselves bear me witness that I said, 'I am not the Christ but have been sent before him.' He who has the bride is the bridegroom; but the friend of the bridegroom, who stands and hears him, rejoices exceedingly at the voice of the bridegroom. This my joy, therefore, is made full. He must increase, but I must decrease" (Jn. 3:28–30).

A few weeks afterwards, it was imprisonment, then death, in the prison of Machaerus.

"Among those born of women, there has not risen a greater than John the Baptist" (Mt. 11:11).

In this remarkable life one sees the whole Old Testament. Elias lives again in John the Baptist (Mt. 17:12–13); the Precursor is as austere as the old prophets. But, since Jesus' baptism, the gentleness of Christ transfigures him; he is the first to recognize in Him the Lamb of God and the Bridegroom. Our Lord will say later to His apostles, "No longer do I call you servants . . . but I have called you friends" (Jn. 15:15); this is henceforth the glory of John: he is "the friend of the Bridegroom" (Jn. 3:29).

4. THE BAPTISM

The baptism of Jesus and His stay in the desert illumine again the mystery which we have just contemplated.

Jesus comes to the Jordan to be humiliated, to mingle with the crowd of sinners, and to receive the baptism of penance. John does not yet recognize Him; but the sanctity of Jesus shines through to eyes capable of discerning it: "It is I who ought to be baptized by thee, and dost thou come to me?" John exclaims. "Let it be so now, for so it becomes us to fulfill all justice," answers Jesus. Then he suffers Him (Mt. 3:14–15). Wondrous humility of John, who does not balk, as St. Peter will, for a moment, at the washing of the feet (Jn. 13:6 ff.). And, above all, incomparable humility of Our Lord: as the Baptist will soon say, He is the Lamb of God who takes away the sin of the world; and, like sinners, He comes to receive the baptism of penance. In this way the Virgin Mary had willed to have herself purified in the Temple. In this soiled and penitent world, the Virgin and her divine Son alone escape the soiling, but they wish to carry their share of the penance. And we know what that share was for them.

On this humility of the Savior the heavens open up and the Father is pleased: "When Jesus had been baptized, he immediately came up from the water. And behold, the heavens were opened, and he saw the Spirit of God descending as a dove and coming upon him. And behold, a voice from the heavens said, 'This is my beloved Son, in whom I am well pleased'" (Mt. 3:16–17). This apparition and this voice were perceived by Our

Lord Himself [16] and also by St. John the Baptist (Jn. 1:32–34), but by no one else, it seems. Of this crowd which hurries to the Jordan, no one knows Jesus, even after this theophany. John the Baptist will soon say, "In the midst of you there has stood one whom you do not know" (Jn. 1:26). Jesus is always the hidden God.

Here we can only repeat the words of St. Paul: "The sensual man does not perceive the things that are of the Spirit of God" (1 Cor. 2:14). The highest revelations are inaccessible to him. The theophany of the baptism, the Transfiguration, the apparitions of our Risen Lord, and His Ascension—all this will be perceived by only a few privileged witnesses, who will make it known to the others.

Likewise the highest revelations made to the saints will be incommunicable. They can only repeat after St. Paul: "I know a man . . . he was caught up into paradise and heard secret words that man may not repeat" (2 Cor. 12:3, 4).

Men who used to construct religions to suit their tastes were wont to screen their mysteries with closely guarded secrets: the name of God was known only to the initiated; it was valuable to them like a talisman. The ceremonies of the rite were shielded behind veils or in sanctuaries hidden in the depths of the temples, access to which was forbidden to common men. The Jewish rite itself was protected by these prohibitions, God wishing in this way to gain respect from the still sensual Jews and to inspire in them the fear of His holiness.

By no means did Our Lord closet Himself with these mysteries. He lived among men by mingling with them; he instituted His Eucharist to stay always in our midst, in temples open to all. But faith alone revealed in Him the Son of God, and in the Holy Eucharist faith alone attains His presence.

Thus at the Jordan, Jesus mingles with the crowd which knows Him not. On Him the heavens open up, the Spirit appears, the Father bends down; no one perceives these divine apparitions, except Jesus and John the Baptist.

[16] In St. Mark (1:11) and in St. Luke (3:22) it is to Jesus that the voice is addressed.

At the beginning of his book to Autolycus, St. Theophilus will write: "You ask me: What kind of God do you have? And I ask you: What kind of man are you? Are your eyes clear-sighted? Are you able to know God?" [17]

"Jesus Christ is holy to God, fearsome to the demons"; but this grandeur can be perceived only by those who see Wisdom.

5. THE TEMPTATION

"And immediately [after the baptism] the Spirit drove him forth into the desert" (Mk. 1:12; Mt. 4:1; Lk. 4:1). This is the only passage in Our Lord's life where the three Synoptics concur in recording the Holy Spirit's action on Him. They recognize, then, in this desert retreat, a very special divine impetus.

Moses had spent forty days on Sinai, in a strict fast, alone with God, from whom he received the law.[18] Our Lord had no need to receive the law; on the Mount He was to promulgate, on His own authority, the new law. But, on the point of beginning His public ministry, He wanted to pray and to fast. Of His prayer He has told us nothing; but He wished to make known to us the temptations which He met with in the desert and which He overcame.

This mystery is one of those which disconcert us the most, one of those, also, which are richest in instruction. Jesus, the "holy one of God" (Mk. 1:24; Acts 3:14), is tempted. No man then is sheltered from this trial; but he can surmount it without contracting any stain.

With men who are sinners, the tempter finds in our concupiscence an accomplice;[19] with the Son of God no evil covetousness, no complaisance in the suggestions of the enemy. These

17 *Ad Autolycum,* I, 1.

18 Ex. 24:18; 34:28. Cf. Dt. 9:9–18. We might also recall the fast of forty days of Elias walking to the mount of God, Horeb (3 Kgs. 19:8).

19 "Let no man say when he is tempted, that he is tempted by God; for God is no tempter to evil, and he himself tempts no one. But everyone is tempted by being drawn away and enticed by his own passion. Then when passion has conceived, it brings forth sin; but when sin has matured, it begets death" (Jas. 1:13–15).

suggestions reverberate on the exterior of the soul which they strive to shake; they fail to penetrate within. Satan has no hold on Him.[20]

And yet the temptations were for the Son of God very grievous: they made Him more keenly aware of His people's opposition to His mission, such that the will of the Father had laid down for Him. This servant of God, gentle and humble, this Man of sorrows, is not the Messias that most of the Jews hoped for and awaited. The beatitudes which He must propose—poverty, hunger, tears, persecutions—their worth will be appreciated by the best among His listeners; the greater number aspire after an easier, more sensual happiness. His very miracles, enveloped in a penetrating but quiet light, will touch pure hearts, those open to the love of God. But proud souls will ask Him for showy prodigies, signs in the heavens (Mk. 8:11). Ordinary souls will have no other concern than to be healed (Lk. 17:17) and fed (Jn. 6:26).

If we wish to understand how grievous such a mission was, let us recall the plaints of Jeremias, laden with a similar message and sinking under the burden:

Thou hast deceived me, O Lord, and I am deceived: thou hast been stronger than I, and thou hast prevailed. I am become a laughing-stock all the day, all scoff at me. For I am speaking now this long time, crying out against iniquity, and I often proclaim devastation: and the word of the Lord is made a reproach to me, and a derision all the day. Then I said: I will not make mention of him, nor speak any more in his name: and there came in my heart as a burning fire, shut up in my bones, and I was wearied, not being able to bear it. For I heard the reproaches of many, and terror on every side: Persecute him, and let us persecute him: from all men that were my familiars, and continued at my side: if by any means he may be deceived, and we may prevail against him, and be revenged on him (Jer. 20:7–10).

Satan recalled these cries of distress of the prophets. He knew that Jesus was the Messias, but he had not yet pierced the mystery of His divinity. He saw in Him only a man—holy, no

[20] Jn. 14:30: *in me non habet quidquam.*

doubt, and beloved of God, but weak like any man. And in his scorn for humanity he did not lose hope of seeing Him sink, like the others, under the weight of too holy a law.

Here is what the three temptations are aimed at (Mt. 4:2–11): that Jesus use for His own profit His power of thaumaturge, that He change the stones into bread; that He cast Himself down from the top of the Temple; finally, that He purchase, by homage to Satan, the empire of the world. This last temptation is a desperate effort that betrays the mad arrogance of the tempter.

Jesus, without revealing Himself, girds Himself with the words of Scripture, with "the shield of faith" in order to "quench all the fiery darts of the most wicked one" (Eph. 6:16).

In these temptations, what was grievous for Jesus was not resisting the extravagant claims which He abhorred; it was beholding, over the entire world, down through all the centuries and henceforth right at His side, countless men who would let themselves be deceived by these mirages, who would prefer the marvels of Satan to the miracles of Christ, the arrogance of the prince of this world to the humility of the Servant of God.

Even those who will be most loyal to Him will be unable, until Pentecost, to get rid of their ambitious dreams, of their claims to the first places of His kingdom (Mk. 10:37). On the day of the Ascension, they will ask Him again, "Lord, wilt thou at this time restore the kingdom to Israel?" (Acts 1:6). The first time this stubborn blindness is manifested, Jesus is deeply moved by it. He has just predicted His Passion; Peter answers Him, "Far be it from thee, O Lord; this will never happen to thee." Jesus replies to him with unusual severity, "Get behind me, satan, thou art a scandal to me; for thou dost not mind the things of God, but those of men" (Mt. 16:22–23). For the tempter himself, Jesus had only disgust and scorn. But, at the thought of this influence, slight and remote though it be, being able to extend over His most beloved apostles, Jesus cannot help trembling with sorrow.

Throughout Christ's life, this struggle against Satan continues: it is evident in the deliverance of the possessed; it is even more dramatic in the conversion or perversion of souls. The fall of Judas is a frightful example of this: already one year before the Passion, Jesus says to the apostles, "Have I not chosen you, the Twelve? Yet one of you is a devil" (Jn. 6:71); at the Last Supper the perversion is accomplished: "The devil having already put it into the heart of Judas Iscariot, the son of Simon, to betray him" (Jn. 13:2); Jesus will make a last effort with him but will be repulsed: "After the morsel, Satan entered into him" (Jn. 13:27).

The other apostles also are tempted; but, protected by the prayer of Jesus, they will not fail irrevocably: "Simon, Simon, behold, Satan has desired to have you, that he may sift you as wheat. But I have prayed for thee, that thy faith may not fail; and do thou, when once thou hast turned again, strengthen thy brethren" (Lk. 22:31–32).

Through the turmoil of the crowds, we divine the influence of the tempter. After the first impressions of docility and even of enthusiasm, there are the failures, the refusals, and the fits of anger which do not come solely from human inconstancy. We recognize in them those counter-attacks of the enemy, which Jesus Himself has described: "When the unclean spirit has gone out of a man, he roams through dry places in search of a resting-place, and finds none. Then he says, 'I will return to my house which I left'; and when he has come, he finds the place unoccupied, swept, and adorned. Then he goes and takes with him seven other spirits more evil than himself, and they enter in and dwell there; and the last state of that man becomes worse than the first. So shall it be with this evil generation also" (Mt. 12:43–45).

We are not surprised to see, then, after one of those counter-attacks of incredulity, Our Lord saying to the Jews of Jerusalem: "The father from whom you are is the devil, and the desires of your father it is your will to do. He was a murderer from the beginning, and has not stood in the truth because there is no truth in him. When he tells a lie he speaks from his very nature, for he is a liar and the father of lies" (Jn. 8:44).

Thus, behind this mobile screen of emotions and passions, there are invisible actors exploiting these human weaknesses so as to set men against God and destroy them.

We see also by means of these incidents, that the suggestions of the demon have, at first, a harmless appearance: thus to Jesus: "Command that these stones become loaves of bread"; it is only gradually that Satan is disclosed: "Adore me." Moreover these promises are at first dazzling—all the kingdoms of the world. In the eyes of the Jews he holds out continual bright prospects for the re-establishment of the kingdom of Israel. There is in it for all a deep national aspiration; for each one, personal ambitions which this dream must realize: the first and the second places of the kingdom. And the people let themselves cling to this confused pressure to which love of country lends its nobility and personal ambition, its greed. It is fairly likely that from this is born the defection of Judas, at the time of the Galilean crisis. And then, little by little, national aspirations grew discouraged before insurmountable obstacles, and there remained only greed and, to satisfy it, theft; and the covetousness, growing ever more intense, is satisfied finally with thirty denarii to make of an apostle a traitor. And all ends in despair and suicide.

The interpretation of this terrible fall Jesus gives us in the words we have just now recalled: the demon is a murderer and a liar.

What forces does Jesus oppose to this diabolic seduction? Truth and love. When He speaks of the two masters who oppose each other, He tells us, "No man can serve two masters; for either he will hate the one and love the other, or else he will stand by the one and despise the other" (Mt. 6:24).

Those who follow Him, love Him and hate Satan; those who follow Satan, support him and scorn God: Jesus takes hold of us by the love He inspires in us; Satan seduces us by the false goods he promises us. We recognize this sway of Jesus in the fidelity of St. Peter: what strengthens him in times of hesitation is love: "Lord, to whom shall we go? Thou hast words of everlasting life" (Jn. 6:69). "If I do not wash thee, thou shalt have no part with me." "Lord, not my feet only, but also my hands and my head!" (Jn. 13:8–9).

This is made clear again by the incident of the sons of Zebedee, and particularly of St. John. The temptation we discern in the petition which it has provoked, the request for the first two places of the kingdom (Mk. 10:37); it is sensual ambition awakened by Satan. Jesus' answer is in the chalice and in service. But of the chalice, He shall be the first to drink (*ibid.,* 38); of service, He gives the example throughout His life (*ibid.,* 45). His example carries along the two young men; love triumphs over pride. And soon, at the Last Supper, John will recline on the heart of Jesus; and the next day, at the foot of the Cross, he will witness His agony, and receive His mother as his share. To the deceptive dream of the first two places is opposed this truly divine gift of Christ's love; but love alone can taste it.

Here we begin to feel the power of that attraction which the heavenly Father instills in the hearts of the faithful: the love of His Son. For Him, the Christian will renounce all that seduces him here below, he will carry his cross and follow Him. This is the glory of Our Lord; it is our strength.

chapter 6

❖❖❖❖❖❖❖❖❖

The Sermon on the Mount

1. THE BEATITUDES

The public teaching of Jesus is inaugurated by the Sermon on the Mount; the first words of this discourse propose to us the beatitudes.[1] These statements are engraved on the Christian conscience; even those who are unfaithful to this law cannot lose

[1] The beatitudes have been transmitted to us under two different forms: in St. Matthew (5:3–12) eight beatitudes, enunciated under the gnomic form ("Blessed are the poor") and understood in the spiritual sense ("the poor in spirit"; "they who hunger and thirst for justice"); in St. Luke (6:20–23) four beatitudes, addressed directly to the hearers ("Blessed are you poor"), and apparently indicating a material condition ("you poor"; "you who hunger now"). There are here two different forms of Christian catechetics, reproducing the teaching of Our Lord with different nuances. These differences may come from the diverse classes to which the catechesis was addressed. The text reproduced by St. Luke aims in particular at the group of disciples such as they appear to us in the first chapters of the Acts: poverty for them is not only detachment from the goods of this world, but deprivation. Cf. *Vie et enseignement de Jésus-Christ*, I, pp. 178–180.

the remembrance of them. But do they all understand them? It would seem not, if we glance through the commentaries, so numerous and so divergent.

The first impression of many readers is that of being confronted with paradoxes. In the beginning of the book of Psalms, we read a beatitude:

Blessed is the man who hath not walked in the counsel of the ungodly . . . but his will is in the law of the Lord, and on his law he shall meditate day and night. And he shall be like a tree which is planted near the running waters, which shall bring forth its fruit . . . and all whatsoever he shall do shall prosper (Ps. 1:1–3).

This beatitude is understood with no difficulty; but in the evangelical beatitudes everything seems to be the exact opposite of the judgments of men. Does happiness consist, then, in being poor, hungry, afflicted, persecuted?

To understand the Master's thought, it is important first of all to consider it in its entirety, as it was transmitted by St. Matthew and St. Luke. The material conditions of life are not indispensable to happiness and do not suffice for it. One can be poor, hungry and persecuted without being a true disciple of Jesus. One must be "poor in spirit," one must "hunger for justice," one must be persecuted "because of the Son of Man"; and one must still be merciful and pure of heart and peaceable. Right there is a religious ideal which is favored, no doubt, by certain living conditions, but not determined by them; it appears more in evidence in them, it is more strongly developed in them, but it does not depend on these accidents of fortune as though on its source.

These considerations are caused by a comparison of the two versions: in St. Matthew, the stress is on moral dispositions; in St. Luke, on the material conditions of life. We might ask whether, and to what extent, these material conditions govern the moral dispositions.

It is quite certain that what matter essentially are the virtues more than the living conditions, detachment from riches more than indigence. But we must add that effective privation is not

an indifferent thing; in an easy, comfortable life it is very difficult not to labor under a delusion concerning the detachment we
think we feel in ourselves. There will be, no doubt, many material things to which we shall attach little value and which we
shall employ without, usually, depending on them; still we shall
want to have them within reach "so as to use them in case of
need." Others will be for daily use and will appear indispensable—
for example, work tools. If, suddenly, all that comes to be missing, we feel how much the detachment, however sincerely desired, was imperfectly realized: this is the experiment which
St. John Chrysostom, for example, made by going from his maternal home into the desert.

We understand, then, that it is easier for the poor, the really
poor, to be poor in spirit; the little flock, beatified in St. Luke,
will be in the most favorable conditions for realizing the beatitudes proposed in St. Matthew. Here is the whole meaning
of the religious state: life therein is organized in such a way
that it is freed from all hindrances here below. When He recommends virginity to His disciples, St. Paul says to them, "I would
have you free from care. He who is unmarried is concerned about
the things of the Lord, how he may please God. Whereas he who
is married is concerned about the things of the world, how he
may please his wife; and he is divided. And the unmarried
woman, and the virgin, thinks about the things of the Lord, that
she may be holy in body and in spirit. Whereas she who is married thinks about the things of the world, how she may please
her husband" (1 Cor. 7:32–34).

The goods of fortune are also sources of anxiety: these are
the thorns which choke the good seed (Mt. 13:22); this is
mammon, the jealous master whose service is incompatible with
that of the heavenly Father (Mt. 6:24). That a rich man enter
the kingdom of heaven is a miracle of grace (Mt. 19:26). We
are not surprised that Jesus asks of him who would be perfect
the actual renunciation of riches (*ibid.*, 21), and that the first
Christians had, for the most part, aspired to that virtuous ideal.

These living conditions can be the object of our choosing;
but there are things in the beatitudes which are in no way the

effect of a human option, but of God's providence: this is true, especially, of persecutions. We can in certain cases choose a type of life which exposes us to persecutions; but we do not have to provoke the persecution ourselves. In the fourth and fifth centuries the Donatists, madly ambitious of martyrdom, will want to force people they meet to kill them or, at other times, they will commit suicide.[2]

These very follies put us on our guard: this beatitude of persecutions does not depend on us, nor does the beatitude of tears. We receive them from the hand of the heavenly Father.

Our life is not in our own hands, but in the hands of God. We can, in many things, search out the conditions most favorable to His service; we commit the others to His wisdom and goodness. A soul attentive to the providence of God soon recognizes that therein she finds the most beneficial and efficacious direction. Wisdom forbids taking every precaution that prudence suggests; but the most attentive foresight is often thwarted by the event: *vana salus hominis.* Only divine Providence imprints on our lives their assured direction. And it is towards this that we are led by the whole effort of detachment which Jesus asks of us: "Blessed are the poor," undoubtedly, because they are not entangled in thorns or hampered with riches; but also because they commit to their heavenly Father all their needs.

Thus in this ideal picture of the Christian—poor, afflicted, merciful, pure, peaceable, and persecuted—we begin to recognize the child of God: "Blessed are the peacemakers, for they shall be called children of God" (Mt. 5:9). This is the reward of all the beatitudes.

From the very beginning, this great lesson appears to us in the example of the Son of God. If we ask Him why the Christian

---

[2] Cf. Monceaux, *Histoire littéraire de l'Afrique chrétienne, depuis les origines jusqu'à l'invasion arabe,* Paris, Leroux, 1901–23, V, pp. 40 ff., quoting *Optatus,* III, 4: "Some, misled by the desire for an imagined martyrdom, pay assassins to kill them. Others, to consummate the sacrifice of their vile souls, hurl themselves from the tops of high mountains." Augustine, *Contra Gaudentium,* I, 28, 32, knew of certain sacred rocks made famous by a long series of suicides.

should place his happiness in the pursuit of so austere an ideal as this, the answer is that which Jesus Himself proposes to us: "Remember the word that I have spoken to you: No servant is greater than his master. If they have persecuted me, they will persecute you also" (Jn. 15:20).

On the day of the Incarnation, the Son of God chose poverty and the Cross; He is the Head of humanity, He has chosen for all. We have already mentioned the reasons for this option; we shall come back to them. Here let it suffice for us to recall that we are engaged in following the Head. Our choice is His own.

We must not however, force the contrast between the Jewish ideal and the Christian ideal. The Jews, who did not have before their eyes the example of Christ, had to be sustained by promises and temporal rewards; but in this provisional economy were already mixed not only the announcement, but the presages, of the suffering of Christ and of His people. We recognize them not only in the books of the prophets but in their lives: Jesus recalls them even here to His disciples: "Blessed are you when men reproach you, and persecute you . . . for so did they persecute the prophets who were before you" (Mt. 5:11–12; cf. Lk. 6:22–23).

In apostolic times, the Christians will be fond of gazing at the examples left them by their fathers in the faith:

. . . Others were tortured, refusing to accept release, that they might find a better resurrection. Others had experience of mockery and stripes, yes, even of chains and prisons. They were stoned, they were sawed asunder, they were tempted, they were put to death by the sword. They went about in sheepskins and goatskins, destitute, distressed, afflicted—of whom the world was not worthy—wandering in deserts, mountains, caves and holes in the earth.

And all these, though they had been approved by the testimony of faith, did not receive what was promised, for God had something better in view for us; so that they should not be perfected without us (Heb. 11:35–40).

Now there appears, at last, this reward: the Son of God relieves all these afflicted, not by delivering them here below from their misery, but by sharing it, by having them experience in all these trials a foretaste of the happiness which He assures them: "Theirs is the kingdom of heaven" (Mt. 5:10).

This prospect gives to the Gospel morality a joyous impetus, but also its limitless requirements. It is brought out from the very beginning of the public ministry, in the Sermon on the Mount: this is what gives to the beatitudes all their meaning: if the poor, the hungry, the afflicted and the persecuted are happy, it is because "theirs is the kingdom of heaven," because their "reward is great in heaven" (Lk. 6:23).

Later on, when Jesus proposes to the rich young man the requirements of the perfect life, He joins to it the promise of the eternal reward: "If thou wilt be perfect, go, sell what thou hast, and give to the poor, and thou shalt have treasure in heaven; and come, follow me" (Mt. 19:21).

The same promise to the little flock of the faithful:

Do not be afraid, little flock, for it has pleased your Father to give you the kingdom. Sell what you have and give alms. Make for yourselves purses that do not grow old, a treasure unfailing in heaven, where neither thief draws near nor moth destroys. For where your treasure is, there your heart also will be (Lk. 12:32–34; cf. Mt. 6:20–21).

This is the conclusion of the parable of the Unjust Steward: "Make friends for yourselves with the mammon of wickedness, so that when you fail they may receive you into the everlasting dwellings" (Lk. 16:9).

All these promises carry us far away from earth, into eternity. This revelation of the Christian's destiny was reserved to the Son of God: the mysteries of His life, His Passion, Resurrection and Ascension, place before our eyes the source and model of this glorious promise to the children of God; but already His teaching reveals it to us. The hope of Israel, sustained and guided by the prophets, reached out to the Messias. The Messias has come; is there anything more to wait for? No other Messias, undoubtedly (Mt. 11:3 ff.); but, of course, the glorious return of Our Lord and the reign which will never end, a reign which the Father has given Him and which He will have Him share with all His own. He willed to take upon Himself our sufferings, and these punishments for sin He has made the seeds of immortality, presages of heaven.

God willed that this mystery of eternal life and its laborious preparation here below be revealed to us by Him who was to be the "author of life" (Acts 3:15); He willed that the secrets of heaven be communicated by Him who "has ascended into heaven . . . him who has descended from heaven: the Son of Man" (Jn. 3:13); "He who comes from above is over all. He who is from the earth belongs to earth, and of the earth he speaks. He who comes from heaven is over all. And he bears witness to that which he has seen and heard, and his witness no one receives. He who receives his witness has set his seal on this, that God is true" (*ibid.,* 31–33).

Up to then man felt grievously the vanity of his ephemeral life, breaking up in a decaying world; he adored the divine liberty, superior to time, eternal; he adored it, but he could not attain it:

Lord, thou hast been our refuge from generation to generation.

Before the mountains were made, or the earth and the world was formed; from eternity and to eternity thou art God.

Turn not man away to be brought low: and thou hast said: "Be converted, O ye sons of men."

For a thousand years in thy sight are as yesterday, which is past. And as a watch in the night, things that are counted nothing, shall their years be.

In the morning man shall grow up like grass; in the morning he shall flourish and pass away: in the evening he shall fall, grow dry, and wither (Ps. 89:1–6).

These flowers of the field we find again in the Sermon on the Mount, but they reveal to us divine Providence, attentive to the humblest creatures, to the lilies of the field, to the sparrows, and

even more, to men: "Of how much more value are you" (Lk.
12:24).

The same theme is taken up again in another Psalm:

Call me not away in the midst of my days: thy years are unto generation and generation.
In the beginning, O Lord, thou foundest the earth: and the heavens
are the works of thy hands.
They shall perish but thou remainest: and all of them shall grow
old like a garment: and as a vesture thou shalt change them, and they
shall be changed.
But thou art always the selfsame, and thy years shall not fail
(Ps. 101:25–28).

We are quite familiar with this beautiful text; it is taken up
again in the Epistle to the Hebrews (1:10–12), as addressed to
the Son of God. Thus this unchanging eternity is His life; it will
be ours. The heavens and the earth wear away and change, like a
garment; we can escape this wear and tear and lay up for ourselves
an imperishable treasure (Lk. 12:32–34).

Henceforth, everything is transformed for us; every trial here
below—poverty, tears, hunger, persecution—ensures for us an
eternal kingdom; united to Christ's sufferings, all these pains become merits, seeds of eternal glory: "Our present light affliction,
which is for the moment, prepares for us an eternal weight of glory
that is beyond all measure; while we look, not at the things that
are seen, but at the things that are not seen. For the things that
are seen are temporal, but the things that are not seen are eternal"
(2 Cor. 4:17–18).

Considered in themselves, all these visible things are stunted
and decaying: of them we can say in all truth: *omnia tempus
habent:* being born, dying, planting, uprooting—all that has
only its day, all that is vanity: *vanitas vanitatum et omnia vanitas* (Eccles. 1:2). And yet, these poor perishable things, when
they are referred to eternal goods, take on a double value therefrom: he who is born and dies, who plants and uproots, who
laughs and cries, is he who is tending toward the kingdom of
God, and he is tending there by this way of afflictions and tears:

from now on, he tastes the earnests of the eternal reward, and those earnests are these fleeting, earthly things, but laden with a promise of imperishable glory; all these accidents, which seem pure vanity, are transformed by faith and clothed with its infinite value.

This relation of temporal goods to eternal goods could not be established if we considered these two orders, infinitely distant, independently of the gratuitous mercy of God. Man, if we see in him only God's creature, is obliged to serve Him without being able to claim an eternal reward:

Which of you is there, having a servant plowing or tending sheep, who will say to him on his return from the field, "Come at once and recline at table!" But will he not say to him, "Prepare my supper, and gird thyself and serve me till I have eaten and drunk; and afterwards thou thyself shalt eat and drink"? Does he thank that servant for doing what he commanded him? I do not think so. Even so you also, when you have done everything that was commanded you, say, "We are unprofitable servants; we have done what it was our duty to do" (Lk. 17:7–10).

St. Francis de Sales expounds this doctrine as follows:

The holy Scriptures, which promise the joys of heaven as a recompense for our actions and exertions here below, frequently repeat that God will render to every one according to his works.

How magnificent is the reward we expect from God! how evidently does it prove the liberality of the Master we serve! He might have exacted our obedience, without promising any salary; we belong to Him on many titles; everything appertaining to us, with the exception of sin, is so completely His, that it is only good in so far as it is done in Him, by Him, and for Him. But His goodness had urged Him to dispose of us otherwise; in consideration of our divine Saviour, He has made a compact with us, promising us an eternal recompense, proportioned to our merits. Not that He requires our services, which are perfectly useless to Him, for after "we shall have done all the things that are commanded" us, we are still obliged to acknowledge ourselves "unprofitable servants": from whom our sovereign Master derives no advantage, since the superabundance of perfection which is essential to Him, admits of no increase (Lk. 17:10). Our services are useless with regard to God, but must be advantageous to ourselves; our most trivial exertions procure us infinite rewards.[3]

The saint rightly adds that God glorifies not only His mercy, but His wisdom, in elevating our works by His grace:

Our actions are like a grain of mustard-seed, which, though the smallest of all seeds, produces the largest of all plants; they bear no proportion to the glory they procure, yet they procure eternal bliss; because the Holy Ghost by infusing His grace into our hearts, renders our actions His, without depriving us of our claim to them. This is because we are members of a Head, of which He is the Spirit; because we are engrafted on a tree, of which He may be called the divine sap.[4]

This account of the holy Doctor clears up the confusions which Protestant theology has accumulated around these texts and in which it entangles them even today.[5]

Let us pause, in conclusion, on this promise of recompense: we find it here, from the very beginning of Jesus' preaching, and many times we shall encounter it again, either in the discourse on the Mount[6] or in the appeals made by Jesus to the apostles

[3] Cf. *Love of God,* ch. VI, p. 449.

[4] *Ibid.,* p. 450.

[5] Thus P. Feine, *Theol. des N.T.,* Leipzig, Hinricks, 1910 and 1934, and Berlin, Evangelische Verlagsanstalt, 1953, p. 102: "The thought of remuneration is a popular conception which Jesus borrowed from His environment. He uses it as one does current money, without testing its real value. But there where He expresses His personal thought, He denies and rejects the idea of remuneration." A little farther on: "Jesus has represented the true relation of man with God as a filiation. Owing to this, there falls into disuse those categories of right or of equivalence between reward and merit. For the fundamental dispositions of the filial relationship are trust, submission, abandon, and obedience. The concept of reward is an element received from Judaism, but which the thinking of Jesus has transcended." Cf. K. Barth, *Hauptproblem des Lebens Jesu,* 1907, p. 49.

[6] "Rejoice and exult, because your reward is great in heaven" (Mt. 5:12); "If you love those who love you, what reward shall you have?" (*ibid.,* 46); ". . . so that thy alms may be given in secret; and thy Father, who sees in secret, will reward thee" (Mt. 6:4).

and disciples.[7] Philosophers who want to strip morality of all prospect of sanction are shocked by these promises, which they deem unworthy of Christian morality.[8] These scruples fail to recognize the deepest aspirations of human nature and the wisdom and goodness of God. Our Creator has linked indissolubly virtue and happiness; every good action is a flowering of our being, and there is no purer happiness than that. But, just as our duty is conceived only in relation to God who imposes it on us, so this flowering is fully understood only if we grasp at the goal of virtuous action, God, better known and better loved. Disinterested love, then, will not be what loses itself in the void while pretending to practise virtue, but what grasps God because it accomplishes its duty for God, in view of God. And the end of a life completely and entirely consecrated to God will be the possession of God, as fully as the weakness of our intelligence permits. For all this, human reason is sufficient for us to be informed. But faith goes much further: it teaches us that God here below lifts us up by His grace, and unites us on high to Himself in glory. This is the message of the Son of God. He knows what it is to possess God; and He who is man and who finds in this sight of the Father all His happiness knows that therein lies human beatitude. Enjoying from the first moment of His life the beatific vision, He marks out for us the way we must follow to rejoin Him: poverty, humility, gentleness, justice, purity.[9]

The experience of all Christians illumines these promises of

[7] "He who receives a just man because he is a just man, shall receive a just man's reward" (Mt. 10:41). "You who have followed me, in the regeneration when the Son of Man shall sit on the throne of his glory, shall also sit on twelve thrones, judging the twelve tribes of Israel. And everyone who has left house, or brothers, or sisters, or father, or mother, or wife, or children, or lands, for my name's sake, shall receive a hundredfold, and shall possess life everlasting" (Mt. 19:28–29). Cf. Mt. 19:21: "If thou wilt be perfect, go, sell what thou hast, and give to the poor, and thou shalt have treasure in heaven . . ."

[8] Thus Hegel in his *Life of Jesus* (1795).

[9] Cf. our book, *La Vie chrétienne au premier siècle de l'Église,* Paris, Grasset, 1927, pp. 91–97.

Christ; here below, the practise of these virtues gives the soul a foretaste of heavenly happiness. Jesus did not mislead us when He said to us, "Come to me all you who labor and are burdened and I will give you rest" (Mt. 11:28). If we wish to understand better the value of this experience and the assurance of these promises, it suffices to consider for a moment the fruit of these virtues to which Our Lord invites us. They seem hard, because they require the renunciation of all those human covetous desires which have given us for so long a time the illusion of happiness. But, it is only too true, happiness is illusory; these covetous desires stifle in us the yearning for heavenly goods, sole source of true happiness.

In the measure that man progresses in this austere way of poverty, tears, gentleness, mercy and peace, he feels his heart being stripped. The justice of God, for a long time so little known, so little desired, seizes him with a hunger and thirst he did not know before. By no means does this attraction sully him as did his former covetous desires; it purifies him. It does not poison him with dangerous illusions, but raises him up by a truly heavenly desire which gives him already an inkling of the possession of God: "Blessed are they who hunger and thirst for justice, for they shall be satisfied . . . Blessed are the pure of heart, for they shall see God" (Mt. 5:6, 8).

Thus, between these virtues and beatitude, there is not only the relationship of trial to reward, but of preparation to perfection. Already we see affirmed here the great law of the spiritual life: when the soul is stripped of all goods here below, God floods it. St. John of the Cross expounds this in regard to the transformation of discursive prayer into passive prayer:

. . . when the soul has completely purified and voided itself of all forms and images that can be apprehended, it will remain in this pure and simple light, being transformed therein into a state of perfection. For, although this light never fails in the soul, it is not infused into it because of the creature forms and veils wherewith the soul is veiled and embarrassed; but, if these impediments and these veils were wholly removed (as will be said hereafter), the soul would then find itself in a condition of pure detachment and poverty of spirit, and, being simple and pure, would be transformed into simple and pure Wisdom, which is the Son of God.[10]

The imitation of the Son of God—this is the ideal goal which the Christian endeavors to reach by the path which Jesus Himself has cleared for him. Taking His word, he enters upon it drawn by love. As he advances on it, he feels that a new intimacy is knit between himself and his Master: he is no longer only His servant, but His friend (Jn. 15:15) and His brother: "Whoever does the will of God, he is my brother" (Mk. 3:35). Stripped, for the sake of His love, of all covetous desires here below, he feels his soul being purified and illumined: this is the savory fruit of the beatitudes.

2. THE NEW LAW

It is thereto, also, that the whole teaching of Our Lord on the Law tends: the Son of God has come, not to abrogate it, but to fulfill it. Taking up all the commandments again, He renders their requirements at the same time more profound and easy; God no longer wishes a servile obedience, but a filial one:

You have heard that it was said, "Thou shalt love thy neighbor, and shalt hate thy enemy." But I say to you, love your enemies, do good to those who hate you, and pray for those who persecute and calumniate you, so that you may be children of your Father in heaven, who makes his sun to rise on the good and the evil, and sends rain on the just and the unjust. For if you love those who love you, what reward shall you have? Do not even the publicans do that? And if you salute your brethren only, what are you doing more than others? Do not even the Gentiles do that? You therefore are to be perfect, even as your heavenly Father is perfect (Mt. 5:43–48).

St. Irenaeus has shown well the transcendence of this filial obedience of the Christian over the servile obedience of the Jew:

---

[10] *Ascent of Mount Carmel,* II, 15, 4, and in tr. *Complete Works.*

The Law, written for slaves, formed man from the outside, by laying hold of the body and attracting the soul by it, as by a chain, to the obedience of the commandments, so that man might learn to serve God. The Word has delivered the soul and thereby has taught the body to purify itself voluntarily. To do this, He had to remove from man the chains of servitude which he was used to wearing, and to teach him to serve God without chains. But it was necessary also that the commandments of liberty extend our subjection to our King, so that no one might fall behind and show himself unworthy of his liberator. The children had to have for the Father of the family as much piety and obedience as the servants, but a greater trust, especially since free activity is nobler and more glorious than servile submission.[11]

Therefore also we have no need of the Law as pedagogue. Behold, we speak with the Father and stand face to face with Him, become infants in malice, and made strong in all justice and propriety. For no more shall the Law say: *Thou shalt not commit adultery,* to him who has not even conceived the desire of another's wife; or *thou shalt not kill,* to him who has put away from himself all anger and enmity . . . Nor will it demand tithes of him who has vowed to God all his possessions, and who leaves father and mother and all his kindred, and follows the Word of God.[12]

We begin to get an inkling of the imperious gentleness of this new Law: it draws us along towards a perfection which surpasses not only our strength but our ambitions, and it has all the intimacy of filial love which raises us up towards the Father. Jesus will tell us so: "My yoke is easy, and my burden light" (Mt. 11:30); and the poet of the *Odes of Solomon* will echo Him: "Thy yoke is the arm of the bridegroom resting on the neck of the bride."

It is, indeed, in the intimacy of a filial life that the Christian will learn to serve the heavenly Father by love: his alms, prayers, fasts, his whole life will be offered in secret, "and thy Father,

[11] *Adv. Haer.,* IV, 13, 2.
[12] *Demonstration,* 96, and in tr. *The Proof of the Apostolic Preaching* (ACW 16), tr. by J. Smith, S.J., Westminster (Md), Newman, 1952, p. 106.

who sees in secret, will reward thee" (Mt. 6:1–18). On the last day of His life, Jesus will say to His apostles, "The hour is coming . . . for you to leave me alone. But I am not alone, because the Father is with me" (Jn. 16:32). This intimacy with the Father was, throughout His lifetime, His strength and joy; in heaven, it is the happiness of the angels: they "always behold the face of my Father in heaven" (Mt. 18:10). It ought to be, also, the life of the Christian. Henceforth no other concern except the kingdom: "Do not be afraid, little flock, for it has pleased the Father to give you the kingdom. Sell what you have and give alms. Make for yourselves purses that do not grow old, a treasure unfailing in heaven, where neither thief draws near nor moth destroys. For where your treasure is, there your heart also will be" (Lk. 12:32–34). In this pressing invitation which St. Luke has recounted, we recognize the emphasis which the beatitudes have also in St. Luke: it is not only detachment, it is deprivation. This is the way of the perfect, and not all the faithful have entered upon it; but those who do so have no other motive than to realize in more assured and complete fashion this ideal proposed to all—God alone. In heaven, God will be "all in all" (1 Cor. 15:28); He ought, beginning here below, to be all for His sons.

All these teachings of Our Lord illumine successively many aspects of the moral and religious life; all shine out with the same light. The soul is not dazzled, but intimately penetrated thereby; all its deepest attractions find therein an echo: the kingdom of God, the possession of God, the sight of God, in a word, supreme and eternal happiness, for so long dreamed of in vain, appears quite close, in the transparency of these promises. Hitherto it seemed full of contradictions, sometimes covered by a paternal, omnipotent goodness, at other times abandoned to blind, wicked forces. Nightmares are dissipated, sufferings are no more than instruments of a divine pedagogy; they are no longer wicked forces which wound us, but the Father forming His children.[13]

13 Cf. Heb. 12:5–8: "You have forgotten the exhortation that is addressed to you as sons, saying, 'My son, neglect not the discipline of the Lord, neither be thou weary when thou art rebuked by him. For whom the Lord

We no longer feel delivered over to the enemy for torture, but abandoned to the Father, who moulds us and makes us worthy of His love. Our heart, up to now, was divided between the different masters from whom it awaited its salary and to whom it hired out its services. Now we have but one Master, our Father. In having us scorn human rewards, He has us reach out for the good in all its purity, with no other desire than to possess it in itself, the infinite Good.[14]

Thus, little by little, is formed the "pure heart," which will see God. The Christian, become a son of God, is a son of light; his whole life becomes transparent: "The lamp of thy body is thy eye. If thy eye be sound, thy whole body will be full of light. But if it be evil, thy body also will be full of darkness. Take care, therefore, that the light that is in thee is not darkness. Therefore, if thy whole body is full of light, having no part in darkness, it will all be illumined, as when a bright lamp illumines thee" (Lk. 11:34–36). "The lamp of the body is the eye. If thy eye be sound, thy whole body will be full of light. But if thy eye be evil, thy whole body will be full of darkness. Therefore if the light that is in thee is darkness, how great is the darkness itself!" (Mt. 6:22–23).

And in the measure that the soul is purified, it grows more eager for the light, it comes to the Son of God, who is the Light. If, on the contrary, it is dark, it flees from Him, and that is the judgment:

---

loves, he chastises; and he scourges every son whom he receives' (Prv. 3:11–12). Continue under discipline. God deals with you as with sons; for what son is there whom his father does not correct? But if you are without discipline, in which all have had a share, then you are illegitimate children and not sons . . ."

[14] Cf. Kierkegaard, *Purity of Heart Is to Will One Thing, Spiritual Preparation for the Office of Confession,* tr. from the Danish by D. Steere, N.Y., Harper, 1938, 1948 and 1956, p. 170: "So different is the Good and the reward, when the reward is separately striven after, that the Good is the ennobling and the sanctifying; the reward is the tempting. But the tempting is never the Good. This reward, that we are talking about here, is the world's reward. For the reward which God for eternity has joined with the Good has nothing bad in it."

The light has come into the world, yet men have loved the darkness rather than the light, for their works were evil. For everyone who does evil hates the light, and does not come to the light, that his deeds may not be exposed. But he who does the truth comes to the light that his deeds may be made manifest, for they have been performed in God (Jn. 3:19–21).

Here, then, is the revelation of the new life; it appears in the teaching of Jesus and in His life. He summons men; the sons of light come to Him, the sons of darkness turn away from Him. But the sides are not settled from the first day; there are many hesitant ones, sometimes hurrying up, at other times fleeing. And among the crowds which throng at His feet on the lake shore, most of those moved by His words are only half-converted. To them is addressed the final warning:

Everyone therefore who hears these my words and acts upon them, shall be likened to a wise man who built his house on rock. And the rain fell, and the floods came, and the winds blew and beat against that house, but it did not fall, because it was founded on rock. And everyone who hears these my words and does not act upon them, shall be likened to a foolish man who built his house on sand. And the rain fell, and the floods came, and the winds blew and beat against that house, and it fell, and was utterly ruined (Mt. 7:24–27).

Thus, from the very beginning of the Gospel, there is presented that option which henceforth will be placed before all men. To listen to Jesus' words, to recognize the exceptional ascendancy in them, to marvel at them—all the listeners at the lake shore went that far (Mt. 7:28–29), but most of them stayed put. They gave Jesus that sincere but slight adherence which they had given to John the Baptist: "He was the lamp, burning and shining; and you desired to rejoice for a while in his light" (Jn. 5:35). And then they returned to their affairs, to their darkness, and even the remembrance was blotted out. What will stamp on the moving soil of souls an indelible imprint? This is the practise of a lifetime, the daily accomplishment of this whole program of action and thought. What appears, throughout such simple preaching as this, is a new life which must be knit between the heavenly Father and that man whom He wills to make His son. The Son of God invites us thereto, He describes for us in broad strokes this existence we aspire to without knowing it, He makes us wonder at it and desire it. It behooves us now to be faithful to that attraction which the Father has put in our hearts and to put this life to the test. This is the whole of Christianity.

chapter 7

Christian Perfection

1. THE ROLE OF THE ELITE ACCORDING TO THE GOSPEL

The Sermon on the Mount is reported by St. Matthew as addressed to the crowd; St. Luke distinguishes in this crowd the group of the twelve apostles, already chosen by Jesus; they are in the first rank of assistants, and it is to them in particular that the Master addresses Himself.

In studying the beatitudes, we have noted that, in St. Luke's wording, they are addressed, not to mankind in its entirety, but to the disciples of Jesus, who are actually poor, hungry, persecuted. The same remark is provoked by many other passages, particularly on the subject of the use of riches: in St. Matthew (6:19), Jesus preaches detachment; in St. Luke (12:33) He exhorts to actual deprivation.

From this time onwards, indeed, we see forming, among Christ's disciples, this elite which is going to be distinguished more and more from the crowd and receive from Jesus reserved teachings and privileged powers. This distinction is further defined at the time of the preaching by parables:

To you it is given to know the mystery of the kingdom of God; but to those outside, all things are treated in parables, that seeing they may see, but not perceive; and hearing they may hear, but not understand; lest perhaps at any time they should be converted, and their sins be forgiven them (Mk. 4:11–12).

The Galilean crisis will again accentuate this distinction. Jesus, driven out of Galilee, retires along the coast, in the region of Tyre and Sidon. The Jewish crowd does not follow Him there; but His apostles are still grouped about Him, and it is then that they receive the great revelations: at Caesarea Philippi and, eight days later, on Thabor. This manifestation of the glory of the Son is not granted to all the others, but reserved to three privileged ones, Peter, James and John.

From day to day is sketched more clearly the divine plan: "To everyone who has shall be given; but from him who does not have, even that which he has shall be taken away" (Lk. 19:26). The unproductive gold piece is taken away from him who did not take care to make the most of it, and is given to him who already has ten gold pieces; the same maxim is already found on Jesus' lips in connection with the teaching in parables (Lk. 8:18). The leveling instinct protests; Our Lord disregards this protest: the Jews, who neither heard nor saw, could only grow poorer; the apostles, having remained faithful to Jesus and confidants of His mysteries, are enriched beyond all measure. Right there is an experience being constantly renewed before our eyes: richness multiplies, influence extends, knowledge grows, prudence is refined and matured, the artistic senses are developed and transcended, while all these gifts are dissipated and all this life wanes in those who possess only their first elements. It is the same in the spiritual order: God's first graces, received with docility, call forth new graces; life, becoming stronger and stronger, grows more rapidly from day to day.

This is the law of life; it is above all the will of the Father, who

is more pleased by the heroic sanctity of one of His servants than
He is displeased by the mediocrity of the many.

Furthermore, this preference accorded the elite does not cause
the crowd to be forgotten. The latter are neither on Thabor nor
at Caesarea Philippi nor in the house of Capharnaum, where
Jesus explains to the apostles the profound meaning of the parables. But these privileged witnesses have received these confidences only to communicate them to all:

Is a lamp brought to be put under the measure, or under the couch?
Is it not rather to be put upon the lamp-stand? For there is nothing
hidden that will not be made manifest (Mk. 4:21–22).

In the Gospel there is no esoteric doctrine which can and
ought to remain the secret of the initiated. But there is a hierarchic organism: those who have received more are the deposi-
tories; they are beholden for these treasures both to the Master
who entrusted them to their safekeeping and to the people to
whom they must transmit them. This responsibility is their glory
and their burden. God does not want to reach men in isolation,
but in the organized, hierarchic body of the Church. He converts
them, enlightens them, sanctifies them—some by others. Because of this, the sanctity of a member will not be his alone, but
the glory and strength of the whole Church.

Hence the seriousness of Christ's instructions to the apostles:
"You are the salt of the earth; but if the salt loses its strength,
what shall it be salted with? It is no longer of any use but to be
thrown out and trodden underfoot" (Mt. 5:13). These graces of
light and sanctity, which have been lavished on certain ones, are
not their treasure for themselves alone; they are the property of
the whole Church, and the whole Church has the right to exact
from these trustees a faithful administration of the goods de-
posited in their care, which they must put to good use.

At this point in the Gospel ministry, the group of the apostles,
which will later constitute the ecclesiastical hierarchy, still appears only as an elite; to these men Jesus promises a leading role
in the establishment and propagation of God's kingdom; in re-

turn, He requires from them a perfection He does not impose on all men.

2. CHRIST'S CALL AND MAN'S RESPONSE

The Engagement and the Refusal

This call to a privileged role and to a higher perfection is evident in the vocation of the apostles. We find it again still evident, though to a lesser degree, in the vocation of the seventy-two disciples (Lk. 10:1–12). We recognize certain of its traits in several episodes of the Gospel ministry; for example, in the story of the rich young man (Mk. 10:17–31; Mt. 19:16–30; Lk. 18:18–30).

Here is one of the most revealing aspects of Jesus' morality. When Our Lord, while passing along the lake shore, said to the Galilean fishermen, "Come, follow me, and I will make you fishers of men" (Mk. 1:17), He gave to human life an impetus it had never known before. These men would be the first of all those bishops and priests who, until the end of the world, would consecrate themselves unreservedly to the service of Christ and the Church. Judaism had known prophets completely devoted to God and to His people; but these were isolated heroes who, raised up by the Holy Spirit, would lay out the great stages of man's march towards Christ. Here there is a whole saintly race which, without ever disappearing here below, will perpetuate the sacrifice of the Cross and propagate the doctrine of the Master. These men will not, like the priests of the Old Law, be tied down to a periodic service which, at stated intervals, will bring them to the Temple; their whole lives will be consecrated to it. Much less can we compare them to those officials of the pagan cities who managed the office of priesthood like the other magistracies of their city, who were priests of Asclepios or of Artemis, as they had been inspectors of the finances or superintendents of the sacred games. Christian priests are wholly and completely taken up with their priesthood. In the third century, after a long period of peace which had caused the rigorous fervor of the Christian life to slacken, St. Cyprian denounces those bishops who, "contemning their divine charge, came under the charge of secular kings; after abandoning their thrones and deserting the people, they wandered through foreign provinces and sought the market places for gainful business." [1] That was the contagion of the pagan morality which, here or there, could contaminate the Church, but which she soon rejected.

At the side of the apostles and disciples we see, already during Jesus' lifetime and more clearly in the origins of the Church, the group of the holy women. They assist Jesus and follow Him right up to Calvary (Lk. 8:2–3; Mk. 15:41); we find them again in the Cenacle around Mary, Mother of Jesus (Acts 1:14). When St. Paul goes to Caesarea, he receives hospitality, at Philip's house, one of the seven; St. Luke remarks on this occasion (Acts 21:9) that Philip had four daughters, virgins, who had the gift of prophecy. We see here that profession of virginity which St. Paul recommends but does not impose.[2]

Thus there appeared, from the first years of the Church, this practice of the perfect life, recommended by the Church, but not imposed by her.[3]

It is important to study in the Gospel the characteristics of this perfect life such as Christ conceived it, and such as the Church will continue to present it to her children.

It is in the story of the apostles that we can understand better the will of Our Lord, the gratuitous mercy of His call, the protracted patience, the wisdom, and the paternal love with which He formed His elect and guided them, little by little, to what exceeded by so much all their ambitions and strength.

---

[1] De Lapsis, 6. Cf. Saint Cyprian: Treatises: the Lapsed (FC 36), pp. 61–62.

[2] 1 Cor. 7:7 ff., 37. Cf. Allo and Bouvet, p. 151.

[3] With regard to actual poverty, the Church's attitude is the same: she praises it, but does not impose it (Acts 5:4). Cf. Heussi, Der Ursprung des Mönchtums, Tübingen, Mohr, 1936, and R.S.R., 1937, p. 481. In the Shepherd of Hermas, part 5 (FC 1, tr. by F.-M. Marique, S.J., N. Y., Fathers of the Church, 1948, pp. 293–294), we notice a great insistence on recommending the practice of works of supererogation. On this distinction between precepts and counsels, cf. La Vie chrétienne au siècle apostolique, p. 76.

We note, first of all, that the initiative comes from Christ: "He called to him men of his own choosing" (Mk. 3:13); "You have not chosen me, but I have chosen you" (Jn. 15:16).[4] Considering their origin and formation, nothing recommended these men to Jesus' choice: more than half were lake fishermen, Matthew was a tax collector; of the others, we know nothing of their previous lives; we do not see any of them distinguished by his birth, fortune, or education. In this recruitment of the kingdom's first workers, we already discern the divine preference for the little and the humble.[5] We should add that, out of the twelve apostles, five at least had been disciples of John the Baptist: this first vocation attested to the urge of their souls, the wish for an entire gift of themselves to the kingdom of God.

This generosity, this unselfish giving, is the indispensable disposition which Jesus requires of anyone wishing to follow Him and, especially, of His apostles: "He who loves father or mother more than me is not worthy of me; and he who loves son or daughter more than me is not worthy of me. And he who does not take up his cross and follow me, is not worthy of me. He who finds his life will lose it, and he who loses his life for my sake, will find it." These words are taken from the discourse to the apostles (Mt. 10:37–39).

Likewise, at Caesarea Philippi (Mt. 16:24–26): "If anyone wishes to come after me, let him deny himself, and take up his cross, and follow me. For he who would save his life will lose it; but he who loses his life for my sake will find it. For what does it profit a man if he gain the whole world but suffer the loss of his own soul? Or what will a man give in exchange for his soul?"

Again, on the day of the Palms: "The hour has come for the

---

[4] Cf. Acts 1:24–26; Gal. 1:1; *Vie et enseignement de Jésus-Christ,* I, 152.
[5] Cf. 1 Cor. 1:26–29: "Consider your own call, brethren; that there were not many wise according to the flesh, not many mighty, not many noble. But the foolish things of the world has God chosen to put to shame the 'wise,' and the weak things of the world has God chosen to put to shame the strong, and the base things of the world and the despised has God chosen, and the things that are not, to bring to naught the things that are; lest any flesh should pride itself before him."

Son of Man to be glorified. Amen, amen, I say to you, unless the grain of wheat fall into the ground and die, it remains alone. But if it die, it brings forth much fruit. He who loves his life, loses it; and he who hates his life in this world, keeps it unto life everlasting. If anyone serve me, let him follow me; and where I am there also shall my servant be. If anyone serve me, my Father will honor him" (Jn. 12:23–26).

What appears to us in the vocations of the apostles is illumined again by the other calls which are reported to us by the Evangelists, especially by St. Luke; in reading these episodes again, we understand better the requirements of Our Lord and the various responses of men:

As they went on their journey, a man said to him, "I will follow thee wherever thou goest." And Jesus said to him, "The foxes have dens, and the birds of the air have nests, but the Son of Man has nowhere to lay his head." And he said to another, "Follow me." But he said, "Lord, let me first go and bury my father." But Jesus said to him, "Leave the dead to bury their own dead, but do thou go and proclaim the kingdom of God." And another said, "I will follow thee, Lord; but let me first bid farewell to those at home." Jesus said to him, "No one, having put his hand to the plow and looking back, is fit for the kingdom of God" (Lk. 9:57–62; cf. Mt. 8:19–22).

What Jesus asks, then, is first and foremost a gift which man makes of himself to the cause he wishes to serve, the kingdom of God. This engagement is so important that we ought not to enter upon it lightly, but only after mature reflection:

Great crowds were going along with him. And he turned and said to them, "If anyone comes to me and does not hate his father and mother, and wife and children, and brothers and sisters, yes, and even his own life, he cannot be my disciple. And he who does not carry his cross and follow me, cannot be my disciple.

"For which of you, wishing to build a tower, does not sit down first and calculate the outlays that are necessary, whether he has the means to complete it? Lest, after he has laid the foundation and is not able to finish, all who behold begin to mock him, saying, 'This man began to build and was not able to finish!' . . . So, therefore, every one of you who does not renounce all that he possesses, cannot be my disciple" (Lk. 14:25–30, 33).

This warning is addressed to the entire crowd: the fidelity asked of every Christian requires, in certain circumstances, heroic courage: thus in times of persecution. But from him who wishes to be perfect, Jesus asks still more; and yet such grave warnings as these tend in no way to discourage good will, but to imprint on it a more powerful impetus. We see it even better in the story of the rich young man (Mk. 10:17–22; Mt. 19:16–22; Lk. 18:18–23).

This young man desires eternal life; he has fulfilled the Law since he "was a child"; he feels that he still lacks something, but what? His approach is sincere, as are his declarations. "Jesus, looking upon him, loved him" (Mk. 10:21); yet He will be unable to get the young man to follow Him. He tells him what He told the apostles: one has to give all; and He adds, as He always does, "Thou shalt have treasure in heaven; and come, follow me." And in spite of this promise, in spite of this attraction, the young man turns glum and goes away quite sad.

Whence comes this failing? This man is a faithful Israelite, like that Nathaniel whom Jesus had recently praised. He knows the commandments and observes them; he knows that eternal life is the goal he must tend towards, and he seeks the way to it. The way he has right before his eyes: it is Jesus: "Follow me." He steals away. We would be tempted to say: this exact observance was an illusion; to this youngster it seemed to suffice; is not this what the lukewarm soul of Laodicea will say: "I am rich . . . and have need of nothing" (Ap. 3:17)? This sufficiency is very dangerous; but we do not find it here: he does not say, "I don't need anything," but "What do I need?" He is aware, then, of his missing something. God loves this young man: He calls him, and this call awakens in his soul an attraction which raises it up and which, at the same time, makes it uneasy: urged on by this still confused desire, he comes to Jesus.

He feels that there is still something to sacrifice; but he does not suspect what it is: it is everything: "Go, sell whatever thou hast, and give to the poor" (Mk. 10:21). He was very rich, and this sacrifice is too heavy for him.

The snare is all the more formidable since thus far he did not feel the danger of this great fortune: it is neither wrongly acquired nor wrongly used; and yet it enslaves him. He is not yet aware of it. Zacheus facing Jesus will feel remorse: "If I have defrauded anyone of anything, I restore it fourfold" (Lk. 19:8). The young man has wronged no one; he has nothing to restore. The publican will precede him into the kingdom of heaven.

Is sin, then, the indispensable condition of a saintly life? Does the faithful practice of the Law, then, close off access to God's kingdom? Surely not; the proof is in the first apostles called by Jesus on the banks of the Jordan: they are the disciples of John; they have shared his penitential life, his fasts, his prayers. As soon as they see the Lamb of God, they give themselves to Him wholeheartedly. Thus, on the one hand and on the other, at the end of a faithful life, Jesus presents Himself, inviting to mount higher. And here the division takes place: some will say, "We have left all and followed thee" (Mk. 10:28); others, like the young man, will go away discouraged.

Let us note, however, that in the different examples we have just considered, the moral preparation is not the same: in the young man, we find a faithful observance of the commandments; in the disciples of the Precursor, there is more: a fervent, mortified life, separated from the world. Though this will not be a guarantee of sanctity for everyone, at least it ensures a personal impetus we do not feel in the case of the rich young man.

His moral life appears to us similar to that of those young people raised in families of faithful Christian tradition. From their childhood they have been formed in the practise of God's law, which has become second nature to them: "Thou knowest the commandments: Thou shalt not commit adultery, Thou shalt not kill, Thou shalt not steal, Thou shalt not bear false witness, Thou shalt not defraud, Honor thy father and mother." "Master, all these I have kept ever since I was a child" (Mk. 10:19–20). This pure life is praiseworthy, and Our Lord rewards it with a look full of love. But it also has its obstacle, and the poor young man will not know how to triumph over it.

Up to then, so protected a life as this, one so well sheltered, has developed, apparently, without resistance or temptation. This innocence has cost little; the young man has adapted himself to his environment with docility and ease. Today, for the first time, a great sacrifice is asked of him; he lacks the heart for it.

The teaching which is given here is of great importance. Continually favorable conditions of moral living often deceive not only the close acquaintances of a person but, above all, the person himself: he is aware of his innocence; he is not aware of his weakness. Furthermore, this irreproachable life often develops a very deep-seated and stubborn self-love: one feels sure of himself, and from that easily results sternness towards one's neighbor. Here we find again those illusions signalized by St. Paul in the case of the Jews:

If thou art called "Jew," and dost rely upon the Law, and dost glory in God, and dost know his will, and dost approve the better things, being informed by the Law, thou art confident that thou art a guide to the blind, a light to those who are in darkness, an instructor of the unwise, a teacher of children, having in the Law the pattern of knowledge and of truth. Thou therefore who teachest another, dost thou not teach thyself? (Rom. 2:17–21).

Before these dangers of conformism, we would easily be carried away and break all those bounds whose protection conceals so many illusions. This is a folly which we are put on our guard against by the teaching of Jesus and, quite as much, by that of St. Paul. "We know that the Law is spiritual" (Rom. 7:14). And back farther the Apostle had written, "What advantage then remains to the Jew, or what is the use of circumcision? Much in every respect. First, indeed, because the oracles of God were entrusted to them" (Rom. 3:1–2). And already Our Lord had said, "The Scribes and the Pharisees have sat on the chair of Moses. All things, therefore, that they command you, observe and do. But do not act according to their works" (Mt. 23:2–3). And what is said there of the privileges of Judaism and of the obedience due its leaders, is still much more true of Christ's Church: her treasures are incomparably more valuable, and her teaching infallible. And yet, we can make bad use of these graces: we can bury them, like a talent, in the ground; that is, let them lie sterile, without causing them to bear fruit; they only dry up. Life conserves itself only by developing, and man, responsible for God's gifts, cannot let them go unproductive without losing them. This is the impressive lesson left to us by the story of the rich young man:[6] on seeing him go away sad, Jesus said to the apostles, "Amen, I say to you, with difficulty will a rich man enter the kingdom of heaven. And further I say to you, it is easier for a camel to pass through an eye of a needle, than for a rich man to enter the kingdom of heaven" (Mt. 19:23–24).

It is, then, not only perfection, but salvation which is jeopardized by this cowardice; this young man, whose life up to now was pure, and on whom Jesus was pleased to rest His look, by his refusal to mount higher, falls from that moral height which he seemed to have attained. This is the lesson of the parable of the Gold Pieces: "I say to you that to everyone who has shall be given; but from him who does not have, even that which he has shall be taken away" (Lk. 19:26).

We shall not conclude from this that perfection is obligatory for all under pain of damnation; but a soul who has closed her hearing to a definite call of Our Lord puts her salvation in great peril.[7]

[6] Like the parable of the Gold Pieces (Lk. 19:12–26).
[7] Cf. *Angela de Foligno*, ed. Doncoeur, Paris, à la Librairie de l'Art Catholique, 1926, p. 97: "A schoolboy was sent to school by his father. And the father pays his expenses and urges him to learn; he has him promoted to a higher teacher. But the schoolboy is negligent; he gives up studying and returns to ploughing; and nothing of what he learned stays with him. Thus is he who at first is taught by preaching or Scriptures, and then is especially enlightened by God, and then is given to understand by a special light how he ought to follow Christ; if he acts negligently and becomes fouled up on purpose, God will take away his light and grace and curse him . . . I considered that doubtful that he could be cursed in this way, and so doubtful that I had suffered much in understanding it. So, I said to my companion that I did not wish to tell it to you, for I feared it was not an illusion. Nevertheless, it was told to me, that I might tell it to you."

chapter 8

Renunciation

We have heard the call of Our Lord; we have recognized the opposing responses made to Him: the generous adherence of the apostles, the discouraged refusal of the rich young man. In all these men Jesus has awakened a sincere desire to follow Him; but this desire is revealed as either efficacious or sterile, according as they had the strength to sustain Our Lord's requirements or, on the contrary, as they found them too costly. These basic requirements are expressed in a word: renunciation. It is this fundamental law of evangelical perfection which we should study more closely.

1. THE LAW OF RENUNCIATION

Renunciation is the first condition of the service of Christ: "If anyone wishes to come after me, let him deny himself" (Mk. 8:34).

After sin, it is, indeed, the first law to be imposed on man.

Everything, in and around him, was created to raise him up towards God, to stimulate his desire and guide his ascent: image of God, he ought to love in himself this likeness, jealously defend it from all deformation, and render it day by day more faithful. In God's creatures, works of God, he ought to recognize and venerate the traces of the Creator. By wishing to enjoy himself and the things of this world, man has failed to recognize and, as much as he can, has effaced this whole orientation towards God. There remain within his grasp only objects more or less pleasant to his taste, more or less pliable in his hands; he will strive to enjoy and use them; he will no longer know how to understand them. He is like an illiterate in front of a beautiful manuscript: these characters are well drawn, but what do they mean? He knows nothing about them. But since the manuscript is made to be read, it will be, in the hands of the illiterate, only a game which will not amuse him for long. And here there is no question of a disappointment which would disturb our lives momentarily; there is question of the whole of life. The man who tries to understand his life without recognizing its orientation towards God comes up continually against walls that block his way, against brutal impacts that break him.

Because he has turned away from God, man finds here below nothing but riddles and, still worse, temptation. Everything we see delights us and deceives us; everything attracts us and wounds us and risks destroying us. The persons whom we may love are often closed to our approach, or evade it; and even if they lend themselves to it, they come empty-handed. *Vana salus hominis.*

In face of this eternal deception, man has tried to shut himself up within himself, to close his eyes to things, and thereby to free himself from them. Delusion still, and the most deceptive of all, enclosing in his heart his desire and his pride.

Out of pity for this immense distress, the God who created us became man and said to us, "Come to me, all you who labor and are burdened and I will refresh you . . . Learn of me" (Mt. 11:28, 29). And what will be the first word of this Master, our only Master? "Deny thyself."

Stern words and liberating ones; all these delightful and deceiving things we have caught in their net. *Laqueus contritus est, et nos liberati sumus.* "Seek first the kingdom of God and his justice, and all these things shall be given you besides" (Mt. 6:33). The lost orientation is found again. In ourselves and in things, we have nothing more to search for again except the image and trace of God. And we begin to understand what life is: *Haec est vita aeterna, ut cognoscant te, solum Deum verum, et quem misisti Jesum Christum* (Jn. 17:3). The other things are the crumbs from His table; He does not refuse them, even to dogs; but for the children He reserves the living Bread.

Consider not thyself as mean, neither pay heed to the crumbs which fall from thy Father's table. Go thou forth from them and glory in thy glory. Hide thee therein and rejoice and thou shalt have the desires of thy heart.[1]

Here is the renunciation of the Christian: he renounces the crumbs for the Bread of life; he hides in the Face of the Father, in His glory.

So much do we live in sin, that we are immersed in ignorance and servitude; our new birth in the Spirit opens our eyes and makes us free. Liberty and knowledge, these are two aspects of the same grace which the Spirit communicates to us. The domain of sin is that world of matter where all is blind necessity. The grace of God illumines this world for us and detaches us from it. Surely, in no way does this grace make us despise the world; quite the contrary, it makes it more revered and dear to us. But what we take more and more pleasure in is the trace of God; this is what fixes our heart above passing seductions and rescues it from them.

Because of this, Christian renunciation will always have the character of a preference, not of a contempt; to love God above all things, we have no need to disdain His works. This is one of the marks by which, in Christian antiquity, the writings of the apostles and the authentic Acts of the martyrs are distinguished from the apocryphal ones. Thus it is that St. Paul teaches that

[1] St. John of the Cross, *Pensées,* p. 193, and in tr. *Complete Works.*

marriage is not a sin, but that virginity is preferable to it, because it permits a more complete attachment to Our Lord (1
Cor. 7:28, 32–34). In the apocryphal Acts of the Apostles, marriage is branded as a shameful defilement and, to dissuade the
readers from it, the writers of these Acts make the most of considerations of common selfishness over the trouble caused by a
woman and children.[2] Likewise in the authentic Passion of St.
Perpetua, the holy woman, urged by her old father who had
remained a pagan, appears deeply moved by his tears;[3] in the
apocryphal Acts she answers him sternly: "Go away, artisans
of iniquity, I do not know you." [4] This disdain, this abruptness,
are signs of weakness; Christian renunciation knows them not.[5]

Renunciation is imposed, then, by the love of God. It extends
as far as the requirements of that love; and since we ought to
love God above all things, we ought to sacrifice all things for
Him. The preaching of Our Lord is, on this point, of such a pre-
cision and insistence as to admit of no hesitation.[6]

[2] Cf. J. Lebreton and J. Zeiller, *Histoire de l'Église,* II, pp. 298–299, and
in tr. *History of the Primitive Church.*

[3] *Passio,* 5: *"Haec dicebat pater pro sua pietate, basians mihi manus, et se
ad pedes meos jactans; et lacrimis me non filiam nominabat, sed dominam.
Et ego dolebam causam patris mei . . . et confortavi eum dicens: Hoc
fiet in illa catasta quod Deus voluerit."* Cf. *The Passion of SS. Perpetua
and Felicity MM.,* London, Sheed & Ward, 1931.

[4] *Actes brefs,* ed. J. Armitage Robinson, p. 102: *"Recidite a me, operarii
iniquitatis, quia non novi vos."*

[5] Father de Grandmaison, in his account of Father Rousselot, wrote: "His
great sacrifice is to leave his family and renounce what he would have
loved to have founded, had not a pressing call summoned him higher. This
last trait is worthy of note in a child so young, so innocent, so full of
fervor: the observation is verified once more, according to which the best
religious are those who sacrifice, and not those who know nothing of great
natural attachments" (Introduction to *l'Intellectualisme de saint Thomas,*
3rd ed., Paris, Beauchesne, 1936.) This remark was suggested to Father
de Grandmaison as much by his own personal experience as by that of
Father Rousselot: the sacrifice of his family had been for him the hardest
of all. On this question one will read with interest an article of Father de
Montcheuil on "Le Ressentiment d'après M. Scheler" (*Recherches de
Science religieuse,* June, 1937, pp. 309 ff.).

[6] Mt. 10:37–39; 16:24–26; Lk. 14:26–33; Jn. 12:24–26.

2. THE OBJECTS OF RENUNCIATION: THE SOCIAL LIFE

If we wish to consider more closely the objects of this renunciation, we shall encounter, first of all, scandal, that stumbling block which closes to us the approach of God; we must avoid it at all costs: "If thy hand is an occasion of sin to thee, cut it off! . . . If thy foot is an occasion of sin to thee, cut it off! . . . And if thy eye is an occasion of sin to thee, pluck it out! It is better for thee to enter into the kingdom of God with one eye, than, having two eyes, to be cast into the hell of fire" (Mk. 9:42, 44, 46). As for the one who gives scandal, if he does so willingly, terrible is his responsibility: "Whoever causes one of these little ones who believe in me to sin, it were better for him if a great millstone were hung about his neck, and he were thrown into the sea" (*ibid.*, 41).

Here we are aware of the infinite distance which separates the kingdom of God from all goods here below. This is what illumines such stern warnings of Jesus to His disciples: if He commands us to hate our parents or even our own lives, it is in the case when all that is opposed to God.[7] He Himself has given us an example of this hatred of scandal in His reply to St. Peter. The apostle is, of all of them, dear to Jesus; he has just confessed Him Son of God and received from Him the highest promises. But, at the announcement of the Passion, he falters; he tries to swerve Jesus from death. Then Christ, turning round, says to Peter, "Get behind me, satan, thou art a scandal to me; for thou dost not mind the things of God, but those of men" (Mt. 16:23). This stern reprimand does not deny Jesus' love for Peter. But this love comes from love of the Father; if Peter opposes it, the love vanishes.

---

[7] In this text, Jesus enumerates all that we hold most dear in the world: on the subject of life, has He not said, "What does it profit a man if he gain the whole world but suffer the loss of his own soul?" (Mt. 16:26). Parents, like life, will be one of the dearest objects of our love, and yet it will be necessary, if a conflict exists, to sacrifice their love for the love of God.

Among His own kin, Jesus encountered more defined cases of opposition: "Not even his brethren believed in him" (Jn. 7:5). He comes up against this unbelief on the occasion of the feast of Tabernacles, and refuses to go up with them to Jerusalem. These domestic conflicts were one of the great trials of the first Christians; we notice them already in the Jewish circles, for example, in the story of the man born blind (Jn. 9:22); we find them again, but much more violent, among the pagans. Hence the Pauline privilege and the explanation that the Apostle gives of it: "If any brother has an unbelieving wife and she consents to live with him, let him not put her away. And if any woman has an unbelieving husband and he consents to live with her, let her not put away her husband. But the unbelieving husband is sanctified by the believing wife . . . But if the unbeliever departs, let him depart. For a brother or sister is not under bondage in such cases, but God has called us to peace. For how dost thou know, O wife, whether thou wilt save thy husband? Or how dost thou know, O husband, whether thou wilt save thy wife?" (1 Cor. 7:12–16). This Pauline privilege is the most evident proof of the rights of God: the peril created for the faith breaks the marriage.

This doctrine is made clear by a story which St. Justin recounts for us (2nd *Apol.*, II): "A woman had a husband who used to live in vice, as she herself had lived before. She had been instructed in Christ's teachings and had changed her life. She sought to bring her husband around to a better frame of mind . . . The husband continued in his debauchery and, by his conduct, drove his wife insane. She had the idea that henceforth it was an impious deed to share the bed of a man who sought, by every means, pleasures contrary to the natural law and to justice, and she resolved to separate from him." The husband accused his wife of being a Christian. All ends in a trial before the town prefect: three Christians were condemned and put to death.

This incident shows us from life what could be the reaction of a pagan family against Christian penetration: in a society where divorce, marriage abuses, and unnatural vices were everywhere rife, we have no difficulty imagining the situation of a Christian wife or husband. The whole morality of the Sermon on the Mount and of the Epistle to the Corinthians must appear pure folly, and the most loving had to say as Pauline to Polyeucte, "Leave this chimera and love me." And if these conflicts were grievous for free men, how much more cruel were they for slaves! These men, protected neither by law nor custom from the immorality of masters and from the promiscuity of other slaves, how could they keep their self-respect without risking their lives?

In these continual struggles, the Christian will maintain the preference he owes to God, but without ever failing to understand the affection and consideration he owes those united to him by blood. And the fruit of these sacrifices will be the intimate union which the Christian faith gives to the family, a union which faces bravely all happenings here below and death itself. The delightful thing about this union is—more so even than its promises of lasting duration—its intimacy, transparency, depth. Wherever souls are not thus of one accord, they must forbid each other certain contacts, certain questions, and these are the most serious. It seems, at first sight, that these tacit agreements are indispensable conditions for peace, and that Christianity by its intransigence provokes war. When Jesus says to Pilate (Jn. 18:37–38): "I have come into the world to bear witness to the truth," Pilate replies, "What is truth?" and by that haughty irony thinks all is appeased. This is not possible; we cannot be satisfied so cheaply: "Everyone who is of the truth hears my voice." The prefect of Egypt, Aemilius, can say to Dionysius, "Adore thy God as much as thou wouldst, but adore ours as well." Men whose religion is so complacent disclose only that they have no religion. There is a true God, and there are false gods; and we cannot found the unity of the home between spouses, nor that of friendship between brothers, on these compromises. The truth alone can give to this union its intimacy and strength.

Beyond this limited but beloved world of the family, there is civil society, one's native land. Here Jesus asks His apostles and all His disciples for a still more painful renunciation than that of the home. How many times have they sung, "How good and how pleasant it is for brethren to dwell together!" (Ps. 132:1); "I rejoiced at the things that were said to me: We shall go into the house of the Lord. Our feet were standing in thy courts, O Jerusalem, Jerusalem, which is built as a city, which is compact together" (Ps. 121:1–3). This unity leads to Christ; Israel rejects it; everything collapses: " 'The stone which the builders rejected, has become the corner stone.' Everyone who falls upon that stone will be broken to pieces; but upon whomever it falls, it will grind him to powder" (Lk. 20:17–18). Their house will be left desolate for them; of the Temple there will not be left a stone upon a stone (Lk. 13:35; 21:6). With a filial piety which nothing can tire the apostles cling to this condemned house, to this rejected people; they will be driven from their midst: "They will expel you from the synagogues" (Jn. 16:2). Does not this become evident in Jerusalem, and later in all the cities evangelized by St. Paul? All that they will be able to do, will be to summon to their side the Israelites who are docile to grace; and like Noah, on the eve of the deluge, get them to enter the ark, the Church. Finally, when the catastrophe foretold by Jesus occurs, when the Jews in revolt against the Romans see their enemies encircle the holy city, the Christians, by order of God, will abandon the cursed city and retire to Pella. This will be the definitive separation; at that time of great chastisement, they will assert to the world's face that they are no longer sons of that Israel whom God rejects. "Every plant that my heavenly Father has not planted will be rooted up" (Mt. 15:13).

If we consider the situation of the converts coming over from pagan society, the conflict is here even more violent: in this world where idolatry has invaded everything, all the trades, or almost all, are suspect; we see in the canons of Hippolytus the list of those who are driven from the catechumenate pending the renunciation of their professions: priests of idols, astrologers, magicians, magistrates, prefects, soothsayers, interpreters of dreams, manufacturers of philtres or amulets, keepers of bad houses. Under pressure from the State, the struggle will become daily more intensified, more bloody. The Christian will never be able to swear by the genie of Caesar, nor repeat like other citizens, "Caesar is Lord." And this is sufficient to have him arrested as a revolutionary. Soon we shall see fulfilled the prediction of the Apocalypse (13:16–17): the image of the beast "will cause all, the small and the great, and the rich and the poor, and the free and the bond, to have a mark on their right hand or on their foreheads, and it will bring it about that no one may be able to buy or sell, except him who has the mark, either the name of the beast or the number of its name."

And yet, rejected by Israel, rejected by the pagan city, the Christians preserve, as far as lies within them, a filial devotedness to those countries that drive them away. Jesus had wept over Jerusalem; St. Paul, in turn, confided his sorrow: "I speak the truth in Christ, I do not lie, my conscience bearing me witness in the Holy Spirit, that I have great sadness and continuous sorrow in my heart. For I could wish to be anathema myself from Christ for the sake of my brethren, who are my kinsmen according to the flesh; who are Israelites, who have the adoption as sons, and the glory and the covenants and the legislation and the worship and the promises; who have the fathers, and from whom is the Christ according to the flesh, who is over all things, God blessed forever, amen" (Rom. 9:1–5).

As for the feelings of the first Christians towards the Roman fatherland, it is sufficient, in order to know them, to read again the prayer of St. Clement of Rome, written at the end of that persecution of Domitian which inflicted such cruelty on the Church: "Grant us to be obedient to Thy almighty and glorious name, as well as to our princes and rulers on earth. Thou, O Master, through Thy transcendent and indescribable sovereignty hast given them the power of royalty, so that we, acknowledging the honor and glory conferred upon them by Thee, may bow to them, without in the least opposing Thy will. Grant to them, O Lord, health, peace, concord, and firmness, so that they may without hindrance exercise the supreme leadership Thou hast conferred on them." [8]

---

[8] *To the Corinthians,* 60–61, in *The Epistles of St. Clement of Rome and St. Ignatius of Antioch* (ACW 1) p. 47.

And, at the same time that we recognize this heroic loyalty to the fatherland, even in the midst of persecutions, we are aware of there being formed among the Christians a new unity, ever so much more intimate, which prepares for the Christian city. From the first days of the Church, at Jerusalem, this hitherto unprecedented unanimity is seen to appear (Acts 2:44–47; 4:32–35). It is by the attraction of this charity that Christianity has won its noblest recruits. But this test, like all tests of religious truth, can be fully understood and experienced only at the cost of a total sacrifice. Surely, one could not read the *Apologia* of Aristides or the *Epistle to Diognetus* (ACW 6, 1948), without sensing the attraction of this Christian community: to live in the society of just, chaste, sincere men, of virgin girls, of pure young men, of chaste spouses, of persons who love one another, who treat their slaves like brothers, even their enemies like friends for whom they strive to do good—this already is the promised hundredfold. But, in order to possess this hundredfold, they must give up everything, leave the home of their father, their social environment, this Roman fatherland which rejects those not accepting its worship. We see in the *Shepherd* of Hermas (FC 1, 1948) the hesitations of the weak, especially of the rich who are afraid to enlist or live in this society of small people. They find themselves at a loss there, outside their social environment, and are always afraid of being asked for alms. Are we not aware there of an indication of the will of Christ? The kingdom of God is the hidden treasure, it is the pearl: we can purchase it only at the price of all we possess; or, if you will, we must value holiness so highly that we are ready to sacrifice for it all goods of fortune, all social relationships, and even, in times of persecution, the security of life.

But we understand also what an intimacy is created by this community of sacrifices: having come over from all classes of Roman society, the neophytes had to renounce everything in order to enter the Church. Because of this, these people, whom until then everything separated, found themselves brothers and sisters; these are the names they give themselves, and they are not simply liturgical formulas. This is an echo of the words of Jesus:

"Who are my mother and my brethren? . . . Whoever does the will of God, he is my brother and sister and mother" (Mk. 3:33, 35).

And what creates this intimacy is not only the esteem and sympathy born of a heroic option; it is, above all, the community of faith and of love. There is not only a common adhesion to the same truths; there is a unanimous orientation of the whole of life: "None of us lives to himself, and none dies to himself; for if we live, we live to the Lord, or if we die, we die to the Lord. Therefore, whether we live or die, we are the Lord's" (Rom. 14:7–8).

Henceforth, all else is accessory. Social inequalities continue to exist and, likewise, distinctions of race, culture and language; but what are these surface divergencies next to this profound unity, next to this faith which illumines the whole of life, next to the love which has taken hold of this whole life in its entirety and sweeps it along? And persecution, which continually hovers over the Church, recalls continually, in face of the common danger, the common hope: slaves or freed, little artisans or rich merchants, commoners or aristocrats—all are menaced equally by that arrest which for them is the guarantee of eternal happiness. Nearby or far away, they hear the voice of their brothers suffering and dying; they wait and hope. The present mode of existence will be for some of them quiet, for others brilliant; but for both it is only an appearance, which faith transcends to attain the reality.

The circumstances in which the Church has been born and has grown up have, undoubtedly, an exceptional character. Still, they convey a lesson. For, willed by God, they reveal His plan to us: this Church, the Spouse of Christ, whom He has loved to the extent of dying for her, has not, without very grave reason, been exposed by Him for three centuries to such murderous persecutions. Our Lord willed that, in this period which would give the Church its decisive impetus, she be propelled from earth to heaven; He willed that all those who would want to pledge Him their faith could do so only at the cost of the option He had imposed from the first day: "If anyone wishes to come after me, let him deny himself, and take up his cross, and follow me" (Mt. 16:24); "If anyone comes to me and does not hate his father and mother, and wife and children, and brothers and sisters, yes, and even his own life, he cannot be my disciple" (Lk. 14:26). And to this heroic sacrifice He has attached that reward whose value no one can appreciate who has not experienced it: the unity of Christians in Christ. All seemed broken; all is restored, but in place of the superficial and fragile unity of human groups, Christ substitutes the profound, eternal unity of His Body.

And already we begin to understand Christian renunciation, the sacrifice it imposes, the happiness it guarantees.

3 . THE RENUNCIATION OF MATERIAL GOODS

In the lessons of Our Lord on renunciation we have considered the sacrifice of human affections: family, home, and country. This is what affects us the most profoundly, but it is not what conditions our whole life. In one of the texts we have pondered, Jesus said, "Everyone of you who does not renounce all that he possesses, cannot be my disciple" (Lk. 14:33). Here there is no question of people who are dear to us, but of objects which belong to us: these also we must renounce.

The story of the rich young man is the best commentary on these words of the Master. Jesus, seeing him go away discouraged, says to His apostles, "Amen I say to you, with difficulty will a rich man enter the kingdom of heaven. And further I say to you, it is easier for a camel to pass through an eye of a needle, than for a rich man to enter the kingdom of heaven" (Mt. 19:23–24).

This text is one of those which have made the deepest imprint on the Christian conscience. One of the oldest homilies we have in our possession is consecrated by Clement of Alexandria to resolve this problem: "How can a rich man be saved?" Already St. Peter had asked this of Our Lord, and Jesus had replied to him, "With men this is impossible, but with God all things are possible" (Mt. 19:26).

Such urgent preaching has been obeyed: from the earliest days of the Church, at Jerusalem, the Christians sell their goods, bringing the price of them to the apostles, and have nothing more which belongs to them as their own. This detachment, which the Church recommends and which the Holy Spirit inspires, has nevertheless never been considered as an obligation, not even in that first fervor of the nascent Church (Acts 5:4). It is important to understand why Jesus has attached so much importance to it, how He has understood it, and what reward He promises us for it.

Many times did Jesus present this doctrine. First of all in the Sermon on the Mount:

"Do not lay up for yourselves treasures on earth, where rust and moth consume, and where thieves break in and steal; but lay up for yourselves treasures in heaven, where neither rust nor moth consumes, nor thieves break in and steal. For where thy treasure is, there thy heart also will be" (Mt. 6:19–21). In St. Luke, the same teaching will be given to the little flock of disciples with more preciseness: "Do not be afraid, little flock, for it has pleased your Father to give you the kingdom. Sell what you have and give alms. Make for yourselves purses that do not grow old, a treasure unfailing in heaven, where neither thief draws near nor moth destroys. For where your treasure is, there your heart also will be" (Lk. 12:32–34).

The danger is obvious: man is the slave of his treasure. The Christian must not suffer this servitude; he must be free. He will succeed in being so only by renunciation.

The same doctrine is expounded in the parables under a slightly different form: "Other seed fell among thorns; and the thorns grew up and choked it, and it yielded no fruit." And Jesus Himself interprets the parable: "Those which are sown among the thorns are they who listen to the word; but the cares of the world, and the deceitfulness of riches, and the desires about other things, entering in, choke the word, and it is made fruitless" (Mk. 4:7, 18–19). It is always the same peril: absorbing cares which stifle life.

The same image will be taken up by Hermas to develop the same theme: "Out of the third mountain, with the thorns and thistles, this type of believer comes: the rich and those involved in too much business." [9]

[9] The *Shepherd* of Hermas: 9th Parable, XX (FC 1), p. 339.

In contrast to this encumbered life is opposed the Christian life, completely free by reason of its concern solely for the kingdom of God, and detachment from all else: "No man can serve two masters; for either he will hate the one and love the other, or else he will stand by the one and despise the other. You cannot serve God and mammon . . . Seek first the kingdom of God and his justice, and all these things shall be given you besides" (Mt. 6:24, 33).

This teaching is quite clear, but it raises a big problem: how can it be that all these things, created by God to help us know, love and serve Him, turn us away from Him? The answer we know already: all these things which are beautiful and nice, ought by this attractiveness to have revealed God to us. But our hearts, wounded by sin, let themselves be captivated by this attractiveness; instead of being induced thereby to mount higher, they are held captive. The saints find in this created world joy and strength; but that is because their souls are pure. Renunciation alone can lead us to that purity. We marvel at the liberty of a Francis of Assisi, of all the true children of God; we aspire to it, and God, indeed, calls us to it. But we shall attain it only by the path of the saints, by Saint Damian, by Alverno.

This doctrine has been fully brought to light by St. John of the Cross:[10]

As in the state of innocence all that our first parents saw and said and ate in Paradise furnished them with greater sweetness of contemplation, so that the sensual part of their nature might be duly subjected to, and ordered by, reason; even so the man whose senses are purged from all things of sense and made subject to the spirit receives, in their very first motion, the delight of delectable knowledge and contemplation of God. Wherefore, to him that is pure, all things, whether high or low, are an occasion of greater good and further purity; even as the man that is impure is apt to derive evil from things both high and low, because of his impurity. But he that conquers not the joy of desire will not enjoy the serenity of habitual rejoicing in God through His creatures and works. In the man that lives no more according to sense, all the operations of the senses and faculties are

10 *Ascent of Mount Carmel,* III, 26, 5 ff., in *Complete Works.*

directed to Divine contemplation. . . . Such a man, being pure in heart, finds in all things a knowledge of God which is joyful and pleasant, chaste, pure, spiritual, glad and loving. From what has been said I deduce the following doctrine—namely that, until a man has succeeded in so habituating his senses to the purgation of the joys of sense that from their first motion he is gaining the benefit afore-mentioned of directing all his powers to God, he must needs deny himself joy and pleasure with respect to these powers, so that he may withdraw his soul from the life of sense. He must fear that since he is not yet spiritual, he may perchance derive from the practice of these things a pleasure and an energy which is of sense rather than of spirit; that the energy which is of sense may predominate in all his actions; and that this may lead to an increase of sensuality and may sustain and nurture it. For, as Our Saviour says, that which is born of the flesh is flesh, and that which is born of the Spirit is spirit.

Such clear instruction as this governs the whole doctrine of St. John of the Cross on mortification, and that of the entire Church. We are acquainted with its requirements:

Strive always to prefer, not that which is easiest, but that which is most difficult; not that which is most delectable, but that which is most unpleasing; not that which gives most pleasure, but rather that which gives least; not that which is restful, but that which is weari-some; not that which is consolation, but rather that which is disconso-lateness; not that which is greatest, but that which is least; not that which is loftiest and most precious, but that which is lowest and most despised; not that which is a desire for anything, but that which is a desire for nothing; strive to go about seeking not the best of temporal things, but the worst. Strive thus to desire to enter into complete detachment and emptiness and poverty, with respect to everything that is in the world, for Christ's sake. And it is meet that the soul embrace these acts with all its heart and strive to subdue its will thereto. For if it perform them with its heart, it will very quickly come to find in them great delight and consolation, and to act with order and discretion. . . .[11]

[11] With these texts of St. John of the Cross we can compare those of M. Olier on interior denial and those of St. John Eudes on humility: *Introduction à la vie chrétienne*, ch. II, p. 146; *Méditations sur l'humilité*, p. 72, quoted by J. Gautier, "Abnégation et adhérence," in the *Revue apologétique*, June, 1937, pp. 647 and 650.

In order to arrive at having pleasure in everything, desire to have pleasure in nothing. In order to arrive at possessing everything, desire to possess nothing. In order to arrive at being everything, desire to be nothing. In order to arrive at knowing everything, desire to know nothing. In order to arrive at that wherein thou hast no pleasure, thou must go by a way wherein thou hast no pleasure. In order to arrive at that which thou knowest not, thou must go by a way that thou knowest not. In order to arrive at that which thou possessest not, thou must go by a way that thou possessest not. In order to arrive at that which thou art not, thou must go through that which thou art not. When thy mind dwells upon anything, thou art ceasing to cast thyself upon the All. For, in order to pass from the all to the All, thou hast to deny thyself wholly in all. And, when thou comest to possess it wholly, thou must possess it without desiring anything. For, if thou wilt have anything in having all, thou hast not thy treasure purely in God.[12]

In this detachment the spiritual soul finds its quiet and repose; for, since it covets nothing, nothing wearies it when it is lifted up, and nothing oppresses it when it is cast down, because it is in the centre of its humility; but, when it covets anything, at that very moment it becomes wearied.[13]

These texts are extremely exacting; what justifies them is the purification they prepare for and the freedom they promise: "We must have our treasure in God"; when we succeed in doing so, we find in all things "a knowledge of God which is joyful and pleasant, chaste, pure, spiritual, glad and loving."

All this is easy to understand, if we recall what we have considered: all that God has created ought to be for us a sign of God's goodness and a help to mount up to Him. But we fail to recognize these intentions of the Creator, so that we see in things only their immediate usefulness or their attractiveness; henceforth, instead of being raised towards God, we are held captive. To free us from this seduction, from this captivity, we must forbid ourselves all pursuits of enjoyment or repose in created things. If

[12] *Ibid.*, I, 13, n. 5 and 10.
[13] *Ibid.*, 10.

we are faithful to this, we shall lose our taste for them and find again their free use.

From our first steps on this path, we turn towards the light; our soul becomes more sincere, more loyal, more transparent. Up to that time we can apply to ourselves the words of Jesus: "If the light that is in thee is darkness, how great is the darkness itself!" (Mt. 6:23). Now there will be this other maxim: "If thy whole body is full of light, having no part in darkness, it will all be illumined, as when a bright lamp illumines thee" (Lk. 11:36). We shall no longer be those who "have loved the darkness rather than the light, for their works were evil," but those who come to the light that their deeds "may be made manifest, for they have been performed in God" (Jn. 3:19, 21). The ideal of this luminous life we shall find in Jesus: a virginal and immaculate human nature, penetrated by the divinity of the Son of God: the Sun of Justice glowing in a vase of crystal.

In the measure that we tend towards that ideal, we free ourselves from material servitude; the truth delivers us. Our gaze, become luminous, penetrates things; it discovers and beholds in them those divine traces it has so long failed to recognize: *Domine, Dominus noster, quam admirabile est nomen tuum in universa terra!* (Ps. 8:2). It is thus that creation is wont to appear to the gaze of Jesus; thus it is that, little by little, it is revealed to those who follow Him and are faithful to Him. And right there, undoubtedly, is the most profound interpretation of the hundredfold promised by Our Lord.

Amen I say to you, there is no one who has left house, or brothers, or sisters, or mother, or father, or children, or lands, for my sake and for the gospel's sake, who shall not receive now in the present time a hundredfold as much, houses, and brothers, and sisters, and mothers, and children, and lands—along with persecutions, and in the age to come life everlasting (Mk. 10:29-30; Mt. 19:29; Lk. 18:29-30).

These words are connected with the episode of the rich young man: the renunciation, which the young man lacks the courage to make, the apostles have accomplished. What will be their reward for it? It has been already nearly two years since the apostles have left everything; they are still waiting for the reward, and again Jesus promises it to them. What, then, is it, and on what condition do we receive it? Let us not talk about eternal life, which belongs to the age to come; but the hundredfold is received now, in this world. In what does it consist?

This hundredfold, Father Lagrange explains very rightly, ought to be understood not from the viewpoint of quantity, but of quality. St. Jerome has already said this: the millenarians are mistaken, then, who imagine an earthly paradise, where the elect would receive the hundredfold, everything they have left. The holy Doctor understands all this of spiritual goods.[14]

This interpretation of St. Jerome has been adopted by other Fathers; and if, indeed, we were acquainted with this statement only from St. Matthew or St. Luke, we would not have to search further: the two Evangelists recount the promise of the hundredfold with no further details. But in St. Mark, this detail appears in its concrete reality: "houses, and brothers, and sisters, and mothers, and children, and lands." Must we delete this? Certainly not, thinks Father Lagrange; we can "take houses, brothers, etc., in the literal sense, but understanding a religious brotherhood, such as existed in the early days of Christianity; this is the meaning in all the moderns, Catholic or independent." [15]

This interpretation is very acceptable, but it does not exhaust the meaning of the Gospel text: the living conditions of the Christians of Jerusalem will last only a few years; Christ's promise will not pass away. Hence, Father Huby, while in complete accord with Father Lagrange's interpretation, has completed it: "Circumstances have changed, but Christ's word continues to be verified in a magnificent sense. Those who leave everything to follow Him are assured of receiving, in exchange for natural goods, which are numbered and weighed, the immeasurable values of

[14] *Sensus ergo iste est: Qui carnalia pro Salvatore dimiserit, spiritualia recipiet; quae comparatione et merito sui ita erunt, quasi si parvo numero centenarius numerus comparetur.*

[15] *Saint Marc,* 4th ed., Paris, Gabalda, 1929, p. 277.

the order of charity." [16] This is quite true, but it brings us back to the purely spiritual interpretation of St. Jerome: Christ will give to His own goods which will be worth a hundred times more than the houses or the fields, but they will be neither houses nor fields.

Can we not preserve the concrete force of these words without limiting their significance to exceptional circumstances? For an orientation towards this solution, we shall recall the Gospel maxim: to find one's soul, one must lose it. It is the same with all the goods here below; if we hoard them jealously, we become their slaves; if we are detached from them, we are their masters. And thereby we win not only freedom but, at the same time, that religious intuition which causes to be discovered in created beings the presence and action of God. Consequently, the most lowly thing gives the soul a joy no miser will ever possess. Having nothing, we possess all things.

Tamquam nihil habentes, et omnia possidentes (2 Cor. 6:10). These words of the Apostle seem to me to reveal the deepest meaning of Christ's words. If you are truly in this world, "as not being of it," you can say with St. Paul, "all things are mine, and I am Christ's, and Christ is God's" (cf. 1 Cor. 3:22–23); "houses, and brothers, and sisters, and mothers, and children, and lands" (Mk: 10:30)—everything is ours; and the goods, whose masters we thus become, are not only what is possessed in common by the religious brotherhood to which we might belong, but the whole of creation.

What Christ must transform is ourselves, much more than the goods we can possess. By renunciation our eyes and hearts are purified; they find in all things that chaste and spiritual relish of God, which is the promised hundredfold.

And all this is illumined again by the personal experience of Jesus. This world, in which He spent His human life, He saw with His eyes, but at the same time He viewed it in the light of glory. The Psalmist could say, "The heavens chant the glory of God"

[16] J. Huby, S.J., cf. *Word of Salvation: Translation and Explanation of the Gospel According to Saint Mark,* tr. by J. Heenan, S.J., Milwaukee, Bruce, 1957.

(Ps. 18:2); no one heard this chant as Christ did. Before this spectacle and this concert, we are blind and deaf. Let night fall, let all be still—little by little we shall see and hear, not, certainly, like the Son, who "carries all by His power and word," but as the children of God can and ought to do in the home of their Father.

And the example of the saints confirms Christ's promise understood in this way. Who, more than St. Francis of Assisi, was stripped of goods here below? Who, more than he, found in them a pure and lofty enjoyment?

Thus in this stripping of all sensible objects, we are led to recognize, once again, the sovereign beneficence of the divine requirements. There is no doubt that abnegation is imposed on us as a duty of reparation for our sins, as a necessary defense against a fragile and wounded nature. But at the same time it elevates, it purifies us. In a Collect of Passiontide Holy Church has us say: "O Almighty God, we beg Thee, grant this grace, that the dignity of our human condition, wounded by intemperance, might be healed by the remedy of a courageous abstinence." Still more often does she show us in the mortification of the flesh an efficacious means to arrive at contemplation; thus in the Collect of St. Peter of Alcantara: "O God, who hast deigned to show us in blessed Peter a glorious example of wonderful penance and exalted contemplation, grant us by his merits the grace to attain, by mortification of the flesh, the more ready contemplation of divine mysteries."

4. SELF-RENUNCIATION

We have studied the renunciation which is asked of us with regard to human affections and material goods. The most difficult remains to be done:[17] we must renounce our very selves. "If any-

---

[17] The author of the *Imitation*, III, II, 3, writes: *Raro invenitur tam spiritualis aliquis, qui omnibus sit nudatus . . . Si habuerit virtutem magnam et devotionem nimis ardentem, adhuc multum sibi deest; scilicet unum quod summe sibi necessarium est. Quid illud? Ut, omnibus relictis, se relinquat et a se totaliter exeat, nihilque de privato amore retineat.* Cf. the *Following of Christ,* tr. by J. Malaise, S.J.,: "Of the Small Number of the Lovers of the Cross of Jesus," pp. 123–124.

one comes to me and does not hate his father and mother, and wife and children, and brothers and sisters, yes, and even his own life, he cannot be my disciple" (Lk. 14:26).

This is the decisive endeavor, which is not separated from the others, but governs them. We must be able to say with St. Paul: *Vivo, iam non ego, vivit vero in me Christus* (Gal. 2:20). This very text reveals to us at one and the same time both the goal to attain and the path to follow: in the end we are still to live, but with the life of Christ. It is necessary, then, that this life become increasingly dear to us and cause us to renounce our own lives. We need, too, the grace of God stimulating and guiding our effort, to transform gradually the orientation of our lives, to forget self in order to seek God.

One sees that it is a question of a profound transformation of the whole being. To understand it better, we can compare this Christian detachment with neo-Platonic asceticism, such as it has been expounded by Plotinus: " 'All duty and all virtue, even courage and justice, which apparently give up their altruistic character, are to make what prevents us from being ourselves disappear. Thus the sculptor works at a statue, hews, chisels, and polishes, carving and scraping.' A theory of radical abnegation: always it is a question of removing, cutting, or fleeing, always the same negative character." [18] Sin is not an "offense committed against God, which is at the same time a deep discord in the depths of the soul; it is a superficial stain, something which is added from the outside, whose presence we must impatiently put up with, but which provokes not this drama of penance, so moving and so tragic." [19] In schools of spirituality which will be deeply affected by the neo-Platonic influence, especially in the Rhenish school, we shall find once more this idea of conversion as a simple scouring, which frees the soul from the stains covering it.

If we go from these texts to those of St. Paul, we feel ourselves

[18] R. Arnou, S.J., *Le Désir de Dieu dans la philosophie de Plotin*, Paris, Alcan, 1921, pp. 38–39. Cf. *Plotinus: The Enneads*, tr. by S. MacKenna, N. Y., Pantheon, 1956, pp. 34–35.
[19] *Ibid.*, p. 39.

in quite a different world: it is no longer a question of rough-hewing a statue, but of transforming a soul. This transformation appears especially in our likings: visible objects, which used to delight us, are indifferent in our eyes; invisible things, which used to seem non-existent to us, absorb all our likings.[20]

Let us read again, for example, the letter of St. Paul to the Philippians (3:4–14): the Apostle recalls at first all the advantages of a Jewish birth and education, which seemed, just a while ago, so valuable to him: "But the things that were gain to me, these, for the sake of Christ, I have counted loss. Nay more, I count everything loss because of the excelling knowledge of Jesus Christ, my Lord. For his sake I have suffered the loss of all things, and I count them as dung that I may gain Christ and be found in him." This is a complete reversal of values and governs not only speculation, but life: it is nothing else but an effort tending towards Christ: "Forgetting what is behind, I strain forward to what is before, I press on towards the goal to the prize of God's heavenly call in Christ Jesus."

Therein lies the meaning of Christian perfection: even as St. Paul himself writes of it here: "Let us then, as many as are perfect, be of this mind" (*ibid.*,15). God, St. Augustine will say, by no means deprives us of all pleasure, but He changes the object of our pleasures.[21]

---

20 *Non contemplantibus nobis quae videntur, sed quae non videntur; quae enim videntur, temporalia sunt, quae autem non videntur, aeterna sunt* (2 Cor. 4:18). St. John of the Cross, quoted above (p. 186): In order to arrive at that wherein thou hast no pleasure, thou must go by a way wherein thou hast no pleasure. In order to arrive at that which thou knowest not, thou must go by a way that thou knowest not.

21 *Tibi converso ad Deum mutatur dilectio, mutantur deliciae (non enim subtrahuntur, sed mutantur): omnes autem deliciae in hac vita nondum sunt in re; sed ipsa spes tam certa est, ut omnibus huius saeculi deliciis proponenda sit, sicut scriptum est: Delectare in Domino (Enarr. 2 in Ps.* 31:5). At the time when St. Francis Xavier is making the decision to return to the island of the Moor, amidst obvious dangers, he writes: "Exposing myself to every danger of death, I place my whole confidence in God Our Lord, desirous of conforming myself, according to my poor, insignificant means, to the words of Christ our Redeemer and Lord, who

The initiative comes from God; if we were not drawn by His attraction, we could not take one step towards Him. This doctrine has been set forth frequently by St. Augustine. The statement of it I borrow from Father Rousselot:[22] "The Holy Spirit works in me the complaisance in, and love of, this supreme and unchangeable good which is God . . . For free will is capable of nothing but sin if the road of truth is hidden from it; and, when the truth has begun to grow clear in our eyes, if there is no pleasure in it, we do not enter, we do not begin to live properly. *Nisi etiam delectet, non agitur, non suscipitur, non bene vivitur.*" [23] And again: "There where the Spirit is, there is no pleasure in sinning, and this is liberty. There where the Spirit is not, there is pleasure in sinning, and this is slavery." [24] And again: "We do not wish to do what is right, either because we do not know whether it is right, or because, knowing it, we do not take pleasure in it . . . But what makes us see what we are ignorant of? What renders easy

---

said, *Qui enim voluerit animam suam salvam facere, perdet eam; qui autem perdiderit animam suam propter me, inveniet eam* (Mt. 16:25). Although the general sense of this saying of Our Lord is easy to understand, still when we examine our personal case and dispose ourselves to be willing to lose our lives for God, then the dangers are presented to the imagination. Everything becomes so obscure, that the Latin, so clear in itself, comes to be itself obscured . . . Then it is that we know the condition of our flesh, and how feeble and weak it is" (May 10, 1546, *Lettres spirituelles,* ed. Brou, Paris, Spes, 1937, pp. 135–36). Then: "All these dangers and sufferings, embraced willingly for the sole love and service of God Our Lord, are treasures and inexhaustible sources of great spiritual joys; . . . I do not recall ever having been so greatly and continually consoled, nor having experienced so few bodily sufferings. And yet, I circulate habitually in islands surrounded by enemies, and peopled with unsure friends, through lands deprived of every remedy for bodily infirmities, and stripped, so to speak, of all helps useful for the preservation of life: better to call these islands, islands of hope in God, than islands of the Moor" (Jan. 20, 1548, *ibid.,* pp. 145–146).

[22] "La grâce d'après saint Jean et saint Paul," in *Recherches de Science religieuse,* 1928, p. 102.

[23] *De spiritu et littera,* III, 5. P.L. XLIV, 203, and in tr. *St. Augustine on the Spirit and the Letter,* tr. by W. Simpson, N. Y., Macmillan, 1925.

[24] *Ibid.,* XVI, 22, 218.

that which gives us no pleasure? It is grace." [25] The proper effect of grace is, in a word, victorious pleasure, *delectatio victrix*.

When we read spiritual books and what is said in them of the happiness of suffering, of being humiliated and scorned, we sometimes have an impression of unreality. And sometimes, indeed, there can be mimesis or suggestion here. But we cannot gainsay in this way all the texts of the saints; they are numerous and sincere. Thus St. Margaret Mary writing to Mother Greyfie, who had been her superior, and thanking her for the humiliations the Mother had inflicted on her:

How can it be that with so many faults and misery, my soul always craves sufferings and mortifications? . . . And when I think that you were doing her the charity of sustaining her with this delicious food, bitter though it was to nature, and that now I see myself deprived of it owing to the bad use I made of it, this fills me with sorrow. Indeed, I can tell you that nothing has so bound me to your charity as that conduct of which I would not know how to think except with a tender gratitude to you, who could not give me more effective signs of a perfect friendship than by humiliating and mortifying me. Although you did only a very little considering the occasions I gave you, still this little used to console me and sweeten the bitternesses of life, and this privation renders it unbearable for me. I would not know how to live without suffering.[26]

The saint was of a very sensitive disposition, and certainly she had suffered these insults keenly; but she felt that each blow dealt to self-love united her to Our Lord and developed in her the divine life, and this was dearer to her than all else. Like a prisoner in a dark cell, with neither air nor water: through an opening he has dug out, he begins to see daylight; to be free, to breathe, to see, he hesitates not to hurt his hands. But still he must perceive something at least; without that, the wounds will pain sharply, and a very costly and constantly renewed effort will be necessary.

---

[25] *De peccatorum meritis et remissione*, I, II, XVII, 26. *P.L.*, XLIV, 167.
[26] *Vie et oeuvres*, II, letter 25, Paris, Poussielgue frères; Paray-le-Monial, Monastère de la Visitation, 1867, p. 84. *Vie* by A. Hamon, Paris, Beauchesne, 1914, p. 230.

It all comes back, then, to the wish of the *Imitation* (III, 47, 4): "Oh, if these truths were agreeable to you and sank deep into your heart, how could you still dare complain?" What is to be done in order to accomplish this? Above all, pray, asking God *recta sapere, et de eius semper consolatione gaudere.* Then tend courageously towards that goal. Supernatural motives will take hold of us only in the measure that we are regularly inspired by them. Deep-rooted habits of life are formed only slowly, imperceptibly. A child who changes his environment, who leaves a worldly family to enter a Christian school, will be assimilated only gradually to his new environment. So it is, *a fortiori,* with supernatural habits, with a judgment inspired by faith and the love of God preferred to all else. In this case the need, when the occasion presents itself for them, is for decisive acts, those sustained, in daily life, by a whole series of choices, judgments, steps.

Instinctively we are led to say that this remissness is not mortal or that this virtuous act is unprofitable. A delusion—in life everything counts for something. Little by little habit is formed, the judgment rights itself or succumbs, the will grows strong or soft. We may say again: I have a dispensation. But no one can dispense us from feeding ourselves, from praying, from loving God. We are led also to prefer what is seen, what counts, to those efforts which seem without effect: rather read or speak, than pray. Thus we neglect profound living for visible activity, the life of God for human life.

Normally our faith has on our life only the grip we give it. If we make great sacrifices to God, like the apostles abandoning all to follow Christ, faith holds large sway over us. But, in order for that rule to be constant, it is necessary for this inspiration to be ever present; if it intervenes only on momentous occasions, it will leave the ordinary course of our life under the sway of natural instincts.

With many sincere but not very fervent Christians, faith intervenes especially by means of the prohibitions it promulgates: no bad desires, no unjust actions, no work on Sunday, no meat on Friday. All this is necessary, but insufficient. God forbids all this to us only in order to open for us the way to Him. Thus the Sun-

296   THE SPIRITUAL TEACHING OF THE NEW TESTAMENT

day rest is ordained for our religious life, for our relations with
God; if this intention is not present, the Sunday observance, like
that of the Sabbath, risks being pharisaical and puritanical. It is
the same with our duties towards our neighbor. We have often
remarked the distance between the Jewish precept "Never do to
another what thou wouldst hate to have done to thee" (Tob. 4:
16) and the Christian precept "Even as you wish men to do to
you, so also do you to them" (Lk. 6:31). The first is a barrier, the
second a spur; but it is a spur we need for developing in ourselves
the spiritual life.[27]

This spur is given to us: God is within us, He abides there, He
pours out His graces there: "We will come to him and make our
abode with him" (Jn. 14:23). How is it that this presence, which
ought to divinize our souls, leaves them, to all appearances, quite
human? It is because we put an obstacle to its action, like a Vene-
tian blind depriving us of the brightness and warmth of the sun.
We ask ourselves, at times, how Christians who live in the state of
grace, who go to Communion every day, remain so imperfect.
The answer is right there, in that obstacle they willfully put in the
way of the divine action. Grace is stored up, but its action is para-
lyzed.

At times the mercy of God is so impelling that it removes all
obstacles; thus with St. Teresa of Avila, who spent more than
eighteen years struggling with God and was finally vanquished by
a more powerful grace. But this merciful pressure is not accorded
to all; no one can promise it to himself.

Greater unfitness and impurity has the soul in its journey to
God if it has within itself the smallest appetite for things of the
world than if it were burdened with all the hideous and persistent
temptations and all the darkness describable, provided that its
rational will refuses them entrance. [28]

This protracted asceticism requires a great deal of firmness, but
also much prudence. We must strip ourselves of everything and
clothe ourselves again with Christ; but we shall strip ourselves

[27] Cf. Col. 2:20–22.
[28] St. John of the Cross, *Aphorismes*, p. 9.

only by putting on Him. We must not remain naked, unattached to thing or person.

This danger is not chimerical; we have been able to experience it ourselves. We are told: "No ambition"; we risk concluding: "No work." "No natural affection"; and we think: "No devotedness." In a word, we are in danger of letting all the ground reclaimed from natural passions be swept away by selfishness and laziness.

Jansenism did not avoid this danger: the Port Royalists claimed to give a purely Christian education, and for this reason, they banished all competition from it; if a child is successful, it will give thanks to God in the silence of prayer. The traditions of our Catholic schools are much wiser, fostering competition, but making an effort to elevate it towards God.

We must watch over this prudence not only in the retrenchments exacted but also in the motives set in play. A great saint will be able to have the strength, not only for himself, but for others, to rely exclusively on the highest motives. Thus St. Paul recommending to the Corinthians the collection for the saints of Jerusalem, suggesting that they imitate Christ, who, being infinitely rich, became poor (2 Cor. 8:9). But more often than not, it is necessary to suport these lofty considerations by other motives.[29]

In all this, no effort of the imagination: *regnum Dei non venit cum expectatione . . . intra vos est* (Lk. 17:20–21). Sacrifice is within us. No fear for the morrow: *sufficit diei malitia sua* (Mt. 6:34). No contention nor stiffness: we recognize Christ's action with its penetrating gentleness: *oleum effusum.* He pervades all, but effortlessly: *Igitur neque volentis neque currentis sed miserentis est Dei* (Rom. 9:16).

---

[29] In the anonymous treatise, *Conocimiento oscuro de Dios,* published in the appendix of the works of St. John of the Cross (Toledo, Gerardo, 1914, III, p. 318), the author advises never acting for a motive other than that of the will of God. St. John himself was wiser: to novices and young religious he used to suggest particular motives, drawn, for example, from the life and passion of Our Lord (*Dictamenes de espiritu,* III, pp. 60–69).

chapter 9

❖❖❖❖❖❖❖❖❖

The Public Life of Our Lord

We have pondered the mysteries of Our Lord's hidden life: His conception and birth, His childhood, His hidden life at Nazareth, His retreat in the desert, His baptism and temptations.

We have gathered together and reflected on His teachings to the crowds surrounding Him, to the disciples He calls to follow Him more closely.

We must now contemplate the mysteries of His public life, the example He sets for His disciples, the spiritual and apostolic formation He continues in them.

1. APOSTOLIC ZEAL

What we admire, first of all, in reading the Gospel is the zealous action of Christ giving Himself unreservedly and untiringly.

From the start of St. Mark's narration (1:21 ff.) we see Jesus at Capharnaum. We can follow Him during this whole day: it is a Sabbath; in the morning Jesus proceeds to the synagogue; He preaches there; He delivers a possessed person there; then He returns to St. Peter's house, cures the mother-in-law of His host, and spends the day with His first apostles. At sunset the house is thronged with the sick, "and the whole town had gathered together at the door." In the morning, long before daybreak, he withdraws apart to pray. Simon goes after him: "They are all seeking thee." Jesus answers, "Let us go into the neighboring villages and towns, that there also I may preach. For this is why I have come." And He went about through all Galilee.

Thus appears this first day, and the whole course of His life—never a single day to Himself: the constant society of the twelve apostles, and the repeated and endless flow of crowds. If He passes by, the people press forward to touch Him: "Who touched my cloak?" He asks, and Peter replies, "Thou seest the crowd pressing upon thee, and dost thou say, 'Who touched me?'" (Mk. 5:31). After the mission of the apostles, He wants to give them a little rest and leads them apart into the desert: "For there were many coming and going, and they had no leisure even to eat" (Mk. 6:31). But the crowd follows them to the desert: and Jesus "had compassion on them, because they were like sheep without a shepherd. And he began to teach them many things" (*ibid.,* 34); and when night came on, seeing them hungry and without food, He fed them miraculously.

Right up to the end, this activity is continued without a day of respite. Sometimes the fatigue is such that it prostrates Our Lord; thus at Jacob's well (Jn. 4:6): *fatigatus ex itinere, sedebat;* thus in the boat, where He falls asleep from fatigue after teaching in parables (Mk. 4:38). And, amidst so much work, He has nowhere to lay His head (Lk. 9:58).

This activity, forgetful of self and completely devoted to the neighbor, appears even more amazing to anyone recalling the hidden life: "How does this man come by learning, since he has not studied?" (Jn. 7:15). His fellow citizens at Nazareth noted nothing in Him, guessed nothing; their witness completes and illumines the silence of the Gospel concerning these thirty years: truly Jesus lived a hidden life. This silent effacement, then this indefatigable activity, could not both be governed by the personal preferences of Jesus, but by His submission to the Father: "I do always the things that are pleasing to him" (Jn. 8:29).

And this constant endeavor encounters endless obstacles He cannot remove: He is attacked first at Jerusalem, at the time of the Passover; the opposition of the Pharisees drives Him away before a month is up. He preaches the Gospel in Judea; the imprisonment of John the Baptist makes Him aware of the danger threatening Him; He must leave. He held on in Galilee for a year; but, after the enthusiasm of the multiplication of the loaves, there is the large defection at Capharnaum and at the same time there are the threats of Antipas. Jesus has to retire with His apostles to the Phoenician coast, then to the country of Philip. For the last six months He multiplies his efforts at Jerusalem, but these are only short missions, on the occasion of feasts, separated by long sojourns in Perea or in the desert.

Even more painful than this opposition of the leaders is the hesitation of the disciples. They gather in large numbers to hear Him; sometimes they follow Him enthusiastically; at other times they fall away and disperse.

"One sows, another reaps" (Jn. 4:37). Jesus willed to be the sower, and to reserve the harvest for His disciples. He willed that the great outpouring of the Holy Spirit be acquired only by the merits of His Passion. Up to then, "the Spirit had not yet been given, seeing that Jesus had not yet been glorified" (Jn. 7:39). Certainly during this public ministry, there are already great graces, great revelations, powerful attractions, especially in the little group of apostles—for example, at the time of their vocation or at Caesarea Philippi or on Thabor; but there is nothing of a Pentecost. Hence, in the crowds, that wavering, fickle faith, waxing enthusiastic for Jesus, then moving away from Him because it has abandoned none of its dreams. Even in those called by Jesus, we occasionally meet timid hesitation: in the rich young man, in the disciple whom He must remind that "no one, having put his hand to the plow and looking back, is fit for the kingdom of God" (Lk. 9:62). The apostles themselves cannot stand the prospect of the Cross. At first they try to thrust it aside (Mt. 16:22); after the stern reprimand by Jesus, they are silent, but without accepting it, without turning away courageously from the mirage obsessing them. On the day of the Ascension they will again say, "Wilt thou at this time restore the kingdom to Israel?" (Acts 1:6). On the contrary, after Pentecost, there will be the joy of suffering (Acts 5:41). There are the mass conversions, of three thousand, five thousand people, and these are not the enthusiasm of a day, but definitive commitments to the most perfect Christianity, these new converts putting in common all their goods to form now but one body and one soul.

Jesus has reserved to His apostles the joy of these bountiful harvests; He is content to prepare them; others will see the crops gathered in. This role, which was His own, is the one He will reserve for His greatest apostles—St. Paul, for example, St. Francis Xavier, and all the pioneers of the Gospel. To carry on continually one's apostolic activity amid these conditions is the achievement of a saint; to have willed and chosen these conditions is the prerogative of the Son of God.

This thankless labor of the first clearing, before the great outpouring of graces, is still saddened by every human misery and, first of all, by rivalries and jealousies. The disciples of John the Baptist come to say to their master, "He who was with thee beyond the Jordan, to whom thou hast borne witness, behold he baptizes and all are coming to him." But John answers them, "The friend of the bridegroom, who stands and hears him, rejoices exceedingly at the voice of the bridegroom. This my joy, therefore, is made full. He must increase, but I must decrease (Jn. 3:26, 29–30). We shall be aware of these jealousies even among the apostles. "Master," John will say to Jesus, "we saw a man casting out devils in thy name, and we forbade him, because he does not follow with us"; and Jesus answers him, "Do not forbid him; for he who is not against you is for you" (Lk. 9:49–50). And especially among the apostles themselves, there will be rivalries, claims to the first place, which will run counter to each other. On this point Jesus is very watchful and strict; He senses in these nascent ambitions one of the most dangerous sources of ferment for the peace and unity of His Church. We have already recalled the incident of Capharnaum (Mk. 9:32–

33). The approach of the sons of Zebedee is even more revealing: immediately after the prediction of the Passion, as they are going up to Jerusalem, James and John say to Jesus, "Master, we want thee to do for us whatever we ask." "What do you want me to do for you?" "Grant to us that we may sit, one at thy right hand and the other at thy left hand, in thy glory." "You do not know what you are asking for." Still the others were indignant; Jesus must settle the dispute by formulating the law of Christian service and by proposing His example (Mk. 10:35–45). At the Last Supper we shall find once more the same rivalries: "A discussion arose among them, which of them was the greatest" (Lk. 9:46). Here again, Jesus interposes His example, in a most solemn way, by the washing of feet and by the interpretation He gives to it: "Do you know what I have done to you? You call me Master and Lord, and you say well, for so I am. If, therefore, I the Lord and Master have washed your feet, you also ought to wash the feet of one another. For I have given you an example, that as I have done to you, so you also should do" (Jn. 13:12–15).

And then, there is still much worse—a betrayal. Already one year before the Passion, at the time of the Passover at Capharnaum, Judas has betrayed His Master: "Have I not chosen you, the Twelve? Yet one of you is a devil" (Jn. 6:71). For one year longer the wretched man lives with Jesus, the witness of His preaching and miracles; he shares that intimacy which Our Lord accords all His apostles; and he is a devil. There is in this hardening a terrible mystery; but also in this patience of the Master an unforgettable lesson. Later on, when people asked St. Martin how he could put up with Brice, the saint replied, "Jesus put up well enough with Judas." And what discretion as well! In this environment of such close unity, no one suspected that downfall; the scandal of Capharnaum has been quickly forgotten. At the Last Supper, when Jesus says, "One of you will betray me," the apostles say, "Is it I, Lord?" (Mt. 26:21–22). No one says, "It is he." We marvel here at the discretion of Jesus, but also at the charity of the apostles. They were, no doubt, ambitious and argued over the first places; but at least they were not suspicious. The betrayal itself is cloaked over in silence and charity.

Nothing is more glorious for God, nothing more sanctifying for men, than a ministry continually pursued among so many enemies, so many infidels, and even traitors. To anyone practising it after the example of Jesus, the apostolic life is at one and the same time the proof and the source of sanctity. It proves sanctity, because it requires sanctity; it is impossible to sustain this activity, disinterested and unsparing of self, unless one is urged on by the love of Christ. And, at the same time, it develops sanctity: nothing that might feed self-love, self-complacency; everything, on the contrary, calls for suppliant prayer, devotedness to God and to souls.

To guide him in so hard a task, the disciple of Christ will behold his Master during His public life, quite particularly in the course of His last months, in the preaching at Jerusalem which St. John describes: there He is attacked in the center of Judaism, where is found the most holiness and the most corruption. He preaches in this Temple, a house of prayer become a den of thieves: to those Scribes who are seated in the chair of Moses and whom He must curse; to those undecided Jews, whose hesitations and vacillations we follow throughout these chapters. Some say, "He is a good man"; others, "No, rather he seduces the crowd" (Jn. 7:12). "He speaks openly and they say nothing to him. Can it be that the rulers have really come to know that this is the Christ? Yet we know where this man is from; but when the Christ comes, no one will know where he is from" (*ibid.*, 26–27). And yet, "when the Christ comes will he work more signs than this man works?" (*ibid.*, 31). And in the midst of this feverish agitation, Jesus stands, on the most solemn day of the feast of the Tabernacles, and cries out, "If anyone thirst, let him come to me and drink" (*ibid.*, 37).

And this supreme effort is carried on amid threats of death, with a superhuman but peaceful strength, forgetful of self: "When you have lifted up the Son of Man, then you will know that I am he, and that of myself I do nothing; but even as the Father has taught me, I speak these things. And he who sent me is with me; he has not left me alone, because I do always the things that are pleasing to him" (Jn. 8:28–29). A word sums up everything: "You are from below, I am from above" (*ibid.*, 23). It is this union of the Son with the Father which we must now consider in the active life of Jesus.

2. THE SON AND THE FATHER

When we consider the life of Jesus, completely engaged in its struggle with men, it seems to end only in failures: at Nazareth His preaching is broken up by the violent wrath of His enemies and by their death-threats (Lk. 4:28–29); on the lake shore, after so many miracles which aroused the enthusiasm of the people and grouped them for a while about Him, there is the desertion, and Jesus has to curse the cities where He preached so much, Corozain, Bethsaida, Capharnaum (Mt. 11:20–24). Jerusalem, finally, the theater of His first preaching and of His supreme efforts, welcomes Him on the day of the Palms, only to put Him to death five days later; and Jesus, upon entering it the very day of His triumph, weeps over it, over the catastrophe which threatens it and which its apostasy will make irrevocable (Lk. 19:41–44).

And yet, when we study the activity of Jesus more closely, we see that it was not deceived; He fulfilled His role of sower: "He went his way, weeping and sowing"; He will say to His Father on the last day, "I have accomplished the work that thou hast given me to do" (Jn. 17:4). In all His life, He had had but one concern: to do the will of the Father; He has been faithful to this right to the end.

In His workshop at Nazareth, He bided the hour of the Father; He bides it still on that day at Cana which is only a prelude to His public ministry (Jn. 2:4). A few months later, on the trip from Samaria, His declarations become categorical: "The hour is coming, and is now here, when the true worshippers will worship the Father in spirit and in truth" (Jn. 4:23); and immediately afterwards, when the woman said that she was waiting for the Messias who will teach her all things, Jesus replies, "I who

speak with thee am he" (*ibid.*, 26). In the Temple, after the healing of the paralytic: "Amen, amen I say to you, the hour is
coming, and now is here, when the dead shall hear the voice of
the Son of God, and those who hear shall live"; and, taking up
that theme again: "Do not wonder at this, for the hour is coming
in which all who are in the tombs shall hear the voice of the Son
of God . . . Of myself I can do nothing. As I hear, I judge; and
my judgment is just because I seek not my own will, but the will
of him who sent me" (Jn. 5:25, 28, 30).

All these passages which crowd together in the Gospel of St.
John—one could mention others—reveal the deepest wellspring
of the Son's action: "Of myself I can do nothing." A superficial
reader will see here a determinism, a constraint; it is the mystery of Jesus' life, it is the vision of the will of the Father and an
acquiescence full of love. On certain more weighty occasions
this acquiescence takes on a note of enthusiasm; thus when Jesus
rejoices in the Holy Spirit and exclaims, "I praise thee, Father,
Lord of heaven and earth, that thou didst hide these things from
the wise and prudent, and didst reveal them to little ones. Yes,
Father, for such was thy good pleasure" (Lk. 10:21).

This filial docility is the fruit of the intuitive vision which illumines, without ever veiling, the whole life of the Son of God.
Thence comes also the assurance with which He tends towards
His goal amidst all the death-threats. He is the only and beloved Son, whom His Father, Master of the vineyard, has sent
among murderous vine-dressers. He knows the destiny which
awaits Him, He goes to meet it; no opposition frightens or upsets
Him. It is thus that He appears from the start of His ministry, in
the Temple, during the feasts of the Passover, cleansing His
Father's shamefully defiled house and driving from it with lashings
the money changers and sellers. Likewise later at Nazareth: the
Jews, shocked by His discourse, carry Him off to hurl Him from
a cliff top. "But he, passing through their midst, went his way"
(Lk. 4:30). And similarly at Jerusalem, on the feast of the
Dedication, the Jews want to lay hands on Him to stone Him:
"They sought therefore to seize him; and he went forth out of
their hands" (Jn. 10:39). And in the course of the next week,

after the parable of the Vine-dressers: "He looked on them and said, 'What then is this that is written, "The stone which the builders rejected, has become the corner stone"? Everyone who falls upon that stone will be broken to pieces; but upon whomever it falls, it will grind him to powder.' And the chief priests and the Scribes sought to lay hands on him that very hour, but they feared the people; for they knew that he had aimed this parable at them" (Lk. 20:17–19).

Where does the Master get this assurance which nothing can shake? From the help He finds in the people? Undoubtedly not: "He himself knew what was in man" (Jn. 2:25); but from the vision of the will of the Father: the hour has not yet come. Thus at the time of the feast of Tabernacles: "No one laid hands on him because his hour had not yet come" (Jn. 7:30); likewise when He is teaching in the Treasury: "No one seized him, because his hour had not yet come" (Jn. 8:20). When, summoned by the sisters of Lazarus, He leaves His retreat and comes up to Bethany, the apostles are frightened; He says to them, "Are there not twelve hours in the day? If a man walks in the day, he does not stumble, because he sees the light of this world" (Jn. 11:9). He had spoken similarly at the time of curing the man born blind: "I must do the works of him who sent me while it is day; the night is coming, when no one can work. As long as I am in the world I am the light of the world" (Jn. 9:4–5). And when His hour shall have come, the hour of darkness (Lk. 22:53), this will be the great temptation and the agony, but it will also be the hour of glory: "Father, the hour has come! Glorify thy Son, that thy Son may glorify thee" (Jn. 17:1).

Thus, in the whole course of Our Lord's life, we see extended over Him the protection of the Father. God had said of old, "Touch ye not my anointed" (Ps. 104:15). How much truer this saying is of the Anointed One, the Christ! Surely the Father spared His Son neither persecutions nor want, from the grotto of Bethlehem and the flight into Egypt up to the grotto of the Agony and Calvary. But, up to the last day, no one touched Him. We could apply to Him the words of the Psalm: "Evil will not touch thee; the flood will not come near thy tent."

The same elements have no power over Him; at the time of the storm on the lake, He sleeps in the boat; the apostles are frightened, not for His sake, but for their own: "Master, we are perishing" (Lk. 8:24). Compare this course with that of St. Paul, five times scourged, three times shipwrecked, sick, at the end of his strength and, apparently, of his hope. With Jesus, on the contrary, it is a life without weakness, without sickness, a life at once manly and divine, thoroughly imbued with a youthful impetus, completely invested with heavenly glory. It is true, this glory is hidden in this humble, gentle Messias; it shines through, nevertheless, and reveals the Son of God, the Heir of the kingdom: "This is my beloved Son, in whom I am well pleased" (Mt. 17:5). And this divine protection covers not Christ alone, but all those whom He wishes to protect: "They shall never perish, neither shall anyone snatch them out of my hand. What my Father has given me is greater than all; and no one is able to snatch anything out of the hand of my Father. I and the Father are one" (Jn. 10:28–30).

We marvel at, we adore, this divine protection; but how can our weakness find in it our assurance? In what it reveals to us of the strength of God. This all-powerful and all-wise Providence, which Jesus beholds unveiled, shines through in the Gospel. It is true, therefore, that not a hair of our head falls without our Father's permission. Surely, we do not lay claim, poor sinners, to the immunity of the only-begotten Son; but, utter sinners though we be, we are children of God, and we well know that our Father will not permit us to be tempted above our strength. In the struggle in which the service of God engages us, we have to fight, not "against flesh and blood, but against the Principalities and the Powers, against the world-rulers of this darkness, against the spiritual forces of wickedness on high" (Eph. 6:12). But for our defense we have all the legions of angels and saints, we have God.

We read in the book of Kings (4 Kgs. 6) that the Syrian cavalry had come to take Eliseus away; in the morning, the servant of the prophet sees them and rushes up terrified; Eliseus answers him, "Fear not: for there are more with us than with them." And the Lord, at the prayer of Eliseus, opens the eyes of the servant and points out to him on the mountains, completely surrounding the prophet, hosts of cavalry and fiery chariots. Our Lord had no need of that vision Himself; neither did He give it to His disciples. But He gave them His word: "Dost thou suppose that I cannot entreat my Father, and he will even now furnish me with more than twelve legions of angels?" (Mt. 26:53). We count on His word and on His presence: "Behold, I am with you all days, even unto the consummation of the world" (Mt. 28:20); have trust, "I have overcome the world" (Jn. 16:33). From this faith there comes to the disciples of Our Lord their unshakeable assurance: and this assurance is all the more glorious for Our Lord as the trials are more cruel.

This is what moves us so poignantly in the Epistles of St. Paul, particularly in the Second to the Corinthians, where the Apostle, who has suffered so much from the ingratitude of his disciples and from the rioting at Ephesus, testifies to his sufferings, but affirms also the assurance he finds in Christ:

In all things we suffer tribulation, but we are not distressed; we are sore pressed, but we are not destitute; we endure persecution, but we are not forsaken; we are cast down, but we do not perish; always bearing about in our body the dying of Jesus, so that the life also of Jesus may be made manifest in our bodily frame. For we the living are constantly being handed over to death for Jesus' sake, that the life also of Jesus may be made manifest in our mortal flesh. Thus death is at work in us, but life in you (2 Cor. 4:8–12).

Let us conduct ourselves in all circumstances as God's ministers, in much patience; in tribulations, in hardships, in distresses; in stripes, in imprisonments, in tumults; in labors, in sleepless nights, in fastings; in innocence, in knowledge, in long-sufferings; in kindness, in the Holy Spirit, in unaffected love; in the word of truth, in the power of God; with the armor of justice on the right hand and on the left; in honor and dishonor, in evil report and good report; as deceivers and yet truthful, as unknown and yet well known, as dying and behold, we live, as chastised but not killed, as sorrowful yet always rejoicing, as poor yet enriching many, as having nothing yet possessing all things (ibid., 6:4–10).

This is the ideal of the apostolic life. How to tend towards it? By faith, having our eyes always fixed on "the author and finisher of faith, Jesus" (Heb. 12:2).

Not only is the setting of this activity of the Son of God determined by the Father, but His teaching and His works are continually dependent on the Father.

He said at the feast of Tabernacles, "My teaching is not my own, but his who sent me" (Jn. 7:16). And a little later on: "When you have lifted up the Son of Man, then you will know that I am he, and that of myself I do nothing: but even as the Father has taught me, I speak these things. And he who sent me is with me; he has not left me alone, because I do always the things that are pleasing to him" (Jn. 8:28–29). And on the day of His entry into Jerusalem: "I have not spoken on my own authority, but he who sent me, the Father, has given me commandment what I should say, and what I should declare. And I know that his commandment is everlasting life. The things, therefore, that I speak, I speak as the Father has bidden me" (Jn. 12:49–50).

What appears in all these discourses is a dependence full of love. But if we wish to reach its source, we find it in the divine nature of the Son of God: "Amen, amen, I say to you, the Son can do nothing of himself, but only what he sees the Father doing. For whatever he does, this the Son also does in like manner" (Jn. 5:19). In the divine nature, the exterior actions are in common, and it is in the Father that this action has its source; likewise, in His human nature, the Son acts only in dependence on the Father.

Let us add that this human nature continually beholds the face of the Father. Suppose one of heaven's elect were to come back to live among us, while enjoying the intuitive vision; he cannot turn his gaze away from it; all he sees, all he says, is radiated from that light. By no means do we have here one of the elect, great as he may be, St. John or St. Bernard or St. Thomas; this is the Son of God Himself, beholding His Father and loving Him. While He speaks to us, He lives with this vision which is imprinted on His soul and fills it. Can He tell us anything else? "My teaching is not my own, but his who sent me."

And it is the same with His works as with His words: these works, the Father gives to Him (Jn. 5:36); He "must do the works of him who sent" Him (Jn. 9:4); "Many good works have I shown you from my Father" (Jn. 10:32; cf. 25). And all this is condensed in these few words: "Dost thou not believe that I am in the Father and the Father in me? The words that I speak to you I speak not on my own authority. But the Father dwelling in me, it is he who does the works" (Jn. 14:10).

This initiative of the Father appears in the works which seem more proper to the Son, for example, in the choice of the apostles; Jesus "called to him men of his own choosing" (Mk. 3:13); and He Himself will recall this to them on the last day: "You have not chosen me, but I have chosen you" (Jn. 15:16). But it is also true that no one can come to Him unless the Father draw him (Jn. 6:44), and that He chooses only those whom His Father has given to Him and who remain His men: "They were thine, and thou hast given them to me, and they have kept thy word . . . I pray for them; not for the world do I pray, but for those whom thou hast given me, because they are thine" (Jn. 17:6, 9).

All these passages reveal to us, not a constraint suffered by Christ, but indeed the deepest impetus of His life. And all that is summed up in the words of Jesus to Philip: "Have I been so long a time with you, and you have not known me? Philip, he who sees me sees also the Father" (Jn. 14:9). This life is completely orientated towards the Father and is understood only by one recognizing its goal; and this goal is not, as it is for us, a distant one, perceived only by faith: "I am in the Father and the Father in me" (*ibid.*, 10).

It is this luminous background which gives to the Gospel of St. John its splendor. We hesitate to fix our eyes on this divine light, and yet we really must do so: it is the very center of Christian faith; it is the mystery of the Son of God. "I have food to eat of which you do not know . . . My food is to do the will of him who sent me" (Jn. 4:32, 34). The angel Raphael said to Tobias, "I seemed indeed to eat and to drink with you, but I use an invisible meat and drink, which cannot be seen by men. It is time therefore that I return to him that sent me" (Tob. 12:19–

20). Jesus speaks not in this way: His humanity is not apparent, but real; in very truth He ate and drank with other men. But at the same time His soul was fed with an invisible food, the sight of the Father. From this ceaseless contemplation there is born in Him a love which never slackens and which sweeps Him along continually towards the Father. This love is a participation in the uncreated love by which the Son and the Father love each other; this love is the Holy Spirit.

Speaking of the spiritual life of the just whom God has made His sons, St. John of the Cross teaches that the Holy Spirit elevates them and disposes them to produce in God the same aspiration of love as the Father in the Son and the Son in the Father.[1]

If this is true of ordinary Christians, how much more so of Jesus Our Lord! Unceasingly He hears in the depths of His heart the words of the Father, "Thou art my beloved Son, in whom I am well pleased," and He rejoices in the Holy Spirit; and in this rejoicing He feels passing into His soul all that infinite love with which the Son eternally loves the Father and eternally produces in Him the Holy Spirit.

3. THE DIVINE ATTRACTION IN JESUS

So far we have considered the public life of Jesus in the divine light which illumines it and guides it from the Jordan to Calvary. This splendor which illumines it radiates, in turn, from Him and draws souls to Him, those at least whom the Father has purified and made sensitive to this light.

When Jesus arrives at the Jordan, He is not yet known by John the Baptist; He will be revealed to him only at the time of the baptism. And yet John exclaims, "It is I who ought to be baptized by thee, and dost thou come to me?" (Mt. 3:14). A few weeks later, when Jesus returns to the Jordan, John says to his disciples, "Behold the lamb of God!" and on the basis of this single utterance, Andrew and John follow Jesus (Jn. 1:36–37). Peter, Philip and Nathanael are going to follow, enthralled likewise by

[1] *Spiritual Canticle,* XXXVIII, 1. Text quoted below, p. 221.

a single utterance. And, after this first call, when the definitive vocation will come, at the lake shore, it will be obeyed with the same impetus: Peter and Andrew abandon all they have; the sons of Zebedee leave their father in their boat, alone with his day-laborers; Matthew quits his counter. All will be able, like Peter, to say to Jesus, "Behold, we have left all and followed thee" (Mt. 19:27). What has thus enthralled these young men, from the first contact? St. Jerome explains it in this way: "The brilliance and majesty of the veiled divinity, which was wont to shine through these human features, could from the first glance draw to Him those who beheld Him." [2] At that first encounter, Jesus has worked no miracle, and He has won men: "Blessed are they who have not seen, and yet have believed" (Jn. 20:29).

Is it not thus that the woman taken in sin was won over? No miracle, not even an utterance; but in that Master seated at the table of Simon the Pharisee she recognized her Savior, the Lamb of God who takes away the sins of the world, and she loved much (Lk. 7:47). And the crowds seem to be enthralled; they follow Jesus right into the desert, without even thinking of bringing provisions there, and Jesus has to feed them: five thousand one time, three thousand another. Even at Jerusalem we shall see around Christ that milling of enthusiastic crowds, especially on the day of the Palms. What is the attraction which has seized all these disciples?

If we consider the Son of God in His divinity, it is the splendor of the Father. But even His humanity is the image of God. Undoubtedly, every man is the image of God; but those who are only men and pilgrims here below are rough images, disfigured by sin, faintly lit by the distant reflection of the fatherland towards which they are tending. He, the Son, whose human soul beholds unveiled the glory of the Father—He is its radiance: "We all, with faces unveiled, reflecting as in a mirror the glory of the Lord, are being transformed into his very image from glory to glory, as through the Spirit of the Lord" (2 Cor. 3:18).

This mystery we are made aware of by the Transfiguration:

2 *Comm. in Evang. Matt. P.L.,* XXVI, 56.

the face of our Lord radiates the glory of the Father; at the sight of this splendor, we can only exclaim, "It is good for us to be here" (Mt. 17:4). This is not only wonderment, it is happiness: this beatific vision which Jesus already possesses and whose splendor shines in Him, is the final end towards which we are tending. If we desire it, if we already have an inkling of it, we shall recognize it in Him, and we shall submit to its attraction. "If the poet could say, *trahit sua quemque voluptas*—not necessity, but pleasure; not obligation, but delight—how much more must we say that man is drawn by Christ, by the attractiveness of truth, beauty, and justice; and all this is Christ!" [3]

Undoubtedly this power of attraction will not seize all souls; there is needed here the grace of the Father: "No one can come to me unless the Father who sent me draw him" (Jn. 6:44). How many saw Him passing along the streets of Nazareth, on the roads of Galilee, in the courts of the Temple, without seeing anything in Him but a worker, an illiterate, or even a seducer! Thereby is man judged: "The light has come into the world, yet men have loved the darkness rather than the light, for their works were evil" (Jn. 3:19). But this very discernment, which judges man, also reveals to us the action of the light. This is what attracts those whose eyes are sound; it is what hurts others. And then, between the just who hasten forward and the obstinate sinners who rebel, there is the crowd of fickle souls who draw near for a moment and pass on. John was "the lamp, burning and shining; and you desired to rejoice for a while in his light" (Jn. 5:35). So, too, for the passage of Jesus: many saw Him, rejoiced for a moment, and then turned away.

These considerations can be of service to us in testing our personal dispositions, in recognizing whether we are children of the light; but we not only have to receive that light, we must also spread it. Our Lord has told us so: "You are the light of the world . . . Let your light shine before men, in order that they may see your good works and give glory to your Father in heaven" (Mt. 5:14, 16).

[3] St. Augustine, *In Joann. P.L.* XXV, 1608–1609.

At first sight, this ideal seems to us above our strength. The Son of God, and He alone, is the true Light; we are witnesses of the light, and that is all. But is it not also of a witness, the Precursor, that Our Lord has said, "He was the lamp, burning and shining"? We also must transmit the light received from another source; we are lamps. If one severs the connection, the lamp is no more than a piece of furniture which can still adorn, but no longer illumines. Likewise, if we do not remain united to Christ, our Light, we burn out.

The sole presence of the Son of God attracted souls who had been well prepared; His words and works revealed to them the Father. It is the same, due allowance being made, with the faithful disciples of Christ: from their presence there radiates an influence, a sanctifying force. Faced with a soul discouraged by her faults or crushed by a trial, a man of God communicates the strength of God; his words are the words of Christ. Others, more often than not, are at a loss; neither experience suffices for this, nor devotedness, nor natural affection.

It is also the life-giving presence of Christ which ensures to apostolic works their fruitfulness and especially their lasting fruitfulness: one has only to think, for example, of the activity of the saintly Curé d'Ars in the Dombes, of St. Francis Regis in Vivarais, of St. Grignion de Montfort in Vendée. Three years after the death of St. Francis Xavier, one of his companions, Father de Quadros, wrote: "It is on this earth, then, that there lived the blessed Master Francis, whose labors, works and virtue bore so much fruit, that I do not see who will ever overthrow what God through him has built in this country. I have definite information on the union with God which this good servant preserved in the midst of his continual labors, and I am amazed at it." [4] We recognize the fulfillment of the words of Our Lord: "I have appointed you that you should go and bear fruit, and that your fruit should remain" (Jn. 15:16).

Vos estis lux mundi (Mt. 5:14): to tend towards the realization of this ideal we must live in the light of Christ. His holy

[4] Brou, S.J., *Vie de saint François Xavier,* Paris, Beauchesne, 1914, II, p. 278.

humanity was a transparent lamp from which radiated the divine light in a splendor which no obscurity dimmed, no weakness deflected, no fright troubled. Let us recall the resurrection laboriously effected by Elias or by Eliseus, the efforts of Eliseus to pass over the Jordan, and let us behold Jesus walking on the waters, calming the storm, raising the child of Naim, or the daughter of Jairus, or Lazarus. It is this sovereign peace which reveals God and captivates men. Likewise, in the preaching, that simplicity of the most sublime or heroic precepts: "You therefore are to be perfect, even as your heavenly Father . . ." (Mt. 5:48). "Let him . . . take up his cross, and follow me" (Mt. 16:24), and at the same time: "My yoke is easy, and my burden light" (Mt. 11:30).

On beholding these works, on listening to these words, we are aware of so much power, so much happiness, so much peace in them, that we are won over. This is what men need—this luminous peace which radiates from Christ. To propagate it, we need first of all to gaze at it and gradually to let it penetrate us, less by violent efforts to remove the obstacles, than by a constant effacement which seeks to disappear before Him who alone must live, act, and be revealed in us. "We all, with faces unveiled, reflecting as in a mirror the glory of the Lord, are being transformed into his very image from glory to glory, as through the Spirit of the Lord" (2 Cor. 3:18).

"You were once darkness, but now you are light in the Lord. Walk, then, as children of light" (Eph. 5:8).

❖❖❖❖❖❖❖❖❖

The Life of Prayer

1. PRAYER

It came to pass, as Jesus was praying in a certain place, that when He had finished, one of the disciples said to Him, "Lord, teach us to pray, even as John also taught his disciples" (Lk. 11:1).

This episode, which St. Luke is the only one to relate, can be neither dated nor situated with certainty; it has, nevertheless, a great importance. It does not take place in the first days of the calling of the apostles, but after several months, perhaps more than a year, of their life in common with Jesus. On more than one occasion, particularly in the discourse on the Mount, Our Lord gave them instructions on prayer; above all, He gave them the example of His life, wholly and completely orientated towards the Father and often interrupted by long hours of solitary re-collection.[1]

---

[1] Every one of Jesus' decisive steps is preceded by a long prayer: He prays at the baptism (Lk. 3:21). Then He retires into the desert led by the Holy

But, in order to complete His teaching in so serious a matter, He waited for God to awaken in their hearts the desire for this divine formation which only the one Master could give them. Hence this scene is parallel to that of Caesarea Philippi: the initiative comes from the Father; Jesus Himself does not anticipate it. He had prepared it by His example and His lessons, and He responds to it at once. This need for prayer, this call of the soul to God and to Christ, will be, in the lives of the saints, one of the most manifest signs of the action of the Holy Spirit; it is like the appetite for food in a fully-developed organism.

But, at the same time that we feel the need to pray, we do not know how to pray: we begin to be conscious of God's attraction, but we are frozen, as it were, before this seemingly inaccessible sanctity. In one of the prayers of the Missal,[2] the Church has us repeat, while giving it a more lofty meaning, a prayer of Esther: *Da sermonem rectum in os meum, ut placeant verba mea in conspectu principis.* This is what the apostles are asking Jesus for here: Tell us how we must pray to God. They have been, half of them at least, disciples of John the Baptist; they recall that the Precursor trained his disciples in prayer. This formation is no longer sufficient for them; the Son of God, they understand full well, is the Master, in deference to whom the Precursor himself stands aside. Jesus answers them: we must speak to God as to our Father. Henceforth, the Church will repeat, humbly, faithfully, the words of the Master: "Schooled in divine teaching, we make bold to say: Our Father."

Spirit and spends forty days there. After the first day's sojourn at Capharnaum, before beginning the evangelization of Galilee, He retires long before daybreak into a desert place to pray (Mk. 1:35). A little while later, He heals a leper, the crowds come flocking and throng Him; He retires apart to pray (Lk. 5:16). He passes the night in prayer before choosing His apostles (Lk. 6:12). After the multiplication of the loaves, in the thick of the Galilean crisis, He retires to pray on the mountain (Mk. 6:46). He prays apart before St. Peter's confession (Lk. 9:18). It is in prayer that He is transfigured (Lk. 9:29). He prays for Peter at the Last Supper (Lk. 22:32), He prays in the Garden (Lk. 22:41–43); He prays on the Cross (Lk. 23:34–46).

[2] Offertory of the 22nd Sunday after Pentecost.

And it will not only be the teaching of the Son of God which will instruct us, it will also be the intimate inspiration of the Holy Spirit: He prays in us with unutterable groanings and makes us cry out to God: "Abba! Father!" (Rom. 8:15, 26; Gal. 4:6). Prayer, then, will be in us like the awakening of the filial spirit; and the more it expands in our souls, the more we shall be conformed to the Son of God, the more docile we shall be to the Spirit of adoption, the more we shall be children of God.

But it does not suffice to know to whom we pray; we must also know what to ask for; and there also we have everything to learn. As long as the soul is not illumined by the grace of God, she has a vivid experience of material needs and of her anxieties, but of spiritual misery she has no awareness, except obscurely and at intervals; she feels no need to pray. "Thou sayest, 'I am rich and have grown wealthy and have need of nothing,' and dost not know that thou art the wretched and miserable and poor and blind and naked one" (Apoc. 3:17). Is not this what we see in the case of the apostles themselves on the evening of the Last Supper? They sense the impending crisis; they consider themselves strong enough to brave anything. To Jesus' warnings Peter replies, " 'Even though all shall be scandalized because of thee, I will never be scandalized' . . . And all the disciples said the same thing" (Mt. 26:33–35; Mk. 14:29–31). And in the Garden, despite the repeated exhortations of Jesus urging them to pray, they fall asleep.

It is necessary for the Holy Spirit to dissipate these illusions, to instill in the hearts of Christians this desire of heavenly goods, this thirst for God which will make them feel their want and will stimulate their prayer: "If anyone thirst, let him come to me and drink," Jesus said to the Jews of Jerusalem (Jn. 7:37). But he must, indeed, thirst; without this, he will not come, nor will he drink. "Blessed are they who hunger and thirst for justice" (Mt. 5:6). How will the Holy Spirit awaken in the soul this hunger and thirst? By prayer.

It is first and foremost towards these heavenly goods that the Lord's prayer raises us: the manifestation of God's name, the coming of God's kingdom, the doing of God's will—these are the primary objects of our prayer. We ask Our Lord that all this may be accomplished perfectly "on earth, as it is in heaven" (Mt. 6:10). But, someone will say, these requests surpass our desires. True, but is not this the law of our prayer? Does he not know that the goods which God reserves for us surpass our merits and our wishes? [3] This is the teaching of St. Paul: "The Spirit also helps our weakness. For we do not know what we should pray for as we ought, but the Spirit himself pleads for us with unutterable groanings. And he who searches the hearts knows what the Spirit desires, that he pleads for the saints according to God." [4]

The first fruit of this prayer will be to develop in the heart of the Christian the concern for God's interests; truly he will be able to say with Jesus: *Mea omnia tua sunt, et tua mea sunt* (Jn. 17:10). Interests, like goods, we share in common: my interests are yours, I surrender them to you; your interests are mine, I pray for them as for my own life.

Elsewhere Jesus again stimulates in the same sense the prayer of His disciples; for example, at the time of His apostles' mission: "Seeing the crowds, he was moved with compassion for them, because they were bewildered and dejected, like sheep without a shepherd. Then he said to his disciples, 'The harvest indeed is abundant, but the laborers are few. Pray therefore the Lord of the harvest to send forth laborers into his harvest'" (Mt. 9:36–38; cf. Lk. 10:2). This exhortation makes us aware of the fact

[3] This is the prayer of the Church: *Deus, qui abundantia pietatis tuae et merita supplicum excedis et vota* . . . (2nd Sunday after Pentecost).
[4] Rom. 8:26–27. Cf. Prat, *Théologie de saint Paul,* I, p. 286, and in tr. *The Theology of St. Paul,* I, 239: "The desires with which he inspires us express themselves in sighs which cannot be voiced in words, because they have for their object that which the eye of man hath not seen, nor his ear heard, nor his heart felt. Neither these desires nor these groanings can be disappointed, for they have for their author the Spirit of truth himself. It is likewise so with the prayers which he forms within us without our aid, knowing better than we what it is fitting that we should ask. When he causes the name of the Father, *Abba, Pater,* to rise to our lips, he testifies to us of our adopted sonship." Cf. Rom. 8:15–16: "You have not received a spirit of bondage so as to be again in fear, but you have received a spirit of adoption as sons, by virtue of which we cry, 'Abba! Father!' The Spirit himself gives testimony to our spirit that we are sons of God."

that, if God bids us pray, it is not at all to be notified of our needs; far more clearly than ourselves, He sees the immensity of the task and the paucity of the manpower. But He wants us to be moved ourselves by this, and that is why He bids us pray.

These sovereign interests which we recommend to God are God's interests; but they are also our own. "The first of all the things," says St. Augustine, "to be requested is this: *Hallowed be Thy name*. This petition is not so worded as if God's name were not already holy, but that men may regard it as holy, that is, that God may become so familiar to them that they will esteem nothing more holy and dread nothing more than to offend that name." [5] The coming of God's kingdom—this is His glory, but it is also our eternal life; it is the reward Our Lord proposes to us in the beatitudes. "Thy will be done"—is not this even here below the supreme happiness of the Son of God? "My food is to do the will of him who sent me" (Jn. 4:34); and when this desire appears in a soul, it is the mark of the divine adoption: "Whoever does the will of God, he is my brother and sister and mother" (Mk. 3:35).

These boundless goods do not represent for us a remote ideal wherein we might be capable of taking only a theoretical pleasure: they are the great forces of our religious life. In proportion as our soul is elevated towards them by faith and desire, it is caught up in the adoration of this most holy God, in love for this King, His reign, His will.

For this action to be fully effective, prayer must be frequent and, as far as possible, continual. This is the teaching of the Master: "They must always pray and not lose heart" (Lk. 18:1). The apostles will recall this frequently to the first Christians: they should be "assiduous in prayer, being wakeful therein" (Col. 4:2); they should "pray without ceasing" (1 Thes. 5:17). Prayer, then, will consist, not only in a few formulas repeated from time to time, but in an orientation of the whole of life.[6]

---

[5] *De Sermone Domini in Monte*, V, 19, and in tr. *The Lord's Sermon on the Mount* (ACW 5), p. 108.
[6] Cf. Huby, *Saint Paul, Les épîtres de la captivité*, p. 99, on Col. 4:2.

This orientation is imprinted on the soul by the Holy Spirit. St. Paul has us recognize His action in these desires and groanings which He has rise up from our hearts towards the Father. But this "guest of our souls" acts there continually; to Him also we ought to apply what the Son of God has said of Himself and of the Father: "My Father works even until now, and I work" (Jn. 5:17). And this continual action is what awakens our prayer, what makes us sigh towards the Father. The Holy Spirit is the mutual Love of the Father and the Son; He instills in our hearts a filial love for the Father, enabling us to participate in this very love by which the Son of God loves His Father. This is the doctrine of the Apostle; it has been commented on by St. John of the Cross in *The Spiritual Canticle* and in *The Living Flame:*

The soul that is united and transformed in God breathes in God into God the same Divine breath that God, being in her, breathes into her in Himself, which, as I understand, was the meaning of Saint Paul when he said: *Quoniam autem estis filii Dei, misit Deus Spiritum Filii sui in corda vestra clamantem: Abba, Pater.* Which signifies: Because you are sons of God, God sent the Spirit of His Son into your hearts, crying in prayer to the Father, which, in the perfect, is according to the manner described. And there is no need to wonder that the soul should be capable of aught so high; for since God grants her the favour of attaining to being deiform and united in the Most Holy Trinity, wherein she becomes God by participation, how is it a thing incredible that she should perform her work of understanding, knowledge and love in the Trinity, together with It, like the Trinity Itself, by a mode of participation, which God effects in the soul herself?

And how this comes to pass cannot be known, nor is it possible to express it, save by describing how the Son of God obtained for us this high estate and merited for us this high office, as Saint John says, of being able to become sons of God. And thus He prayed to the Father, as says the same Saint John, saying: *Pater, volo ut quos dedisti mihi, ut ubi sum ego, et illi sint mecum: ut videant claritatem meam quam dedisti mihi.* Which signifies: Father, I will that they whom Thou hast given Me may be also with Me where I am, that they may see the brightness which Thou gavest Me. That is to say, that they may work in Us by participation the same work which I do by nature, which is the breathing of the Holy Spirit.[7]

In truth our divine adoption is not an empty word; we are called children of God, and so we are. All that we have just seen of Christian prayer, such as Our Lord has taught it to us and such as the Holy Spirit breathes in us, unites us to the heavenly Father by ties of filial intimacy which we had been incapable of ambitioning and even of imagining. The Father whom we implore, the goods which we ask for—all surpass us and yet take hold of us. We cannot aspire so high; but from the moment the Holy Spirit raises us there, we cannot detach our hearts from it: "To whom shall we go? Thou hast the words of everlasting life" (Jn. 6:69).

This holy God, this sovereign King, is our Father. At the start of these studies, we noted in Christian revelation the union of those two traits which our human conceptions have so much trouble in reconciling: the transcendence of the one adorable God, the intimacy of our Father. We shall rediscover them both in the *Pater Noster*.

And the second part of the prayer makes that intimacy appear under a new and no less touching aspect: Our Lord uses our misery itself to awaken in us the filial instinct which attaches us to the Father. From Him the Christian implores all and expects all, not only those heavenly treasures which will be fully possessed only in heaven—the hallowing of God's name, the coming of His kingdom, the doing of His will—but also those daily helps which are necessary here below for our weakness: the daily bread which must sustain the life of our bodies and souls, preservation from temptations, and the defense against the enemy of God and man. "Watch and pray, that you may not enter into temptation," Jesus will soon say to His apostles; "the spirit indeed is willing, but the flesh is weak" (Mk. 14:38). The more faithful the soul is, the more clear-sighted will it be, and consequently the more conscious of its weakness and the dangers surrounding it. The great temptations, such as the Passion was for the apostles, make us more keenly aware of the imminence of danger and the

7 *The Spiritual Canticle*, XXXVIII, 3–4, in *Complete Works*.

necessity of prayer; but in the whole course of our lives, we have to maintain a constant effort against the continual pressure of flesh and sin.

They who are according to the flesh mind the things of the flesh, but they who are according to the spirit mind the things of the spirit. For the inclination of the flesh is death, but the inclination of the spirit, life and peace. For the wisdom of the flesh is hostile to God, for it is not subject to the law of God, nor can it be. And they who are carnal cannot please God.

You, however, are not carnal but spiritual, if indeed the Spirit of God dwells in you. But if anyone does not have the Spirit of Christ, he does not belong to Christ. But if Christ is in you, the body, it is true, is dead by reason of sin, but the spirit is life by reason of justification. But if the Spirit of him who raised Jesus Christ from the dead dwells in you, then he who raised Jesus Christ from the dead will also bring to life your mortal bodies because of his Spirit who dwells in you.

Therefore, brethren, we are debtors, not to the flesh, that we should live according to the flesh, for if you live according to the flesh you will die; but if by the spirit you put to death the deeds of the flesh, you will live. For whoever are led by the Spirit of God, they are the sons of God (Rom. 8:5–14).

What St. Paul depicts so vividly for us becomes clear to each of us from our daily experience: in our souls, in our very bodies, everything reacts and everything vibrates; the inspirations of God, the temptations of the devil, the attractions of the world— nothing can reach us which does not leave us better or worse. Sustained by God, our souls in face of temptation are confirmed in Him and are attached more closely to Him from whom Satan would like to separate us. A sinner, on the other hand, whom grace attracts and who resists it, hardens himself against God and yields himself more to the devil. Thus Judas at the Last Supper; by a supreme effort, Jesus tries to recapture the wretched man by a sign of friendship: "When he had dipped the bread, he gave it to Judas Iscariot, the son of Simon. And after the morsel,

Satan entered into him" (Jn. 13:26–27). The obstinacy in which he becomes hardened shuts him off from Jesus and surrenders him to Satan.

Conscious of our weakness and of the incessant risks in our lives, what ought we to do, if not pray? "My eyes are ever towards the Lord: for he shall pluck my feet out of the snare" (Ps. 24:15). Our frailty, like our love, impels us: we must pray without ceasing.

St. Paul tells us so in the text we have just read: if we live according to the flesh, we shall die; if by the spirit we mortify the works of the flesh, we shall live, "for whoever are led by the Spirit of God, they are the sons of God." This decisive option between death and life is not settled once and for all. Continually menaced by the flesh and the devil, it must be continually renewed, under the influence of the Spirit, by our free will. And it is at this price that we are sons of God. But it is impossible, without prayer, to rest continually under the motion of the Spirit: if He urges us to act for God, He urges us first of all to pray to God, and we cannot remain docile to His motion if we shut our hearts to prayer.

We have no trouble recognizing in this urgent necessity of ours the effect of a divine will: God uses our very frailty to form us in the filial life. Such intimate relations as children have with their parents are created and developed by the dependency of their living: at birth, they have received everything from their parents; and, as long as they cannot support themselves, they must continually ask for and receive the food which sustains their physical existence and the affection and human experience which carry them along and guide them in life. Children of God, we have received all from Him at baptism, and we shall always live by His graces.[8] Never shall we be able to suffice for ourselves. This

---

[8] On this essential dependency of man with regard to God, we like to read St. Irenaeus: "If even in this created world, there are some things which God reserves for Himself and other things which our knowledge can attain, is it surprising that, among the questions which Scripture raises, when the whole of Scripture is spiritual, there are some which we can resolve with the grace of God, but there are some also which are reserved to God,

subjection which we have gazed at in the Child Jesus is the law of our life, forever. This is what recalls to us the commandment of prayer; this is what renders it so burdensome to pride, so sweet to filial love.

The Christian who is docile to the teachings of Jesus has no trouble yielding to this law of prayer. He knows that God watches over him like a father, that not a hair can fall from his head but that He looks out for it; he knows, too, that the Father wants His child to have recourse to Him and to invoke Him in trustful prayer. It is in this trust that we are encouraged by the instructions of Our Lord: a man awakened in the dead of night by his friend, refuses to get up; let the friend but insist, and he will have all that he asks for: "And I say to you, ask, and it shall be given to you; seek, and you shall find; knock, and it shall be opened to you. For everyone who asks receives; and he who seeks finds; and to him who knocks it shall be opened" (Lk. 11:9–10). And, having recourse again to daily experience, Jesus emphasizes the point: "If one of you asks his father for a loaf, will he hand him a stone? or for a fish, will he for a fish hand him a serpent? or if he asks for an egg, will he hand him a scorpion? Therefore, if you, evil as you are, know how to give good gifts to your children, how much more will your heavenly Father give the Good Spirit to those who ask him!" [9]

This is what our prayer ought to be—an act of trust, and also of filial regard. Our Lord has told us in His Sermon on the Mount, "Your Father knows what you need before you ask him" (Mt. 6:8). We have nothing to teach Him, but we have everything to ask from Him; it is our duty and our happiness: we are His children, we want to receive all from His hand.

---

not only in this world, but even in the future world, so that God has always to teach, and man has always to learn from God?" (*Adv. Haer.,* II, 28, 2–3; cf. *Histoire du Dogme de la Trinité,* II, 538.)

[9] *Ibid.,* 11–13. On another occasion, Jesus clarifies the same lesson by the example of the godless judge: he feared neither God nor men; and yet, overcome by the importunities of a widow, he did her justice: "And will not God avenge his elect, who cry to him day and night? . . . I tell you that he will avenge them quickly" (Lk. 18:7, 8).

Here, especially, our model is the Son of God. This world, wherein He dwells, is His heritage; He can say to His Father, "And thine are mine" (Jn. 17:10). First-born of creation, He did not enter this domain except as its King. He is life; he can by His own power resurrect whom He will. From His sacred body there goes forth a power that heals all sicknesses (Lk. 6:19). And yet all these powers of healing and resurrecting He wishes to exercise only in dependence on His Father. Before His most striking miracle, the resurrection of Lazarus, He will pray, "Father, I give thee thanks that thou hast heard me. Yet I knew that thou always hearest me; but because of the people who stand round, I spoke, that they may believe that thou hast sent me" (Jn. 11:41–42).

To that prayer of the Son of God, the Christian conforms his own and unites himself to it; he prays in the name of Jesus, relying on His all-powerful intercession.[10] And yet, above all personal desire, he repeats to the Father, "Thy will be done," and if that will of the Father is not conformable to the will of His child, the child repeats with Christ in the Garden, "Not what I will, but what thou willest" (Mk. 14:36).

Thus is formed and opened up that filial trust, at once so assured and so submissive. Certain theoreticians of prayer have wanted to reduce our relations towards God to an adoration, silent and without acts. This is a dream which belies the teaching of Our Lord and, quite as much, the conditions of our existence. As long as we are on earth, we are voyagers; our life, marked by the rhythm of time, must continually be renewed and enriched under penalty of perishing. To wish to reduce everything to a silent, peaceful contemplation, where one cannot distinguish any

---

[10] "Amen, amen, I say to you, he who believes in me, the works that I do he also shall do, and greater than these he shall do, because I am going to the Father. And whatever you ask in my name, that I will do, in order that the Father may be glorified in the Son. If you ask me anything in my name, I will do it" (Jn. 14:12–14). "If you abide in me, and if my words abide in you, ask whatever you will and it shall be done to you" (Jn. 15:7).

succession of acts—this is to want to transport onto earth the intuitive vision which will make us live in the eternity of the very life of God. We tend there by desire, by effort, and especially by prayer.[11] This is the teaching of the saints; it is, above all, that of Our Lord in His Gospel.

2. THANKSGIVING

The same filial spirit which animates prayer gives rise also to thanksgiving. The first canticles which the Gospel presents to us are cries of gratitude: the *Benedictus,* the *Magnificat,* the *Nunc Dimittis.* The great prayer of the Christian will be the Eucharist. We bless God for all His benefits, for His creation, His providence, above all, for the mission of His divine Son, for His incarnation, birth, life, death, resurrection and ascension, for the gift of the Spirit which fructifies the Church and remits sins. And all these benefits appear to us in this living memorial which the Son of God has left us, and which is the Eucharist.

This institution governs the whole of Christian worship and imprints on it its character; this is the same teaching which Jesus gives us in the Gospel, and St. Paul in his Epistles. When Jesus cured the ten lepers, only one returned to Him to bless God; Jesus replied, "Were not the ten made clean? But where are the nine? Has no one been found to return and give glory to God except this foreigner?" And he said to him, "Arise, go thy way, for thy faith has saved thee" (Lk. 17:17–19). "Even today," says St. Bernard, upon recalling this narrative, "we see many

[11] We might recall here that definition of prayer by St. Jeanne de Chantal in her conference on the excellence of prayer: Prayer is "the way by which we ask of God and of Jesus Christ, who is our sole liberator, that He save us, because we feel in ourselves such great movements of infirmity that, if He did not sustain us at every moment by new graces, we would perish" (*Entretiens,* XXX, Paris, 1875, p. 323. Cf. *Saint Jane Frances Frémyot de Chantal. Her Exhortations, Conferences, Instructions and Retreats,* tr. from the French ed. printed at Paris in 1875, Chicago, Loyola Univ. Press, 1928).

people asking, with importunity, for what they need; but we find very few of them who know how to give fitting thanks for benefits received." [12]

This ingratitude deprives God of His glory; it deprives the Christian of his life. God's benefits were only the foreshadowings of more valuable graces; by attaching himself through gratitude to his benefactor, the child of God is assured the help of this infinite liberality seeking only to pour itself out. If he turns away from it, he falls back into his need and into his pride.

During the whole ministry of Jesus, this gratefulness is quite rare and quite brief; the canticles which rise up around His crib find no more echo: Mary, Zachary, the shepherds, and Simeon extol the glory of God, the light and peace poured out on the earth, the redemption of Israel, the exaltation of the humble and the poor. These great religious themes are scarcely seen any longer in the eyes of those crowds often milling around Jesus: "Amen, amen, I say to you, you seek me, not because you have seen signs, but because you have eaten of the loaves and have been filled" (Jn. 6:26). The miracle is utilized, it is not understood: if any prospect yawns before these enthusiastic crowds, it is that of the restoration of the Davidic monarchy, the reestablishment of the kingdom of Israel. Sometimes, especially in the eyes of the apostles, more lofty views are discovered: they are moved with a deep feeling of adoration and of fear,[13] or even, as at Caesarea Philippi (Mt. 16:16) or on Thabor (Mt. 17:4, 6), by a revelation which suddenly transforms their faith. But even then, we do not see in them the peaceful, radiant thanksgiving of the *Magnificat,* the *Benedictus,* the *Nunc Dimittis.*

We must wait for Pentecost to find again these outpourings of the Holy Spirit, and henceforth they will no longer be only promises, but the apparition of a new life. The apostolic Church is resplendent with this light; joy and thanksgiving overflow from Christian hearts; that from the time of the first narratives of the Acts:

[12] *In Cantica, Sermo XXVII,* 6. *P.L.,* CLXXXIII, 615.
[13] For example, on the occasion of the miraculous draught of fishes (Lk. 5:8) or of the walking on the waters (Mt. 14:33).

Continuing daily with one accord in the temple, and breaking bread in their houses, they took their food with gladness and simplicity of heart, praising God and being in favor with all the people (2:46–47).

They departed from the presence of the Sanhedrin, rejoicing that they had been counted worthy to suffer disgrace for the name of Jesus (5:41).

And likewise frequently in the Epistles of St. Paul; for example:

Be filled with the Spirit, speaking to one another in psalms and hymns and spiritual songs, singing and making melody in your hearts to the Lord, giving thanks always for all things in the name of our Lord Jesus Christ to God the Father (Eph. 5:18–20).

And so many times later on in the Acts of the martyrs; for example, in the supreme prayer of St. Polycarp:

O Lord God, O Almighty, Father of Thy beloved and blessed Son Jesus Christ, through whom we have received the knowledge of you—*God of angels and hosts and all creation*—and of the whole race of saints who live under your eyes! I bless Thee, because Thou hast seen fit to bestow upon me this day and this hour, that I may share, among the number of the martyrs, the cup of Thy Anointed and rise to eternal life, both in soul and in body, in virtue of the immortality of the Holy Spirit. May I be accepted among them in Thy sight today as a rich and pleasing sacrifice, such as Thou, the true God that cannot utter a falsehood, hast prearranged, revealed in advance, and now consummated. And therefore I praise Thee for everything; I bless Thee; I glorify Thee through the eternal and heavenly High Priest Jesus Christ, Thy beloved Son, through whom be glory to Thee together with Him and the Holy Spirit, both now and for the ages yet to come. Amen.[14]

The most ancient Christian prayers have the same emphasis: a cry of filial gratitude and joy.[15]

[14] *The Martyrdom of St. Polycarp* (ACW 6), p. 97.
[15] St. Clement of Rome (*Ep. ad Cor.*, LIX–LXI, and in tr. ACW 1, pp. 45–47), and the morning hymns: the φῶς ἱλαρόν, and the evening ones: the *Gloria in excelsis*. Cf. *Histoire de Dogme de la Trinité*, II, pp. 220–222.

❖❖❖❖❖❖❖❖❖

The Life of Union with God in Jesus Christ

1. THE REVELATION OF GOD IN JESUS CHRIST

This life of prayer which develops in the soul, penetrated entirely with adoration, desire and gratitude, gradually fosters a very close intimacy between the Christian and God. It is this intimacy which we must study more closely.

"This is everlasting life, that they may know thee, the only true God, and him whom thou hast sent, Jesus Christ" (Jn.17: 3). Here Jesus reveals to us the beatitude to which He calls us and which is the end of all our efforts and all our desires: it is the knowledge of God and of Jesus Christ. Here we do not have two objects to distinguish, unequal and successively attained, Jesus Christ, whom we would go beyond to reach the Father. There is only one act of knowledge, only one beatitude—the possession of God. The beatific vision clearly distinguishes therein the divine Persons; but it sees also that among them the nature is single and that consequently there are no inequalities at all in them; they radiate from the same holiness. They are equally inaccessible to us, naturally speaking; they are revealed only by a grace which is an effect of love.

The Son, splendor of the Father, is made man; He has come to reveal to us both Himself and His Father: "No one has at any time seen God. The only-begotten Son, who is in the bosom of the Father, he has revealed him" (Jn. 1:18). He reveals Him to us by His teaching; He reveals Him to us better still by the intimate manifestation of Himself which He accords us. This is what Jesus, at the Last Supper, taught St. Philip: to the apostle who said to Him, "Lord, show us the Father and it is enough for us," He replied, "Have I been so long a time with you, and you have not known me? Philip, he who sees me sees also the Father. How canst thou say, 'Show us the Father'? Dost thou not believe that I am in the Father and the Father in me? . . . Otherwise believe because of the works themselves" (Jn. 14:8–10, 12).

This teaching of Our Lord determines the whole of the Christian's spiritual life: the Son of God will never be for him an intermediary which he may thrust aside or go beyond. Between man and God there is a chasm; but over that chasm God's love has extended the holy humanity of His Son. Through Him and through Him alone we can have access to God.[1]

The reason for this economy of divine revelation has been grasped in its depths by St. Irenaeus:

The Son shows God to men and He presents man to God; He safeguards the invisibility of the Father, so that man does not come to despise God, and so that he might always have to draw nearer to Him; and, on the other hand, He shows to men, by many means, God visible, so that man might not lose his being by being separated from God. For the glory of God is the life of man, and the life of man is the vision of God. And if, by showing Himself by means of creation, God gives life to all those living on earth, with how much greater rea-

[1] Eph. 2:13. The metaphor of the chasm and bridge is dear to St. Catherine of Siena, who often proposes it to us in her *Dialogue* (ch. XXI and LI, ff.). Cf. *Treatise on Purgatory* and the *Dialogue,* London, Sheed & Ward, 1946.

son the manifestation of the Father which is effected by the Word gives life to those who see God.[2]

This revelation must be brought by Him who is the "splendor of the Father"; it must reach us under the veil of that humanity which tones down its brightness. Finally, and above all, this knowledge of Him who, by nature, is the Son of God ought to make of us, by grace, sons of God. God would not appear to us only in His relations with men, in His inaccessible transcendency of Creator; He would be revealed in the Person of the Son completely orientated towards the Father. We could not know the Son without knowing Him as Son, without being caught up by Him in that love of the Father which is His whole life.

Also, the only words addressed by the Father to the disciples of Jesus are the words of the Transfiguration: "This is my beloved Son, in whom I am well pleased; hear him" (Mt.17:5). St. John of the Cross has given an unforgettable commentary on these words; he recalls the text of the Epistle to the Hebrews (1:1) and adds:

Herein the Apostle declares that God has become, as it were, dumb, and has no more to say, since that which He spake aforetime, in part, to the prophets, He has now spoken altogether in Him, giving us the All, which is His Son. Wherefore he that would now enquire of God, or seek any vision or revelation, would not only be acting foolishly, but would be committing an offence against God, by not setting his eyes altogether upon Christ, and seeking no new thing or aught beside. And God might answer him after this manner, saying: If I have spoken all things to thee in My Word, Which is My Son, and I have no other word, what answer can I now make to thee, or what can I reveal to thee which is greater than this? Set thine eyes on Him alone, for in Him I have spoken and revealed to thee all things, and in Him thou shalt find yet more than that which thou askest and desirest . . . For since that day when I descended upon Him with My Spirit on Mount Tabor, saying: *Hic est filius meus dilectus, in quo mihi bene complacui, ipsum audite* (which is to say: This is My Beloved Son, in Whom I am well pleased; hear ye Him), I have left off all these manners of teaching and answering, and I have entrusted

[2] *Adv. Haer.,* IV, 20, 7. *P.G.,* VII, 1037; cf. *ibid,* IV, 6, 3–7, 987; *Histoire du Dogme de la Trinité,* II, pp. 590 ff.

this to Him. Hear Him; for I have no more faith to reveal, neither have I any more things to declare. For, if I spake aforetime, it was to promise Christ; and, if they enquired of Me, their enquiries were directed to petitions for Christ and expectancy concerning Him, in Whom they should find every good thing . . . but now, any who would enquire of Me after that manner, and desire Me to speak to him or reveal aught to him, would in a sense be asking Me for Christ again, and asking Me for more faith, and be lacking in faith, which has already been given in Christ. . . .[3]

Here, indeed, is the meaning of the Gospel: the Son has brought to us a total and definitive revelation; we have nothing more to expect from another; and this revelation is absolutely necessary for us: "No one comes to the Father but through me" (Jn.14:6). We shall dismiss, then, the example of a "holy man," recounted in the *Institutions* of Tauler:

It happened one day as he was weeping with an abundance of tears, that two angels appeared to console him. He said these words: "O Lord, my God, I do not ask for any consolation, and I shall be happy enough if I can guard the place where You dwell in my soul, so that no one besides Yourself ever enters and appears there." At these words, he was surrounded with so great a light that it is impossible to find the terms to express it; and the heavenly Father said to him: "I shall give you My Son, so that He might ever accompany you wherever you may be." "No, my God," replied this holy man, "I desire to dwell in You and in Your very essence." Then the heavenly Father answered him: "You are My beloved son, in whom I have placed all my affection." [4]

In this text we recognize the neo-Platonic mysticism which has at times contaminated Rhenish mysticism. From this source comes the ambition which has seemed so fascinating to certain minds: to remove every intermediary, not only the angels,[5] but

[3] *Ascent of Mount Carmel*, II, 22, 4–5, in *Complete Works*.
[4] *Institutions*, ch. I. Cf. *The Sermons and Conferences of John Tauler, of the Order of Preachers, surnamed "the illuminated doctor"; being his spiritual doctrine*, tr. by W. Elliot, Brookland Station, Washington, D.C., Apostolic Mission House, 1910.
[5] Here is seen a pride which is opposed to the Gospel: the Son of God did not spurn the angel of the Agony (Lk. 22:43).

even the Son, so as to dwell in God's essence. This is to fail to recognize the whole order of supernatural revelation: the only way which leads to the Father is the Son; it is in Him that we have been adopted. If we brush Him aside, we are no more than creatures and sinners, standing before the most holy God, who dwells in inaccessible light.[6]

The life of union with God, such as it appears to us in the Gospel, is governed entirely by this supreme law. Jesus has said, "I am the way, and the truth, and the life" (Jn.14:6). From the time He appears in this world, privileged souls whom God has chosen for Himself, hasten to Christ and rejoice in His light. The spirit of Christ is poured forth on His elect, and on the earth —silent for so long a time—there resound the first Christian canticles: the *Magnificat,* the *Benedictus,* the *Nunc Dimittis.* There is an outpouring of graces which already causes a foreshadowing of Pentecost; these are the first fruits of the Messianic era. The first one to be filled with these graces is the Mother of Jesus; then John the Baptist and Elizabeth, at the visit of Mary; St. Joseph, enlightened by an angel; then the shepherds, Simeon and Anna, the Magi. We have tried to follow, in the hidden life of Our Lord and in the baptism, the progress of these graces in Mary and in John the Baptist. Here we do not have to resume that study, but only to underline one or two of its traits.

The first and most manifest is that the source of all these graces is Jesus. In all these narratives we see no religious life which does not tend towards Him, which does not live by Him. After a long wait and many prayers, He whom all were calling for finally appears, gives Himself to them and fills all their desires. All can repeat the words of the Psalmist: "What have I in heaven, and besides thee what do I desire on earth?

---

[6] The problem of the mediation of the Son of God is often presented under a different form; without wishing to thrust aside this essential mediation, a certain number of mystics have thought that the humanity of Christ had to be surpassed, the soul beholding in Our Lord only His divine nature. We shall see below (p. 248) that Christ's humanity, which is for the docile disciple a valuable help, can become for him who stops there an obstacle.

. . . Thou art the God of my heart, and the God that is my portion for ever" (Ps. 72:25, 26). This is the meaning of Simeon's *Nunc Dimittis*.

And these first revelations have a character of total illumination which we shall not find again for a long time in the Gospel. This is particularly evident in the holy Virgin: she is full of grace; she is open to the divine revelation with a purity and an ardor of desire which no other creature has ever shown. In Simeon and Anna, God wanted to crown the long expectation, the long prayers of a whole lifetime. By a heroic training in penance and silence St. John the Baptist purchased the signal grace of a meeting with Our Lord. And then for the Precursor, as for Simeon and Anna, this great grace marks the supreme stage of a life which is drawing to a close; in just a few months, the sword of the executioner will cut off that noble flower blooming under the first gaze of Jesus. In the apostles, on the contrary, the first impressions will appear less profound, but the soul will be strengthened slowly on contact with Jesus, during several years' time.

We shall endeavor to follow this formation through its laborious stages. But before retracing the progress, it will be useful to consider in the story of Christ's ministry, other meetings which themselves are also full of instruction: in the apostles we shall see the conduct of the Master gradually penetrating the souls of the disciples and transforming them; in sinners, we shall see the grace of Our Lord purifying their souls and uniting them to Himself. This grace will not ordinarily appear to us in its progressive development; more often than not, we shall be able to grasp only its decisive phase. But such brief scenes as these are revealing.

2. THE SAVIOR AND SINNERS

It is in the house of a pitiless Pharisee that the mercy of the Savior is first revealed (Lk. 7:36–50).

Jesus accepts the invitation of Simon. A woman sinner, known as such in the town, hears of Him and comes to Him. She comes there, to the home of the Pharisee, she whom all condemn; she presents herself as a sinner, to make reparation. She approaches Jesus and, having taken her place behind, near His feet, she breaks out in sobs and begins to bathe the feet of Jesus with her tears, wipes them with her hair, kisses them, and anoints them with a fragrant oil. She came well provided with a token of respect, but on entering she had been seized with a fit of sobbing; she thinks only of her sorrow and of her love.

"Why have we fasted, and thou hast not regarded: have we humbled our souls, and thou hast not taken notice?" (Is. 58:3).

Jesus is silent, and yet He fails not to notice these gestures of repentance which He will soon recognize publicly; and already He backs her up, and she feels herself forgiven, and love impels her: "Her sins, many as they are, shall be forgiven her, because she has loved much." Who can tell what her love was on hearing these words? Who can tell her sorrow? To have offended so good a God! To have wounded so merciful a Savior! The heart seemed closed, hard as stone; sorrow has opened it and has caused to gush forth from it that fount of love which will never dry up:

> *Quo fonte manavit nefas*
> *fluent perennes lacrimae,*
> *si virga paenitentiae*
> *cordis rigorem conterat.*

We have the same revelation in the reconciliation of the prodigal son (Lk. 15:11–32): the shame of his fall, the pain of his poverty and hunger have put him in mind of his paternal home and hearth, open even to mercenaries. He returns; his father runs down to meet him and does not let him finish his confession but falls on his neck and kisses him. In that hour of pardon, there is a new intimacy between God and His repentant child. It is truly a second baptism, when the soul, if it is completely sincere and generous, is aware of the freshness of recovered innocence, of new-born filial love.

Let us recall again the reconciliation of the adulteress, alone with Jesus (Jn. 8:1–11): the accusers, the judges, have gone away, abandoning their prey. The Savior stands alone with the sinner. The soul gives herself to God with a humility, a gratitude, a tenderness she did not suspect until then. This first emotion will pass; but, if the sinner perseveres in humility, repentance and gratitude, she will be able to go on tasting the recollection and intimacy of this union with God.

And, at the same time, she feels lighting up within herself a new flame: her life, which until then was sterile and knew only the enjoyment of sin, will become fruitful and dedicated. Thus the woman with five husbands, encountered near Jacob's well, "left her water-jar and went away into the town, and said to the people, 'Come and see a man who has told me all that I have ever done. Can he be the Christ?' " (Jn. 4:28–29). Thus the man possessed by a whole legion of impure spirits: delivered by Jesus, he entreated Him that he might remain with Him; Christ sent him back to his own relatives: " 'Tell them all that the Lord has done for thee, and how he has had mercy on thee.' And he departed, and began to publish in the Decapolis all that Jesus had done for him" (Mk. 5:19–20).

Of all the conversions, the most touching is undoubtedly that of the good thief: a criminal, justly condemned by men, and who on his cross seems cursed by God. Like the other thief, he joins in the blasphemies and insults of the Pharisees; and then, of a sudden, grace breaks through this closed soul and fills it with humility and faith: "Dost thou not even fear God," he said to the other condemned man, "seeing that thou art under the same sentence? And we indeed justly, for we are receiving what our deeds deserved; but this man has done nothing wrong." And in a supreme effort, he adds, "Lord, remember me when thou comest into thy kingdom." And Jesus said to him, "Amen I say to thee, this day thou shalt be with me in paradise" (Lk. 23:40–43). For the first time, a sinner feels the blood of Christ falling on his cross. All is appeased; already this is paradise.[7]

---

[7] Here one might read the story of St. Catherine and the two condemned men of Siena. These two brigands were driven on their carts through the streets of Siena; the executioners tortured them with red-hot iron pincers. The wretched men had refused to confess; they blasphemed God and the

This conversion of the thief, passing thus from Calvary to Paradise, is a miracle of grace wrought by the Cross. We can only marvel at it and thank God for it. It would be rash to promise ourselves for the last hour a similar conversion; the warnings of Jesus in the Gospel show us that, more often than not, death does no more than render definitive the option to which we have pledged our lives.[8]

The other conversions which we contemplate in the Gospel take hold of some sinners in the midst of their course and imprint on them a new direction towards God. We would like to be able to follow them on this path and be assured that they have not deviated from it. The apocryphal writings have tried to satisfy the pious curiosity of the faithful, making of Zachary a bishop of Caesarea and of Mary Magdalen the confidante of Our Lord's revelations.[9] Sometimes, on the contrary, we see a conversion

---

saints. St. Catherine, nonetheless, prayed for them. Suddenly they were seen to ask for a priest, confess their sins, praise God and blame themselves. The bystanders were dumbfounded: "The executioners themselves relented and, confronted with such contrition, no longer dared to continue with their tortures."

Do we not recognize the divine mercy in this passage? It waits only for our contrition in order to let us off. We can compare with this account the recollections of Jacques Rivière in *A la trace de Dieu*, Paris, *Nouvelle revue française*, 1925, and Gallimard, 1939, pp. 274–275: "At the time when worries I was suffering from threatened to turn my heart and poison me, they stopped, by some peculiar miracle or other. And I found out that this happened every time that I used to accept the threat of them with good dispositions, with a submissive heart, loving, hoping. That seemed to daunt them. God was satisfied, then, with indicating the trial; He withdrew it at once; He caused me to be rid of it."

[8] This is the meaning of the urgent exhortations to vigilance: Christians must always have their loins girt and their lamps lit, like the servants awaiting the return of their Master (Lk. 12:35–38; Mt. 24:42), like the virgins awaiting the arrival of the spouse (Mt. 25:1–13); they must continually be on the alert, like the man wishing to defend his house against the thief (Lk. 12:39).

One can read St. Catherine of Siena's *Dialogue*, ch. XXXVII, on the death of the sinner, and ch. XLIV on the death of the sinner and the death of the just.

[9] *Evangile de Marie-Madeleine* (cf. *Histoire du Dogme de la Trin.*, II, p. 119).

which seemed sincere yield before fresh temptations; this is, apparently, the case with Simon the Magician.[10] Here we can only repeat the words of Our Lord: "The last state of that man becomes worse than the first" (Mt. 12:45). The long experience of the Church warns us, indeed, that in the whole course of life man is exposed to relapses, no matter what the sincerity of the first conversion.

To converts, as to the newly-baptized, the first fruits of the Christian life often bring an impetus, a gladness, a freshness which gives them an inkling of a new life. And this presentiment is not false; God wills that these valuable gifts lead the neophyte and the converted sinner to maturity in Christ. All do not reach that goal; in the case of more than one the fervor of the first days slackens, and the soul falls again. Thus Marcion, scarcely converted, gives 200,000 sesterces to the Roman community, but soon he is led astray by his dreams and his ambition. He defects and founds a new sect.

Without going as far as apostasy, many new converts let themselves be recaptured by their old weaknesses. The attraction of Christian truths and virtues no longer has the allure of novelty, and the soul, no longer feeling their attractiveness, finds the obligations imposed on her by her new faith burdensome. The automation of old habits reacts and solicits the will which is too much accustomed to yield to them. And then, if the soul whom God weans and from whom He asks a staunch effort, does not take by means of prayer His help in grace, she soon feels discouraged; Christian practise, but lately pursued eagerly and generously, is reduced to a minimum, and faith secures no more than a sterile adherence which soon withers and dies.

It would be easy to pick out in the Epistles of St. Paul, particularly in those to the Corinthians and Galatians, traces of these infirmities which were so grievous to the Apostle, so dangerous to his Christians. And the *Shepherd* of Hermas would confirm them

[10] To the grave reproaches of St. Peter, he replied, "Do you pray for me to the Lord, that nothing of what you have said may happen to me" (Acts 8:24). This fear could lead him to conversion; the sequence of his life shows him, on the contrary, a deadly enemy of the Christian preaching.

by what it reveals to us of the Roman community and its weaknesses.

But besides these weak and poorly converted sinners, there are those who have yielded completely to grace; the conduct of the Savior appears to them in all its power, mercy and wisdom. The past remains present to their recollection, not at all worrisome or in such detail as would prove unhealthy,[11] but in a general view which keeps them in a state of mind that is untroubled and full of trust in their Savior. They repeat with St. Paul, "Jesus Christ came into the world to save sinners, of whom I am the chief. But for this reason I obtained mercy, that in me first Christ Jesus might show forth all patience, as an example to those who shall believe in him for the attainment of life everlasting" (1 Tim. 1:15–16).

Thus, until the end of his life, the Apostle will acknowledge his past; and this confession will be not only an act of humility, but above all an act of love and gratitude. God has been lavish with grace in his regard, and this grace has not been unproductive; but this is the work and glory of God, so that whoever is glorified, is glorified in the Lord. The more abundant this grace, the brighter will be the light and consequently the more clearly will man recognize that his salvation comes, not from himself, but from the Savior who ransomed him and each day preserves him.

Even in heaven we shall not forget Him. The immense happiness of being united with God, of knowing Him as we are known, will appear to us as acquired by the blood of the Son of God; we shall love to repeat eternally to Him that we are His redeemed and that we belong to Him:

Worthy art thou to take the scroll and to open its seals; for thou wast slain, and hast redeemed us for God with thy blood, out of every tribe and tongue and people and nation, and hast made them for our God a kingdom and priests (Apoc. 5:9–10).

Thus is consummated eternally that union between man and his Savior. The joy of conversion gave an inkling of its intimacy, and

[11] Cf. St. Catherine of Siena, *Dialogue,* ch. LXVI.

at first we experienced especially the forgiveness of sin, the cancellation of the debt. Then, in proportion as the light grows brighter, we distinguish this new life which the death of Our Lord communicates to us; henceforth, He appears to us as our "inseparable life." [12] This is the foretaste of paradise.

3. THE MASTER AND HIS DISCIPLES

The conversions we have studied revealed to us the close relations created between the Savior and the sinner by contrition and pardon. But this intimacy appeared to us in an episode, decisive undoubtedly but isolated, whose preparation and fruits we are, most of the time, unable to know.

It is quite otherwise with the relations which we must study now between the Master and His disciples. We perceive them throughout all the Gospel narratives, and a little attention suffices to discern their birth, their progress—which is at times rapid, at other times uncertain and laborious—and finally their blossoming.

What strikes us at first is the sovereign role which, from the first day, the Master assumes in the lives of His disciples: "He who does not take up his cross and follow me is not worthy of me" (Mt. 10:38); "If anyone wishes to come after me, let him deny himself, and take up his cross, and follow me" (Mt. 16:24); "He who does not carry his cross and follow me, cannot be my disciple" (Lk. 14:27); "If anyone serve me, let him follow me; and where I am there also shall my servant be" (Jn. 12:26). We already perceive, in these moral precepts, the theological background which the final talks will reveal: "I am the way, and the truth, and the life" (Jn. 14:6). Salvation and, with greater reason, Christian perfection, can be conceived of only as a life united to Christ and by Him carried along in His path.

It is not only the disciple whom Jesus wishes thus to form, it is the apostle; He has in view not only a man's moral and religious elevation, but his preparation for the role He reserves for him in the conversion of Israel and of the world. The men on

[12] St. Ignatius of Antioch, *To the Ephesians*, III, 2 (ACW 1), p. 61.

whom He calls for assistance will be not only bearers of His message, but companions and witnesses of His life. This trait has in His thought and in that of His apostles such an importance, that, when there is question of replacing, in the apostolic college, the wretched man who was a traitor, they require the new apostle to be "of these men who have been in our company all the time that the Lord Jesus moved among us, from John's baptism until the day that he was taken up from us" (Acts 1:21–22).

None of Jesus' disciples can foresee what Our Lord will ask of him and, much less, what He will give to him. To all Jesus could say what He said to Nathanael, "Greater things than these shalt thou see" (Jn. 1:50); and later on, to St. Peter: "What I do thou knowest not now; but thou shalt know hereafter" (Jn. 13:7). In the course of that slow formation of the apostles, we shall be ever aware of the patience of the Master, reserving for later the revelation of secrets still too divine for their weakness (Jn. 16:13), but giving them an inkling, from the first, of those prospects which He has them gradually glimpse and then desire.

What carries them along, by those roads they are ignorant of, towards that end which is unknown to them, is the knowledge and love of the Master, who gradually reveals Himself to them: "No one can come to me unless the Father who sent me draw him" (Jn. 6:44). This first step has been inspired by the Father; He it is who has given a decisive force to the words of John the Baptist: "Behold the lamb of God" (Jn. 1:36), or to the promise of Jesus: "I will make you fishers of men" (Mk. 1:17). They have come, they have stayed. When recalling his first recollection, the apostle St. John gives us still the vivid impression of that timid step when he pledged his whole life: " 'Rabbi . . . where dwellest thou?' 'Come and see.' They came and saw where he was staying; and they stayed with him that day. It was about the tenth hour" (Jn. 1:38–39). That is all. The next day, Andrew, the companion of John, says to his brother Simon, "We have found the Messias" (Jn. 1:41), and he leads him to Jesus, who looks at him and says to him, "Thou art Simon, the son of John; thou shalt be called Cephas (which interpreted is Peter)" (*ibid.*, 42). At that time, no doubt, they believed themselves already at the goal; it was only the first step. Eighteen months will elapse before the solemn confession of St. Peter: "Thou art the Christ, the Son of the living God" (Mt. 16:16), and it will need a revelation from the Father.

A new stage is marked by the miraculous draught of fishes (Lk. 5:1–11). There again we meet, next to Jesus, those fishing companions whom we saw as disciples of John the Baptist. After a laborious, fruitless night, they see Jesus coming to them. The Master climbs into the boat and says to Simon and Andrew, "Put out into the deep, and lower your nets for a catch." They obey, and the catch is so plentiful that they have to call John and James to come and help them. Seeing the two boats laden with fish to the point of bursting, Peter falls down at Jesus' feet, exclaiming, "Depart from me, for I am a sinful man, O Lord."

The vocations of the apostles arise in very diverse circumstances: in the company of St. John the Baptist, on the banks of the Jordan, on the lake shore, in a fishing boat or in a customhouse; the call is always the same: "Follow me." The past of these men, their social situation, even their moral preparation—everything is different. Apparently in the eyes of the Master all this is of no consequence; He asks for one thing only: a good will which gives itself to Him without reserve. What does He want of them? That they follow Him. What will they do in His company? What He will tell them to do day by day. Above all, they will share His life, see Him in action, hear Him teach.

By no means is this a clerical school, a seminary, where one learns the sacred sciences while receiving the training in life which holy Church asks of its clerics; nor is it a novitiate, where one is penetrated with the spirit of a religious order while conforming oneself to its spiritual methods and its asceticism. The setting is neither a house nor a chapel; it is Galilee, which they roam with no preconceived plan, with no other end than the evangelization of the people they will meet. The sole but sovereignly efficacious means of formation is the company of the Master: "Follow me."

It is not unprofitable, if we wish to have a good understanding of this method, to recall the formation which the prophets, and later the teachers of the Law, impose on those who wish to become their disciples. The distance, no doubt, is infinite between Christ Our Lord and the jurists whose memory has been preserved for us by the Talmud; but the divine Master deigned to use the traditions which He already found familiar to His people and which He quickened with His spirit. What He retained of them is the continual contact which the master had with his disciples, whereby He willed to render still more tangible the reality of His Incarnation. Far from isolating Himself among men, He mingled with them like yeast in dough, and it is thus that He transformed mankind.[13]

The Jewish law as interpreted by the rabbis was so detailed that a theoretical instruction could not suffice for a schooling in it. The young man who put himself at the feet of a teacher was attached to him in order to serve him in everything; but, at the same time, he watched him and stamped on his memory the solution of innumerable cases of conscience which daily life tended to raise. To succeed in this, the studious disciple let no gesture, no word of the master escape. We understand what a constraint Our Lord imposed on Himself by calling the apostles to follow Him: except for the time He reserves for prayer, He will no longer have in His life a single moment of solitude.

Besides, this new Master, so independent with regard to the Pharisees and the Scribes, is observed not only by disciples who wish to understand Him, but also by adversaries who wish to destroy Him.[14]

[13] On the formation which the rabbis prescribed for their disciples, one may read Medebielle, art. "Apostolat" in the *Supplément au Dictionnaire de la Bible,* t. I, col. 550 ff.

[14] They notice that some of Jesus' disciples are eating without washing their hands: "Why do not thy disciples walk according to the tradition of the ancients?" And Jesus replies, "There is nothing outside a man that, entering into him, can defile him; but the things that come out of a man, these are what defile a man" (Mk. 7:1–5, 15). Another day: "Why does your master eat and drink with publicans and sinners?" "It is not the healthy who need a physician, but they who are sick." "Why do the disciples of John and of the Pharisees fast, whereas thy disciples do not fast?" "Can the wedding guests fast as long as the bridegroom is with them?"

This community of life has been for the Son of God a servitude; but it has also been a great force: by living under the eyes of His disciples and by sharing their lives, He has been able to guide them in delicate cases of conscience of daily occurrence; and, above all, He has been revealed to them, and this revelation was the essence of His message. His role was not that of Moses, transmitting to men the will of God; it is the role of the Son of God, saying with sovereign authority, "You have heard that it was said . . . But I say to you . . ." (Mt. 5:21–47). He is the Legislator and the living law; He is also the supreme object of revelation: let us recall the last talk in the Cenacle: "Lord, show us the Father and it is enough for us." Jesus said to him, "Have I been so long a time with you, and you have not known me? Philip, he who sees me sees also the Father . . ." (Jn. 14:8–11).

We perceive, through these moving and profound words, the intimacy and sublimity of the mystery of the Son of God; we also discern the goal towards which this communal life is tending and, despite the daily efforts of Our Lord, the imperfection of the revelation: "Have I been so long a time with you, and you have not known me?" Here no human words can suffice: there is needed in a docile soul that enlightenment of divine grace which causes to appear, in the treasure of daily experiences, the latent truth for which the soul thirsts and which, nevertheless, it is incapable of disengaging. The progress of this faith in St. Peter has been marked out by the Evangelists, and they allow us to discern the divine illumination.

There is, first of all, after the multiplication of the loaves of bread and the discourse on the bread of life, the Galilean crisis: in face of the desertion of the crowd, but lately so enthusiastic, Jesus says to the apostles, "Do you also wish to go away?" "Lord," replies Peter, "to whom shall we go? Thou hast the words of everlasting life" (Jn. 6:68–69). Divine grace makes

---

One Sabbath day, the disciples, while going through a field, plucked some corn to eat: "Why are they doing what is not lawful on the Sabbath?" "The Sabbath was made for man, and not man for the Sabbath. Therefore the Son of Man is Lord even of the Sabbath" (Mk. 2:16–28).

him more clearly conscious of the treasure he possesses, which temptation threatens. Soon afterwards, there is the decisive revelation of the Father, and the great confession: "Thou are the Christ, the Son of the living God" (Mt. 16:16). Eight days later, there is the Transfiguration: Peter, beside himself, exclaims, "It is good for us to be here!" The cloud overshadows him; the voice of the Father makes itself heard: "This is my beloved Son, in whom I am well pleased; hear him" (Mt. 17:1–5). On these two solemn occasions, at Caesarea Philippi and on Thabor, the prediction of Our Lord's Passion follows immediately the revelation of His divine filiation. These two great mysteries—of the sorrowful death of Christ and of His glory—are closely linked one with the other; they support and complement each other. Their revelation is reserved to the apostles, and even the revelation of Thabor is reserved to the three privileged ones who will be witnesses of the Agony. Thus, according as the revelation is more lofty, it calls for a greater docility, a closer intimacy with the Son of God. The apostles, and St. Peter in particular, have been prepared for it by their daily contact with the Master. Unconsciously, day by day, there is formed a treasury of admiration, gratitude, love, faith. This is the wood of the sacrifice; the fire of heaven has kindled it and caused to flare up therefrom that great light which illumines us even today.

We must admit, however, that during the lifetime of Jesus, the souls of the apostles are not yet fully luminous; we do not recognize in them the ideal which Jesus has proposed to us (Lk. 11:35–36): a light in which there is no more darkness. Right after the glorious confession of Caesarea Philippi, Jesus presented to Peter and to all the apostles the prospect of the Passion. They did not want to face up to it, and Peter strove to turn his Master away from it: "Far be it from thee, O Lord; this will never happen to thee." And Jesus answered him with painful severity, "Get behind me, satan, thou art a scandal to me; for thou dost not mind the things of God, but those of men" (Mt. 16:22–23).

Peter yields and is silent; the other apostles do the same. But their silence remains unsubmissive; the repeated predictions of

Jesus, on the day of the Transfiguration (Mt. 17:12, 21) and on the occasion of the trip from Jericho to Jerusalem (Mt. 20:18–19), will not bend this stubbornness at all.

The death of Jesus will break the hearts of the apostles and open them up to grace; then light will be diffused there in waves. Until then the highest graces will be only promises, the treasures entrusted to them, only deposits. When the Passion shall have fully converted them, the Holy Spirit will be poured forth in them, will recall to them and make them understand the discourses and the life of Jesus; and, faithful servants, they will draw from these treasures, and therefrom enrich all men.

"Thou dost not mind the things of God, but those of men": this grave warning given by Jesus to St. Peter reveals to us the obstacle which a single stubborn refusal can oppose to the divine light.

From this source arise the misunderstandings which separate Jesus from His people and, oftentimes, from His disciples themselves. One has only to recall, for example, the discussions carried on in the Temple, on the feast of Tabernacles:

Jesus therefore said to the Jews who had come to believe in him, "If you abide in my word, you shall be my disciples indeed, and you shall know the truth, and the truth shall make you free." "We are the children of Abraham, and we have never yet been slaves to anyone. How sayest thou, 'You shall be free'?" "Amen, amen, I say to you, everyone who commits sin is a slave to sin" (Jn. 8:31–34).

Do we not feel here that Christ and His hearers live in two different worlds, that He is from above, that they are from below? Likewise, with the apostles, near Jacob's well: "I have food to eat of which you do not know . . . My food is to do the will of him who sent me" (Jn. 4:32–34). Likewise, in the course of the lake crossing:

They had forgotten to bring bread, and they had but one loaf with them in the boat. And he began to charge them, saying, "Take heed; beware of the leaven of the Pharisees, and the leaven of Herod!" And they began to argue among themselves, saying, "We have no bread."

But Jesus knowing this, said to them, "Why do you argue that you have no bread? Do you not yet perceive, nor understand? Is your heart still blinded? Though you have eyes do you not see, and though you have ears do you not hear? And do you not remember? When I broke the five loaves among five thousand, how many baskets full of fragments did you take up?" They said to him, "Twelve." "And when I broke the seven loaves among four thousand, how many large baskets of fragments did you take up?" They said, "Seven." And he said to them, "How is it that you do not yet understand?" (Mk. 8:14–21).

This little incident has been retained by the three Synoptics; and indeed it is revealing: the preoccupations of the apostles are not those of Jesus: they remain encumbered by those cares of earth from which so much preaching, so many miracles, would have to free them. Their ambitions are as tenacious as their cares, which are, continually and up to the last day, the pursuit of the first places they dream of and beg for, and argue about (Mk. 9:33; 10:37; Lk. 9:46; 22:24). All this, despite the warnings, the reproaches, the example of the Master.

And the ambitions which they have for themselves, they also have for their Master: they endure with great difficulty and do not understand so humble a life as this, this care which Christ takes to defer the decisive revelations, to tone down the brilliancy of His miracles, to moderate the enthusiasm of the crowds. On the eve of the great feast of Tabernacles, His brethren say to Him, "Leave here and go into Judea that thy disciples also may see the works that thou dost; for no one does a thing in secret if he wants to be publicly known. If thou dost these things, manifest thyself to the world" (Jn. 7:3–4). After the Last Supper, St. Jude says again to Jesus, "Lord, how is it that thou art about to manifest thyself to us, and not to the world?" (Jn. 14:22).

To him who lets himself be stopped by these human horizons, the very humanity of Jesus can become an obstacle: to the eyes of faith it reveals the divinity; to human eyes, it obscures it. This is what Jesus Himself had to make the apostles understand at the Last Supper: "It is expedient for you that I depart. For if I do not go, the Advocate will not come to you; but if I go, I will send him to you" (Jn. 16:7). As long as Jesus lived among them, they followed Him only from afar; after His death, they were truly faithful to Him. This apparent enigma is the whole mystery of faith, which the mission of the Holy Spirit and His presence in souls illumines.

It is certain that the visible and tangible presence of Our Lord was an immense grace. Jesus Himself will recall this to the disciples who enjoy this happiness without understanding it: "Blessed are the eyes that see what you see! For I say to you, many prophets and kings have desired to see what you see, and they have not seen it; and to hear what you hear, and they have not heard it" (Lk. 10: 23–24). Is not this what Simeon had already sung: "Now thou dost dismiss thy servant, O Lord, according to thy word, in peace; because my eyes have seen thy salvation" (Lk. 2:29–30)?

All the desires of the faithful Jews are fulfilled; but why is it necessary to advise them of this? Simeon understood at once: "My eyes have seen thy salvation"; he has nothing more to wait for here below. The hearers to whom Jesus' announcement is addressed are less clear-sighted.

Among them, some are completely closed to the light; they are offended by what they see and hear. Thus the people of Nazareth: "Where did he get all this? What is this wisdom that is given to him? What mean such miracles wrought by his hands? Is not this the carpenter, the son of Mary, the brother of James, Joseph, Jude, and Simon? And are not also his sisters here with us?" (Mk. 6:2–3). We shall hear the same murmurings at Capharaum: "Yet we know where this man is from; but when the Christ comes, no one will know where he is from" (Jn. 7:27). From the first day, when Philip had said to Nathanael, "We have found him of whom Moses in the Law and the Prophets wrote, Jesus the son of Joseph of Nazareth," Nathanael had replied, "Can anything good come out of Nazareth?" (Jn. 1:45–46).

Apparently this very incarnation and the closed nature of its human setting are a motive for distrust: Him they know too well, He is from their village and from their family. To the Jews of Jerusalem, on the occasion of the feast of Tabernacles, Jesus replied, "You both know me, and know where I am from. Yet I have not come of myself, but he is true who has sent me, whom you do not know" (Jn. 7:28). It is necessary, then, while retaining completely the firm reality of this human flesh and this human birth, to mount up higher, up to the Father. We must not be offended by this humanity, nor must we stop there; we must penetrate more deeply. This is the work of faith; the faithful alone apply themselves to it.

The apostles are faithful; they have all heard the confession of St. Peter at Caesarea, and have echoed it: "Thou art Christ, the Son of the living God" (Mt. 16:16). Yet even with them, this faith, illuminating now and again their knowledge of Christ, has not transformed it entirely: on the last day, Philip will say to Him again, "Lord, show us the Father and it is enough for us." And Jesus answers him sadly, "Have I been so long a time with you, and you have not known me? Philip, he who sees me sees also the Father. How canst thou say, 'Show us the Father'? Dost thou not believe that I am in the Father and the Father in me? The words that I speak to you I speak not on my own authority. But the Father dwelling in me, it is he who does the works. Do you believe that I am in the Father and the Father in me? Otherwise believe because of the works themselves" (Jn. 14:8–12).

Here we find the same movement of thought as on the occasion of the feast of Tabernacles: from this real, visible humanity Jesus seeks to raise His hearers up to the Father and to His union with Him. And this effort is here even more revealing, addressed as it is, not to adversaries, but to the apostles; and provoked, not by an isolated incident, but by a habitual attitude: "You have not known me?"

The very request of Philip points clearly to that deficiency in his knowledge of the Son of God: if he were habitually attentive to that great mystery which he has little knowledge of, he would ask Jesus to reveal it to him. But no, he thinks he knows his Master; all he asks for is to see the Father. Here our attention is drawn to a point of very great importance: nowhere in the Gospel do we see the apostles asking Jesus to reveal Himself to them more plainly. They live with Him, they see His miracles, they listen to Him; it seems to them that He has nothing more to reveal to them. And yet He will tell them in His crowning talk, "Many things yet I have to say to you, but you cannot bear them now" (Jn. 16:12).

They have given themselves to Him unreservedly; not only have they left all, but they are ready to sacrifice their lives. When Jesus, threatened by the Jews' hatred, decides, nonetheless, to go up to Bethany to Lazarus, the frightened apostles try to dissuade Him from going. Since Christ persists in His design, Thomas exclaims, "Let us also go, that we may die with Him" (Jn. 11:16).

Their hearts are won over to Christ, but their intelligence is poorly enlightened. Their Master, with whom they live continually, appears to them as the head of the great enterprise to which they have been passionately devoted. He is going to establish the kingdom of heaven. They add: He is going to re-establish the kingdom of Israel. How will this take place? They do not know, they rely on Him; but they already envisage His triumph and their own: that Messianic feast which the parables recall to them, those twelve thrones on which they will be seated, judging the twelve tribes of Israel (Mt.19:28). Besides these prophecies in which they take pleasure, there are others which are incomprehensible to them and which they reject: Christ delivered over to the Gentiles, despised, scourged, put to death, crucified (Mk. 8:31–33; 9:11, 30–31; 10:33–34; Mt. 20:18–19).

If they had understood their Master better, if to them faith had more habitually revealed in Him the Son of God, they would have been neither beguiled by the symbolic descriptions of the triumph, nor frightened by the predictions of the Passion. For want of penetrating that far, they do not ask to know Him better whose life they share; they look without seeing, listen without hearing and, despite so many warnings, the shock of the Cross will fall on them unexpectedly and fill them with dismay.

Temptations will be all the more dangerous as the apostles rely on the fidelity which they feel sincere and consider unshakeable. Alas! they rely on flesh, and flesh is weak. Despite the urgent warnings of Jesus, they neither watch nor pray; they are not aware of that absolute need of prayer on which, in this hour above all, their salvation depends.

Jesus sees this lamentable fall of those men who are so dear to Him and who love Him so sincerely: His exhortations will not be able to preserve them from it. In any case, He will lift them up again. This is what the discourse after the Last Supper already prepares for: "Abide in me, and I in you" (Jn. 15:4).

"Follow me," He said to them a short while ago; now: "Abide in me." Their Master will no longer be in front of them like the head leading them; He will be within them like the life quickening them. This is the decisive transformation.

Long hours of walking when suddenly there is seen to appear, at the top of the hill of Naim, the widow following the bier of her child; or, on the lake shore, at Capharnaum, the crowd shoving the apostles, pressing the Master, so as to steal from Him the cure of a hemorrhage; or those troops of children flocking to Him; or, after the heavy day's preaching of the parables, Jesus asleep on the cushion of the boat, in the storm. All that is the past, a very dear past, truly divine, but which has not yet yielded its secret. And all these talks, parables, long discourses, brief statements, treasures sleeping in the innermost recesses of souls almost oblivious of them—these the Spirit will cause to revive and come forth into the open light. Yes, indeed, St. Ignatius of Antioch had good reason to say, "Nothing that I see is good. Our God Jesus Christ certainly is the more clearly seen now that He is in the Father." [15]

On that same evening, when Jesus promises the Spirit to His apostles, when He exhorts them to abide in Him, He gives Himself to them for the first time in the Eucharist: a presence which escapes the senses, but which has never been so intimate; a presence not only of the divinity of Our Lord, but of His holy humanity, of His body and soul; a real presence with which our soul and body are nourished, but which we perceive only by faith. And like every presence of faith, this one, the most valuable of all, is

[15] *To the Romans,* 3 (ACW 1), p. 81.

not only a leaven transforming us, but a force uplifting us; it is a pledge of eternal life, a murmuring of living waters, the voice of the Son of God saying to us again in the depths of our hearts, "Come to the Father."

The terrible day which is going to follow that evening in the Cenacle—the Agony, the Praetorium, Calvary—will seal this gift of the Cenacle. What we receive is the Body given to us, the Blood shed for us, the Blood of the Alliance. "Abide in me, and I in you": you, united to My sacrifice; I, offering you with Myself to the Father. "It is the spirit that gives life, the flesh profits nothing" (Jn. 6:64); or rather, yes, it profits as a sacrifice: flesh and blood, this is our offering for the sacrifice; it is ourselves, Head and members, Body of Christ.

After the resurrection of Jesus, for forty days, He is going to show Himself to His disciples; by no means will this be the life of old which He will take up again; it will be the new life which He will inaugurate. His presence will be attested to firmly enough so as to banish all doubts, even those of Thomas; but it will not be as formerly, handed over to men. When Magdalen wishes to touch Him, Jesus will not permit it. No longer will He make His abode with men; but He will appear by apparitions which will take by surprise those whom they reach and which will be suddenly withdrawn from them.

Men learn to know Jesus in those visits which He accords them, such sweet visits but so brief, preceded by long waits and followed by such sorrowful separations. When Jesus has withdrawn, the Christian lives no more in memory, but in hope; he does not try at all to recall the past, he aspires to heaven. Thus already St. Paul, stretched towards Him who has taken hold of him and who calls him. What animates his life is not at all the recollection of the apparition at Damascus; it is the expectation of the eternal presence: "We shall ever be with the Lord" (1 Thes. 4:16); "Henceforth we know no one according to the flesh. And even though we have known Christ according to the flesh, yet now we know him so no longer" (2 Cor. 5:16). This is the desire which stirs the Apostle writing to the Ephesians, or to the Philippians:

I bend my knees to the Father . . . that he may grant you from his glorious riches to be strengthened with power through his Spirit unto the progress of the inner man; and to have Christ dwelling through faith in your hearts: so that, being rooted and grounded in love, you may be able to comprehend with all the saints what is the breadth and length and height and depth, and to know Christ's love which surpasses knowledge, in order that you may be filled unto all the fullness of God (Eph. 3:14–19).

I count everything loss because of the excelling knowledge of Jesus Christ, my Lord. For his sake I have suffered the loss of all things, and I count them as dung that I may gain Christ . . . so that I may know him and the power of his resurrection and the fellowship of his sufferings: become like to him in death, in the hope that somehow I may attain to the resurrection from the dead. Not that I have already obtained this, or already have been made perfect, but I press on hoping that I may lay hold of that for which Christ Jesus has laid hold of me (Phil. 3:8–12).

Life is completely enthralled by the desire to know Christ, to possess Christ; and henceforth, throughout the history of the Church, we shall be conscious of this irresistible current that raises souls towards the knowledge of Christ. This desire is the fruit of faith; by faith we possess the pledge of eternal beatitude and a sort of faint outline of the intuitive vision. This is a matchless treasure by what it gives us, and above all, by what it promises us. The more we are aware of its value, the more impatient we are to possess in its plenitude what we do not yet possess except in hope. Also, the deeper the faith, the more urgent the desire; mystical contemplation is nothing else but a very lofty and pure faith; the more luminous and ardent it becomes, the more it consumes the soul with desire.

By this trait faith is distinguished from sense knowledge: "Blessed are they who have not seen, and yet have believed" (Jn. 20:29): this bliss does not consist only, nor especially, in the merit of a soul who believes on the testimony of God what she does not attain through a personal experience; it consists even more in the foretaste communicated by God of that divine mystery which here below we believe on His word and which in heaven we shall see in His light.

Spiritual authors commonly give as one of the marks of mystical knowledge the heavenly savor which it causes the soul to taste, and one asks: How does a man living on earth recognize that savor, an experience of which he has never had up to then? He recognizes it by the desire he feels awakening in his soul: "This heavenly food is sweet to his taste." From the time he has tasted it, he is enthralled by its delight; here is the secret of the attraction by which the Father takes hold of us: "No one can come to me unless the Father who sent me draw him" (Jn. 6:44). And if he is docile to this attraction, he feels increasing within himself the desire of heavenly goods, that is to say, the love of God and of Christ, the foretaste of eternal beatitude: "This is everlasting life, that they may know thee, the only true God, and him whom thou hast sent, Jesus Christ" (Jn. 17:3).

chapter 12

❖❖❖❖❖❖❖❖❖❖

The Holy Eucharist

The last evening of Christ's mortal life has an exceptional importance: in the intimacy of the Cenacle, He gives Himself and reveals Himself to His apostles and, through them, to holy Church, more fully than ever before. We shall first consider the institution of the Holy Eucharist, then we shall ponder the Discourse after the Last Supper.

In the mystery of the Eucharist, we adore the most valuable remembrance that the Son of God has left us of His benefits, the surest pledge of His promises. This remembrance of His benefits is not a simple memorial of them; it is their reality: the gift of the Incarnation is continued here and is applied to each of us: the redeeming sacrifice is actually re-enacted, and its fruits distributed to us. Thus our whole Christian life finds its center in the Eucharist: baptism orientates us to it,[1] and all the other sacraments are derivations from this source.[2]

[1] St. Thomas, *Summa Theologica*, III, q. 73, a. 3.
[2] The Roman Catechism [Catechism of the Council of Trent] part 2, chap-

A year before the Last Supper, Jesus in His discourse at Capharnaum had given His disciples a glimpse of, and then promised to them, the supreme gift of the Eucharist. He proposes it to them in the perspective of the Incarnation: the Son of God is the living bread which has come down from heaven and which gives life to the world. Jesus responds thus to our deepest desires: we need life, and eternal life; Jesus offers it to us. It is not that perishable life which the manna gave to the Israelites: "Your fathers ate the manna in the desert, and have died. This is the bread that comes down from heaven, so that if anyone eat of it he will not die" (Jn. 6:49–50).

For a moment the Jews are moved by the desire which Jesus awakens in them: "Lord, give us always this bread" (*ibid.*, 34); thus a short while ago the Samaritan woman: "Sir, give me this water that I may not thirst, or come here to draw" (Jn. 4:15). With the Samaritan woman, this desire was so strong that it broke down all resistance. The Jews of Capharnaum are more selfish and, consequently, more hesitant: they said, "Is this not Jesus the son of Joseph, whose father and mother we know? How then does he say, 'I have come down from heaven'?" (Jn. 6:42).

Here again we are conscious of the decisive option: from the start of the discourse Jesus puts before His listeners the great task of faith: "This is the work of God, that you believe in him whom he has sent" (*ibid.*, 29). Confronted with this trial, the Jews of Capharnaum fail as had failed those of Nazareth, and

---

ter 4, n. 47–48, exhorts pastors to have their faithful understand that the Eucharist "contains, in a marvelous manner, the source of all heavenly gifts, the author of all the Sacraments, Christ Our Lord: from this source the other Sacraments derive whatever goodness and perfection they contain." On the other hand, the Eucharist causes grace only through utilizing the ministry of the other sacraments: they prepare the subject for the universal grace which comes from the Eucharist: *"Per sanctificationes enim omnium sacramentorum fit praeparatio ad suscipiendam vel consecrandam eucharistiam"* (St. Thomas, *ibid.;* cf. M. de la Taille, S.J., *Mysterium Fidei,* Paris, Beauchesne, 1923, and in tr. *Mystery of Faith: regarding the most august Sacrament and Sacrifice of the Body and Blood of Christ,* N. Y., Sheed & Ward, 1940).

trip on the same obstacle: they think they know all about Jesus, and thrust aside from the first word the mystery He proposes to them.

And yet, these are "words of everlasting life" (*ibid.,* 69); it is here especially that we are aware of the value and reward of faith: "Blessed are they who hear the word of God and keep it" (Lk. 11:28).

What we notice, first of all, is a new and touching aspect of the mystery of the Incarnation. The Eucharist consummates it and makes it bear all its fruits of union: the Son of God, in becoming man, has taken on our nature; by giving Himself to us in the Eucharist, He takes hold of each one of us and becomes incorporated, so as to give us life. The Discourse after the Last Supper will take up the same teaching: He will repeat to the apostles during those first "Graces" of thanksgiving: "Abide in me, and I in you" (Jn. 15:4).

Thus, between Jesus and ourselves there is not only that union which humanity constitutes among all men; there is not only that action which His example ought to exercise on us or which the merits of His death ought to produce. He is our model, He is our victim, but He is also our inseparable life, and that not only by His divinity but by His flesh. This flesh He did not take up save for the salvation of the world, for the salvation of each one of us. God the Father, who takes infinite pleasure in this gift of His Son, wants to apply Him, as a matter of fact, to each of us. Every man ought to be a member of Christ; every man is called to a physical union with his Head. This union will be renewed frequently and, if possible, daily; it will be transitory, but its fruits will remain engraved not only on our souls but on our bodies, and it will be the principle of their resurrection.

And yet this union of our humanity with the holy humanity of Christ, of our flesh with His flesh, is not a carnal union; it is knit, not by the senses, but by faith. All that we have seen hitherto of the economy of the Incarnation prepares us for this mystery which is the completion of the great divine work. "Blessed are they who have not seen, and yet have believed"

(Jn. 20:29). It is to this beatitude that Our Lord wishes to lead us. He has appeared to us so deeply hidden that His holy Mother herself, in order to behold the depth of the mystery, must meditate in her heart the words of her divine Son. It is thus that He gives Himself to His Mother, it is thus that He gives Himself to all Christians. His presence in the Holy Sacrament does not depend on our faith, any more than His Incarnation does; but it is perceived only by our faith. In the Son of God, the Jews of Capharnaum believe they see the son of Mary and Joseph; in the sacred Host the unbeliever sees a piece of bread. And yet this is the beloved Son in whom the Father is well pleased; this is the living Bread come down from Heaven. In Him are "all the treasures of wisdom and knowledge," but they are hidden (Col. 2:3). He offers them to us by giving Himself to us. And our souls, if they believe, participate in them; but only faith can discover them.

It is not at all by means of the senses, but by faith, that we can unite ourselves to our Head. Our piety will be a worship "in spirit and in truth" (Jn. 4:24), a spiritual homage which faith governs and enlightens. Sensible affection is not banished therefrom; but this is not what leads us, it is faith. We are men, and we must consecrate to the service of God all our powers, hence also our powers of the senses; but in the order which reason makes known to us and which the teaching of Our Lord renders still more imperative: "It is the spirit that gives life; the flesh profits nothing" (Jn. 6:64). And yet "unless you eat the flesh of the Son of Man, and drink his blood, you shall not have life in you" (*ibid.,* 54). "My flesh is food indeed, and my blood is drink indeed" (*ibid.,* 56). All is real in the gift of God, nothing is purely symbolic; but this reality is perceived only by faith, and it is first and foremost eternal life which is thus communicated to us. The body also is attained: it receives a seed of resurrection; it is sanctified and, if God so wills, it is cured. In the Communion antiphon on the feast day of Saints Fabian and Sebastian, holy Church has us read the text: "Power had gone forth from him and healed them all" (Lk. 6:19). But all these miracles worked by the flesh of the Son of God were accorded to faith; it is faith which obtained them and which made the bodies of the sick benefit by them. In the Holy Eucharist, the Body of Christ has the same virtue and acts according to the same law. The Eucharist is the Mystery of faith. In the Office of St. Agnes, the Church has us say: "When I love Him, I am chaste; when I touch Him, I am pure; when I receive Him, I am a virgin." These words apply fully to the Eucharistic communion: the believer who receives the body of Christ is united to Him; and the fruit of this union is that Christ and Christian are now but one spirit.

And just as the soul is the spouse of Christ, the Church in its entirety is, in full truth, the spouse of Christ; this union is not at all the imitation of, but the exemplar of, the union between husband and wife. Christ has given His body to the Church, His Spouse; the ministers of the Church have power over the body of Christ and give it to the faithful. And this union consecrates the virginity of the Church; the ancient Fathers loved to venerate the Church like the Virgin Mary.[3] Of herself as of Mary we can say that the Son of God, far from hurting her virginity, has consecrated it.

The whole Church, like each Christian, must make an effort to tend toward that divine and heavenly purity to which her Spouse calls her; the communion of the Body of Christ leads her there. This divine body is a memorial; we shall emphasize this point in speaking of the sacrifice. But it is also a seed of immortality and resurrection; it is the bread of angels; it prepares us for that virginal life where we shall all be like "angels of God in heaven," as Jesus taught the Sadducees (Mt. 22:30).

These considerations lead us towards a more complete comprehension of this great mystery: there is nothing in the Incarnation of the Son and in His redemptive work which is not communicated to us by the Eucharist, and this union is consummated in faith.

[3] For example, Clement of Alexandria, *Pedagogus,* I, 6, 42, 1. *P.G.*, VIII, 300, and in tr. *Christ the Educator* (FC 23), tr. by S. Wood, C.P., N. Y., Fathers of the Church, 1954, p. 40.

We are brought back to the text of Osee (2:20), dear to St. John of the Cross: "I will espouse thee to me in faith."

But this life-giving union is well understood only if we consider in the Eucharist the memorial of the redemptive death of the Savior.

"Unless the grain of wheat fall into the ground and die, it remains alone. But if it die, it brings forth much fruit" (Jn. 12:24–25). These words of Jesus refer directly to His death but they shed a powerful light on the Eucharistic mystery. The bread of life descended from heaven is this grain of wheat; it must fall in the ground, it must die, in order to bear fruit. This great law—the whole Gospel story proposes it to us; but it is in the Eucharist especially that it fully comes to light. At Capharnaum we have only the promise; the institution will take place only at the Last Supper, *ea nocte qua tradebatur,* at the time when the Passion had already begun.

"On the great day of the feast of Tabernacles, Jesus stood and cried out, saying, 'If anyone thirst, let him come to me and drink. He who believes in me, as the Scripture says, "From within him there shall flow rivers of living water." ' He said this, however, of the spirit whom they who believed in him were to receive; for the Spirit had not yet been given, seeing that Jesus had not yet been glorified" (Jn. 7:37–39).

At the Last Supper He will say, "All of you drink of this; for this is my blood of the new covenant, which is being shed for many unto the forgiveness of sins" (Mt. 26:27–28). This is no longer a promise; it is an urgent invitation. But this blood which we must drink is the blood shed for the forgiveness of sins. Likewise: "This is my body, which is being given for you" (Lk. 22:19). This is what we already catch a glimpse of in the discourse of Capharnaum: "The bread that I will give is my flesh for the life of the world" (Jn. 6:52). The promise is now realized: Jesus is already the victim of Calvary, and it is as such that He is given.

This relation of the Eucharist to the Cross is essential to it: in this Body given, in this Blood shed, there is a real sacrifice offered to God. This oblation does not consist in the offering of bread and wine, but in the offering of the Body and Blood of Our Lord truly given and shed for us.[4]

The repercussion of this dogma on our spiritual life is immeasurable. "The love of God impels us, because we have come to the conclusion that, since one died for all, therefore all died; and that Christ died for all, in order that they who are alive may live no longer for themselves, but for him who died for them and rose again" (2 Cor. 5:14–15).

This teaching of the Apostle is already very impelling, if we consider the death of Christ on Calvary; but it takes on a new force with the Eucharist. By the celebration of this mystery we "proclaim the death of the Lord, until he comes" (1 Cor. 11-26). That is what gives this rite its divine and tragic grandeur; it is in order to lead the Corinthians back to a more religious celebration that the Apostle recalls it to them.

And this is not only a liturgical drama which is performed in front of the faithful; it is an actual re-enactment of the offering of the Cross, and St. Paul will straightway draw the conclusion therefrom: "Whoever eats this bread or drinks the cup of the Lord unworthily, will be guilty of the body and blood of the Lord . . . He who eats and drinks unworthily, without distinguishing the body, eats and drinks judgment to himself" (ibid., 27–29).

These practical conclusions are those called forth by the irreverence of the Corinthians. But they are not the only ones: as soon as we have understood that what we thus receive is the Body and the Blood of the Son of God immolated for us, we begin to understand all that the celebration of and participation in this divine sacrifice asks of us.

First of all, adoration and thanksgiving. Bossuet thus expounds it:

These words of the Savior: "Take, eat, this is my body given for you," show us that, as the Jews of old were not only united in spirit

[4] Cf. M. de la Taille, *Mysterium Fidei, elucidatio* 3[a], pp. 33–39, and in tr. *The Mystery of Faith*, N. Y., Sheed & Ward, 1940.

to the immolation of the victims offered for them, but that, as a matter of fact, they used to eat the sacrificed flesh, which was a sign to them of the part they had in this oblation, so Jesus Christ, being made Himself our victim, has willed that we eat in reality the flesh of this sacrifice, so that the actual communication of this adorable flesh might be a perpetual witness to each of us in particular that it is for us that He has taken it up, and that it is for us that He has immolated it.[5]

Here again we find, in the application which is made for us of the redemptive sacrifice, what we recognized in the application of the Incarnation: it is by means of the Eucharist, we said, that the fruits of the Incarnation are applied to each of us; it is also by the Eucharist that we take in the redemption wrought for us on the Cross.

Already in baptism we get an inkling of this intention of Our Lord; wishing to unite the neophyte to Himself, He unites Him to His death and resurrection; the divine life of Jesus is grasped in that decisive moment when He is immolated for us. In the Eucharist there is manifested the same will, and in a still more expressive way: what we receive is the Body given, the Blood shed, the victim of Calvary; and the liturgical mystery which gives it to us is a sacrifice, an actual re-enactment of the sacrifice of the Cross.

It is, therefore, by this supreme gift, by this homage rendered to the Father, that the Son of God has wrought our redemption. God willed that all the other mysteries of Christ's life receive their efficacy from this sacrifice. And He willed that the actual union of our flesh with the flesh of His divine Son cause us to take hold of it in His death. It is there that it gives us life.

There is an unforgettable lesson here, one which governs our whole life. Communion tends to assimilate us to Our Lord; consequently, to cause us to die with Him. Again, it is the fruit of baptism, to which the real presence of the Body of Christ gives a still greater efficacy. We receive an immolated victim, and in the very act of its immolation; this victim is our Head, and His whole

[5] *Exposition de la doctrine catholique sur les matières de controverse,* Paris, Desprez, 1761.

endeavor aims at uniting us to His sacrifice, at immolating us with Himself. Can we, without slipping from His embrace, turn ourselves away from His sacrifice?

Here the priest is tied to his Master by still more sacred bonds: "This is the chalice of my blood . . . shed for you and for many . . ." The priest pronounces these words in the name of Christ: this is not a mere delegation, it is the close union of Head and member. Our Head wishes to offer Himself by our lips in order to bring us along in His offering. This is the glory of God and of Christ; it is our own glory too.[6]

This daily offering ought to govern our life. St. Gregory explains this duty of priests as follows:

Recalling the eternal judgment, [the saints] are immolated each day to God as a sacrifice of compunction. They chastize their bodies to fulfill what the Apostle of the nations prescribes for us: "Present your bodies as a sacrifice, living, holy, pleasing to God" (Rom. 12:1). The sacrifice is put to death to be offered. But the living sacrifice, this is the body put to death for the Lord; it is called sacrifice and living sacrifice, because it is alive with virtue and dead to vice. Sacrifice, because dead henceforth to the world and to all wicked actions; living, because it carries out every good work within its power.[7]

This duty of mortification is imposed on every Christian by the fact of his baptism: "We are debtors, not to the flesh, that we should live according to the flesh, for if you live according to the flesh you will die; but if by the spirit you put to death the deeds of the flesh, you will live" (Rom. 8:12–13). The Eucharist renders this duty more urgent, especially for the priest, but at the same time it gives to our mortifications an outstanding value by uniting them to the sacrifice of Christ:

No trouble endured by the sinner, however serious, however prolonged it may be, can by itself blot out the stain of sin or the obliga-

6 Cf. M. de la Taille, *Eucharistia et Mortificatio. "Dratio habito ad sacerdotes in congressa eucharistico Amstelodamensi."*
7 *In Ezech.*, I, 1, 2 *Hom.*, 10, 19. *P.L.*, LXXVI, 1069–1070. M. de la Taille, *ibid.*, p. 8.

tion of punishment. But also the troubles of this life, however brief or light they may be, troubles we patiently submit to or spontaneously choose, as soon as they are united to the sacrifice of Christ, as soon as they are joined to the propitiatory offering made by our Head, as soon as they have been changed, like the water of Cana, into the wine of salvation, into the blood of Our Lord, the price of the world, the libation of our Priest—it is impossible for them not to produce all the efficacy of the Cross.[8]

Let us add that this mortification to which Christ invites His priest will be all the more perfect as the offering is more sincere and generous: *Qui seminat in benedictionibus, de benedictionibus et metat.* This is the fruit which the Church often has us ask for in her Postcommunions, for example: *Ut quidquid in nobis vitiosum est [sacramentalis] medicationis dono curetur* (24th Sunday after Pentecost) or: *Munera tua nos, Deus, a delectationibus terrenis expediant* (4th Sunday after Epiphany).

But, at the same time as the work of death, there is continued the work of life: the Body which we receive has been crucified and put to death; now it is glorious. It gives us life, not only because it is the living Head come down from heaven, but also because it is the first of the resurrected bodies, the first fruits of the Resurrection.

Hence, in Holy Communion, that heavenly delight which Christ often has those enjoy who are united to His death.[9] Among the fruits of the Eucharist, the Council of Florence (Denz. 698) counts this delectation which is a foretaste of heaven.[10] This is what the Church has us repeat in her Postcommunions: *Caelestibus, Domine, pasti deliciis, quaesumus ut semper eadem per quae veraciter vivimus, appetamus.*[11] A friend of St.

[8] M. de la Taille, *ibid.*, p. 10.
[9] Cf. M. de la Taille, *ibid*, pp. 12–14.
[10] *"Omnem effectum, quem materialis cibus et potus quoad vitam agunt corporalem, sustentando, augendo, reparando et delectando, sacramentum hoc operatur quoad vitam spiritualem"* (Denzinger, *Enchiridion Symbolorum definitionum et declarationum de rebus fidei et morum,* Friburg (im Breisg.), Herder, 1955, n. 698).
[11] Sixth Sunday after Epiphany.

Bernard, Ernaldus of Bonneval, has us ask: *"Nos pascant ac reficiant maturatae resurrectionis laetabunda solemnia."* [12]

If we do not taste this delight, let us take care that it be not because of our lack of mortification: "We do not wish to taste in our souls the sweetness which is prepared for us, and we love our hunger." [13]

These delights ought to be dear to us, less for the present pleasure they bring us than for the future happiness they betoken for us. This is what we repeat in the Common for Pontiff Confessors: *Ut, de perceptis muneribus gratiae exhibentes, beneficia potiora sumamus.*

Here again are verified the words of the Apostle: "In hope were we saved" (Rom. 8:24), and the very happiness we feel in this embrace of Christ does not satiate our desire, but purifies and exalts it. This is what St. Bernard taught the monks of Clairvaux:

I also receive the Word, but in the flesh; to me also is given the truth, but in the Sacrament. The angel is sated with wheat-oil, with pure grain; while I must content myself with the husk of the Sacrament, with the mincemeat, with the shavings of the letter, the veil of faith . . . It is the spirit which vivifies and makes me live by means of all these things; but although they make us taste, indeed, the abundance of the spirit, we do not taste the same happiness in the husk of the Sacrament and in the oil of the wheat, in faith and in vision, in the remembrance and in the presence, in eternity and in time, in the face and in the mirror, in the image of God and in the form of the slave . . . Do you not see that the foods are as distant from one another as the places? And just as heaven is above earth, so those who dwell there enjoy the greatest goods.[14]

This Body of Christ, completely invested with heavenly glory, sweeps us on high. *Ego sum resurrectio et vita* (Jn. 11:25):

[12] *Lib. de card. oper. Christ.,* 6. P.L., CLXXXIX, 1646 (*ibid.,* p. 14).

[13] *"Quia gustare intus nolumus paratam dulcedinem, amamus foris miseri famem nostram"* (Greg., *Hom. 36, In Evang.*).

[14] *In Cantica Hom.,* 33, 3. P.L., CXXXIV, 952, and in tr. *On the Song of Songs.*

this is the One we receive. Also, never will our joy leave us a feeling of satiety, but, on the contrary, a more pressing desire to be with Christ. We shall repeat with St. Ignatius of Antioch: "Him I seek who died for us . . . *Bread of God* is what I desire; that is, the Flesh of Jesus Christ, *who was of the seed of David;* and for my drink I desire His Blood, that is, incorruptible love." [15]

In sketching Christian perfection, such as it appeared to us in the vocation of the apostles, we have kept insisting on the total seizure of man's life by Christ. This becomes even more manifest in the light of the Eucharist: from the day when the apostles received from Jesus—when the priests receive from the bishop —the power to consecrate Our Lord's Body, their lives are transformed: they will say, "This is My Body, this is My Blood," and under the sacramental species, the Body and Blood of Christ will be really present.

A man who has received such a power no longer belongs to himself; he is Christ's man. While beholding the Son of God living and acting in the world, we have seen Him wholly and completely penetrated with the thought and action of the Father: His doctrine is not his doctrine, but the doctrine of Him who sent Him; His works are not his works, but the works which the Father does in Him and by means of Him. Human nature, taken up by the Son of God, is entirely possessed and quickened by Him; He alone is responsible for His words and acts. And if we consider the divine nature of the Son of God, it is the same in the Father and in the Son: in the Father, as in its source; in the Son, as in Him in whom it overflows fully and necessarily, and at the same time in a movement of complaisance and infinite love. Here is the ideal model of the Christian and, first and foremost, of the priest. In the act of Consecration, the man disappears; the priest acts, or rather Christ in him and by means of him. And likewise when he says: *Ego te baptizo* and *Ego te absolvo.* St. Augustine, arguing against the Donatists, showed them that it was Christ who baptized, and not man: "Peter baptizes, it is

---

[15] *To the Romans* 6–7, in ACW 1, p. 83.

Christ who baptizes; Paul baptizes, it is Christ who baptizes; Judas baptizes, it is Christ who baptizes." [16]

It is the same with the remission of sins: we can grant to Jesus' adversaries that no one, except God, can remit sins (Mk. 2:7); but this divine power can be delegated to a man: "Receive the Holy Spirit; whose sins you shall forgive, they are forgiven them; and whose sins you shall retain, they are retained" (Jn. 20:23). This power, conferred on the priest over the Body of Christ and over His members, is not an accidental delegation like that which, in case of necessity, makes of any man the minister of baptism; it is a function which imprints on him a character, which makes of him Christ's man. The human person remains distinct, no doubt, from God, who delegates him; he is responsible for his acts; he can withdraw from His sway, act without Him and against Him. But he cannot do so without being unfaithful to the divine vocation, to the sanctity which it calls for. Hence his priesthood tends justifiably to penetrate his life and to make of it a unity; it is not a sporadic function, but a vocation which summons all his powers and elevates them all by uniting them to Christ.

This is the doctrine which Pius XI recalls to us in his letter on the Priesthood:

These elevated powers are conferred on the priest by a sacrament instituted especially for this purpose. They are in him not transitory and passing, but stable and perpetual, united as they are to an indelible character imprinted in his soul, by which he has become "a priest for eternity," in the likeness of Him who possesses the eternal priesthood of which he is made a participant. This is a character which the priest, even in the most deplorable aberrations wherein human frailty can fall, can never efface from his soul. But, with this character and these powers, the priest also receives, through the sacrament of Orders, a new and special grace together with particular helps by which, if his free and personal cooperation seconds faithfully the divinely powerful action of grace itself, he will be able to acquit himself faithfully of all the difficult obligations of the sublime

16 *In Joann. Tract.* 6. Cf. *Contra Litteras Petiliani,* III, c. 49. *Contra Cresconium,* III, c. 8.

state to which he has been called. He will also be able to bear, without breaking under them, formidable responsibilities, which are inherent in the priestly ministry and which make even the strongest athletes of the Christian ministry tremble, like St. John Chrysostom, St. Ambrose, St. Gregory the Great, St. Charles and so many others.

chapter 13

❖❖❖❖❖❖❖❖❖

The Discourse After the Last Supper

1. CHRIST AND CHRISTIANS

On the threshold of His public life, Our Lord inaugurated His teaching to His apostles by the Sermon on the Mount. On the last day of His life, He consummated that teaching by the Discourse after the Last Supper.[1]

This discourse will not have for a setting, like the first one, the broad horizons of Galilee, its verdant slopes and flowering lake shore; it will be in a house of Jerusalem, in a closed chamber. The audience, too, will be contracted: it is no longer the flocking throng "from all Judea and Jerusalem, and the sea coast of Tyre and Sidon" (Lk. 6:17); it is the small group of the Twelve. Here more than ever we recognize that effort, more and more profound and intimate, which characterizes the apostolic activity

[1] Cf. J. Huby, S.J., *Le Discours de Jésus après la Cène, suivi d'une étude sur la connaissance de foi dans saint Jean* (*Verbum Salutis*), Paris, Beauchesne, 1932 and 1942. —Msgr. Moisson, *Entretiens sur le Discours après la Cène,* Langres, 1935.

of Our Lord. For a long time it is carried on under the open skies, through the fields and villages of Palestine, sowing on all types of soil, giving lavishly to all and sundry; now it is reversed: to intimate friends, in a Cenacle.

The very moving occasion of this talk gives it the poignant note of a farewell. The remembrance will remain stamped on souls by the sorrow of the separation. Throughout that evening, the apostles felt the anguish of the darkness which was descending upon them; and that very anguish opened them to the love of their Master. Never had they felt its power so deeply. Can we not recognize an echo of this recollection in the promise of Jesus to St. John, sixty years later: "Behold, I stand at the door and knock. If any man listens to my voice and opens the door to me, I will come in to him and will sup with him, and he with me" (Apoc. 3:20)? [2]

This is a farewell banquet, and the whole discourse is characterized by this fact. And yet, it contains even more promises than recollections. If He illumines the past (for example, Jn. 15:16), He does not tarry there; He recalls it only in order to give them a glimpse of the future and to bear along thither the hope of His disciples.

And this Cenacle, indeed, where all of Jesus' activity seems to die out, is the fertile furrow where the grain of wheat is buried but whence it will soon sprout up: in forty days, the Spirit is going to descend in the Cenacle, the Church is going to be born, to radiate and to spread throughout the world.

This is what we have an inkling of, henceforth, in that triumphal cry which opens the whole discourse: "Now is the Son of Man glorified, and God is glorified in him" (Jn. 13:31). And the last words will be the assurance of victory: "In the world

---

[2] This very insistence recalls the emphasis of Our Lord: "Abide in me, and I in you" (Jn. 15:4 ff.). In his commentary (*Saint Jean: l'Apocalypse,* Paris, Gabalda, 1921 and 1933, p. 56), Father Allo has underlined the intimacy of this Supper: "There is no image, in all these Letters, which has a character more intimate, more personal, and more touching." We can compare with it, too, in the *Canticle* of St. John of the Cross, str. 14 (*Complete Works*), "*la cena que recrea y enamora.*"

you will have affliction. But take courage, I have overcome the world" (Jn. 16:33).

This triumph achieved by Christ over His enemies is the presage of the eternal beatitude which He assures to all His own. In heaven, whence He comes and where He dwells, He is going to prepare a place for them. This heaven, so greatly desired, is not described as it appeared to the Jews in their apocalyptic dreams, at the end of a long and perilous ascent beyond the walls of ice and snow; it is the house of the Father, where the dwellings are numerous and where Jesus goes to prepare a place for His disciples. Undoubtedly, He is leaving them, but just for a while; He will come back to take them, that where He is, they also may be (Jn. 14: 2–3).

2. THE UNION OF CHRISTIANS WITH CHRIST

He is leaving them: the apostles see only this separation, which is so painful for them and veils the whole future from them; the road, the goal—all appears to them equally mysterious. Jesus lays stress, then, both on the intimacy, quite close and already present, and on the happiness of heaven. This Father, whom they would like to see, they already see in Jesus; these works, which they marvel at and which have illumined their faith, these are the works of the Father. And soon they themselves will do these same works, and even greater, because Jesus is going away to the Father (Jn. 14:12). And under a thousand various forms, the Master strives to make His disciples understand the whole benefit of this separation which discourages them: a benefit, first of all, for Jesus: "If you loved me, you would indeed rejoice that I am going to the Father" (14:28); a benefit for them too: "I speak the truth to you; it is expedient for you that I depart. For if I do not go, the Advocate will not come to you; but if I go, I will send him to you" (16:7).

Thus, beyond this present, already so rich in graces, we catch a glimpse of a more divine future: after the separation, there will be the return of the risen Christ; there will be Pentecost, and the gift of the Spirit; there will be eternal life, in the abode of the Father, with the Son, who will receive in His glory all those whom He has made the children of God. In the eschatological discourse, the frightful perspectives of the ruin of Jerusalem and of the end of the world were superimposed, and the first disaster seemed like the presage and rough sketch of the final catastrophe. It is the same with the glorious perspectives which Jesus reveals to us here: His glorious return on the day of the resurrection; the foundation of His Church on Pentecost; the definitive coming of the kingdom of God—these are by no means disparate episodes in the course of history, with nothing linking them together; they are the successive phases of that glorification of God and of His Son, of which the death of Jesus is the prelude.

For the apostles and all the elect, this will be the birth of a new life: they do not yet know either the Son or the Father; they shall know Him, and this will be eternal life. The promise of this knowledge and of this life is the principal theme of the Discourse after the Last Supper. After Pentecost, the emergence of this life will be manifest; the accounts of the Acts, the Epistles of the Apostles, and especially of St. Paul, will unfold it before our eyes; the great light of the death and resurrection of Our Lord will give to this Christian dawn its splendor. In the Discourse we are studying, we do not yet grasp these miracles of grace except in a mirror, in the promise which Christ has made of them to the apostles. But this mirror is more luminous than ever before; at one time, the apostles exclaim, full of joy: "Now thou speakest plainly, and utterest no parable" (16:29). This is saying too much: Jesus still speaks in parables (16:25); but the light is so intense and the veil so transparent that all seems to be revealed.

For us, moreover, the accomplishment of these promises not only confirms but clarifies them. The life of Christ, said St. Justin, is the best interpretation of the prophecies; in the same way the birth and the life of the Church enable us to understand all that Jesus promises us here of the action of the Advocate. And these promises, in turn, enable us to grasp better the source, the law, and the goal of this new life which is soon to appear. He who speaks to us is the Author of life; no one can reveal its mystery to us as He can.

"This is everlasting life, that they may know thee, the only true God, and him whom thou hast sent, Jesus Christ" (17:3). This knowledge will render the elect like to God,[3] but it presupposes the assimilation which, here below, makes them children of God. In the measure they are faithful to the graces of this adoption, they receive an intuition, a "view," which reveals their Master to them. This supernatural knowledge has for its principle their participation in His life: "Yet a little while and the world no longer sees me. But you see me, for I live and you shall live" (14:19). And, taking up this promise again, Jesus reveals more explicitly the conditions and the law of this life: "In that day you will know that I am in my Father, and you in me, and I in you. He who has my commandments and keeps them, he it is who loves me. But he who loves me will be loved by my Father, and I will love him and manifest myself to him" (14:20–21).

What appears first and foremost, and what is imposed on the disciple as the condition of this revelation to which he aspires, is the accomplishment of the will of Our Lord: this fidelity is the fruit and the proof of love; love, fruitful in works, docile to its Master, opens the eyes of the disciple and draws down upon him the gaze of the Master who is revealed. This promise of Christ is recalled by St. Catherine of Siena in the prologue of her *Dialogue*[4]: it is the response of Our Lord to the desire which He Himself has awakened in the soul: her whole ambition is to know Him and, in Him, the Father; this is "everlasting life" (17:3); it is already the life of grace, in the measure in which God deigns to grant it to the soul.

[3] Cf. 1 Jn. 3:2: "We know that, when he appears, we shall be like to him, for we shall see him just as he is."

[4] "By following the marks of Christ crucified, by desire, by affection, by a union of love, the soul becomes another self. Is not this what Christ wanted to teach us when He told us: To him who will love me and will keep my word, I shall manifest myself; he will be one and the same thing with me and I with him" (*Dialogue*, Prologue, pp. 3–4. Cf. *Treatise on Purgatory* (*and*) *the Dialogue*).

Then this immanence—till then veiled—of Christ within us, of us in Christ, begins to be revealed and, at the same time, the immanence of the Father in the Son. These two mysteries are closely linked together not only here, but again and repeatedly in the supreme prayer of Jesus: "That all may be one, even as thou, Father, in me and I in thee; that they also may be one in us" (17:21); "That they may be one, even as we are one: I in them and thou in me; that they may be perfected in unity" (22–23); "I have made known to them thy name, and will make it known, in order that the love with which thou hast loved me may be in them, and I in them" (26).

In all these texts, the supreme unity of the Father and the Son is seen as the ideal model, but also as the fruitful source and as the efficacious principle of the unity of Christians with Christ and among themselves. The bond of this unity is love. Love born of knowledge of God tends to the accomplishment of His will; when this tendency is efficacious, when the soul is completely docile to Him, God reveals Himself.

These eyes which are opened, this faith which becomes luminous and which contemplates God and His Christ, this love which embraces the supreme Good and gives itself to Him without reserve—this is a new life which transforms the soul into Jesus Christ. Knowledge flowers from it necessarily: "You see me, for I live and you shall live" (14:19); "He is not the God of the dead, but of the living" (Lk. 20:38).

We see here, more clearly than in any previous text, the goal towards which we are tending; here also we see the road: in this supreme union which is the aim of all our efforts and of all God's graces, everything is so strongly linked that we have trouble distinguishing among all these divine gifts—life, knowledge, love—a priority of one over the other: all this is eternal life. But, if we consider the progressive blossoming of this life, we can distinguish, in their successive appearance, the elements constituting it.

What we recognize at the point of departure is the love which the Father inspires in us for His Son: He has given us to Him, He has placed in our hearts a little of the knowledge which He bears for Him; in a word, He has drawn us to Him. If we are docile to this attraction, we give ourselves to Christ. This means not only that we are pleased to live with Him and hear Him, but, above all, that we want, sincerely and integrally, to do His will: "He who has my commandments and keeps them, he it is who loves me" (Jn. 14:21). A short while before, Jesus had already said, "If you love me, keep my commandments" (14:15); and again, a little later on, He will repeat, "If anyone love me, he will keep my word" (14:23).

This insistence is very worthy of attention: in this supreme discourse, when Our Lord reveals His highest secrets, He tires not of repeating these first elements of the spiritual life, so familiar to all the Jews: the first duty of man is to obey God. And if God grants us the grace to adopt us as His sons, this adoption by no means frees us from this duty of obedience, but renders it more strict, more sacred.

Here is recalled to us the discourse on the Mount. At the conclusion of that discourse, Jesus taught us what would give to our Christian life its depth and stability: the faithful accomplishment of His law. He who puts this in practice, he alone builds on rock. Outside of this, there is only a frivolous complaisance which the least storm sweeps away (cf. Mt. 7:21–27).

This teaching of the Master prepared us for what He gives us today: the courageous and faithful accomplishment of the will of Our Lord is the proof of our love; it is also its support. If our love is only a barren complaisance, it withers; if, on the contrary, it is the law of our life, if it imposes on us and secures from us strenuous efforts, it takes deep root in our soul. The great statements of Christ, "If anyone wishes to come after me, let him deny himself, and take up his cross, and follow me" (Mt. 16:24), could often be piously reread, as a splendid ideal which we admire; but when we must put them in practice, tear ourselves away from all those we love, break up our life, carry our cross and follow Jesus, all seems then unattainable. Those lofty heights, which kept calling us and which seemed so close, rear before us their steep walls to defy our efforts, and we come away asking ourselves whether we had quite understood and whether the requirements of Christ, which now seem to us inhuman, really extend to this total sacrifice. But if love governs this anguish and raises us up to the Cross, what a triumph it is for grace and what a blossoming! Urged on by love, the heart dilates; Christ bends over His disciple and reveals Himself to him in an intimacy hitherto unsuspected.[5]

These decisive sacrifices mark the great stages of the soul's ascent; but it is necessary that from one to the other the ascent be continued by a daily fidelity to the manifestations of His will each day better understood, better loved and better followed.

If we are docile to the teaching of Our Lord, it will reform not only the exterior conduct of our lives, but our interior dispositions, abolishing every bad desire, every hate, every bitterness, and at the same time developing in our hearts a filial obedience, an avid love, and each day a closer intimacy with the heavenly Father. And in the measure that this filial spirit is formed in us, we shall be able to begin to understand the Son of God. Our prayer will support our action, and will give to it not only its impetus, but its direction towards God.

"Thou hast held me by my right hand; and by thy will thou hast conducted me" (Ps. 72:24). These words of the Psalm reveal the meaning of this whole life: Christ's faithful are in His hand, and no one can snatch them from it (cf. Jn. 10:28). From day to day the clasp is tightened; throughout the obscure melee of life—all its clashes, all its shocks, all its joys—the march is continued towards this goal which is always more avidly desired and of which everything gives an inkling. The first steps—was it not yesterday?—were so uncertain, so timid. Alas, O Lord, I was afraid of You; afraid of no longer belonging to You, of being swept away far from myself, far from life, far from all that I love here below. Oh, it is quite true, I no longer belong to myself, but I do belong to You; and in You I have found everything. Everything becomes disengaged, little by little, from the fog, and is seen in the transparency of Your light.

"He who does the truth, comes to the light" (Jn. 3:21): these

[5] Here we might again read the fragments of the letters of St. Francis Xavier, quoted above, pp. 192–193 n.

two steps govern each other: I cannot do the truth without coming to the light; I cannot come to the light unless I do the truth. It is not enough to contemplate truth, not enough to take pleasure in it; one must do the truth; one must respond manfully to its call, one must act in God and for God. "Not everyone who says to me, 'Lord, Lord,' shall enter the kingdom of heaven; but he who does the will of my Father in heaven" (Mt. 7:21). This warning of the discourse on the Mount is echoed by the repeated instances of the discourse after the Last Supper; to the text already recalled (Jn. 14:21, 23), we must add the present exhortation of Chapter 15; after proposing to the apostles the allegory of the vine and the branches, Jesus repeatedly says to them, "Abide in me" (15:4, 7, 9, 10). But how can they do it? By keeping His commandments: "If you keep my commandments you will abide in my love, as I also have kept my Father's commandments, and abide in his love" (15:10).

Always the same ideal is proposed to us: the union of the Son with the Father is the model of the union of Christians with Christ; and, on His part, this second union is, like the first, inseparable: "They shall never perish, neither shall anyone snatch them out of my hand" (Jn. 10:28). But the Christian can withdraw himself from this powerful and faithful embrace by shirking Our Lord's commandments: the love of Christ will be for him only a passing haven, a tent pitched for a night. It ought to be an atmosphere of light and joy which envelops and penetrates him.[6]

These lessons of Our Lord will be taken up by the beloved apostle: "This is the love of God, that we keep his commandments . . . (1 Jn. 5:3); "This is love, that we walk according to his commandments" (2 Jn. 6). St. John has taken care to add, as did the Master Himself, "His commandments are not burdensome" (1 Jn. 5:3). Here are not simply echoes of the Gospel, they ought to be piously recollected. If we remain attentive to them, we receive purely and submissively the teaching of Our Lord; if we

[6] Here I reproduce the commentary of Father Huby, *Discours de Jésus après la Cène*, p. 88.

turn away from them, we lose our way. In place of the light yoke of Christ, we are laden with the intolerable burden of men; or else we reject every burden and let ourselves be carried away by dreams.

What are we to understand by these "commandments of God"? When the rich young man asked Jesus, "What good work shall I do to have eternal life?" Our Lord replied to him, "If thou wilt enter into life, keep the commandments" (Mt. 19:16–17). Today this is the same formula, but its meaning is more ample: there is no longer question of the keeping of the decalogue, but of total submission to the will of God. We understand this by the example of Jesus which He Himself proposes to His apostles: "I also have kept my Father's commandments, and abide in his love" (Jn. 15:10).

This paternal will, obeyed with so much love, led the Son of God to the Cross. The disciple is no greater than the Master; the servant cannot claim to be treated better than the Son. The apostles, too, will have to accomplish the wishes of the Father in their regard; at this price, they will abide in His love. This is what Jesus was teaching, one or two weeks before, to the sons of Zebedee: "Can you drink of the cup of which I drink?" (Mk. 10:38).

What this cup will be which the Father will hold out to them, they hardly have an inkling of; Jesus has not revealed it more clearly to James and John. But He has all the apostles, in this talk at the Last Supper, catch a glimpse of the worst treatment, expulsion, death (Jn. 16:2), tears, cruel tribulations, like labor pains. But, in the end, the joy of a new birth, of the meeting with Christ; this joy no one shall take from them (16:20–22).

All this is spoken "in parables" (16:25); they could not yet bear more light. What they must understand is that this will of the Father is sovereign, and that it is full of love. If they want to remain in the love of the Father, in this atmosphere of joy and light which He has had them taste already, they must remain in a filial docility to the will of the Father. So they must not only keep the commandments, as they have long had the habit of doing;

but comply with every divine wish, however austere it may be. The grace of the Passion will strengthen them: in St. Peter such weak flesh as this, which for so long a time shut its eyes to the Cross, will become the unshakeable rock on which the Church will be built.

And, what is perhaps still more remarkable, with the firmness of the rock will be combined the pliancy of the flame: his head-strong attachment for so long a time to the traditional practises of Judaism will yield before the divine will. Peter had heard the words of Jesus: "There is nothing outside a man that, entering into him, can defile him; but the things that come out of a man, these are what defile a man" (Mk. 7:15); he had heard them, he had not understood them. But in the vision of Joppa, the Spirit illumines the teaching of Jesus: "What God has cleansed, do not thou call common" (Acts 10:15). And soon Peter himself, at the Council of Jerusalem, will say, "Why then do you now try to test God by putting on the neck of the disciples a yoke which neither our fathers nor we have been able to bear?" (Acts 15:10).

He hesitates to mingle with the pagans, to give them baptism; but, led by the Holy Spirit, he enters the house of Cornelius and baptizes him (Acts 10:1–48). Paul, too, would like to reserve his apostolate to his racial brethren; but Our Lord orders him to go out of Jerusalem and preach to the Gentiles (Acts 22:18–21).

The whole book of the Acts is a testimony of this action of the Spirit. Jesus, at Capharnaum, had promised His disciples that they would be taught by God (Jn. 6:45); at the Last Supper, He repeatedly emphasized these great promises: "The Advocate, the Holy Spirit, whom the Father will send in my name, he will teach you all things, and bring to your mind whatever I have said to you" (14:26). When it resounded in the ears of the apostles, this teaching had delighted them; but it had been only half understood and quickly forgotten; now it will be engraved in their hearts.

And this new law, this law of love, will become the law of their lives: "If you keep my commandments you will abide in my love" (15:10). Here it is not a question of absorption in prayer, but of a penetration by it of the whole of life; it is not only a mysticism of contemplation but also, and perhaps even more, a mysticism of action.

3. THE MANIFESTATION OF CHRIST

Seized by the will of Our Lord, stabilized in it and modeling itself on it, the will of the disciple is no longer distinguished therefrom. The apostle can, like St. Paul, be thrown into the most grievous conflicts; he is not upset by them, receiving his assurance from Our Lord Himself. Jesus has promised this: "I am with you all days, even unto the consummation of the world" (Mt. 28:20).

It is above all in the confessors and martyrs that this assistance of Our Lord will be manifest: when St. Stephen appears before the Sanhedrin, which is going to condemn him, looking up to heaven he cries out, "Behold, I see the heavens opened and the Son of Man standing at the right hand of God" (Acts 7:55); St. Paul, when a prisoner, likewise sees Jesus standing before him: "Be steadfast; for just as thou hast borne witness to me in Jerusalem, bear witness in Rome also" (Acts 23:11). How the martyrs, in their turn, will be sustained by their Master! Thus the martyrs of Smyrna, in the year 155: "Some, again, proved themselves so heroic that not one of them uttered cry or moan, and thus they made it clear to all of us that in the hour of their torture the most noble martyrs of Christ were no longer in the flesh, or rather that the Lord stood beside them and conversed with them";[7] thus St. Blandina: "She was tossed about for some time by the animal, but was insensitive to what was happening to her because of her hope and hold upon what had been entrusted to her and her communion with Christ";[8] thus Sanctus, the deacon of Vienne: "He himself remained unbending and unyielding, strong in his confession, refreshed and strengthened by the

---

[7] Cf. *The Martyrdom of St. Polycarp* (ACW 6), p. 91.

[8] Eusebius, V, 1, 56. Cf. *Ecclesiastical History* (FC 19), N. Y., Fathers of the Church, 1953, pp. 284–285.

heavenly spring of the water of life which comes forth from the breast of Christ. And his body was a witness of what happened to him, being all one wound and bruise, wrenched and torn out of human shape, and Christ suffering in him manifested great glory." [9]

This miraculous assistance Jesus has never refused to His martyrs; they could remind Him of His promise and say to Him, "By going to Your death, You have accomplished what Your Father commanded You; the same commandment urges me; I wish to accomplish it, manifest Yourself to me." [10] And Our Lord was faithful. The martyrs are the privileged ones of Our Lord, the primary objects of holy Church's veneration,[11] and the models of Christian perfection. In the first three centuries of the Church, "the martyr is the perfection and ideal towards which one must tend." [12] When peace was restored to the Church, one understood better that "peace too has its crowns" and its martyrdom.[13] But, by giving to Christian asceticism the help of monastic rules, they strove to carry it along towards the same goal, which

[9] *Ibid.*, 22–23 (FC 19, p. 278). To these passages we could add many more; cf. M. Viller, *"Martyre et perfection," Revue d'Ascétique et Mystique,* 1925, pp. 3–25, and our *Histoire du Dogme de la Trinité,* II, pp. 229–234.

[10] The martyrs were conscious of this right which their confession gave them: St. Ignatius of Antioch wrote: "It is the same with me: just because I am in chains and able to grasp heavenly things—the ranks of the angels, the hierarchy of principalities, *things visible and invisible*—it does not immediately follow that I am a disciple" (*To the Trallians,* V, 2 [ACW 1], pp. 76–77). Likewise the brother of St. Perpetua, who goes to visit her in her prison, said to her: "My honored sister, you are now possessed of great dignity; you can ask for a vision"; the saint asked for this and indeed obtained it (*Acts,* IV; cf. *The Passion of SS. Perpetua and Felicity, MM.*).

[11] Even now they alone are mentioned in the Canon of the Mass, in the diptychs.

[12] Viller, *art. cit.,* p. 17.

[13] Already Cyprian had said: *"Habet et pax coronas suas";* St. Jerome stresses: *"Habet et pax martyrium suum"* (*De Persecutione Christiana,* in *Anecdota Maredsolana,* ed. by Dom Morin, III, 402). These texts have been quoted by Father Viller in his article on *"Le Martyre et l'Ascèse," Revue d'Ascétique et de Mystique,* 1925, p. 113.

always remained the Christian ideal: "The monks, too, are
martyrs." [14]

It is not, then, to resurrect the past that we have looked first
of all into martyrdom for this revelation of Our Lord: *manifestabo meipsum* (Jn. 14:21): these great athletes have arrived suddenly at the goal by means of the "short cut of a consecrated death: *mortis sacrae compendio.*" This goal is the one
towards which we are tending; if we see Christ revealing Himself to them, He will reveal Himself also to all those who ac-

---

[14] St. Jerome, *Tractatus de Psalmo CXV. Anecdota Maredsolana,* III, 218–
219, quoted *ibid.,* p. 120.

[The basis for this comparison of the monk, the virgin, and the
ascetic with the martyr has been well stated by Father Elmer O'Brien,
S.J., in his article on "Ascetical and Mystical Theology, 1956–57," *Theological Studies,* March, 1958, pp. 58–59: "As Brilioth noted some years
ago, sacrifice in primitive Christianity was identified with what was done
in the Eucharist and not with what was done on Calvary. Now this directly
'eucharistic' understanding of martyrdom which Kettel has so splendidly
put in evidence offers us perhaps the final clue to much in primitive
spirituality that has hitherto remained so confusing. For instance, the
martyr's sacrifice did not consist essentially in his suffering and dying, and
yet he was held to be the perfect imitator of Christ in His dying; the virgin
and the ascetic did the same as the martyrs, theirs was a consummate
'sacrifice,' and yet death and suffering were as such not involved; the first
monks were esteemed as the successors to the martyrs, and yet the sufferings they imposed upon themselves were precautionary in purpose,
medicinal, and as such disassociated from the sufferings of Christ. And so
on. But now all such seemingly conflicting data can finally be resolved
into a harmonious and intelligible pattern; for the conflicts were born, it
would seem, only of our having read back into the documents a later
notion of sacrifice that was immediately derived, not from the Eucharist,
but from the Crucifixion and thus included the historical concomitants
of the sacrifice of Calvary, Christ's suffering and death. Sacrifice, however,
is dedication. Sacrifice to God is one's freely and irrevocably making something God's. Although this may sound strange to our post-Reformation
ears, it is at least historically true: thus did the primitive Church understand 'sacrifice.' And thus, in varying temporal circumstances, are the
monk, the ascetic, the virgin at one with the martyr; for the essence of the
martyr's act was dedication, not death (or suffering), as is clear from its
primary referent being, not Calvary, but the Eucharist."—Trans. note.]

complish sincerely and heroically the commandments of God.

Besides, the letters of St. Paul teach us this clearly enough: they reveal to us not only the visions which, at decisive moments, illumine the life of St. Paul and guide it,[15] but throughout this life, an action which is more and more profound and powerful:

The love of God impels us, because we have come to the conclusion that, since one died for all, therefore all died; and that Christ died for all, in order that they who are alive may live no longer for themselves, but for him who died for them and rose again (2 Cor. 5:14–15).

I through the Law have died to the Law that I may live to God. With Christ I am nailed to the cross. It is now no longer I that live, but Christ lives in me. And the life that I now live in the flesh, I live in the faith of the Son of God, who loved me and gave himself up for me (Gal. 2:19–20).

This life of Christ has taken hold of everything; it is so intimate and so dear to the Apostle that he exclaims, "Who shall separate us from the love of Christ? Shall tribulation, or distress, or persecution, or hunger, or nakedness, or danger, or the sword? . . . But in all these things we overcome because of him who has loved us. For I am sure that neither death, nor life, nor angels, nor principalities, nor things present, nor things to come, nor powers, nor height, nor depth, nor any other creature will be able to separate us from the love of God, which is in Christ Jesus our Lord" (Rom. 8:35–39).

This assurance is not illusory; it echoes the words of Jesus: "They shall never perish, neither shall anyone snatch them out of my hand. What my Father has given me is greater than all; and no one is able to snatch anything out of the hand of my Father. I and the Father are one" (Jn. 10:28–30). In the same

[15] There is first of all the apparition of Jesus to Saul, which made of the persecutor an apostle (1 Cor. 15:8; cf. 9:1); then there is the vision of, and rapture to, the third heaven (2 Cor. 12:1–6); we can join to these the answer of Our Lord to the entreaty of the Apostle: "My grace is sufficient for thee, for strength is made perfect in weakness" (2 Cor. 12:9).

sense, St. Ignatius of Antioch will call Jesus his "inseparable life." [16]

Thence comes, in the language of St. Paul, that phrase so often repeated and, for the Apostle, so rich in meaning: "in Christ Jesus," "in the Lord".[17]

Today these expressions have become commonplace, and for many Christians have lost their force; but what must have been the mystical life of the one who created them![18] Twenty years only after the death of Jesus, Paul—that Paul who has come so far: from Pharisaism, from earnest persecution—can no longer act or think or talk except in this Jesus whom so many people were able to know alive, were able to see in agony on His Cross. And this religious life has penetrated the whole Church, which henceforth lived only "in Christ Jesus." There is here a unique factor, which we cannot account for unless we recall what Jesus Himself has taught us:

Abide in me, and I in you. As the branch cannot bear fruit of itself unless it remain on the vine, so neither can you unless you abide in me. I am the vine, you are the branches. He who abides in me, and I in him, he bears much fruit; for without me you can do nothing (Jn. 15:4–5).

In viewing the wonderful constancy, and often the cheerfulness of the martyrs, we are compelled to recognize that a divine

---

[16] *To the Ephesians*, III, 2; ACW 1, p. 61.

[17] This phrase has been frequently studied, particularly by Deissmann, *Die neutestamentliche Formel in Christo Jesu* (Marburg, 1892); Prat, *Théologie de saint Paul*, II, pp. 476–480; A. Schweitzer, *Die Mystik des Apostles Paulus* (Tübingen, Mohr, 1930), pp. 122–126, and in tr. *The Mysticism of Paul the Apostle*, tr. by W. Montgomery, N. Y., Macmillan, 1955.

[18] Cf. Schweitzer, *ibid.*, p. 125: "The fact that the believer's whole being, down to his most ordinary everyday thoughts and actions, is thus brought within the sphere of the mystical experience has its effect of giving to this mysticism a breadth, a permanence, a practicability, and a strength almost unexampled elsewhere in mysticism. Certainly in this it is entirely different in character from the Hellenistic mysticism, which allowed daily life to go its own way apart from the mystical experience and without relation to it."

force animates them, and we are not surprised to see them conversing familiarly with Our Lord or beholding Him beside them. A Christian life, especially a heroic life like that of St. Paul, is as evident a miracle as that of martyrdom. The presence of Christ in the Apostle can alone explain it. And if we see this presence being revealed to one who lives by it, we marvel at this divine life, we are happy to behold it, we recognize in it the source of all those virtues which today still form the adornment of the Church.

These great lights illumine the whole of Christian spirituality: we might recall the prayer of St. Catherine of Siena, invoking the promise of Jesus and imploring its fulfilment: "He who has my commandments and keeps them, he it is who loves me. But he who loves me will be loved by my Father, and I will love him and manifest myself to him" (Jn. 14:21). We know full well that, if we keep Our Lord's commandments, if we love Him, it is to His grace that we owe it: "Without me you can do nothing" (15:5). We ask Him to make us conscious of this action which He exercises in us, and which is the source of all our merits.

It is, on His part, a boundless grace to dwell in wretched people like ourselves, to live there, to act there, there to feed our Christian life as the vine nourishes the branches. This action is so intimate that it escapes our consciousness; a special grace from God is needed to make it appear in our souls. This grace is one of the distinctive characteristics of the mystical life; it enables us to take note of what faith alone up to then revealed to us. It is not at all essential to the development of our spiritual life, but it brings thereto a very efficacious help; it is not out of curiosity, but out of piety, that we beseech Our Lord to manifest Himself to us.

When God awakens this pious, humble desire, the soul ought to welcome it and pray. How will she be able to come to this intimacy which she begs for? St. Teresa of Avila answers: "At first, by recognizing ourselves as unworthy of it." [19] It is here,

---

[19] "As well as acting, then, as do those who have dwelt in the Mansions already described, have humility and again humility! . . . The first way in which you will see if you have humility is that if you have it you will not

especially, that the soul should repeat with the Apostle: *Non volentis neque currentis, sed miserentis est Dei* (Rom. 9:16).

The soul, then, will not reach out for these graces by an effort of the imagination or by ambition; if God calls her, He will let her experience in the depths of her heart a peaceful, humble desire which only He can give. This first call will be recognized instinctively by the soul which the Holy Spirit renders docile to her Lord: "The sheep hear his voice, and he calls his own sheep by name and leads them forth . . . and the sheep follow him because they know his voice" (Jn. 10:3–4).[20]

Whoever has heard this first call of Our Lord can no longer, as long as he is faithful, hear another master: "To whom shall we go? Thou hast the words of everlasting life" (Jn. 6:69). This sovereign voice draws him and detaches him: the Good Shepherd "calls his own sheep by name and leads them forth":

---

think you merit these favours and consolations of the Lord or are likely to get them for as long as you live. 'But how,' you will ask, 'are we to gain them if we do not strive after them?' I reply that there is no better way than this one which I have described. There are several reasons why they should not be striven for. The first is because the most essential thing is that we should love God without any motive of self-interest. The second is because there is some lack of humility in our thinking that in return for our miserable services we can obtain anything so great. The third is because the true preparation for receiving these gifts is a desire to suffer and to imitate the Lord, not to receive consolations; for, after all, we have often offended Him. The fourth reason is because His Majesty is not obliged to grant them to us, as He is obliged to grant us glory if we keep His commandments, without doing which we could not be saved. . . . The fifth reason is that we should be labouring in vain; for this water does not flow through conduits, as the other does, and so we gain nothing by fatiguing ourselves if it cannot be had at the source." (*Interior Castle,* "Fourth Mansion," ch. II, in *Complete Works,* tr. by E. A. Peers, London, Sheed, 1946).
[20] St. Teresa has spoken on several occasions of this first call of Christ; she refers to this text of St. John; she describes the senses and powers as spread throughout the interior castle: "Like a good Shepherd, with a call so gentle that even they can hardly recognize it, He teaches them to know His voice and not to go away and get lost but to return to their Mansion; and so powerful is this Shepherd's call that they give up the things outside the castle which had led them astray, and once again enter it." (*Ibid.,* ch. III).

this is always the same sovereign call, which detaches and unites: it is the call which the virgins, too, hear in the middle of the night: "Behold, the bridegroom is coming, go forth to meet him" (Mt. 25:6). In his *Adornment of the Spiritual Nuptials,* Ruysbroeck describes the progressive requirements of divine Love disengaging its disciple from the world, from his family, and finally from himself. It is always the same call which resounds: "Behold the bridegroom is coming, go forth to meet him! Go forth . . . Go forth . . ." If the soul is thus urged to detach herself from everything, it is in order to become attached to Him who calls her: "The love of God impels us, because we have come to the conclusion that, since one died for all, therefore all died" (2 Cor. 5:14).[21]

Under the sway of a burning charity, faith is engraved more deeply in the heart. God reveals no new mysteries at all; He has told us everything through His Son. But the mysteries of our faith, which too often have glanced off our souls, finally penetrate them: before this mystery of a God having died for him, of a God living for him, the child of God feels himself incapable of responding to such a love: "The ardor of this intimate touch and of His love is such that it wants to consume us entirely; it cries out unceasingly to our spirit: 'Pay your debt, love the love which has eternally loved you.' " But how to pay that debt? "Then when that humble man sees and understands that he cannot accomplish what God craves for him, he falls at the feet of Our Lord, saying: 'Lord, I cannot acquit myself towards Thee; I abandon myself and deliver myself into Thy hands.' " [22]

It is always the same avowal of humility which God asks of us: *non habentibus illis unde redderent donavit utrisque.* The contrition of the sinner, the burning desire of the mystic—deliver them both over, in the same trustful humility, to the mercy of Our Lord. This is the fundamental truth which we must often recall

---

[21] On these progressive requirements of the love of God, one may read Ruysbroeck, *The Seven Steps of the Ladder of Spiritual Love,* tr. from the Flemish by F. Taylor, Westminster (London), Dacre (A & C Black), 1944.

[22] Ruysbroeck, *op. cit.*

to souls whom God leads by this way. God's appeals, when they are pressing, give rise to great distress. "Lord, what wilt thou have me do?" (Acts 9:6). This cry of St. Paul rises instinctively to all lips: from the moment we begin to understand what the love of God is and that we must respond to it, we can only repeat, "Please, Lord, what shall I do for this? You see clearly that I have nothing!" God, then, bends over His child humiliated at His feet, and lifts him up again.

His love is his whole response; if we say to Him, "What do you want of me?", He has but one word to say to us: "Yourself!" This gift of self is said in a word; it is realized only by the whole of life.

Here we shall not undertake to describe this mystical life and to follow its progressive development. The New Testament does not furnish us, along this lengthy route and its stages, descriptions which we might compare with those of the great mystical doctors, particularly of St. Teresa of Avila and St. John of the Cross; it is to these masters that we must be referred. What Our Lord does reveal to us in His Discourse are the high summits which dominate this whole mountain range.

The first is the manifestation which He promises us of Himself: *manifestabo ei meipsum* (Jn. 14:21). We have mentioned it briefly; we must dwell on it more at length.

What we shall pick out, first of all, is the decisive role of this manifestation of the Son of God: "No one comes to the Father but through me" (14:6). There is here a fundamental maxim we must not lose sight of. Souls eager for mystical contemplation would gladly repeat the ambitious, naive request of St. Philip: "Lord, show us the Father and it is enough for us." Jesus can only reply to us what He replies to His apostle: "Have I been so long a time with you, and you have not known me? Philip, he who sees me sees also the Father" (14:8–9). It is in the Son that we know the Father. It is, then, an illusion to claim to reach the Father without beholding the Son; it is an illusion to consider this contemplation of the Son as an inferior knowledge which one would go beyond to reach the Father. [23]

[23] Cf. above, pp. 248–249.

We must dismiss, then, those factitious oppositions which certain historians picture—in St. Paul, for example—between a *Christusmystik* and a *Gottesmystik* and, in like manner, between a Christocentric contemplation and a theocentric contemplation. The Gospel knows nothing of these oppositions: it tells us, "He who sees me sees also the Father . . . Dost thou not believe that I am in the Father and the Father in me?" (14:9–10).

Here we encounter the fundamental opposition between Christian mysticism and neo-Platonic mysticism: Platonism, and especially neo-Platonism, pictures between the human soul and God a natural affinity which permits us to arrive at the contemplation of God and at ecstasy through our own efforts.[24] From its first contact with it, Christianity has rejected this claim: to arrive at this knowledge of God to which we aspire, it is necessary for God to reveal Himself, and for this revelation to reach us, and for our souls to be illumined interiorly by the grace of the Holy Spirit.[25] The revealer of the Father is the Son: no one knows "the Father except the Son, and him to whom the Son chooses to reveal him." [26] This revelation is proposed to us by Our Lord's teaching, and better still, by His life here below.[27]

---

[24] This is what Justin, before his conversion, explains to the old man he met. "Plato says that the eye of the spirit is such that it has been given to us to be able to contemplate by its own transparency Being itself. This Being is the principle of all our concepts; it has neither color, nor exterior form, nor extension, nor anything like that whereby the eye of the body perceives. But, he adds, it is a Being above every essence, indescribable and ineffable; it alone is Beautiful and Good; it is found immediately innate in souls of good disposition, by a certain affinity and desire to see it" (*Dialogue,* IV. 1. Cf. *Justin Martyr, The Dialogue with Trypho,* tr. by A. Williams, N. Y., Macmillan, 1930).

[25] Cf. *Histoire du Dogme de la Trinité,* II, pp. 412–415.

[26] Mt. 11:27. One might read again on this text the commentaries of St. Irenaeus: *Adv. Haer.,* IV, 6, 3–7; II, 30, 9; IV, 20, 7. These texts are quoted and studied in *Histoire du Dogme de la Trinité,* II, pp. 590–595.

[27] "We could not know the things of God, unless our Master became man, while remaining the Word. For no one else could reveal to us what is from the Father, except His Word . . . And, on the other hand, we could only learn by seeing our Master and by hearing, through listening, the sound of His voice" (Irenaeus, *ibid.,* V, 1, 1, quoted *ibid.,* p. 599).

Under the veil of His flesh will appear to us the Son of God; He accommodates Himself in this way to our infirmity and "accustoms us to perceive God." [28] The gift of the Holy Spirit illumines for us this revelation of God Incarnate; our weakness is lifted up to God.[29]

The contemplation of the Son of God is not, then, for the Christian an inferior stage of religious knowledge, which we must go beyond to reach the Father directly; it is by means of the Son and in the Son that we know the Father. If we consider its object, which is God Himself, this knowledge is sovereign and cannot be transcended; if we consider the man who perceives it, this knowledge is always, here below, capable of progress: the more lofty and pure it is, the more avid it will be to grasp fully at last through the intuitive vision Him whom it still knows only through faith. Thereby, again, Christian mysticism will be distinguished from neo-Platonic mysticism. The Platonist claims to arrive, while still in this present life, at that complete and untroubled possession which he pursues; this is a dream which he has striven in vain to realize. The Christian, on the contrary, will always repeat the words of St. Paul: "Not that I have already obtained this, or already have been made perfect, but I press on hoping that I may lay hold of that for which Christ Jesus has laid hold of me. Brethren, I do not consider that I have laid hold of it already. But one thing I do: forgetting what is behind, I strain forward to what is before, I press on towards the goal, to the prize of God's heavenly call in Christ Jesus" (Phil. 3:12–14). This goal is always the Son of God, never surpassed and never so much as fully grasped. Still, when the promise of the Master is fulfilled for the disciple, *manifestabo ei meipsum*

---

[28] "The Word of God gives to man the power to grasp the Father; He has dwelt in man, He was made the son of man, in order to accustom man to perceive God, to accustom God to dwell in man, according to the good pleasure of the Father" (Irenaeus, *ibid.*, III, 70, 2, quoted *ibid.*, p. 600).
[29] "Without the Spirit there is no seeing the Word of God, and without the Son there is no approaching the Father; for the Son is knowledge of the Father, and knowledge of the Son is through the Holy Spirit" [Irenaeus, *Demonstration 7*, quoted *ibid.*, p. 601, and in tr. *Proof of the Apostolic Preaching* (ACW 16), pp. 51–52].

(Jn. 14:21), then at last he knows Him and is conscious of possessing Him.

This knowledge is a treasure which transforms the whole of life. Already, in the whole course of his lengthy endeavors, the Christian, fully docile to the commandments of Our Lord, is conformed to His will: thus it is, we have seen, that in St. Peter whatever had made for constraint in that practice of Judaism eases up so as to open completely to the liberty of the Gospel; thus it is that St. Paul comes to the point of seeing nothing but prejudices in what he had for so long a time considered as privileges. He can no longer place his confidence in the flesh, nor glorify himself in the flesh, when he considers the "excelling knowledge of Jesus Christ" (Phil. 3:8). In face of this transcendent value, all human values are diminished in the world, all judgments transformed, and gradually the Christian acquires the "mind of Christ" (Phil. 2:5 ff.; cf. 1 Cor. 2:16).

All that was still only a preparation. In manifesting Himself to man, Christ brings to him a new gift—Himself. To the Marcionites, who asked what the Incarnation of the Son of God had given us, St. Irenaeus replied:

Know that He has given us every newness, in giving Himself, He who had been announced: a new principle had to come, which would renew and vivify mankind. The servants who are sent in front of the king announce his coming, so that the subjects can get ready to receive their Lord. But, when the King has come, when His subjects have been filled to overflowing with that joy which had been foretold to them, when they have received from Him their freedom, when they have gazed on His countenance, when they have heard His words, when they have enjoyed His gifts, they no longer ask—not, at any rate, if they have any sense—what this King has given more than the precursors had announced. He has given Himself, He has given to men those gifts which had been promised, and for which even the angels pine.[30]

[30] Irenaeus, *Adv. Haer.*, IV, 34, 1, quoted in *Histoire du Dogme de la Trinité*, II, pp. 598–599.

This history of mankind, or rather of the Church, appears to us reproduced by God in the life of each of the faithful: to each Christian He wills to give His Son; He prepares him for this gift by that lengthy formation we have described: He accustoms him gradually to think, feel, and act like Christ, and, under the action of the Holy Spirit, to acquire the "mind of Christ." The end of this lengthy series of graces is the manifestation of Christ Himself.

This manifestation transforms the whole of life: whatever up to that time had been scattered and obscure becomes clarified in the light of Christ and is unified in Him. "I determined not to know anything among you, except Jesus Christ and him crucified" (1 Cor. 2:2). This concentration of the whole of his thought, of the whole of his life in Christ, is not explained, in the case of St. Paul, by a few occasional considerations, by the remembrance of the failure at Athens or by the very keen awareness of the moral miseries in which the Corinthians were involved. These encounters could have awakened in the soul of the Apostle his total adherence to Christ and given him more fervor; they did not create it.

The source of this fervor is the revelation of Christ, perceived by St. Paul, which illumines his whole life. If, amid mankind, in the world, Jesus Christ was only a person—eminent no doubt, but on the level of the others—this exclusive preoccupation of a life, of a thinking wholly and completely centered on Him, would be a dangerous mono-ideology. But if Christ is in fact the Head of mankind and the Lord of the world, this attitude is the only one fully in accord with faith. All other things, and especially all men, are by no means forgotten, but are contemplated in Christ, in the essential relation which every man has to Him: created by Him, saved by Him, he lives only by Him and for Him. Hence, is it not true that we do not really understand anyone, unless we know Christ, who is his beginning and end, his first cause and final goal?[31]

31 When Father de Grandmaison, at the age of twenty-one, was finishing his literary studies and getting ready to begin his philosophical studies,

Reason suffices to justify this view of all things in Christ; it does not suffice to bring it to birth in the soul: there is needed that manifestation which transforms the whole of life, by letting its source in Jesus Christ be seen. We must be able to say with St. Paul, "To me to live is Christ" (Phil. 1:21); "It is now no longer I that live, but Christ lives in me. And the life that I now live in the flesh, I live in the faith of the Son of God, who loved me and gave himself up for me" (Gal. 2:20). At one and the same time with this inward action, the Apostle contemplates the radiating of the Son of God in the whole world: "All things have been created through and unto him, and he is before all creatures, and in him all things hold together. Again, he is the head of his body, the Church; he, who is the beginning, the firstborn from the dead, that in all things he may have the first place . . ." (Col. 1:16–18).

The fruit of this revelation of Jesus Christ appears to us in the teaching and activity of the Apostle; everything tends towards orientating Christians towards that unique source of light and life: in the apostolic Church the remembrance of Christ is constantly present and active.[32] Moral exhortation is backed up by His example[33] and, more still, illumined by His presence, which faith reveals; obedience, so burdensome to the slaves and often so degrading, is ennobled by the homage rendered to Christ:

---

his professor of French literature, Father Longhaye, wrote him with all the fervor of his friendship and with all the authority of his experience and talent: "If this testament had—what it has not—an obligatory force, I would enjoin on you one thing, one single thing: to seek in every object of study the connection with Jesus Christ, the means, more or less direct, but always existing, of making every bit of knowledge acquired a witness in favor of Jesus Christ. All the rest is curiosity, more or less incomplete or debased" (J. Lebreton, *Le Père L. de Grandmaison,* Paris, Beauchesne, 1932, pp. 39–40).

[32] I take the liberty of referring to what I have said about this in the *Histoire de l'Eglise* (Fliche-Martin), I, *L'Eglise primitive,* pp. 259 ff., and in tr. *The History of the Primitive Church.*

[33] We must forget ourselves in order to imitate Jesus Christ, who, being by nature God, took the nature of a slave (Phil. 2:6–7); we must give alms generously, following the example of Christ, who, being rich, became poor (2 Cor. 8:9).

"Slaves, obey your masters according to the flesh, with fear and trembling in the sincerity of your heart, as you would Christ: not serving to the eye as pleasers of men, but as slaves of Christ, doing the will of God from your heart, giving your service with good will as to the Lord and not to men, in the knowledge that whatever good each does, the same will receive back from the Lord, whether he is slave or freeman" (Eph. 6:5–8).

This teaching of the Apostle is recalled by St. Ignatius Loyola to his religious in the Letter on Obedience; and, indeed, it gives us the light we need: the force, the dignity of our obedience consist in a deep and complete sincerity, which takes hold of all our powers and makes them all tend to the same end, with no reserves, no regrets, the will giving itself with all its energy and the judgment adhering in all docility.

How to arrive at that? How to love with the same sincerity, with the same heart, Pius X, Benedict XV, Pius XI, Pius XII, John XXIII? By seeing Our Lord Himself in him who commands us in His name:

Just as we are inclined with all our heart and all our judgment to believe what the Catholic faith proposes to us, so we are inclined to do unhesitatingly all that the superior tells us, with the force of will which aims only at obeying; in all things, of course, except where they would command us to do a manifest sin.[34]

This view of faith enlightens every Christian and gives to his obedience its dignity and merit; but when, by a higher grace, this faith is illumined, when Christ, as He has promised, manifests Himself to His faithful disciple, then the soul is carried along towards God with a force it never knew before.

In the life of St. Catherine of Siena, Blessed Raymond of Capua recounts to us that one day, hearing the words of the saint, he was quite astounded at them and had difficulty giving credence to them:

[34] St. Ignatius Loyola, *Letter on Obedience*.

While I had these thoughts and was looking at Catherine's countenance, her face was suddenly transformed into that of a man who, fixing on me a stern look, frightened me greatly. This countenance was of an oval shape and of a middle-aged man. The sparse beard had a golden tinge to it. Majesty, which was reflected over this whole physiognomy, revealed clearly Our Lord. I could not, at that moment, recognize in that vision any other face but His. While trembling and afraid, I raised my hands shoulder-high and cried out, "Oh, who is this who looks at me?" The virgin answered me, "It is He who is." So speaking, this face disappeared at once, and I saw again clearly the face of the virgin, which a moment before I could not see.[35]

This vision, miraculous but transitory, enables us to understand this view of faith which the grace of Christ illumines: man disappears, Our Lord is revealed.

Like obedience, fraternal charity is transformed by this manifestation of Christ. On the last day Jesus will say to His faithful, "You gave me to eat . . . gave me to drink . . . took me in . . . visited me." And they will say to Him, "Lord, when?" And He will answer them, "As long as you did it for one of these, the least of my brethren, you did it for me" (Mt. 25:35– 40). Admirable mercy of our Head, who rewards as done to Himself whatever is done to one of His members! But how much more perfect is fraternal love, when it recognizes Our Lord in the neighbor it assists! This is that love which St. Paul admires in his faithful: "You received me . . . even as Christ Jesus" (Gal. 4:14). The view of faith, consequently, is no longer only a reflection of heaven come to color an earthly view, or a Christian remembrance giving more nobility and purity to a natural sympathy. The whole of life in its entirety, seized by Christ, attains Him, first of all, and men in Him. We marvel at the heroic charity of a St. Paul, of a St. Vincent de Paul, of a Father Damien. We marvel at it; we cannot imitate it without taking from Him its inspiration: if this torrent of love is so powerful, it is because it falls from heaven.

But humility, more than any other virtue, is illumined by the

[35] *Life,* ch. IX.

light of Christ and transformed. We have heard the cry of fright from St. Peter feeling so wretched before his Lord: "Depart from me, for I am a sinful man, O Lord" (Lk. 5:8). This first seizure subsides, but each day the contrast is more keenly felt between the sinner and his Lord:

My soul has always known that it was the nothing to which the All was pleased to grant mercy, because He is not a respecter of persons, and I have always believed in, and seen, in the same knowledge, the nothingness of the creature, being quite at ease in being this nothingness and in knowing that this great God was all. And in my loving activity, it was one of my canticles to say to Him: "My chaste Love, it is my glory that Thou art all and I am nothing. Blessed art Thou, O my Love!" These feelings of lowliness have given me some fears, granted the proportion of the two beings so opposed. As I talked of it with my divine Spouse, He signified to me by interior words: "I will that you praise Me and sing My praises as the blessed spirits praise Me in heaven" . . . I was thirty-eight to thirty-nine years old at the time.[36]

The Virgin Mary, more than any other human creature, has been illumined by this light; her humility too, has been incomparable. She saw growing up beside her that Child in whom she adored her God; she beheld in Him "all the treasures of wisdom and knowledge" (Col 2:3), hidden treasures, and all the more admirable. Under this rather plain veil of silence, peace, and love of the Father, she penetrated those unfathomable riches which no human gaze can pierce to their depths. In face of such majesty and such humility, one can only adore, love, and serve.

[36] Marie de l'Incarnation, *Relation de 1654, Ecrits spirituels,* II, p. 266.

❖❖❖❖❖❖❖❖❖❖

chapter 14

The Discourse after the Last Supper: Fraternal Charity

A new commandment I give you, that you love one another: that as I have loved you, you also love one another (Jn. 13:34).

It is the course of the final evening, in the Discourse after the Last Supper, that Jesus has willed to promulgate His new commandment: on this evening when He institutes the Holy Eucharist, when already He gives Himself up to death for men, He brings out the inner meaning of these divine examples and the lesson which they leave us. This teaching, an echo of His whole life, is also His last will and is going to stamp on the memories of His disciples an indelible impression.

It is in this light that we must study this precept in which is summed up the whole law of Christ.

It is new, and yet the whole teaching of Our Lord, like His whole life, tended towards it. His first step had been the gift which He made to us of Himself at the Incarnation, and already

His example involved us in fraternal charity, going as far as the sacrifice of ourselves for our brethren: "We likewise ought to lay down our life for the brethren" (1 Jn. 3:16).

The first discourse of Our Lord, on the Mount, dwelt with great emphasis on this duty of charity: He urged us to love not only those who do us good but those who persecute and calumniate us, and the example He proposed to us was that of the heavenly Father, "who makes his sun to rise on the good and the evil, and sends rain on the just and the unjust." To love those who love you, to love your brethren—even sinners do that, and the Gentiles; "you therefore are to be perfect, even as your heavenly Father is perfect" (Mt. 5:43–48).

To this duty of the love of enemies, Our Lord added the duty of the pardon of offenses: "If you forgive men their offenses, your heavenly Father will also forgive you your offenses. But if you do not forgive men, neither will your Father forgive you your offenses" (Mt. 6:14–15). This duty, so costly to human pride, is recalled by Jesus with the utmost emphasis and without reserve: St. Peter will ask Him one day, "Lord, how often shall my brother sin against me, and I forgive him? Up to seven times?" Jesus replied, "I do not say to thee seven times, but seventy times seven" (Mt. 18:21–22); and, to understand His thinking better, He proposed the parable of the Unmerciful Servant: in debt to the sum of ten thousand talents which he could not pay, he had obtained from his master a release from this huge debt. Meeting, then, one of his fellow servants who owed him a hundred denarii, he laid hold of him and throttled him, saying, "Pay what thou owest." The poor man, not being able to pay, was cast by him into prison. The master, hearing what had happened, was indignant:

"Wicked servant! I forgave thee all the debt, because thou didst entreat me. Shouldst not thou also have had pity on thy fellow servant, even as I had pity on thee?" And his master, being angry, handed him over to the torturers until he should pay all that was due to him. So also my heavenly Father will do to you, if you do not each forgive your brothers from your hearts (Mt. 18:23–35).

To render more continually present and dear to us the remembrance of this duty, Jesus willed to have us repeat in our prayer: "Forgive us our debts, as we also forgive our debtors" (Mt. 6:12; cf. Mk. 11:25).

What gives force to these precepts is the close bond which attaches them to our divine adoption; we cannot be sons of God if we do not imitate our Father. His beneficent love covers all men; our charity cannot know any exclusion. And if our selfishness claims to defend its rights while nursing grudges, our Father recalls to us our debts towards Himself.

In his short letter to Philemon, St. Paul, interceding for a fugitive slave and thief, said to his master, "If he did thee any injury or owes thee anything, charge it to me" (Phlm. 18). It is thus that our heavenly Father acts towards us: "If you forgive men their offenses, your heavenly Father will also forgive you your offenses" (Mt. 6:14).

And here again there appears to us the drastic exigency, at the same time as the great kindness, of this law of charity: the paternal heart of God is open to all men; the prodigal son, as low as he might fall, can come back to the paternal house; if he is sincerely repentant, his Father will welcome him with open arms and restore him to his place in the home. It is necessary, then, that the other children welcome him also: the elder son may not harden himself in his pharisaic pride, and even if he has a personal grievance, he must renounce it: he himself has need of pardon, and the pardon is at that price.

This duty of pardon seems very burdensome to selfish and easily offended souls. But, when the love of God has touched them, they cannot on this point turn a deaf ear to His call. They can be slow to get rid of their other faults; but if they are faithful to God, it is impossible for them still to nurse their grudges.[1]

---

[1] Cf. St. Teresa of Avila, *Way of Perfection*, XXXVI, 13 (*Complete Works*): "I know many persons to whom Our Lord has granted the grace of raising them to supernatural experiences and of giving them this prayer, or contemplation, which has been described; and although I may notice other faults and imperfections in them, I have never seen such a person who had this particular fault, nor do I believe such a person exists, if the fa-

In the small society of the apostles, gathered together by the call of Christ and sustained by His teaching and example, one does not see those stubborn obstinacies closing the soul to charity —the hatred of enemies, the pitiless resentment for offenses. Not even suspicions affect these souls deeply. After the sorrowful scene at Capharnaum, when Jesus declared to the Twelve that one of them was a devil (Jn. 6:71), Judas remained an entire year in the apostolic college, living in the intimacy of Jesus and of the other apostles, without rousing, on their part, any suspicion, and yet without abandoning his projects of treason and without returning to the heart of his Master. At the Last Supper, when Jesus repeats His warnings: "One of you will betray me," the apostles in consternation ask, "Is it I, Lord?" (Mt. 26:21–22). Not one of them says, "It is he." They still were aware of their innocence, they believed in the prophecy of Our Lord, but instinctively they forbade any inquiry one of the other. We feel here the power of those habits of mutual respect, reserve, and charity which Jesus had created around Himself.

And yet these men still had much to do in order to raise themselves to that ideal of charity which their Master was going to propose to them in His example: "As I have loved you, you also love one another" (Jn. 13:34). This was truly a "new commandment." We understand it better by noting a few passages pointed out by the Evangelists in the course of their narratives.

At the multiplication of the loaves, "when he landed, Jesus saw a large crowd, and had compassion on them, because they were like sheep without a shepherd" (Mk. 6:34). He pitied their moral misery, but also their poverty and need. The apostles saw it just as well, but they conclude therefrom: "The hour is already late; send them away, so that they may go to the farms and villages round about and buy themselves food to eat." Jesus

---

vours he has received are of God." *Ibid.,* 12: "I cannot believe that a soul which has approached so nearly to Mercy Itself, and has learned to know itself and the greatness of God's pardon, will not immediately and readily forgive, and be mollified and remain on good terms with a person who has done her wrong." Cf. St. Francis de Sales, *The Love of God,* Bk. 10, ch. 8, pp. 407–410.

answered them, "You yourselves give them some food" (*ibid.*, 37). But how? All they have is the scant provisions of a child: five barley loaves and two fishes; what is that for so many? Thus Moses of old: "Whence should I have flesh to give to so great a multitude? They weep against me, saying: 'Give us flesh that we may eat?' I am not able alone to bear all this people, because it is too heavy for me" (Nm. 11:13–14). The apostles begin to understand what this pastoral charge is to which the Master initiates them.

A little later on, in the country of Tyre, before the importunities of the Canaanite woman: "Send her away," they said, "for she is crying after us" (Mt. 15:23). But, when the children besiege them, it is necessary for Jesus to come to the little ones' defense. The instinctive reaction of human selfishness will always be: You are bothering us; go away.

More dangerous even than this selfishness are rivalries and jealousies: the disciples of St. John the Baptist say to him, "Rabbi, he who was with thee beyond the Jordan, to whom thou hast borne witness, behold he baptizes and all are coming to him." John has to answer them, "The friend of the bridegroom, who stands and hears him, rejoices exceedingly at the voice of the bridegroom. This my joy, therefore, is made full. He must increase, but I must decrease" (Jn. 3:26–30). Later, the apostle St. John will say, "Master, we saw a man casting out devils in thy name, and we forbade him, because he does not follow with us." Jesus replies, "Do not forbid him; for he who is not against you is for you" (Lk. 9:49–50).

The most dangerous reef for charity is ambitious claims: the apostles quarrel over the first places, they oppose each other, they take offense. Jesus must intervene in order to propose to them, in the light of His example, unselfishness, service, charity.

After the ambitious request of the sons of Zebedee, "when the ten heard this, they were at first indignant at James and John" (Mk. 10:41). Even at the start of the Last Supper, "there arose also a dispute among them, which of them was reputed to be the greatest" (Lk. 22:24). When we consider these weaknesses, we can say with St. Francis de Sales: "Souls which have attained a place among the happy number of perfect lovers sometimes fall off so considerably, as to commit many imperfections, and even serious venial sins. We may judge of this by the angry disputes and bitter contests occasionally carried on between eminent servants of God. The apostles themselves were not exempt from these and other imperfections. Yet, as they were usually animated with a pure and generous love for God, they should not, on account of their human frailties, be retrenched from the number of the most perfect lovers." [2]

These are human weaknesses, which the "new commandment" bids us transcend. "It is more blessed to give than to receive" (Acts 20:35). These words of Jesus, illumined by His example, release us from this whole entanglement of petty preoccupations in which self-love imprisons us. Self-love is a miser and is conscious of its impoverishment; it wants always to receive, and not to give; and, if it gives, it will want to reimburse itself by the familiarities it covets: the first and the second place in the kingdom. Experience, however, ought to give us a distaste for all these beggarly schemes: this begging has never enriched anyone. We shall angle for a little gratitude, a little affection, a little esteem; we do not always obtain it and, even when we succeed in doing so or think we have succeeded, we hear the sovereign voice warning us: "They have had their reward" (Mt. 6:16).

Opposed to that, the charity of Christ gives without expecting anything in return, except the heavenly Father, and this gift goes as far as death: "The Son of man also has not come to be served but to serve, and to give his life as a ransom for many" (Mk. 10:45). This prospect of the redemptive death hovers over the final evening, and the institution of the Eucharist renders it present; it is the light which gives to the "new commandment" all its force. "The love of Christ impels us, because we have come to the conclusion that, since one died for all, therefore all died; and that Christ died for all, in order that they who are alive may live no longer for themselves, but for him who died for them and rose again" (2 Cor. 5:14–15). This death of Christ

[2] Cf. *The Love of God,* X, ch. 5, pp. 402–403.

frees us from the whole past; this resurrection of Christ involves us in a new life; members of Christ, we owe all to the Body and Head, nothing to the flesh, nothing to the world.

From men the Apostle expects nothing more; he well knows that, loving them more, he is "loved less"; and yet he "will most gladly spend and be spent" for their souls (2 Cor. 12:15).

He gives, and it is already the mark of the divine blessing. How much do we have? The provisions of a child: five loaves and two fishes, and God will give us five thousand men to feed, and He will feed them, as a matter of fact, through our hands; or, like the widow of Sarephta to whom God entrusted the prophet Elias, they have only a "little oil in a cruse," only a "handful of meal in a pot," and with that they will live and they will cause to live for ten years (3 Kgs. 17:12).

And whence comes that unexpected fecundity to such poor works, if not from the death and the resurrection of Our Lord? The light of the Cross is poured out on all those unknown souls, for whom Christ has died. The charity of Christ impels us, we said a while ago; but at the same time it precedes us, it calls us. Having come to Troas and not knowing where he must go, St. Paul sees in a vision a Macedonian standing before him and saying to him, "Come over into Macedonia and help us" (Acts 16:9). These souls, ransomed by Christ, have rights over the Apostle: "To Greeks and to foreigners, to learned and un-learned, I am debtor" (Rom. 1:14). Begotten to a new life, they still impel him: "My dear children, with whom I am in labor again, until Christ is formed in you!" (Gal. 4:19). And for years to come, they will be mere children whom he must feed with milk (1 Cor. 3:2); he will have to preserve their weakness from all scandal, at the cost of any sacrifice: "If, then, thy brother is grieved because of thy food, no longer dost thou walk according to charity. Do not with thy food destroy him for whom Christ died" (Rom. 14:15). In this concern for Christ which absorbs all else, selfishness disappears: "None of us lives to himself, and none dies to himself; for if we live, we live to the Lord, or if we die, we die to the Lord. Therefore, whether we live or die, we are the Lord's" (ibid., 7–8).

The foundation of the Church, the Body of Christ, is going to draw these bonds of charity tighter and compel all Christians thereto by a new title: "Bear one another's burdens, and so you will fulfill the law of Christ" (Gal. 6:2).

In this whole new life, nothing surpasses the ideal proposed by Jesus on the Mount: one does not surpass a divine ideal. But, in the light of Christ having died and risen for us, this ideal of charity appears closer to us, more imperative and dear: forgiveness is commanded us by the forgiveness of God, as it was in the parable of the Unmerciful Servant (Mt. 18:35); but this forgiveness of God appears to us in Christ:

"Be kind to one another, and merciful, generously forgiving one another, as also God in Christ has generously forgiven you" (Eph. 4:32). The example we must reproduce is always the supreme ideal, the sovereignly good God; but this example seems to us even more compelling in Christ, who died for us: "Be you, therefore, imitators of God, as very dear children and walk in love, as Christ also loved us and delivered himself up for us an offering and a sacrifice to God to ascend in fragrant odor" (Eph. 5:1–2).

Pure eyes, luminous eyes, enlightened by this light of Christ, succeed little by little in recognizing the image and traces of God in their brethren, as Rachel recognized in the features of the young Tobias the likeness of the father he loved.[3]

If we compare our natural blindness to this clearsightedness given by grace and by the love of God, what a contrast! No one has felt this more keenly than St. Augustine:

What is there more human than the inability to look into another human heart and, in our powerlessness to scan its recesses, very often to suspect there something other than what is going on in it.

---

[3] Tob. 7:2 ff. Cf. St. Francis de Sales, *Love of God,* 1, X, ch. XI, pp. 416–417: "The love of God not only frequently commands the love of our neighbor but produces and diffuses it in the heart, as its image and likeness. For as man is the image of God, so the perfect and holy love of our neighbor is the image of the love which inflames the heart of man for God."

The darknesses of the heart are responsible for a surprising and deplorable fact. Sometimes we suppose a person unjust, and yet he is just; and loving the justice in him which we are in ignorance of, we avoid him, turn our backs on him. . . I have caused wrong without knowing it; it is not a lack of discernment of virtues and vices which causes my error, it is the darknesses of the human heart.[4]

How many times have the souls of the most saintly been misunderstood by those surrounding them! Thus St. Thérèse of Lisieux: a Carmelite of her convent said of her towards the end of her life: "When this little Sister is dead, what shall we be able to say of her?" Sometimes this goes much further; thus for St. Geneviève, St. Germain had to intervene with his authority for her defense. We may recall again the persecutions undergone at Paray by St. Margaret Mary. And these misunderstandings are not encountered only in the cloisters; the active life, by the conflicts it provokes, has often given birth to them: St. Epiphanius lets himself become involved in the secret meeting of the Council that wishes to depose St. Chrysostom; Manning will write one day: "Newman is the most dangerous man in England."

The excuse for these mistakes is the obscurity in which we live. If we wish to preserve ourselves from it, we must mount towards the divine light and strive to see everything in God.

This intuition will be perfect only in heaven, just as this divine likeness will be without blemish only among the elect;[5] but faith

---

[4] *Tractatus in Joann.*, XC, 2–3, col. 1859–60. Cf. *Confessions*, I, 6, 8 (FC 21, p. 9).

[5] On the happiness of the elect, one may read St. Catherine of Siena, *Dialogue*, 41 and 148: "Oh, how fraternal is that charity! How closely it unites to Me all these souls and all among themselves, since it is from Me that they hold it, and they recognize with holy fear and perfect respect that it is from Me that they have received it. This communication embraces them with love for Me; and in Me henceforth they see and know the dignity to which I have raised them. The angel enters into communication with man, with the blessed soul, and the blessed with the angels; united as they are by the bonds of charity, each rejoices with the happiness of the other; and all together exult in the possession of Myself. This is a jubilation, a joy without sadness, a sweetness without bitterness, be-

and grace prepare us for it. To him who lives in the light of Christ, everything, and especially men, appear no longer as those dark shadows in which our susceptibilities and ambitions are in conflict, but like children of God, sons of light, whom the grace of God penetrates and transforms, or at least impels. We may still experience, but much less keenly, those manifold shocks of vessels of flesh, which are cramped for room and jostle each other, and we begin to catch a glimpse of those immense areas of charity expanding before us.

Thus we attain, before anyone, those whom a divine election ennobles, and whom a select grace raises and gradually transforms into the image of Christ; then, all the sons of holy Church, known or unknown: in heaven each one of them will appear to us in his special brightness, just as star differs from star (1 Cor. 15:41). But from now on we admire this huge constellation of the saints; how many friends of God who do not know each other and whom, at times, a providential meeting causes us to discover! *Domine, Dominus noster, quam admirabile est nomen tuum in universa tua!* And even among sinners, what a marvelous working of grace! No one can escape His rays. *Nec est qui abscondat a calore eius.*

And then our gaze is detached from earth. In heaven will be those who have preceded us, our friends already crowned by God and the saints. We do not seek to relive with them times gone by; all that vanishes; *prima abierunt.* It is the future that summons us, the eternal future; God is not the God of the dead, but of the living; in Him all live (Lk. 20:38). We aspire to live among them, to see them, to hear them. They are no longer but a flame, a voice: Glory to God and to Christ! [6]

It is up to heaven, in the house of the Father, that the Dis-

---

cause in their life and death, they have tasted Me, My very Self, through the consciousness of love, in the love of neighbor."

[6] One may read again concerning paradise, St. Francis de Sales, *The Love of God,* pp. 154–155. One may also read in the memorial of St. Alphonsus Rodriguez, the account of his visions: the saints of paradise, whom he had never known, all manifest themselves to him as intimate friends whose souls he penetrates to the depths.

course after the Last Supper raises us (Jn. 14:2 ff.), and to that place, indeed, we must ascend in order to arrive at the source whence charity is poured forth. All those who have seen a little of the first Christians have wondered at this new life, so joyous, so unified, so profound; the will of Jesus has been accomplished: "By this will all men know that you are my disciples, if you have love for one another" (Jn. 13:35). In this pagan world of disunited men without love or mercy (Rom. 1:31), a life as intimate, charitable, and social as this has been a revelation: "See how they love one another!" [7] We envy them this charity, but we cannot arrive there without sharing their faith. "Their founder has made them believe that they are all brothers." These words of the satirist Lucian were truer than he thought: it is from the revelation of Christ that this charity is born and on which it depends. We can, by separating from Him, still dream of brotherhood among men; it is only a dream. If we are brothers, it is because we are all children of the heavenly Father, united to Him through the death and the resurrection of the only Son.

[7] Tertullian, *Apologeticum*, XXXIX, 7, and in tr. the *Apologetical Work* (FC 10), tr. by R. Arbesmann, O.S.A., N.Y., Fathers of the Church, 1950, p. 99.

chapter 15

❖❖❖❖❖❖❖❖❖

The Passion and the Death
of Jesus

"I determined not to know anything among you, except Jesus
Christ and him crucified" (1 Cor. 2:2). This affirmation of St.
Paul gives us a faithful echo of the first Christian preaching—not
only the message of the Apostle, but that of the whole Church:
its privileged object is Christ, and Christ crucified. During the
whole lifetime of Jesus, the sorrowful mysteries of His passion
and death had frightened the apostles; despite Jesus' most urgent warnings, they dared not fix their thoughts on them. Since
His death and resurrection, all is changed: what was for them
an object of scandal is now the foundation of their faith. Their
love of Jesus could not support the prospect of His torments;
now this fearsome mystery of His Cross and of His death is
the hearth from which radiates His love, illuminating and embracing them. In the four Gospels, we can pick out many divergencies in the narration of the incidents and in the unequal importance assigned to them; but all are unanimous in the exceptional importance they attach to this last day: this is what

reveals to the faithful the whole meaning of the life of the Son of God and of His mission here below.

Holy Church has religiously assured to the mystery of the passion and the death of Jesus this privileged veneration: the birth of Our Lord, His baptism, His teachings, His miracles and Transfiguration are recalled for our adoration in the course of the liturgical year; His passion and death are put before our eyes each day in the Holy Sacrifice of the Mass: "As often as you shall eat this bread and drink the cup, you proclaim the death of the Lord, until he comes" (1 Cor. 11:26). In this, moreover, the Church obeys the will of the Master. The reason of this will is evident: of all the mysteries, the mystery of the death of Jesus is that which reveals to us most manifestly the love of God and the salvation of man.

No other mystery, then, will have in the spiritual life of the Christian a place comparable to that which the passion and the death of Christ ought to occupy. This mystery must be the "daily food of our souls." [1]

It is our food, our light, and yet it will always remain for us a mystery; the more intimately it is revealed, the more mysterious it appears. Is there, indeed, any more unfathomable mystery than that of the religion of the Son of God, especially when the Gospel shows Him to us as offering Himself to His Father as a victim of reparation for our sins?

If the whole drama were acted out between Jesus and His enemies here below or in hell, we could understand it better: from the first days of His public ministry, Jesus runs into the opposition of the leaders of the Jewish nation, the high priests, the ancients, the Pharisees; behind these men we have no trouble distinguishing the impetus of Satan and his demons. From year to year and even from month to month, one is aware of these hatreds growing beyond all measure. From the time of the first Passover, Jesus had to leave Jerusalem; then, at the end of a few weeks, Judea; a year later, Galilee. Henceforth we see

---

[1] This phrase is borrowed from the Directory of the *Exercises* of St. Ignatius Loyola; but it is not peculiar to one school of spirituality; it is a formula of Christian spirituality.

no more prolonged stays, but trips along the Phoenician coast, in Samaria, Judea, Perea. He appears in Jerusalem only at the time of the feasts, when the concourse of pilgrims intimidates His enemies. He goes up to Bethany, at the call of Martha and Mary, only at the risk of His life (Jn. 11:8, 16); the raising of Lazarus again exasperates the priests and, on the advice of Caiphas, they decide on the death of Jesus; Christ having withdrawn to the desert, they had ordered anyone knowing His whereabouts to denounce Him to the high priests and Pharisees (*ibid.*, 53–56). After that, we cannot be surprised either by the condemnation which Caiphas will hand down, or by the brutal hatred from his accomplices and henchmen.

But what, from the first centuries of Christianity, has disconcerted many readers of the Gospel, are the moral sufferings of Jesus, so painfully acknowledged, in the Garden and on Calvary. What makes them even more inexplicable in their eyes is that Jesus makes no effort to avoid the condemnation and the punishment: He marches willingly to death, and yet that death horrified Him. From the second century, Celsus objected: "If Jesus consented to His lot, if He underwent death only to obey His Father, it is evident that being God and willingly accepting all that, He could not complain of the cruelty of His tortures." [2] Origen answered that Jesus undoubtedly was God, but that He was man too, that He could experience fear, and that He willed to experience it in order to sustain us by His example. He adds that of this prayer to His Father one might give another explanation: He sees that His death, the guilt of which Israel would incur, would save the world, but lose Israel. To save His people from this catastrophe, He prayed, "If it is possible, let this cup pass away from me." [3]

One might follow in patristic exegesis these two interpretations: the first, which recognizes Jesus' human fear, is encountered in most of the Fathers, especially the Greeks; a few Latin Fathers, following St. Hilary, dismiss this explanation as

[2] Cf. Origen, *Contra Cels.*, II, 23; cf. 9. *P.G.*, XI, 841; cf. 808; and in tr. *Origen: Contra Celsum*, pp. 87–88.
[3] *Ibid.*, II, 25. *P.G.*, XI, 845.

seeing in Jesus' fear and moral suffering only feelings inspired in Him by His compassion for men.[4]

The second opinion is, today, generally abandoned: exegetes and theologians caution us not to look for the glory of Christ in an opinion which is in poor agreement with Scripture.[5]

This lesson, of inestimable worth, is interpreted by the Apostle: he explains to us, thereby, the priesthood of the Son of God:

Jesus, in the days of his earthly life, with a loud cry and tears, offered up prayers and supplications to him who was able to save him from death, and was heard because of his reverent submission. And he, Son though he was, learned obedience from the things he suffered; and when perfected, he became to all who obey him the cause of eternal salvation, called by God a high priest according to the order of Melchisedech (Heb. 5:7–10).

We must bear in mind, however, that these considerations do not entirely clarify the description of the agony as proposed to us by the Gospel. What disconcerts us the most, in the scene of Gethsemani and in that of Calvary, is the attitude of Jesus with respect to His Father. During His whole lifetime, His most ardent desire and keenest joy has been to accomplish the will of His Father: this is His "food" (Jn. 4:34); it is in His union with His Father that He has found the ever-present help which enables Him to bear without flinching all the desertions of men, even those of the apostles (Jn. 16:32). But then how interpret those words in the Garden: "Yet not as I will, but as thou willest" (Mt. 26: 39; Mk. 14:36; Lk. 22:42)? How interpret the words on the

---

[4] These texts are quoted in *Vie et enseignement de Jésus-Christ,* t. II, pp. 323–325. This exegesis is explained, I think, at least in part, by the fear of scandal which the fact of Jesus' fear would awaken in a hard, heartless world (Rom. 1:31), where only strength was held in admiration; cf. *Revue pratique d'apologétique,* March 15, 1922, pp. 715 ff., and G. Joussard, *"L'abandon du Christ,"* in *Revue des Sciences philosophiques et théologiques,* 1934, p. 324.

[5] Father Voste, *De Passione et Morte Jesu Christi* (Rome, 1937, p. 35), reaffirms approvingly this judgment of Father Knabenbauer: *"Cavendum est, ne pietatis et gloriae Christi id esse arbitremur quod S. Litteris non concordat."*

Cross: "My God, my God, why hast thou forsaken me?" (Mt. 27:46; Mk. 15:34)? The submission of the Son to the paternal will is, as it has always been, unlimited and unconditional. But so far this will was presented to the soul of Christ all radiant with light and attractiveness; now it appears to Him obscure and distant. We should say with Maldonatus: "Christ in this prayer has spoken as a man to whom the divine will might have been imperfectly known, and who might not have had enough strength to surmount death." The sensible contact is lost; His Father seems far from Him.

This contemplation of the sadness of Our Lord and of the abandonment He felt has been dear to the saints; it is, indeed, an inexhaustible source of adoration and love.

St. Francis de Sales proposes this great mystery to us as follows:

Notice, I beg of you, Theotimus, that just as Our Savior, after the prayer of resignation that He made in the Garden of Olives and His capture, let Himself be handled and led at the mercy of those who crucified Him, with an admirable abandonment of His body and life into their hands; so He puts His soul and will, by a very perfect indifference, into the hands of His eternal Father. For although He said, "My God, my God, why hast thou forsaken me?" it was to make us know the real bitterness and afflictions of His soul, and not to contravene the very holy indifference in which He found Himself, just as He will demonstrate soon after, concluding His whole life and passion with these incomparable words: "Father, into thy hands I commend my spirit" (Lk. 23:46).[6]

In this sorrowful abandon of Christ, St. Francis de Sales has us adore the heroic and peaceful docility of the Son of God. St. John of the Cross dwells even more on this mystery; he recognizes in it the ideal model of Christian renunciation, and he extols its unlimited fruitfulness: by contemplating it, we learn to die to ourselves, to our sensible and spiritual nature:

In the first place, it is certain that Our Lord died as to sense, spiritually, in His life, besides dying naturally, at His death. For, as He

[6] *The Love of God,* Bk. 9, ch. 5.

said, He had not in His life where to lay His head, and at His death this was even truer. In the second place, it is certain that, at the moment of His death, He was likewise annihilated in His soul, and was deprived of any relief and consolation, since His Father left Him in the most intense aridity, according to the lower part of His nature. Wherefore He had perforce to cry out, saying: "My God! My God! Why hast Thou forsaken Me?" This was the greatest desolation, with respect to sense, that He had suffered in His life. And thus He wrought herein the greatest work that He had ever wrought, whether in miracles or in mighty works, during the whole of His life, either upon earth or in Heaven, which was the reconciliation and union of mankind, through grace, with God. And this, as I say, was at the moment and the time when this Lord was most completely annihilated in everything. Annihilated, that is to say, with respect to human repu-tation; since, when men saw Him die, they mocked Him rather than esteemed Him; and also with respect to nature, since His nature was annihilated when He died; and further with respect to the spiritual consolation and protection of the Father, since at that time He for-sook Him, that He might pay the whole of man's debt and united him with God, being thus annihilated and reduced as it were to nothing. . . . This he said that the truly spiritual man may under-stand the mystery of the gate and of the way of Christ, and so become united with God, and may know that, the more completely he is annihilated for God's sake, according to these two parts, the sensual and the spiritual, the more completely is he united to God and the greater is the work which he accomplishes. And when at last he is reduced to nothing, which will be the greatest extreme of humility, spiritual union will be wrought between the soul and God, which in this life is the greatest and the highest state attainable. This consists not, then, in refreshment and in consolations and spiritual feelings, but in a living death of the Cross, both as to sense and as to spirit—that is, both inwardly and outwardly.[7]

This teaching of the great mystical doctor sheds a powerful light on the mystery of the Passion of the Son of God; it leaves in the dark a question which has been asked later on, and which we must consider: this agony of the Son of God, did it

[7] *Ascent of Mount Carmel,* Bk. II, ch. 6, n. 7. —Concerning Christ on the Cross "happy and sorrowful," one may read also St. Catherine, *Dialogue,* ch. LXXVIII.

embrace Him only in His Passion or did it cover His whole life? If the second interpretation must be retained, our whole conception of the life of Jesus has to be transformed: the hour of darkness no longer lasts only for a day; it extends over the whole mortal life of Jesus, from Bethlehem till Calvary.

This thesis has been defended by a certain number of spiritual authors, belonging, for the most part, to the seventeenth century and to the Dominican school; the most eminent of them is Chardon, in his magisterial work *The Cross of Christ.* [8]

Father Florand, in the introduction he has given to the new edition of this work, pp. lxxxvii–xci, has grouped around Chardon other theologians of this period and school who have defended the same view. This research is interesting; but we must admit that, taken as a whole, tradition is not favorable to this interpretation of the Gospel. We can say with the author of the *Imitation: Tota vita Christi crux fuit et martyrium.*[9]

But we do not mean by this that Christ had habitually experienced the feeling of His Father's abandoning Him; we recognize only that His whole life was transversed with trials, contradictions, and sufferings.[10]

The view of Chardon, then, cannot be authorized by tradition; and, what is decisive, it does violence to the Gospel. Any reader of the account of the Agony notes there a state of soul entirely new in Jesus. Undoubtedly He has always regarded the Cross as the goal towards which His life tends, but He marches to it unafraid. Upon entering Jerusalem, He experiences a first shudder, as it were, of anguish. But He controls it immediately: "Now my soul is troubled. And what shall I say? Father, save me from this hour! No, this is why I came to this hour" (Jn. 12:27). He adds at once, "Father, glorify thy name!" Much less still shall we

---

[8] *La Croix du Christ,* where the finest truths of mystical theology and of grace have been laid down; and in tr. *The Cross of Christ,* I.

[9] II, 12, 7.

[10] This is the view of St. Bernard, *In Cantica, Hom.* 43, 3. *P.L.,* CLXXXIII, p. 994. Cf. St. Robert Bellarmine, *De Gemitu Columbae,* Bk. II, ch. III; cf. *Sur les sept paroles de Jesus en croix,* tr. by Brignon, Avignon, 1835, pp. 94 ff., and in tr. *Seven Words Spoken by Christ on the Cross,* tr. from the Latin, Westminster (Md.), Newman, 1950.

see agony in these words (Lk. 12:49–50): "I have come to cast fire upon the earth, and what will I but that it be kindled? But I have a baptism to be baptized with; and how distressed [*pressé*] I am until it is accomplished!" This is the expression which St. Paul will use later on: "The love of Christ impels [*presse*] us" (2 Cor. 5:14); and St. Ignatius of Antioch: "If anyone holds Him in his heart, let him understand what I am aspiring to; and then let him sympathize with me, knowing in what distress I am (*me presse*)." [11] There is, in these texts, the same eager desire, expressed by the same term.[12]

Thus, in the whole course of His life, Jesus had His passion before His eyes, even on the day of the Transfiguration (Lk. 9:31). But this prospect becomes overwhelming only in Gethsemani; then only was His soul "sad, even unto death"; then only did He say to His Father, "Father, if it is possible, let this cup pass away from me" (Mt. 26:38–39). Up to then He feels the weight of the Cross; but the will of the Father, in which He took His pleasure, caused Him to find the burden light; and the glorification of the Father, assured by His passion, caused Him to love its ignominy. We can apply to him literally the words of St. Paul: "Our present light affliction, which is for the moment, prepares for us an eternal weight of glory that is beyond all measure; while we look not at the things that are seen, but at the things that are not seen. For the things that are seen are temporal, but the things that are not seen are eternal" (2 Cor. 4:17–18). Jesus, ever so much more than St. Paul, was in His mortal life a contemplator of the invisible. On the day of His Passion, the sensible happiness of this contemplation was withdrawn from Him; and this was the agony. But up to then His soul was wholly and completely immersed in it, and found therein a continual strength and joy.

Thereby Our Lord is our master and our model; He reveals to us the price of union with God by a faithful submissiveness and

---

11 *To the Romans,* VI, in ACW 1, p. 83.

12 πῶς συνέχομαι (Luke), ἡ αγάπη τοῦ Χριστοῦ συνέχει ἡμᾶς (2 Cor.), εἰδὼς τὰ συνέχοντά με (Ignatius).

a constant prayerfulness. The Christian who, with Christ and in Christ, is united to the Father, can take up his yoke and find repose in it.

In His agony, too, Jesus is our model; the dearest friends of God know the torment of His absence. Like the Psalmist, they repeat, "O God, my God . . . why hast thou forsaken me?" (Ps. 21:2). But the example of the Son of God sustains them; they understand, by beholding it, the valuable lesson of this example:

It became him for whom are all things and through whom are all things, who had brought many sons into glory, to perfect through sufferings the author of their salvation (Heb. 2:10). It was right that he should in all things be made like unto his brethren, that he might become a merciful and faithful high priest before God to expiate the sins of the people. For in that he himself has suffered and has been tempted, he is able to help those who are tempted (*ibid.*, 17–18).

This fine text reveals to us another fruit of this agony, more valuable still than the example it gives us: the Son of God made man, King and High Priest of mankind, has experienced human sufferings in their most terrible and interior aspects: "He, Son though he was, learned obedience from the things that he suffered; and when perfected, he became to all who obey him the cause of eternal salvation" (Heb. 5:8–9).

In viewing the Incarnation of the Son of God, we marveled at this merciful and frightful exchange whereby the Son of God took on our death to give us life. We recognize Him here in what He has that is most grievous for Him, but most beatifying for us. Between man and God sin has hollowed out an abyss; the death of Christ has filled that abyss. We were far away from God, we become close to God. But Christ worked this reconciliation only by making Himself jointly responsible with man: "For our sakes he made him to be sin who knew nothing of sin, so that in him we might become the justice of God" (2 Cor. 5:21). That does not mean that the Son of God is a sinner, or sinned personally, but "as a member of a sinful family with which He identifies himself." [13] This solidarity, which by a divine condescension He willed to contract with us, is the source of our salvation, but also the cause of His sufferings. With regard to His Father, it is a filial homage of reparation which, as the Head of guilty mankind, He offers to Him; God receives it and pardons us.[14]

Never will we be able fully to understand the weight of that responsibility assumed by the Son of God. If we wish to conceive at least some idea of it, let us recall what the Gospel tells us: Jesus himself "knew what was in man" (Jn. 2:25). God is good, men are bad (Mt. 7:11). With regard to God, they are debtors, and insolvent debtors (Lk. 7:42). If we do not regard mankind in general, but the Jewish people, the object of God's mercies, Jesus finds in them only ingratitude and stubbornness: "O unbelieving and perverse generation, how long shall I be with you and put up with you?" (Lk. 9:41). "Jerusalem, Jerusalem, thou who killest the prophets, and stonest those who are sent to thee! How often would I have gathered thy children together, as a hen gathers her young under her wings, but thou wouldst not!" (Lk. 13:34). It is with these ungrateful, obstinate and wicked sinners that the Son of God has made Himself jointly responsible, and it is in order to save them that He goes to die! And those whose Head He thus becomes, are not only this perverse generation, but all human generations, from Adam up to the last human being. And His death will not stop this contagion of sin; the disciples whom He will send will be treated as the prophets were treated: "Some of them you will put to death, and crucify, and some you will scourge in your synagogues, and persecute from town to town; that upon you may come all the just blood that

[13] Prat, *Théologie de saint Paul,* 6th ed., II, p. 245, and in tr. *Theology of St. Paul,* p. 205.
[14] Prat, *ibid.,* p. 256, and in tr. p. 213: "It is no longer a question of a substitution by which the innocent should undergo the punishment of the guilty, but of a sublime condescension which leads the Son of God to identify his cause with that of sinners; nor is it a question of an external satisfaction given to God in order to extort from him the pardon of criminals, but of a filial homage which, thanks to Jesus Christ, the human race pays of itself and which God accepts because he initiated it and has the principal part in it."

has been shed on the earth, from the blood of Abel the just unto the blood of Zacharias the son of Barachias, whom you killed between the temple and the altar" (Mt. 23:34–36). This is spoken to the Pharisees by Jesus a few days before His death, and it is for these people that He offers Himself and is going to die.

In the silence of the Garden of Gethsemani and in the silence of Calvary, He will hear rising up from the land all those cries of hate and pain; and in order to expiate those hatreds and to assuage those pains, He delivers Himself over to the hate of His enemies, to the brutality of His executioners; and the Father will hear the voice of "Jesus, mediator of a new covenant," and that of the "sprinkling of blood which speaks better than Abel" (Heb. 12:24).

Jesus willed, by shouldering the crushing weight of the sins of men, to allow us to approach God with a filial trust. We are soiled with blood and filth; we are washed with the Blood of Christ. We go before God in all confidence, "looking towards the author and finisher of faith, Jesus, who for the joy set before him, endured a cross, despising shame, and sits at the right hand of the throne of God" (Heb. 12:2).

To ensure this reconciliation, nothing has been spared: the Son of God gazes on the holiness of God; He knows the infinite gravity of the offense against God, and, in order to repair it, engages without hesitation all that He has—this human nature which He has taken only to offer it in sacrifice to God, His Creator and supreme end. And as for Himself, the Holy One of God, He does not wish at this time to go before the Father except as the ransom of men, His brethren, with whom He is jointly responsible and with whom He wishes to bear the punishment. The shame and sorrow He feels here is unutterable; but, at this price, He repairs the honor of God which we had violated, and He saves us.

And God the Father bends over the sacrifice with an infinite love; He takes pleasure in this immaculate offering, radiating with filial piety towards God and brotherly devotedness towards mankind. Never had earth produced such a bloom, never had God received such homage.

In the Office of Good Friday, holy Church tires not of chanting this mystery of pain and glory:

Crux fidelis, inter omnes arbor una nobilis: Nulla silva talem profert, fronde, flore, germine. Dulce lignum, dulces clavos, dulce pondus sustinet.

Flecte ramos arbor alta, tensa laxa viscera, Et rigor lentescat ille, quem dedit nativitas: Et superni membra Regis tende miti stipite.

Sola digna tu fuisti ferre mundi victimam: Atque portum praeparare, arca mundo naufrago: Quam sacer cruor perunxit, fusus Agni corpore.

O Crux, ave, spes unica, hoc Passionis tempore, Piis adauge gratiam, reisque dele crimina!

It is with these sentiments that every child of the Church ought to approach the Passion of Our Lord: contrition and profound sorrow in face of this suffering of which we are the cause; but, at the same time, wonderment and happiness in the radiance of such glory: never has the holiness of God been so worthily honored, never has Christ's love shone with such bright splendor.

Pain and glory—here everything infinitely surpasses us, and yet nothing overwhelms us: because all these divine mysteries appear to us in the sacred humanity of Jesus, which tempers their brightness. Let us not fear to prolong that contemplation and, if possible, to resume it each day. Is it not each day that Our Lord immolates Himself on the altar and unites us by Holy Communion to His sacrifice?

In the lives of several saints, we see Our Lord inviting them to be united to Him, and offering them the choice of a union full of joy or of sorrow: and at the same time that He proposes this choice to them, He Himself suggests to them the option which He prefers: joy will be for heaven; sorrow is for earth.[15] Let us not complain about this: the union which is formed in sorrow is

15 Thus in the *Autobiographie* of St. Margaret Mary, n. 66 (Paris, Gauthey, 1915), pp. 78, 79.

quite close, and the intimacy it creates is undoubtedly the most profound that can be cemented on earth. Our Lady and St. John have, at the foot of the Cross, tasted this intimacy with Our Lord; it will be, henceforth, their treasure.

The agony of Jesus has bid us contemplate this prospect of the Passion. It is not an anticipation; Jesus, no doubt, has not at Gethsemani exhausted the painful pruning: He must submit again, at the hands of Ananias and Caiphas, to the ignominious condemnation decreed by the religious authorities of His nation. Then a night of insults and tortures; next the appearance before Pilate, the scourging, the crowning with thorns, the condemnation to the Cross; finally the sufferings of the dolorous way and of Calvary. But all this shame and all these punishments have been proposed to Him in the Garden; He has subscribed to this frightful program: He will do nothing to back out of it or even to soften its rigor.

The attitude of Jesus, in the course of this day of physical and moral tortures, is governed in its entirety by the choice He made in the Garden: "Not my will but thine be done" (Lk. 22:42).

In the letter of the Church of Lyons recounting the Acts of the martyrs of the year 177, we see how the pagans' hatred, very bitter from the start, was provoked beyond measure by the calumnies hurled against the Christians. "Then finally," adds the narrator, "the holy martyrs endured punishments beyond all description." [16] Thus it is with every Christian in face of life's great trials: he has defended himself; he has fought; a time comes when there is nothing more to do but suffer. This is a terrible hour; but for those who are fully submissive to the will of God, it is the hour of heroic sanctity.

Of this heroic sanctity, Jesus willed to give us an example we may never forget. In His Agony, His sensitive nature is frightened by the terrible program presented to Him. He prays, "Remove this cup from me." Then He adds, "Yet not my will but thine be done" (Lk. 22:42). This will is evident; the Son of God accepts it as He has always done: "My food is to do the will

[16] Eusebius, *Ecclesiastical History,* V, I, 16, in FC 19, p. 276.

of him who sent me" (Jn. 4:34). The cup has not lost its mortal bitterness: but this is the cup which the Father presents to Him; He will not utter a prayer, nor take a step to avoid it: "Shall I not drink the cup that the Father has given me?" (Jn. 18:11).

He knows that He is the sovereign Master of heaven and earth; a word from Him and the Father would furnish Him "with more than twelve legions of angels" (Mt. 26:53). Besides, He has no need of this help: at His single reply, "I am he," the guards "drew back and fell to the ground" (Jn. 18:6). But He willed to use this power only to make visible the spontaneity of His sacrifice.

Even without recourse to this supernatural power, He could have foiled the snares of His enemies. Before Caiphas, His silence alone upset the conflicting statements of the false witnesses. He could be condemned only on His solemn declaration; He might have refused it, as He had done so many times. Before Pilate, He would have been able, on many occasions, to take advantage of the hesitation of the Procurator and of his obvious reluctance to issue the condemnation which the Jews' hatred was demanding. But He was silent, silent even before Herod, whom He could so easily have set at odds against the Jews.

If we wish to understand this attitude of Jesus, we can compare it with that of St. Paul before the Sanhedrin (Acts 23:6–10). The Apostle, hounded by the Jews' hatred, is handed over to the Supreme Court. He knows that his judges are divided: some are Pharisees, others Sadducees; the first believe in the resurrection and in angels; the others deny them. He cries out, "Brethren, I am a Pharisee, the son of Pharisees; it is about the hope and the resurrection of the dead that I am on trial." Immediately the dispute breaks out: among the Pharisees, some rise to protest: "We find no evil in this man; what if a spirit has really spoken to him, or an angel?" Such is the confusion that they have to adjourn the session. How easy it would have been for Jesus to set at odds the rival powers of Romans and Jews, and to escape them! He did not even attempt it; no endeavor at all to recapture the crowd which at certain times (for example, at the time of the Barabbas episode) hesitates and could, by a vigorous intervention, be torn away from its guides. The people had said recently: "No man has spoken like this man"; but today He is silent.

In this silence we are aware of no discouragement; Jesus is neither crushed nor vanquished: let us recall His sovereign answer to the interrogation of Caiphas: "Art thou the Christ, the Son of the Blessed One?" "I am. And you shall see the Son of Man sitting at the right hand of the Power and coming with the clouds of heaven" (Mk. 14:61–62); and to Pilate: "Thou sayest it; I am a king. This is why I was born, and why I have come into the world, to bear witness to the truth. Everyone who is of the truth hears my voice" (Jn. 18:37). But this sovereign force Jesus employs, not for defending Himself, but for asserting His authority: He is the King of martyrs; He owes to Himself His own witness; He gives it to Himself. He knows, too, that He will have to seal it with His blood; He does nothing to postpone His taking this chalice; it is the chalice which the Father holds out to Him; He will drink it.

This decision is not for a single moment troubled by dread of the agony: Jesus is, as He was in the Garden, "sad, even unto death" (Mt. 26:38); but He sees clearly the will of His Father; He yields to it with all His soul. This is the hour of darkness; but throughout this night, Jesus perceives the light which has been the strength of His whole life and which, in this supreme hour, is its law: at the time of His arrest, He said to Peter, "Shall I not drink the cup that the Father has given me?" (Jn. 18:11); to Pilate, who is going to condemn Him: "Thou wouldst have no power at all over me were it not given thee from above" (Jn. 19:11); and at the moment of death: "Father, into thy hands I commend my spirit" (Lk. 23:46).

All is summed up in those words of the Epistle to the Hebrews, which we have already recalled: "He, Son though he was, learned obedience from the things that he suffered" (Heb. 5:8). This lesson, more than any other, was necessary for us; Jesus spared nothing to give to it an irresistible force.

That is why He willed that this obedience appear to us in that sensible abandonment by the Father. How many martyrs will be led to death, through every torture, by a joyful gladness. Such the young virgin of Lyons, the slave Blandina:

But the blessed Blandina, last of all, like a noble mother who has encouraged her children and sent them forth triumphant to the king, herself also enduring all the conflicts of the children, hastened to them, rejoicing and glad at her departure, as if called to a marriage feast and not being thrown to the beasts. And after the scourging, after the wild beasts, after the roasting seat, she finally was placed in a net and thrown to a bull. She was tossed about for some time by the animal, but was insensitive to what was happening to her because of her hope and hold upon what had been entrusted to her and her communion with Christ.[17]

This gladness is undoubtedly remarkable; it is a gratuitous gift of God. Christ has often given it to His martyrs; but He did not will to enjoy it Himself, in order to give us the example of His filial resignation to the good pleasure of God, in pain, pure and simple. "Let him deny himself, and take up his cross, and follow me" (Mt. 16:24); this is the rule He imposes on every Christian. Such an austere rule as this is transformed by His example: we see Him carrying His Cross, abandoned by all men, without tangible help from the Father, covered with the shame and pain of our offenses and, in that extreme suffering and want, completely at peace.

"When the sixth hour came, there was darkness over the whole land until the ninth hour" (Mk. 15:33). The three Synoptics have noted this obscurity which covers the agony of Jesus: silence reigns, enemies have stepped aside, Jesus is alone. God wishes to give us to understand the depth and holiness of this mystery. Here one might recall some great examples, the least unworthy of being compared to this death of the Son of God. At the death of some great servants of Christ, we again meet with this solitude and silence. Thus at the time of the last captivity of St. Paul: the Apostle, so unsparing in affection and devotion, is nearly abandoned on the last day of his life. The last lines we have from him reveal to us the sorrow he feels

[17] *Ecclesiastical History,* V, I, 55, in FC 19, pp. 285–286.

on this account: "Make haste to come to me shortly," he writes to Timothy (2 Tim. 4:8 ff.), "for Demas has deserted me, loving this world, and has gone to Thessalonica, Crescens to Galatia, Titus to Dalmatia, Luke only is with me . . . At my first defense no one came to my support, but all forsook me; may it not be laid to their charge." Other saints have suffered, unto death, similar abandonment: St. Francis Xavier, on Sancian; St. John of the Cross, at Ubeda, and many others. They have thus imitated the Passion of their Lord; they have not, nevertheless, felt all its bitterness. In that decisive hour, Jesus follows each one of His own, those whom He has filled to overflowing with His graces, whom He has raised to such heights of faith and love, and who totter, then, in disarray, when all disappears. "We were hoping," the disciples at Emmaus will say two days after the Crucifixion (Lk. 24:21); this is what all of them are repeating at that time. In our Lady faith and hope remained bright; in all the others these were veiled. Surely, they still love their Master; the tears of Peter are proof enough of that. But that love finds not the means for its support.

This abandonment by the best is rendered even more painful by the violent infidelity of others. At the Praetorium, in the streets of Jerusalem and on Calvary, how many, carried away by fear and discouragement, join in the cries of death, in the jeers and insults, who had been, but a few days before, on the feast of the Palms or in the Temple, devoted disciples and enthusiastic listeners! And this apostasy breaks out at a decisive moment in the destiny of Israel, when there is question of the Jewish nation's being saved or lost. "His blood be on us and on our children" (Mt. 27:25). And Jesus sees, from the height of His Cross, that unfortunate city stretched out at His feet, proud of the splendor of its Temple, and especially of the concourse of its children and faithful on this day of the Passover. In forty years, of this Temple "there will not be left here one stone upon another" (Mt. 24:2), and the Israelites, gathered together in crowds in the holy city, will waste away there in slow agony, to die of starvation, be massacred by the Romans, or be sold into slavery. This prevision had caused Jesus to weep in the very midst of the triumph of the

Palms (Lk. 19:41); what was His sorrow on the Cross, when the Jews' hatred made Him more aware of the imminence and severity of the punishment! This is that sorrow which breaks out in His reply to the women of Jerusalem: "Daughters of Jerusalem, do not weep for me, but weep for yourselves and for your children . . . If in the case of green wood they do these things, what is to happen in the case of the dry?" (Lk. 23:28–31).

In this darkness, solitude, and silence, Jesus seems to have lost everything: then it is that He opens heaven to the Good Thief: "This day thou shalt be with me in paradise" (Lk. 23:43); then it is, too, that seeing near the Cross His Mother and His beloved disciple, He says to Mary, "Woman, behold thy son" and to St. John, "Behold thy mother" (Jn. 19:27). This mystery reveals to Christians the boundless treasure of the Cross: it is there that the faithful disciples of Our Lord penetrate into His intimacy and are bequeathed by Him to Mary as her children.

All is consummated in a supreme prayer; for the last time, Jesus repeats the invocations of the Psalms while giving them a deeper and more touching accent. There is, first of all, Psalm 21, at first sorrowful like a cry of anguish and then blossoming out into praise of God and into thanksgiving:

O God, my God, look upon me: why hast thou forsaken me? Far from my salvation are the words of my sins . . . In thee have our fathers hoped: they have hoped, and thou hast delivered them . . . But I am a worm, and no man: the reproach of men, and the outcast of the people. All they that saw me have laughed me to scorn: they have spoken with the lips, and wagged the head. "He hoped in the Lord, let him deliver him: let him save him, seeing he delighteth in him." . . . Many dogs have encompassed me: the council of the malignant hath besieged me. They have dug my hands and feet . . . They parted my garments amongst them; and upon my vesture they cast lots. But thou, O Lord, remove not thy help to a distance from me; look towards my defense . . . I will declare thy name to my brethren: in the midst of the church will I praise thee. Ye that fear the Lord, praise him: all ye the seed of Jacob, glorify him . . . because he hath not slighted nor despised the supplication of the poor man. Neither hath he turned away his face from me: and when I cried to him he heard me (Ps. 21:2–25).

Hearing this prayer, *Eloï, Eloï,* the soldiers jeer; one of them, in derision and also, no doubt, out of pity, soaks a sponge in a vessel full of vinegar water, and puts it to the lips of Jesus, saying, "Wait, let us see whether Elias is coming to take him down" (Mk. 15:36). Having taken the vinegar, Jesus said, "It is consummated" (Jn. 19:30). Then He cried out, "Father, into thy hands I commend my spirit" (Lk. 23:46). Here again, He echoed the prayer of the Psalmist,[18] while giving it a more filial accent. The first of the martyrs, St. Stephen, will, in the act of dying, address the same prayer to Jesus: "Lord Jesus, receive my spirit" (Acts 7:58).

We are at the summit of the religious history of the world: all converges there, the prayers of the Psalmist and the prayers of the martyrs. Everything seems buried in the darkness and silence which cover the earth with a veil of mourning: "All the crowd that collected for the sight, when they beheld what things had happened, began to return beating their breasts" (Lk. 23:48).

This was not a sterile dejection; it was already contrition awakening in their souls. After his first miracle, St. Peter will say to the Jews:

The God of Abraham and the God of Isaac and the God of Jacob, the God of our fathers, has glorified his Son Jesus, whom you indeed delivered up and disowned before the face of Pilate, when he had decided that he should be released. But you disowned the Holy and Just One, and asked that a murderer should be granted to you; but the author of life you killed, whom God has raised up from the dead; whereof we are witnesses . . . And now, brethren, I know that you acted in ignorance, as did also your rulers. But in this way God fulfilled what he had announced beforehand by the mouth of all the prophets, namely, that his Christ should suffer (Acts 3:13–18).

One feels in this discourse that the apostle is addressing men whom the tragedy of Calvary has profoundly touched and upset. It will, no doubt, take a great power of the Holy Spirit to transform into Christian faith these feelings of shame and of

[18] Ps. 30:6: "Into thy hands I commend my spirit: thou hast redeemed me, O Lord, the God of truth."

sorrow. But again it is because these feelings are deep-seated and living. A few weeks later, when Peter, miraculously released, is preaching in the Temple, the high priest has him arrested, he and the other apostles, and says to them, "We strictly charged you not to teach in this name, and behold, you have filled Jerusalem with your teaching, and want to bring this man's blood upon us" (Acts 5:28). The high priest affects not to mention Jesus: but one feels that this preaching of the apostles, which is hateful to him, finds an echo in the people.

This religious impression produced in the Jewish people by the Passion of Our Lord ought to make us attentive to the lessons of this great mystery. What Calvary teaches us, first of all, is horror of sin and adoration of the holiness of God. No lesson is for us more necessary. When we let ourselves be carried along by the flood of human life and human judgments, sin no longer appears to us except as an inevitable weakness for which God cannot be hard on us. We feel in and around us not only so much frailty, but so much selfishness and even so much pretense and falsehood, that the Gospel morality, when we understand it, seems to us like an unattainable ideal whose purity is incompatible with the exigencies of the world. And yet we must, indeed, live in the world; God, we imagine, cannot be hard on us for that. The passion of Christ upsets this flimsy scaffolding: it makes us reflect upon the agony and tortures of the Son of God: if the will of His Father has been so rigorous for Him, it is because the offenses to be expiated were quite serious. In this relentless light, let us examine our lives, and reform them. If Jesus permitted the kiss of Judas, it is to cure us of all hypocrisy and falsehood; faced with this desperate wretch, we see the unpitying hardness of the high priests: "I have sinned in betraying innocent blood." "What is that to us? See to it thyself" (Mt. 27:4). Our Lord has permitted it to make us abhor our selfishness. Jesus Himself has summed up in a word this lesson of our moral misery compared to His holiness, a painful but supremely beneficial lesson: "If in the case of green wood they do these things, what is to happen in the case of the dry?" (Lk. 23:31).

Purified by contrition for our offenses, we ought to go on contemplating the Passion in order to adore in it the mystery of God's love, and to recognize therein the inexhaustible source of our gratitude and hope:

Why did Christ, at the set time, die for the wicked when as yet we were weak? For scarcely in behalf of a just man does one die; yet perhaps one might bring himself to die for a good man. But God commends his charity towards us, because when as yet we were sinners, Christ died for us. Much more now that we are justified by his blood, shall we be saved through him from the wrath. For if when we were enemies we were reconciled to God by the death of his Son, much more, having been reconciled, shall we be saved by his life (Rom. 5:6–10).

Love, thanksgiving, hope—these are the divine fruits of the Cross; but we cannot gather them without uniting ourselves forever to Him who will be for us the principle of death and of life:

The love of God impels us, because we have come to the conclusion that, since one died for all, therefore all died; and that Christ died for all, in order that they who are alive may live no longer for themselves, but for him who died for them and rose again (2 Cor. 5:14–15).

The mystery of the Resurrection of Our Lord will make us understand better that great law of Christian destiny, its exigencies and its fecundity; but from now on, His death lets us catch a glimpse of it:

None of us lives to himself, and none dies to himself; for if we live, we live to the Lord, or if we die, we die to the Lord. Therefore, whether we live or die, we are the Lord's. For to this end Christ died and rose again, that he might be Lord both of the dead and of the living (Rom. 14:7–9).

In the teaching of St. Paul, these two mysteries of death and of life are always closely united, as they are in the plan of God. But after pondering this definitive synthesis, it is well to consider more closely its progressive flowering and to return to Good Friday before going on to Easter Sunday.

The death of Jesus brings to His whole preaching a new and decisive force: that of His example. It is good to read again at the foot of the Cross the precepts given to the apostles and, in their person, to all Christians:

He who loves father and mother more than me is not worthy of me; and he who loves son or daughter more than me is not worthy of me. And he who does not take up his cross and follow me, is not worthy of me. He who finds his life will lose it, and he who loses his life for my sake, will find it (Mt. 10:37–39).

If anyone comes to me and does not hate his father and mother, and wife and children, and brothers and sisters, yes, and even his own life, he cannot be my disciple. And he who does not carry his cross and follow me, cannot be my disciple (Lk. 14:26–27).

This heroic program frightened many of Christ's first hearers; and yet it was imperfectly understood. Today many Gospel readers find in it phrases which are worn by long liturgical usage and of whose sharp relief they are no longer aware. But whoever takes up these texts while meditating on the way of the Cross, understands that he can neither reduce in this way the requirements nor escape them. "Let him deny himself, and take up his cross, and follow me" (Mt. 16:24). He who speaks to us in this way is passing before us, covered with blood and sinking under the weight of His Cross. He knows what He is asking of us, but He imposes on us only the lot which He Himself has chosen; we have only to follow Him.

To understand fully this lesson of the Cross, we ought to meditate on the Gospel. Those surrounding Jesus, and the disciples, indifferent or hostile, had only to open their eyes; and for many years the great lesson of Calvary is continually repeated before them: "He who does not carry his cross and follow me, cannot be my disciple." We noted in the first recitals of the Acts the sympathetic remembrance and even the veneration which many Jews kept of Jesus; of these numerous sympathizers, very few had the courage to join the tiny nucleus of the primitive Church.[19] Whence came their hesitation, if not from this teaching and frightening reminder: "Let him deny himself, and take up his cross, and follow me"?

Christ willed to keep His Church for a long time under that threat of persecutions in order to ensure its fervor. The benefit of this painful formation was so evident that, when this deadly opposition began to wane, the Church more than once regretted it.[20] It is then that monasticism appeared and developed, striving to secure, by a spontaneous asceticism, the deprivation and sufferings which the persecutions no longer imposed.

At the same time as the monastic constitutions, and more severe than these, the appeals of Christ Crucified make themselves heard to His most faithful friends: "He who does not carry his cross and follow me, cannot be my disciple." What will this cross be for each man? Our Lord will show it to him; the disciple will have only to shoulder it and follow his Master.

---

[19] Cf. Acts 2:47: They were "praising God" and were "in favor with all the people"; 5:13: "No one dared to associate with them, yet the people made much of them."

[20] Thus Origen in the course of the peaceful years which preceded the persecution of Decius; recalling past struggles, he said to his listeners: "Then they were faithful, when martyrdom was striking at the time of the birth of the Church, when, coming back from the cemeteries whither we had accompanied the bodies of the martyrs, we entered the assemblies again, when the whole Church stood up there, unshakeable, when the catechumens were baptized in the midst of the martyrs, in face of the dying Christians who confessed the truth unto the end, and when these catechumens, surmounting trials, attached themselves unflinchingly to the living God. It is then that we were conscious of having seen remarkable and wondrous marvels. It is then that the faithful were less numerous, no doubt, but truly faithful, advancing by the narrow, rough way that leads to life" (*Hom. in Jerem.* IV, 1, 3. *P.G.,* XIII, 288–289).

chapter 16

❖❖❖❖❖❖❖❖❖

The Resurrection and the Glorious Life of Our Lord

The death of the Son of God is the source of our life; it is, in fact, inseparably united to His resurrection, which is the pledge of our own.

Jesus is handed over for our sakes to death; the Father has approved this sacrifice. By resurrecting His Son, He showed that all was appeased in heaven and on earth: God is reconciled to man, the princes of this world are vanquished and routed, mankind is delivered from the yoke of sin and vivified. This is what the Church recalls to us in having us repeat, throughout the Paschal time, the Commemoration of the Cross: "The Crucified has risen from the dead and ransomed us. Alleluia! O God, who hast willed that Thy Son be attached for our sake to the gibbet of the Cross, so as to remove far from us the power of the enemy, grant us, Thy servants, the grace of the resurrection."

This "grace of the resurrection" we shall enjoy fully in heaven; but, even while on earth, we taste its first fruits; it is the fruit of our baptism:

Do you not know that all we who have been baptized into Christ Jesus have been baptized into his death? For we were buried with him by means of baptism into death, in order that, just as Christ has arisen from the dead through the glory of the Father, so we also may walk in newness of life (Rom. 6:3–4).

You were buried together with him in baptism, and in him also rose again through faith in the working of God who raised him from the dead (Col. 2:12).

If we have died with him, we shall also live with him (2 Tim. 2:11).

This mystery was made palpable to the first Christians by the rite of immersion, and later by the liturgical custom of baptizing neophytes on Holy Saturday. But, whatever be the rite and the date of baptism, it is always from the death of Christ and from His resurrection that it draws its efficacy. Even today the Church continues to remind us, during Paschal time, of our baptism, in order to have us adore, in the mystery of Our Lord's death and resurrection, the source of the new life which He bestows on us.[1]

This "new life" appears to us in Christ leaving the tomb: in Him it is perfect from the first moment; it will know neither loss nor growth. In us, this gift of life is definitive, in this sense that sin no longer holds any sway over the newly baptized, and that grace, from the first moment, makes him a child of God. But this life-giving union of the Christian with Jesus can be broken by sin: in the just, it is susceptible of indefinite growth, and all our efforts ought to lead to the development of this life.

This progress we understand better by considering the character of our new life and, first of all, its freedom. Resurrected with Christ, we are delivered from the bondage of the flesh, we must live by the spirit.[2]

---

[1] Thus in the Mass of Easter Saturday: "You, then, putting off all malice, all deceit, dissimulation and envy, all slander, like new-born children desiring simply spiritual milk to grow up by means of Him and be saved, if only you have tasted the sweetness of the Lord."

[2] "We are debtors, not to the flesh, that we should live according to the flesh, for if you live according to the flesh you will die; but if by the spirit you put to death the deeds of the flesh, you will live" (Rom. 8:12–13).

The ideal model of this freedom we behold in the risen Christ: He is delivered from every bondage here below; He experiences neither weakness nor fatigue of the flesh; He has conquered death; He escapes from the world and His enemies; He makes Himself known immediately or slowly, as to Magdalen or to the disciples of Emmaus; He is recognized only by those He wishes to affect; the others are roused, frightened, put to flight; He troubles Himself over them no longer. He said recently, "You are from below, I am from above" (Jn. 8:23). These words now take on a new force: He has from above not only His origin but His abode.

This is ever so distant an ideal, one exceeding our reach; yet it does not exceed our hope, and henceforth the risen Christ instils this desire in our hearts. In the chapter of the Epistle to the Romans recalled above, St. Paul shows us creation as a whole tending towards its liberation:

Creation was made subject to vanity—not by its own will but by reason of him who made it subject—in hope, because creation itself also will be delivered from its slavery to corruption into the freedom of the glory of the sons of God. For we know that all creation groans and travails in pain until now. And not only it, but we ourselves also who have the first-fruits of the Spirit—we ourselves groan within ourselves, waiting for the adoption as sons, the redemption of our body (Rom. 8:20–23).

This teaching reveals to us the goal of our desire; it transcends our strength infinitely. But if we cannot grasp it, we cannot give up hoping for it and tending towards it: "In hope were we saved" (*ibid.*, 24); and this hope is the Holy Spirit, who instils it in our hearts and who raises us up towards this naturally inaccessible goal: "We do not know what we should pray for as we ought, but the Spirit himself pleads for us with unutterable groanings. And he who searches the hearts knows what the Spirit desires, that he pleads for the saints according to God" (*ibid.*, 26–27).

This hope appears to us in our Head, the risen Christ: He is the first-born among the dead; He lives, and He calls us to share His life. It is by gazing at Him that we understand what that liberty is which He has won for us. The first Christians had often seen around them, in the pagan world, freed slaves putting their liberty, ransomed at the cost of money, under the protection of a god. At the price of a fictitious ransom, whose expenses they themselves had paid, the god used to guarantee them freedom to "go where they wanted" and "do what they wanted." [3] This fiction brings out by way of contrast the price of the Christian redemption: the recovered liberty is not paid for by man, but by the Son of God; the price is not a sum of money, it is the blood of Christ; the liberty is not a legal guarantee, it is life. We are members of the risen Christ; He dies no more; if we are faithful to Him, we share His immortality.

That is what gives to the life of the Christian risen in Christ its assurance and its impetus. This life is so holy that no law can constrain it; it is so powerful that no force can stifle it.

Who shall make accusation against the elect of God? It is God who justifies! Who shall condemn? It is Christ who died; yes, and rose again, he who is at the right hand of God, who also intercedes for us! Who shall separate us from the love of Christ? (Rom. 8:33–35).

Such is Christian liberty: it is not the liberty of the flesh, which knows only how to divert and disperse itself; it is the liberty of the spirit, which is freed from its servitudes and raised towards God. In the measure that the goal draws closer, its attraction is more powerful; in the end, it will be irresistible, and this will be perfect liberty.

It is at the revelation of this life that the forty days' apparitions aim: Jesus multiplies these encounters not only to convince some slow disciples to believe, but above all to reveal Himself more profoundly to them. He wills that the last tangible remembrances they keep of His passage on earth be these glorious and familiar remembrances; that is why He shows Himself in

[3] Cf. A. Deissmann, *Licht von Osten*, Tübingen, Mohr, 1923, p. 276, and in tr. *Light from the Ancient East: the New Testament illustrated by recently discovered texts of the Graeco-Roman world,* tr. by L. Strachnan, N. Y., Doran, 1927, and our *Histoire du Dogme de la Trinité,* I, pp. 407 ff.

all those places which He sanctified by His earthly and suffering life: the Cenacle, the lake, the hills of Galilee, and finally this Mount of Olives recently cloaked with the night of the Agony and now radiant with the glory of the Ascension.

And in the course of these talks, He lavishes the divine gifts which transform the lives of the apostles and which will be the treasure of the Church:

Peace be to you! As the Father has sent me, I also send you . . . Receive the Holy Spirit; whose sins you shall forgive, they are forgiven them; and whose sins you shall retain, they are retained (Jn. 20:21–23).

Feed my lambs . . . Feed my sheep (Jn. 21:15–17).

All power in heaven and on earth has been given to me. Go, therefore, and make disciples of all nations, baptizing them in the name of the Father, and of the Son, and of the Holy Spirit, teaching them to observe all that I have commanded you; and behold, I am with you all days, even unto the consummation of the world (Mt. 28:18–20).

In all these apparitions there shines out the divinity which undoubtedly had been manifested already, but not with such splendor. And this splendor does not hurt our eyes, it delights them; Our Lord wishes not only to found our faith, but to captivate our hearts and to take hold of our lives.

He who appears to us, completely radiating divine life, is the Vine of which we are the branches, the Head of which we are the members; His life is the principle of our own and its model. Henceforth, the spiritual life is not only mortification but also, and especially, vivification. For too long a time we have had only a stagnant life where everything ferments and grows bitter, where the least scratch of self-love festers and becomes a wound. Henceforth we feel in our souls a new life, a living fount whose waters sweep everything along. *Quasi modo geniti infantes*. Little children delight us by this freshness of life: their fits of impatience are only a passing cloud. Even violent attacks of fever are allayed more often than not without leaving any trace. This fresh young life sweeps everything along. Likewise with the Christian whom the risen Christ vivifies.

Here is what was manifested with special prominence in the martyrs and gave to their witness an irresistible ascendency. The pagans could not understand how so many dreadful tortures could be endured not only heroically but joyfully. Such was the example which, among the martyrs of Lyons whose Acts we have already recalled, was given by the deacon Sanctus:

When the wicked hoped through persistence and the severity of the tortures that they would hear something from him which should not be said, he resisted them with such firmness that he did not even tell his own name nor of what race or city he was, nor whether he was a slave or free, but to all their interrogations he answered in the Latin language: "I am a Christian." . . . They fastened plates of heated brass to the tenderest parts of his body. And these were burning, but he himself remained unbending and unyielding, strong in his confession, refreshed and strengthened by the heavenly spring of the water of life which comes forth from the breast of Christ. And his body was a witness of what happened to him, being all one wound and bruise, wrenched and torn out of human shape, and Christ suffering in him manifested great glory, routing his Adversary and for the example of the rest showing that there is nothing to be feared where there is love of the Father and nothing painful where there is Christ's glory.[4]

Our trials are not comparable to this martyrdom; the power animating us is the same: it is the "heavenly spring of living water which comes forth from the breast of Christ." This is what another great martyr tasted, St. Ignatius of Antioch: "My Love has been crucified, and I am not on fire with the love of earthly things. But there is in me a *Living Water,* which is eloquent and within me says: 'Come to the Father.' "[5]

These great examples fill us with admiration at the inestimable worth of the glorious life of Christ and, consequently, at the

---

[4] Eusebius, *Ecclesiastical History,* V, 20–23, in FC 19, pp. 277–278.
[5] *To the Romans,* 7, in ACW 1, p. 83.

338 THE SPIRITUAL TEACHING OF THE NEW TESTAMENT

infinite value of the sacrifice of the Cross, which has won for us these treasures. But one must note, too, that these signal favors were bestowed, during the forty days, on but a small number of people. Jesus is manifested, then, only to the select witnesses whom He has chosen: the apostles, the holy women, a few disciples. The first alone were prepared to see Him. These privileged witnesses themselves are not suddenly set before Our Lord; at first they wend their way towards Him. Thus the holy women see the empty tomb and the angels; then Jesus presents Himself to them: "Hail!" He said to them, "do not be afraid; go, take word to my brethren that they set out for Galilee; there they shall see me" (Mt. 28:9-10). In the apparition to Magdalen, we follow this careful preparation even better. Magdalen is weeping near the empty tomb; she sees two angels. Then, turning around, she notices, but does not recognize, Jesus standing near her: "Woman, why art thou weeping? Whom dost thou seek?" "Sir, if thou hast removed him, tell me where thou hast laid him and I will take him away." "Mary!" "Rabboni!" (Jn. 20:15-16). As soon as He spoke her name, she recognized Him. With the disciples at Emmaus, the preparation is more lengthy and painstaking: Jesus joins them on the road and explains the Scriptures to them; at their invitation, He reclined at table with them and made Himself recognized at last in the breaking of the bread (Lk. 24:13-32). Undoubtedly Our Lord wished to have them merit this great grace by the charitable invitation which the disciples address to the stranger encountered on the road. But above all He wanted to lift up their faith again by the consideration of the Scriptures and in this way to inflame their desire. They understood this themselves: "Was not our heart burning within us while he was speaking on the road and explaining to us the Scriptures?"

Wonderful pedagogy of Christ and, for us, a valuable lesson. It is not sufficient that Jesus appear: He must first lift souls up to Himself, make them desirous of possessing Him and fit to understand Him. This is what we are taught, too, by the apparition at the lake shore (Jn. 21:1-7). The long toil of the night is not only a test; it evokes remembrances. After the miraculous draught of fishes, John, the beloved disciple, recognizes Our Lord and noti-fies St. Peter. We, too, need that intuition of love: just as to the heart of St. John the miracles of Galilee and the intimacy of the Cenacle and Calvary reveal the Master waiting for him on the bank, so it is necessary for a faithful soul to preserve piously the remembrance of so many kindnesses from Our Lord, of so many desires awakened in her heart, of so many prayers and thanks-givings, and, at the first sign, to recognize Him: *Dominus est!*

This lesson will be better grasped by contrast if we consider the apparition of Jesus to Paul on the road to Damascus. This is a persecutor who is overthrown by Christ; the divine light does not flood him peacefully like John and Peter, it blinds him. Here we recognize what St. Ignatius Loyola teaches in the rules for the discernment of spirits: on sinners the grace of God falls like water on a rock; in the just it penetrates like water penetrating a sponge.[6] And certainly, after the first splash, it is possible for the stone to soften and split; but it is a great and rare miracle. The small number of the apparitions of Jesus confirms what the study of Jesus' ministry has already revealed: the Spirit has not yet been diffused, conversions are sparse. It will require the breath of Pentecost to soften these hearts of stone and to make of them hearts of flesh.

[6] Cf. *Spiritual Exercises,* tr. by L. Puhl, S.J., Westminster (Md.), Newman, 1951.

chapter 17

❖❖❖❖❖❖❖❖❖

The Ascension

The forty days' apparitions enable us to behold the glory of Christ and give us an inkling of the profusion of the gifts of the Spirit. The Ascension of Our Lord prepares the apostles for this effusion of graces; the apostles are going to understand what Jesus said to them the evening of the Last Supper: "But I speak the truth to you; it is expedient for you that I depart. For if I do not go, the Advocate will not come to you; but if I go, I will send him to you" (Jn. 16:7).

These words of Jesus become clear when we compare them with the teaching of St. Paul:

To each of us grace was given according to the measure of Christ's bestowal. Thus it says, "Ascending on high, he . . . gave gifts to men . . ." He who descended, he it is who ascended also above all the heavens, that he might fill all things. And he himself gave some men as apostles, and some as prophets, others again as evangelists, and others as pastors and teachers, in order to perfect the saints for a work of ministry, for building up the body of Christ (Eph. 4:7–12).

From heaven whither He is going to ascend, Jesus will pour forth on the apostles those gifts and graces which will render them capable of the divine ministries with which they are going to be charged; at the same time it opens to their hope that paternal house where He goes to prepare a place for them.

Let not your heart be troubled. You believe in God, believe also in me. In my Father's house there are many mansions. Were it not so, I should have told you, because I go to prepare a place for you. And if I go and prepare a place for you, I am coming again, and I will take you to myself; that where I am, there you also may be (Jn. 14:1–3).

Thus in the desert the Ark of the Covenant departed before the Israelites; it made a journey "for three days providing a place for the camp" (Nm. 10:33).

We can also recall the exhortation of the Epistle to the Hebrews (6:18–20): "This hope we have, as a sure and firm anchor of the soul, reaching even behind the veil where our forerunner Jesus has entered for us, having a high priest forever according to the order of Melchisedech."

This is the symbolic meaning and the fruit of the mystery of the Ascension: Our Lord had no need of opening for Himself the entrance to Heaven: He lives there, He reigns there: "No one has ascended into heaven except him who has descended from heaven: the Son of Man who is in heaven" (Jn. 3:13). He mounts up to heaven by right of nature; He wills that we follow Him there by grace. "Father, I will that where I am, they also whom thou hast given me may be with me; in order that they may behold my glory, which thou hast given me, because thou hast loved me before the creation of the world" (Jn. 17:24).

These promises of the Last Supper, this supreme and sovereign prayer of the Son of God, are consecrated by the Ascension. Jesus wishes to mount up to heaven under the eyes of His apostles in order to make perceptible to them His personal glorification, the foundation of our hope. He disappears into the cloud, that world which until then was inaccessible to all men, and whither He calls us to follow Him.

This mystery has transformed our whole life. Until the coming of Christ, the horizon beyond the grave appears closed and obscure; it seems that one can praise God only on earth:

I said: In the midst of my days I shall go to the gates of hell: I sought for the residue of my years.

I said: I shall not see the Lord God in the land of the living. I shall behold man no more, nor the inhabitant of rest.

My generation is at an end, and it is rolled away from me, as a shepherd's tent. My life is cut off, as by a weaver . . .

Thou hast delivered my soul that it should not perish, thou hast cast all my sins behind thy back.

For hell shall not confess to thee, neither shall death praise thee: nor shall they that go down into the pit, look for thy truth.

The living, the living, he shall give praise to thee, as I do this day: the father shall make thy truth known to the children.

O Lord, save me, and we will sing our psalms all the days of our life in the house of the Lord (Is. 38:10–20).

Let us compare these words with those of the Apostle:

We know that if the earthly house in which we dwell be destroyed, we have a building from God, a house not made by human hands, eternal in the heavens . . . knowing that while we are in the body we are exiled from the Lord . . . we even have the courage to prefer to be exiled from the body and to be at home with the Lord (2 Cor. 5:1–8).

He does not bewail his uprooted tent; he glories in his loss because Our Lord has prepared for him an eternal dwelling.

Henceforth all the troubles of life appear as the light ransom of this huge weight of glory: "Esteem it all joy, my brethren, when you fall into various trials" (Jas. 1:2). "Blessed is the man who endures temptation; for when he has been tried, he will receive the crown of life which God has promised to those who love him" (*ibid.,* 12).

This is the teaching of Jesus: "Blessed are you when men reproach you, and persecute you, and, speaking falsely, say all manner of evil against you, for my sake. Rejoice and exult, because your reward is great in heaven" (Mt. 5:11–12). In the first days of Our Lord's preaching, this teaching could seem inaccessible; the Ascension makes clear, and brings nearer to us, this prospect: "Did not the Christ have to suffer these things before entering into his glory?" (Lk. 24:26). The servant is no greater than the Master; our whole ambition is to be treated like Him and, better still, to be with Him.

Between sufferings and glory, there is not only the relationship of work to reward; there is the growth of one and the same life, at first suffering, then glorious: after the labor pains, the joys of birth (Jn. 16:20–22). Christ is formed little by little in me; He must increase, I must decrease (Jn. 3:30). In the hymn of the feast of the Ascension, the Church sums up this lesson in a word, a prayer: *Sis lacrimarum guadium:* Be thou the joy of our tears.

This joy, it is hope that gives it to us. "In hope were we saved" (Rom. 8:24); and from now on we possess the earnest of salvation, we commence to live. Our whole endeavor will be to develop in ourselves this heavenly life whose first-fruits the Ascension of Our Lord has us taste: *"Ipsi quoque mente in caelestibus habitemus."* But how, still living on earth, can we taste the joy of heaven? By weaning ourselves from the joys of earth, so as to desire more ardently and more purely the joys of heaven; and here again is the fruit of the Ascension: "It is expedient for you that I depart" (Jn. 16:7).

Let us understand well what this separation takes away from us; we shall grasp better what it gives us. The Ascension caused the apostles and all of us to lose the visible and tangible presence of Our Lord; we can no longer reach Him except by faith: this is a blessing.

St. Catherine of Siena shows us in St. Peter the model of the penitent soul, whom Our Lord sustains at first with His visits, then purifies by His absence:

> The sorrow of Peter was still imperfect, and it remains imperfect for forty days, until after the Ascension. But, when My Truth was returned to Me according to its humanity, Peter and the other disciples went back home to await the coming of the Holy Spirit, which My Truth had promised them. So does the soul who wishes to arrive at perfection . . . She is always imperfect, and, to lead her to perfection, after forty days, I go away from her, not by grace, but by feeling . . . I tell you, it is thus that I conduct Myself in this matter. To make the soul go out of its imperfection, I withdraw from her, by depriving her of the consolation she felt before.[1]

This spiritual doctrine is illumined by the whole Gospel story. Surely the sensible presence of the Son of God on earth was an immense grace: "Blessed are the eyes which see what you see!" (Lk. 10:23). And yet this is not the highest gift: "Blessed are they who have not seen, and yet have believed" (Jn. 20:29). The sensible presence of Our Lord will have to set the disciples on their way to this faith; when they arrive there, God will withdraw the sensible help He had loaned them, and invite them to follow Him in the night.

If we wish to grasp the necessity of this progress, let us recall how difficult it was for the Jews, in the time of Jesus' sensible presence, to elevate themselves to spiritual realities. They follow Him in the desert and, from there, to Capharnaum; but it is because they "have eaten of the loaves and have been filled" (Jn. 6:26). Among those who follow Him, how few ask Him for the graces of conversion or of faith! What they expect from Him is the curing of an ill or the resurrection of a dead person; or it is the re-establishment of the kingdom of Israel. Sometimes it is even less—like arbitration for the division of an inheritance between two brothers (Lk. 12:13). Jesus answers simply, "Who has appointed me a judge or arbitrator over you?" He discourages, likewise, national ambitions; He mercifully bestows the graces of resurrection and healing, but He profits from them, above all, to

---

[1] *Dialogue,* ch. 33.

bestow that forgiveness of sins about which so few are concerned, and to elevate the faith from life here below to eternal life. To Martha weeping over her dead brother He announces: "Thy brother shall rise." "I know that he will rise at the resurrection, on the last day," "I am the resurrection and the life; . . . whoever lives and believes in me, shall never die. Dost thou believe this?" (Jn. 11:23–26).

Thus such touching miracles as these are, no doubt, works of mercy; but, above all, they aim at procuring faith and at sustaining it. Alas! among the Jews who throng Jesus, the majority take advantage of the miracle without understanding its teaching; they admire the beautiful characters of this divine script without grasping the words which are thus traced. Do we not thus pass through this sensible world, a work of so much wisdom and goodness? We enjoy ourselves in it, we understand not its lesson.

These straight and narrow views appear even in the apostles, and even on the day of the Ascension, when they ask Jesus, "Wilt thou at this time restore the kingdom to Israel?" (Acts 1:6). Jesus dismisses this question, which betrays so painfully the preoccupations of men of earth, blind still to the mysteries of heaven. He leaves them, He ascends on high, and this departure, by weaning them, is going to transform them. By withdrawing from them these sensible realities which hide from them the divine mystery, He is going to stimulate them to a deeper intuition. He could repeat to them, then, what He said to them in the Cenacle, "Have I been so long a time with you, and you have not known me? Philip, he who sees me sees also the Father" (Jn. 14:9). Soon they will reach that far, with the light of the Holy Spirit.

The decisive grace will be this gift of the Holy Spirit, merited by Christ's death; but the apostles will have been prepared for this grace by the detachment which Our Lord's departure imposes on them. They will no longer be able to see or touch their Master, whom they love so ardently; they will no longer reach Him except by faith. This will be a painful privation, and a great grace.

As long as Jesus shared their lives, they undoubtedly loved Him, they believed in Him; but they did not fully understand Him. They begin to understand Him now that they are no longer looking for Him except by faith; for only by this can the mystery be revealed. Now their prayer, their longing, their entire religion is transformed; they will no longer beg for the restoration of the kingdom, but for the salvation of souls, of all souls: "There is no other name under heaven given to men by which we must be saved" (Acts 4:12). St. Paul will say, "Henceforth we know no one according to the flesh. And even though we have known Christ according to the flesh, yet now we know him so no longer" (2 Cor. 5:16). And St. Ignatius of Antioch: "Nothing that is seen is good. Our God Jesus Christ certainly is the more clearly seen now that He is in the Father." [2]

Jesus, if He had so wished, could have perpetuated His sensible presence here below or renewed it from time to time, just as He had done during the forty days. He did not will to do so. He dwells among us, God and man, with His body, His soul, His divinity; but this mysterious presence does not depend, like ours, on sensible conditions, and can be grasped only by faith. And that gives to Christian worship its character: one can have access to Christ only in faith. This essential condition raises the soul to Christ and wards off from Our Lord all contact unworthy of Him.

[2] *To the Romans,* 3, ACW 1, p. 81.

chapter 18

❖❖❖❖❖❖❖❖❖

Pentecost

Jesus has left us forever; it is now that He is going to manifest Himself. At the Last Supper He had advised the apostles of this: "I am going to him who sent me . . . It is expedient for you that I depart. For if I do not go, the Advocate will not come to you; but if I go, I will send him to you" (Jn. 16:5–7). And again, on the day of the Ascension, He had repeated this to them: "I send forth upon you the promise of my Father. But wait here in the city, until you are clothed with power from on high" (Lk. 24:49).

When the days of Pentecost were drawing to a close, they were all together in one place. And suddenly there came a sound from heaven, as of a violent wind coming, and it filled the whole house where they were sitting. And there appeared to them parted tongues as of fire, which settled upon each of them. And they were all filled with the Holy Spirit and began to speak in foreign tongues, even as the Holy Spirit prompted them to speak (Acts 2:1–4).

This great mystery, like that of the Incarnation, is the work of the entire Trinity: the Father has promised the Holy Spirit, the Son sends Him, and the Spirit indeed gives Himself.[1] We shall not find in this gift the wondrous condescension of a God being made man, being born and dying for us; but we shall adore therein the incomparable efficacy of the divine gifts. Jesus has told us, "It is the spirit that gives life; the flesh profits nothing" (Jn. 6:64); He spoke thus of His Eucharist; in order to make His thought understood by sensual men who were scandalized, He said to them, "What then if you should see the Son of Man ascending where he was before?" (*ibid.*, 63). These words, at that time obscure, become clear in the light of the Ascension.[2]

The flesh of Christ which we receive in the Eucharist, this is His glorious flesh which is living in heaven, freed from the material conditions of earthly existence; it vivifies us by the life of the Spirit which it pours forth in us. It will be the same with the activity of the Holy Spirit, a completely spiritual and heavenly activity.

And indeed the radiation of this activity in the apostles is wondrous: it is manifested by the gift of languages, by miracles, but above all by the spiritual transformation that it works. Jesus had advised His apostles to stay in the city until they had received power from on high; they had not yet either the strength

---

[1] One will, however, note this essential difference between the two mysteries: namely, by the Incarnation, the Son has taken on a human nature; henceforth He is God and man; on Pentecost the Spirit pours forth His gifts on men, but without taking on their nature, without becoming one of them. Because of this, the bond which unites us to the Holy Spirit is a bond of dependency and of thanksgiving, but not a bond of nature like that uniting us to Jesus Christ.

[2] Cf. the note of Joüon: "If [men] stumble, if their faith vacillates, it is because they think only of the eating of a flesh subjected to the ordinary conditions of matter. If they saw Jesus mounting up to heaven, they would have the idea of a human body completely exempt from these conditions. Jesus hints that it is in this state that He will give His body as food." *L'Evangile de Notre Seigneur Jésus-Christ, trad. et commentaire du texte original grec, compte tenu du substrat sémitique,* 2nd ed. (Verbum Salutis 5), Paris, Beauchesne, 1930, pp. 498–99.

or the light which that completely new mission required of them. The Holy Spirit gives them this "power from on high."

The missions which they had received from Jesus during His life were only trial missions: their message was confined to the announcement of the kingdom of God; it relied on miracles and deliverances of the possessed. But in all the cities and villages they passed through, they had nothing to found; these were sowings, not the harvest. And the field they sowed was only the land of Israel: "Do not go in the direction of the Gentiles, nor enter the towns of Samaritans; but go rather to the lost sheep of the house of Israel" (Mt. 10:5-6). Now all the barriers are down: "Go, therefore, and make disciples of all nations, baptizing them . . ." (Mt. 28:19). In this completely new apostolate, what initiatives they will have to take, which until then had made them recoil! They do not think about this; they lead the way, relying on the Holy Spirit. They address, first of all, the Jews; then they see the Jews closing their eyes to their message and soon rejecting it with all their might. Driven out by Israel, they go to the pagans, and find hearts opening up. They are surprised, they are full of admiration, at one and the same time joyful and sorrowful; they say with St. Peter, "Can anyone refuse the water to baptize these, seeing that they have received the Holy Spirit just as we did?" (Acts 10:47), or with St. Paul, "It was necessary that the word of God should be spoken to you [Jews] first, but since you reject it and judge yourselves unworthy of eternal life, behold, we now turn to the Gentiles" (Acts 13:46).

Such bold initiatives as these which Jesus Himself had objected to during His mortal life, the apostles take up, although all their Jewish past might be hurt by it. Do we not feel here the irresistible force of the Spirit living and speaking in them? And this gift of the Spirit has been bought with the death, the resurrection, and the ascension of Jesus.

What is most wondrous and divine in this force is its docility. On more than one point the teaching of Jesus had remained misunderstood by the apostles. Now the Spirit causes them to understand the words of the Master, just as He Himself had promised them (Jn. 14:26). Thus will it be with the legislation about the clean and the unclean, so sacred until then to the Jews. This barrier had for a long time protected them from pagan contagion: now they must win over the pagans; the barrier must fall. But for those Jews, careful for such a long time about these observances, what a scandal! Yet Jesus had said to them, "What goes into the mouth does not defile a man; but that which comes out of the mouth, that defiles a man" (Mt. 15:11). They had once been frightened by these words: "Dost thou know that the Pharisees have taken offense at hearing this saying? Every plant that my heavenly Father has not planted will be rooted up. Let them alone; blind guides they are of blind men" (*ibid.,* 12–14). Since then, many months have passed; the vision at Joppa clarifies for Peter the statement heard of old but not understood, and he finally grasps its full significance: at Caesarea he enters the house of the centurion: "You know it is not permissible for a Jew to associate with a foreigner or to visit him; but God has shown me that I should not call any man common or unclean; therefore I came without hesitation when I was sent for" (Acts 10:28–29). We see the same docility in St. Paul at the time of the vision which he had at Jerusalem: "When I was praying in the temple, I was in ecstasy and saw him as he said to me, 'Make haste and go quickly out of Jerusalem, for they will not receive thy testimony concerning me.' " Paul then reminds Jesus of all the pledges He had given the Jews and which, he thinks, will recommend his testimony in their eyes. Our Lord is insistent: "Go, for to the Gentiles far away I will send thee" (Acts 22:17–21). This order tore him away from all that he loved and revered on earth. He obeyed at once.

This docility in action is perhaps less remarkable even than docility in thought. These Jews, whose monotheism is so jealous, are led by the Holy Spirit to the revelation of the Trinity, with no shock, no surprise, with nothing of the faith of Israel turning into something strange for them. On the contrary, they understand better each day, in the new light penetrating them, the prerogatives of the chosen people who have "the adoption as sons, and the glory and the covenants and the legislation and the worship and the promises; who have the fathers, and from whom is the Christ according to the flesh, who is over all things, God blessed forever" (Rom. 9:4–5). They are conscious of "the mystery of Christ, that mystery which in other ages was not known to the sons of men, as now it has been revealed to his holy apostles and prophets in the Spirit" (Eph. 3:5). But these new revelations neither blind nor exalt them; they spread their boundless light over the whole past of humanity and all its future; better still, over the whole world: "He is the image of the invisible God, the firstborn of every creature. For in him were created all things in the heavens and on the earth, things visible and things invisible, whether Thrones, or Dominations, or Principalities, or Powers. All things have been created through and unto him" (Col. 1:15 ff.). The whole universe is completely radiant with the splendor of Christ's resurrection. And all this glory, far from overwhelming man, lifts him up: Christ is in him, and it is from Christ that all this light shines forth.

The supreme fruit of this transformation will be, here below, liberty: with regard to human constraints, the cross of Christ releases the Christian from them; with regard to human traditions, the docility of Christ, the sole Master, sets him free; with regard to all the qualms which the mystery of the world awakens in us, the light of Christ dissipates them. "I am sure that neither death, nor life, nor angels, nor principalities, nor things present, nor things to come, nor powers, nor height, nor depth, nor any other creature will be able to separate us from the love of God, which is in Christ Jesus our Lord" (Rom. 8:38–39).

chapter 19

The Body of Christ

In viewing the mystery of the Ascension, we have marveled at the beneficent and wise action of Our Lord Jesus, pouring out His divine gifts on all men, making of them evangelists, pastors and teachers, "for building up the body of Christ" (Eph. 4:12). The building up of the Body of Christ is the principal work for which Jesus paid with His blood and which He is going to continue in the whole world until the end of time. It is in the progressive construction of this immense, eternal edifice that there will appear the wisdom and love of Our Lord, at the same time as the boundless fecundity of the sacrifice of Calvary.

What strikes us from the first day of Pentecost is the completely divine boldness of the plan. The death and the resurrection of Jesus open henceforth to the Gospel an immense perspective: "Go, therefore, and make disciples of all nations" (Mt. 28:19). This divine will is clearly signified from the day of Pentecost:

They were all together in one place. And suddenly there came a
sound from heaven, as of a violent wind coming, and it filled the
whole house where they were sitting. And there appeared to them
parted tongues as of fire, which settled upon each of them. And they
were all filled with the Holy Spirit and began to speak in foreign
tongues, even as the Holy Spirit prompted them to speak (Acts
2:1–4).

The bystanders are astounded:

Behold, are not all these that are speaking Galileans? And how have
we heard each his own language in which he was born? Parthians and
Medes and Elamites, and inhabitants of Mesopotamia, Judea, and
Cappadocia, Pontus and Asia, Phrygia and Pamphylia, Egypt and
the parts of Libya about Cyrene, and visitors from Rome, Jews also
and proselytes, Cretans and Arabians, we have heard them speaking
in our own languages of the wonderful works of God (*ibid.*, 7–11).

This miracle was the presage of a preaching which, before the
end of the century, was going to be spread throughout the Medi-
terranean world, propagated among all these peoples, carried by
all these languages which resound today in the ears of the pilgrims at Jerusalem. Such a rapid and extensive propagation as
this will be a great miracle; but what will be still more remarkable,
will be the unity of the Church built up from all these peoples:
all these men, because on that day of Pentecost in Jerusalem they
receive the gifts of the Spirit, will be able to return to their distant countries and live there, separated from each other, having
but one body and one soul.

There were at that time in Jerusalem many Jews closed to the
preaching of the Gospel; if any one of them assisted at this
scene or heard tell of it, what could he say except that these
people were drunk or mad[1] or, more politely, that it was a new
Babel. And yet this was Pentecost; it will be judged by its fruits:
these men, filled on that day with the gifts of the Spirit, will return to their countries, Mesopotamia, Cappadocia, Pontus, Asia,

[1] Acts 2:13; cf. 1 Cor. 14:23.

Phrygia, not like human dust which the wind scatters at random, but like seeds which the Spirit fecundates, which He bears where He will and which He will cause to germinate there.

The most remarkable feature in these young churches, vibrant with faith and love, will be their unity. During His life, Jesus had maintained unanimity in the little flock of the apostles; but He needed for this all His vigilance, all His love, all His sovereign authority. He had stifled, from the time of their first manifestations, the ambitious schemings, the seeking after the first places (Mk. 9:32–36; 10:41–45; Lk. 22:24–27). With Jesus gone, who would ensure this humble, peaceful unity? And it is not a matter of maintaining it henceforth in a group of a dozen persons, but in a Church which spreads its branches everywhere and counts by the hundreds and then by the thousands its faithful, of whom she will be able to say with pride: "The multitude of the believers were of one heart and one soul" (Acts 4:32); and the pagans themselves will soon say of the Christians, "See how they love one another." [2]

What will ensure this unity is the mystery of the Church, the Body of Christ. In order to participate in the divine life which the Son of God offers to communicate to them, men must die to themselves and live to Christ. And this new life, which is given to them at baptism and developed by the Eucharist, is essentially a social life, which makes of all Christians a single body whose sole Head is Christ and whose members are all Christians. No one, then, will be able to receive the grace absolutely necessary for life without that incorporation; no one can be vivified by Christ without being completely taken up by Him, without consecrating to the development of the entire body what he himself has of strength and activity. There is in it for each member a social function of which he continually becomes more conscious and more dearly enamoured, in the measure that he is more deeply transformed by the life-giving influence of the Head. This Head is the Son of God, who for our sakes was made man, who for our sakes died and came to life again, who gives Himself in the Eu-

[2] Tertullian, *Apologeticum*, XXXIX, 7, and in tr. FC 10, p. 99.

charist to each of His members so as to vivify him, so as to make Himself known and loved by him. The spiritual life cannot penetrate and transform the Christian without uniting him more intimately to his Head, without revealing Him to him, and without causing him to love Him. This new life, then, will be for him not only a vital impulse summoning him to the service of the Church, the Body whose member he is; it will be above all the communication of the life of the Son of God, the Head of the Church and the Savior of men. This huge undertaking of salvation is unveiled gradually before our eyes; it is so sublime that God sacrificed for it the life of His Son, and He so honors men that He invites all of them to collaborate in so holy a work as this, to save themselves and their brethren. United to the Son of God, we cannot fail. He wills that this union be efficacious and that we pledge our lives thereto as He has pledged His own. This is the whole meaning of the Christian vocation.

chapter 20

❖❖❖❖❖❖❖❖❖

The Life of Christ in Christians, His Members

Jesus had repeated many times to His disciples the fundamental law of salvation: "He who finds his life will lose it, and he who loses his life for my sake, will find it." [1] The death and the resurrection of Jesus have brought to this law a decisive confirmation. No disciple, henceforth, can escape it; none can elude these words by seeing in them, under a bold metaphor, only the general law of renunciation. The death of Christ bears witness to their literal meaning: here it is a question, in the proper sense, of death and of life. But death appears fruitful; it is by death that life must germinate:

Amen, amen, unless the grain of wheat fall into the ground and die, it remains alone. But if it die, it brings forth much fruit. He who

[1] This maxim is encountered six times in the Gospels: Mt. 10:39; 16:25; Mk. 8:35; Lk. 9:24; 17:33; Jn. 12:25. On the different forms of these maxims and their Semitic substratum, cf. Joüon, *Recherches de Science religieuse*, 1927, pp. 225–227.

loves his life, loses it; and he who hates his life in this world, keeps it unto life everlasting (Jn. 12:24–25).

Jesus spoke thus on the day of the Palms, when the shadow of the Cross was falling on Him; and, in order to carry along in His wake all His disciples, He added:

If anyone serve me, let him follow me; and where I am there also shall my servant be. If anyone serve me, my Father will honor him (*ibid.*, 26).

We are aware in these warnings of Jesus, in the Discourse at the Last Supper, in the institution of the Eucharist, and above all in His death and resurrection, of a mystery in which everything infinitely surpasses us—the requirements and, still more, the promises. Everything surpasses us, but everything takes hold of us; and if our faith wills to be docile, it cannot evade this clasp.

To live, we must die with Christ and rise with Him. "Abide in me, and I in you," Jesus told us at the Last Supper (Jn. 15:4); this immanence is the condition of our lives; but the Eucharist and Calvary make us understand the sovereignly tremendous and beneficial radiance of this presence. We no longer belong to ourselves; ransomed by Christ, we are His. He takes hold of us, He unites us to His death and life, so as to make us die to ourselves and live by Him. And this death, no doubt, is shown to be much more profound than we at first suspected; but this life, this union with Our Lord, surpasses all our hopes.

St. Paul takes pleasure in this mystery of death and of life; he tires not of reminding his disciples of it in phrases whose bold relief has been carved forever in the Christian conscience:

The love of Christ impels us, because we have come to the conclusion that, since one died for all, therefore all died; and that Christ died for all, in order that they who are alive may live no longer for themselves, but for him who died for them and rose again (2 Cor. 5:14–15).

None of us lives to himself, and none dies to himself; for if we live, we live to the Lord, or if we die, we die to the Lord. Therefore, whether we live or die, we are the Lord's. For to this end Christ died and rose again, that he might be Lord both of the dead and of the living (Rom. 14:7–9).

This life of God in the Christian is a gift of God; we misunderstand it entirely if we see in it only the charm of a pleasant remembrance, of a satisfied wish. This is not an affective state which man induces and fosters; it is the gift of a divine Guest who comes into us, so as to transform us into Himself.[2]

It is by baptism that God bestows on men this gift of the

[2] Schweitzer has vigorously refuted the purely psychological and affective conception of the life of Christ in the Christian, expounded by many liberal Lutherans. After recalling that Paul never spoke of the "mystical body" of Christ, he continues: "Without admitting it, the explanation of Paul's mysticism has always come to an end at the point where the mystical body of Christ came in. The way in which it was attempted to explain it could not lead to the goal. The idea was to drive it from the belief in Christ and the being-in-Christ. The belief in Christ was supposed to become a being-in-Christ, and from the being-in-Christ of the many believers Paul was supposed to have arrived at the conceptions of the mystical body of Christ."

All these attempts, he thinks, are fruitless: "That the being-in-Christ arises out of such an enhancement of belief in Christ is nowhere indicated by Paul and is nowhere presupposed by him. The relationship of faith in Christ to union with Christ is for him thus: that belief in Christ being present, union with Christ automatically takes place—under certain circumstances, that is to say, when the believer causes himself to be baptized. Without baptism there is no being-in-Christ!" (*Die Mystik des Apostels Paulus,* pp. 117, 118, and in tr. *The Mysticism of Paul the Apostle*). All is not exact in this critique; the conferring of grace at baptism is not "automatic"; it is true, at any rate, that there is in it a conferring of grace whose source is in God and not in man; and this grace is the principle of the indwelling of Christ in the Christian and, consequently, of the "body of Christ."

As for the term, "mystical body of Christ," we know that it is foreign to St. Paul and that it has been applied to this mystery only in the theology of the Middle Ages, which has given exact expression to its full significance. Cf. H. de Lubac, S.J., *"Corpus Mysticum, Etude sur l'origine et les premiers sens de l'expression," Recherches de Science religieuse,* 1939, pp. 257–302; 429–480; 1940, pp. 40–80, 191–226. Cf. his *Corpus mysticum, l'Eucharist et l'Eglise au Moyen-Age, étude historique* (Théologie 3), Paris, Aubier, 1944.

presence and life of His Son; it is at this time that the Christian, united to the death of Christ, dies to sin and rises with Our Lord to a new life. St. Paul recalls thus to the Romans this fundamental belief:

Do you not know that all we who have been baptized into Christ Jesus have been baptized into his death? For we were buried with him by means of baptism into death, in order that, just as Christ has arisen from the dead through the glory of the Father, so we also may walk in newness of life. For if we have been united with him in the likeness of his death, we shall be so in the likeness of the resurrection also. For we know that our old self has been crucified with him, in order that the body of sin may be destroyed, that we may no longer be slaves to sin; for he who is dead is acquitted of sin. But if we have died with Christ, we believe that we shall also live together with Christ; for we know that Christ, having risen from the dead, dies now no more, death shall no longer have dominion over him. For the death that he died, he died to sin once for all, but the life that he lives, he lives unto God. Thus do you consider yourselves also as dead to sin, but alive to God in Christ Jesus (Rom. 6:3–11).

Baptism by immersion, such as it was commonly practised at that time, would suggest this mystery by its symbolism: the neophyte, immersed in the piscina, buried therein his whole past; uniting himself to the death of Christ dying with him, he did not emerge from the baptismal water except restored to life with Him. But the symbol is secondary, and, from that period, immersion was no longer considered as an indispensable ritual.[3] Grace was always the same, independent of the symbol: with Christ, the Christian dies to sin; with Christ, he is reborn to divine life. The baptismal piscina, then, is for him what the tomb was for Christ: he is buried therein, but so as to leave it restored to a new life. St. Paul again sets forth this doctrine to the Colossians:

[3] We read in the *Teaching of the Twelve Apostles* (*The Didache*), 7 (ACW 6, p. 19): "If you have no running water, baptize in other water; and if you cannot in cold, then in warm. But if you have neither, pour water on the head three times in the name of the Father and of the Son and of the Holy Spirit."

In him, too, you have been circumcised with a circumcision not wrought by hand, but through putting off the body of the flesh, a circumcision which is of Christ. For you were buried together with him in baptism, and in him also rose again through faith in the working of God who raised him from the dead. And you, when you were dead by reason of your sins and the uncircumcision of your flesh, he brought to life along with him, forgiving you all your sins (Col. 2:11–13).[4]

By describing in this way the effect of baptism, the Apostle makes clearly understood what this life "in Christ" is, which baptism inaugurates. We have been "baptized into Christ, that is to say, plunged into the mystical Christ, as into the natural element of our new life." [5] Henceforth the Christian who is faithful to his baptism lives in Christ. This is even better understood when we continue with the reading of St. Paul's text: the neophytes who have been "baptized [plongés] into Christ Jesus have been baptized [plongés] into his death" (Rom. 6:3). Indeed, we are associated with Christ and we become His members at the precise moment when He Himself becomes our Savior. But, this moment coincides for Jesus with that of death, acted out and mystically realized for us in baptism. From then on, everything for us is in common with Jesus Christ: we are crucified, buried, restored to life with Him; we share His death and His new life, His glory, His reign, His heritage.[6] But we must go even further: the death of Christ, in which baptism plunges us, unites us to His death by

[4] This transformation which makes a man die to sin so as to make him live to God in Jesus Christ is the proper fruit of baptism, but it implies, necessarily, faith: "It is indeed union with Christ which makes us children of God, and this union is effected by faith and by baptism; but neither can the effective union of baptism be produced without the affective union of faith, nor the affective union of faith be produced without some intrinsic relation with the effective union of baptism; it is because the affective union of faith tends essentially to the effective union of baptism that it becomes itself effective; and the two conceptions, far from being opposed, are reunited." (F. Prat, Théologie de saint Paul, 6th ed., II, pp. 314, 315, and in tr. The Theology of Saint Paul, II, p. 261.)

[5] Prat, ibid., II, p. 266, and in tr. II, 258.

[6] Prat, ibid.

making us die to ourselves; it is at this price that we are united to the life of the risen Christ, to His glory and to His reign.[7]

What baptism inaugurates, the Eucharist consummates: baptism unites us to the Savior in the very act of His sacrifice, in His death offered for us; likewise the Eucharist, which incorporates us in Him, causes us to partake of the immolated victim. This is the teaching of St. Paul, in Chapter 10 of the First Epistle to the Corinthians (16–22); he stresses it in the subsequent chapter:

As often as you shall eat this bread and drink the cup, you proclaim the death of the Lord, until he comes. Therefore whoever eats this bread or drinks the cup of the Lord unworthily, will be guilty of the body and the blood of the Lord (1 Cor. 11:26–27).[8]

At baptism, the union of the neophyte with Christ is consummated in his participation in the death of Christ; it is by His death that Christ has purchased it, and it is by being united to this mystery that the Christian participates in the redemption. The same law is applied to the Eucharist: "The cup of blessing that we bless, is it not the sharing of the blood of Christ? And the bread that we break, is it not the partaking of the body of the Lord?" (1 Cor. 10:16). If we are incorporated in Christ, it

---

[7] This symbolism of baptism is thus expounded by St. Augustine commenting on the text of the Epistle to the Romans: *"Sacri baptismatis in cruce Christi grande mysterium commendavit eo modo, ut intelligamus, nihil aliud esse in Christo baptismum, nisi mortis Christi similitudinem; nihil autem aliud mortem Christi crucifixi, nisi remissionis peccati similitudinem; ut quemadmodum in illo vera resurrectio, ita in nobis vera justificatio"* (*Enchiridion Symbolorum* 52. P.L., XL, 256).

[8] Cf. Allo, *Saint Paul, Première Épître aux Corinthiens*, p. 305: "The Eucharistic ceremony, renewed in all the churches for as long a time as the Church will last, until the Parousia, has, then, in the spirit and letter of St. Paul, all it needs in order to realize fully the notion of sacrifice, a commemoration, no doubt, of that of the Cross and a recall of the Last Supper, but real, absolutely real, because the sacrifice of Calvary is found there mysteriously renewed, by the presence of the same victim, acted out in the same state of immolation, and offered on that altar which is called the τράπεζα τοῦ χυρίου."

is, then, like being so in a victim sacrificed for us. We cannot conceive of the sharing without the sacrifice, and this sacrifice is nothing else but the sacrifice of the Cross. If, then, the Eucharist is the supremely efficacious means to unite us to our Head and to make us His members, we understand that the first law of this incorporation is the sharing in His passion.[9] The mystery of baptism had taught us this, the mystery of the Eucharist reveals it to us with even greater clarity.

The first fruit of this participation of Christians in the death of Christ is the unity which it creates among all of them and of them all with Christ and with God His Father:

All you who have been baptized into Christ, have put on Christ. There is neither Jew nor Greek; there is neither slave nor freeman; there is neither male nor female. For you are all one in Christ Jesus (Gal. 3:27–28).

There is not Gentile and Jew, circumcised and uncircumcised, Barbarian and Scythian, slave and freeman; but Christ is all things and in all (Col. 3:11).

This is already the effect of baptism; it is also that of the Eucharist:

Because the bread is one, we, though many, are one body, all of us who partake of the one bread (1 Cor. 10:17).

In this sacramental action of baptism and, above all, of the Eucharist we must recognize much more than a symbolic meaning. At baptism, the immersion of the neophytes in the baptismal piscina signified the abolition of the past; here the unity of the grains of wheat in a single bread is the symbol of the unity of

---

[9] St. Augustine only develops this teaching of the Apostle, when he presents to us, in the Eucharist, Christ, at one and the same time, priest and victim, and the Church, united to Him as the Body to the Head, and offering herself with Him: "[Christus] et sacerdos est, ipse offerens, ipse et oblatio. Cujus rei sacramentum quotidianum esse voluit Ecclesiae sacrificium; quae cum ipsius capitis corpus sit, se ipsam per ipsum discit offerre" (De Civitate Dei, X, 20. P.L., XLI, 298; cf. ibid., X, 6, 284, in FC 14, p. 153; Mersch, Le Corps mystique du Christ, II, p. 108, n. 2, and in tr. The Whole Christ).

Christians in the Church. But in these two sacraments we must attain, through the symbols, the reality they signify: at baptism, the neophytes are incorporated in the death of Christ so as to be reborn, by His resurrection, to a new life; in the Eucharist, they communicate in the victim of the redemptive sacrifice and, by uniting themselves to Him, they are united to each other.

We are baptized in the death of Christ; we communicate in the death of Christ. That is the first aspect of the sacramental action. Incorporation in Christ has for its effects, then, death to sin, death to the old man and to all his tendencies. If this grace develops all its efficacy, the union is consummated, both with God and with each other, through Jesus Christ, in whom we are dead to our whole past.

He himself is our peace, he it is who has made both one, and has broken down the intervening wall of the enclosure, the enmity, in his flesh. The Law of the commandments expressed in decrees he has made void, that of the two he might create in himself one new man, and make peace and reconcile both in one body to God by the cross, having slain the enmity in himself. And coming, he announced the good tidings of peace to you who were afar off, and of peace to those who were near; because through him we both have access in one Spirit to the Father (Eph. 2:14–18).

This universal pacification is the fruit of Christ's death; by being united to this death, through baptism and the Eucharist, we imbue its efficacy. What separates us from God is sin and the evil inclination we harbor for it: if sin is dead, if this evil inclination is effectively mortified, the wall of enmity is broken down between God and ourselves. It is the same between ourselves and the other members of Christ: the "intervening wall" which separates one man from another is the selfishness which raises and defends it. Let us recall the cliques of the Corinthians and the protests of St. Paul: "Has Christ been divided up?" (1 Cor. 1:13); "You are still carnal. For since there are jealousy and strife among you, are you not carnal, and walking as mere men? For whenever one says, 'I am of Paul,' but another, 'I am of Apollos,' are you not mere men?" (*ibid.*, 3:2–4).

The grace of baptism and the Eucharist is powerful, but it desires docile souls. A persecutor thrown from his horse can still kick against the goad; if he prays like Saul, if he is docile, he will be mortified; he will still be able to feel the pain of the former wounds and to exclaim, "Unhappy man that I am! Who will deliver me from the body of this death?" But he will reply at once with a cry of triumph, "The grace of God through Jesus Christ our Lord" (Rom. 7:24–25). This work, inaugurated on the day of conversion by baptism and the Eucharist must be continued during the whole of life, so that in the end "what is mortal may be swallowed up by life" (2 Cor. 5:4). But we marvel, from the first day, at the efficacy of these graces; they make us die to ourselves and thereby they unite us to God and to each other, in such a way that we form but one body and one soul.

More powerful still than this work of death there appears to us the work of life which is continued in us by the risen Christ. At baptism, we acknowledged Him as Our Lord; we were handed over to Him and He took hold of us; and this embrace grows tighter in the whole course of the Christian life:

It is now no longer I that live, but Christ lives in me. And the life that I now live in the flesh, I live in the faith of the Son of God, who loved me and gave himself up for me (Gal. 2:20).

This life is not individualistic, but social; at baptism, Christians have been united to Christ only in order to form one body; and in the Eucharist, they are fed by Christ only as members of His body. Race barriers are abolished in the unity of the Church; but we distinguish in this single body diverse members whose functions are complementary and who all aim at the blossoming of the social life of the whole body.

This great mystery is recalled by the Apostle to the faithful of Corinth as a teaching which is familiar to them: "Do you not know that your bodies are members of Christ?" (1 Cor. 6:15). This doctrine forms part of the elementary catechesis of St. Paul; the Corinthians are only children in Christ, and yet they cannot ignore it. This is not, then, a mystery reserved to the initiated; it is the milk of children. And yet what loftiness! "He who cleaves to the Lord is one spirit with him" (*ibid.*, 17). The union of Christians with Christ takes hold of them completely, body and soul; and this union, whose principle is the spirit, is so intimate that the Christian and Christ now form but one spirit. The Eucharist consummates this mystery of baptism: "Because the bread is one, we, though many, are one body, all of us who partake of the one bread" (1 Cor. 10:17). In this single body, all the members are differentiated by the various graces which God has communicated to each of them in view of the complete building up of the body:

Now there are varieties of gifts, but the same Spirit; and there are varieties of ministries, but the same Lord; and there are varieties of workings, but the same God, who works all things in all. Now the manifestation of the Spirit is given to everyone for profit. To one through the Spirit is given the utterance of wisdom; and to another the utterance of knowledge, according to the same Spirit; to another faith, in the same Spirit; to another the gift of healing, in the one Spirit; to another the working of miracles; to another prophecy; to another the distinguishing of spirits; to another various kinds of tongues; to another interpretation of tongues. But all these things are the work of one and the same Spirit, who divides to everyone according as he will.[10]

[10] 1 Cor. 12:4–11. This doctrine is clarified, in the rest of the chapter, by the analogy of the human body and its members. This analogy was inspired neither by the Bible nor by the Rabbinic literature (cf. Mersch, *Le Corps mystique*, I, p. 114, n. 1). E. Käsemann, *Leib und Leib Christi* (Tübingen, 1933), especially pp. 50–93, thought he recognized in this Pauline theology a gnostic influence: the body is a particle of material substance possessed by demons; the soul, on the contrary, is connected to man who, like Eon, constitutes the unity of all spiritual substances. This mythology did not appear under this determined form and it is impossible to prove its influence on St. Paul: moreover, it is profoundly different from the doctrine expounded in *1 Corinthians:* the "body" is not conceived as a universal substance, but as an individual body having its own activity and finality, and all its particular activities appear there as converging for its life and its good.

The interpretation which Schweitzer gives of the Pauline conception of the body of Christ is different from that of Käsemann, but is no longer

This theology, recalled by St. Paul to the Corinthians and to the Romans,[11] is taken up again by the Apostle in the letters of the Captivity[12] and put in sharper focus. These lofty mystical views

---

admissible. Here is how he himself expounds it: "The original and central idea of the Pauline Mysticism is therefore that the Elect share with one another and with Christ a corporeity which is in a special way susceptible to the action of the powers of death and resurrection, and in consequence capable of acquiring the resurrection state of existence before the general resurrection of the dead takes place. . . . The enigmatic concept, which dominates that mysticism, of the 'body of Christ' to which all believers belong, and in which they are already dead and risen again, is thus derived from the pre-existent Church (the 'Community of God')" (*Die Mystik des Apostels Paulus*, pp. 116, 117, and in tr. *The Mysticism of Paul the Apostle*).

This material conception of the body of Christ, involves, for the incorporation of the Christian in Christ, a strictly physical interpretation: "For him [Paul] every manifestation of the life of the baptized man is conditioned by his being in Christ. Grafted into the corporeity of Christ, he loses his creatively individual existence and his natural personality. Henceforth he is only a form of manifestation of the personality of Jesus Christ, which dominates that corporeity. Paul says this with trenchant clearness when he writes, in the Epistle to the Galatians, 'I am crucified with Christ, so I live no longer as I myself; rather, it is Christ who lives in me'" (*ibid.*, pp. 125, 126).

This interpretation is ruled by materialistic imaginings which distort the thought of St. Paul. The Church is not a "privileged bodily substance" in which one is incorporated by baptism; the incorporation of the Christian in Christ does not involve a suppression of his personality. Sudden incorporation is not, for the Christian, an "isolated step"; it makes of him a member of the body. But this incorporation is not "automatic"; it is a grace of God, accorded to the good will of man, capable of growth, but also of loss. This moral and religious conception of the incorporation in Christ is implied necessarily by the life of the Apostle and by his teachings: this life in Christ requires a constant effort, stimulated by desire, sustained by an invincible hope, and yet always penetrated with fear and a humble vigilance: "Not that I have already obtained this, or already have been made perfect, but I press on hoping that I may lay hold of that for which Christ Jesus has laid hold of me" (Phil. 3:12). This experience of St. Paul, and of all Christians, does not allow us to forget that the soul which Christ has laid hold of does not lose its personality; it stays free in its choice, and it is conscious of this freedom.

[11] 1 Cor. 12:4–31; Rom. 12:3–8.
[12] Col. 2:10–14; Eph. 2:11–22; 4:4–16.

appear in the great Epistles only for the purpose of backing up a moral lesson; here, they are expounded for their own sake, the moral precept being no more than their fruit. The body is presented not only as one, but as universal; mankind is the people of God. This grand idea, developed especially in Eph. 2:11–22, is completed by the description of the immanent life and growth of the body:

One body and one Spirit, even as you were called in one hope of your calling; one Lord, one faith, one baptism; one God and Father of all, who is above all, and throughout all, and in us all. But to each one of us grace was given according to the measure of Christ's bestowal. . . . And he himself gave some men as apostles, and some as prophets, others again as evangelists, and others as pastors and teachers, in order to perfect the saints for a work of ministry, for building up the body of Christ, until we all attain to the unity of the faith and of the deep knowledge of the Son of God, to perfect manhood, to the mature measure of the fullness of Christ. And this he has done that we may be now no longer children, tossed to and fro and carried about by every wind of doctrine devised in the wickedness of men, in craftiness, according to the wiles of error. Rather are we to practise the truth in love, and so grow up in all things in him who is the head, Christ. For from him the whole body (being closely joined and knit together through every joint of the system according to the functioning in due measure of each single part) derives its increase to the building up of itself in love (Eph. 4:4–16).[13]

In this text, the theology of the Body of Christ and of its Head is proposed in its fullness; the life-giving action of the Head appears under a double aspect: Christ is the source of life which, "through every joint of the system," is poured forth into all the members and gives to each of them its growth for the building up of the whole Body; but Christ is also the Head, who gives to each of the members his special function:[14]

[13] On the progress of the Pauline theology of the body of Christ in the epistles of the Captivity, one may read A. Wikenhauser, *Die Kirche als der mystische Leib Christi nach dem Apostel Paulus,* München in Westfalen, Aschendorff, 1937, especially p. 152.

[14] In the great Epistles this specification of the members was attributed

To each of us grace was given according to the measure of Christ's bestowal. Thus it says, "Ascending on high, he led away captives; he gave gifts to men" (Eph. 4:7–8).

The comparison of these texts is revealing: Christ is at one and the same time, then, the vital principle which animates each Christian and the personal Head who assigns to each his role. Thus the study of the social role of Christ, the life of the Church, brings us back to the fundamental dogma of the divinity of Our Lord, just as the study of the individual role of Christ, the life of the Christian, had done. Under these two aspects, the theology we are studying proposes to us the same mystery: Jesus Christ is our Head and our life: if we consider Him in His humanity, He appears to us as the Head who chooses His servants and assigns to them their roles; if we reflect on His divinity, He is more intimate to us than we are to ourselves, He is the divine life which is poured forth in us, which ripens there, which is consummated there. Thus St. Paul depicts to us the action of Our Lord Jesus in his life: He is the Head who, on the road to Damascus, overthrows him and enlists him in His service; He is the Head who, throughout his career, leads him and, oftentimes, appears to him and intimates to him His orders; and He is also the inner principle of his life, He of whom it can be said, "It is now no longer I that live, but Christ lives in me" (Gal. 2:20).

In the interpretation of the doctrine of St. Paul we must respect its richness and depth. Undoubtedly, it would be much easier to see in these aspirations of the Apostle only the attraction of an ideal model, the recollection of which calls for imitation and sustains the endeavor; one might even recognize here the intervention of a superhuman being governing the life of the Apostle and guiding it. But all that is incomplete and insufficient;

either to God the Father, or especially to the Spirit; here it is to Christ that this distribution of gifts is attributed, and it is closely linked to the glorious Ascension of Our Lord: "To each one of us grace was given according to the measure of Christ's bestowal. Thus it says, 'Ascending on high, he led away captives; he gave gifts to men.'" On this rather free quotation from Psalm 67:19 and its interpretation, cf. Huby, *Saint Paul: Les Épîtres de la Captivité,* p. 199.

St. Paul, and each Christian, and the whole Church, are ruled and animated by this Head who imposes on them His will and vivifies them by His intimate action.

The doctrine of St. Paul, which we have just studied, illumines many lessons of his life and many practical instructions he gives his disciples. The Apostle and Christians live in Christ; but, at the same time, they live in a pagan world which they are endeavoring to illumine and to convert. In these contacts and in these daily endeavors the Christian life is revealed, mortified and vivified, such as the doctrine of St. Paul enables us to catch a glimpse of it.

In the Apostle there appears, above all, the striking contrast of death and life: in his Epistles, all pulsating with his sufferings and triumphs, we behold a life handed over completely to Christ, captivated and mortified by Him, and, at the same time, rich with a divine sap whose fecundity will never be equaled by any human action. To open the eyes of the Christians to this mystery, St. Paul has only to draw their attention to the contrast, humanly inexplicable, between a life men hold in contempt and the fruits of salvation which it produces.

In the two Epistles to the Corinthians, these great lessons are proposed to us:

I think God has set forth us the apostles last of all, as men doomed to death, seeing that we have been made a spectacle to the world, and to angels, and to men. We are fools for Christ, but you are wise in Christ! We are weak, but you are strong! You are honored, but we are without honor! To this very hour we hunger and thirst, and we are naked and buffeted, and have no fixed abode. And we toil, working with our own hands. We are reviled and we bless, we are persecuted and we bear with it, we are maligned and we entreat, we have become as the refuse of this world, the offscouring of all, even until now! (1 Cor. 4:9–13).

And in the subsequent letter, the Apostle takes up the same theme and unveils its mystery more intimately:

We carry this treasure in vessels of clay, to show that the abundance of the power is God's and not ours. In all things we suffer tribulation, but we are not distressed; we are sore pressed, but we are not destitute; we endure persecution, but we are not forsaken; we are cast down, but we do not perish; always bearing about in our body the dying of Jesus, so that the life also of Jesus may be made manifest in our bodily frame. For we the living are constantly being handed over to death for Jesus' sake, that the life also of Jesus may be made manifest in our mortal flesh. Thus death is at work in us, but life in you (2 Cor. 4:7–12).

To anyone considering it from the outside, this life of continual mortification and humiliation appears despicable. But to the one experiencing it, it reveals itself as divine: the Apostle admires in it a fatherly Providence which does not allow temptation to exceed our strength.[15] "It is an existence in which we live while dying, where the forces which come to life replace those which are spent, where an invisible hand lightens the burden at the moment when it threatens to become overwhelming, where the heavenly gleam of hope pierces through the clouds darkening the soul, where God is close by when friends are hidden and enemies advance. Behold what one might call the life of Jesus . . . It is this serenity of spirit, this steadfastness of character, this energy of will, which triumphs by its very resignation, and which the Master pours out abundantly, like an inexhaustible sap, into the body of the disciple, into this earthen vessel, so that his mortal flesh, this weak, fragile instrument, can still continue to do its duty." [16]

A still more decisive sign of the action of Christ in His Apostle is the fruitfulness of these trials: "Death is at work in us, but life in you." This is what Jesus Himself has taught His Apostle: "My grace is sufficient for thee, for strength is made perfect in weakness" (2 Cor. 12:9); and St. Paul echoes the words of the Master: "Gladly therefore I will glory in my infirmities, that the strength of Christ may dwell in me. Wherefore I am satisfied, for Christ's sake, with infirmities, with insults, with

[15] Cf. 1 Cor. 10:13: "God is faithful and will not permit you to be tempted beyond your strength."

[16] E. Reuss, *Les Épîtres pauliniennes,* I, p. 311, on 2 Cor. 4:7–15.

hardships, with persecutions, with distresses. For when I am weak, then I am strong" (*ibid.,* 9–10).

This teaching, so dear to St. Paul, relies on a Jewish and, above all, prophetic tradition: God is jealous of His strength and glory, He denies them to human instruments too sure of themselves; He wills that he "who takes pride, take pride in the Lord." [17] But, seeing His Son in the world, God gave to this providential law a new guarantee and a universal bearing: He made of it the fundamental law of redemption:

The foolish things of the world has God chosen to put to shame the wise, and the weak things of the world has God chosen to put to shame the strong, and the base things of the world and the despised has God chosen, and the things that are not, to bring to naught the things that are; lest any flesh should pride itself before him. From him you are in Christ Jesus, who has become for us God-given wisdom, and justice, and sanctification, and redemption; so that, just as it is written, "Let him who takes pride, take pride in the Lord" (1 Cor. 1:27–31).

This law of the Incarnation is imposed on all Christ's members, because the Head has made of it His law. The Son of God, by becoming man, was reduced to nothing, veiling the divine majesty underneath the infirmity of human flesh and, for that flesh itself, choosing the most despicable conditions of life, the poorest and the most cruel. This is the example which St. Paul never tires of putting before the eyes of his disciples: what he recalls to them is less the detail of the words and actions of Jesus as that incomparable splendor, that piercing, gentle brightness of the Son of God, who lowered Himself to us, who lived amongst us, who suffered for us and who now lives in us.[18]

This divine lesson is proposed to us, above all, in the Epistle to the Philippians: wishing to exhort his beloved disciples to humility and to mutual respect, St. Paul says to them:

[17] Jer. 9:24, quoted by St. Paul in 1 Cor. 1:31.
[18] Father Pinard de la Boullaye, S.J., studying the *Imitation de Jésus-Christ* (*Revue d'Ascétique et de Mystique,* 1934, p. 339), has rightly emphasized this point.

Have this mind in you which was also in Christ Jesus, who though he was by nature God, did not consider being equal to God a thing to be clung to, but emptied himself, taking the nature of a slave and being made like unto men. And appearing in the form of man, he humbled himself, becoming obedient to death, even to death on a cross. Therefore God also has exalted him and has bestowed upon him the name that is above every name, so that at the name of Jesus every knee should bend of those in heaven, on earth and under the earth, and every tongue should confess that the Lord Jesus Christ is in the glory of God the Father (Phil. 2:5–11).

The Incarnation has been an emptying through love; it has been also an impoverishment. Thus, in order to urge the Corinthians to give alms to the poor of Jerusalem, the Apostle says to them:

May you excel in this gracious work also . . . For you know the graciousness of our Lord Jesus Christ—how, being rich, he became poor for your sakes, that by his poverty you might become rich (2 Cor. 8:7–9).

In this text, as in the preceding one, we recognize the habitual object of St. Paul's contemplation: it is the Son of God at the decisive moment when He becomes incarnate and when He has imprinted on His human life or, more accurately, on the whole of human life, the sole orientation which henceforth may be fruitful.

The whole endeavor of the Christian will aim at being penetrated with this life: renouncing every personal gain in which he has until now taken pleasure, he will have no other ambition but "to gain Christ" (Phil. 3:8). This desire rules the life of the Apostle more and more and animates all his Epistles. No text reveals this better than the confidences of St. Paul to the Christians of Philippi; writing to his most devoted disciples, the prisoner of Christ reminds them of his past and of all the sacrifices he has made in order to possess Christ:

If anyone else thinks he may have confidence in the flesh, yet more may I: circumcised the eighth day, of the race of Israel, of the tribe of Benjamin, a Hebrew of Hebrews; as regards the Law, a Pharisee; as regards zeal, a persecutor of the Church of God; as regards the justice of the Law, leading a blameless life. But the things that were gain to me, these for the sake of Christ, I have counted loss. Nay more, I count everything loss because of the excelling knowledge of Jesus Christ, my Lord. For his sake I have suffered the loss of all things, and I count them as dung that I may gain Christ and be found in him, not having a justice of my own, which is from the Law, but that which is from faith in Christ, the justice from God based upon faith; so that I may know him and the power of his resurrection and the fellowship of his sufferings: become like to him in death, in the hope that somehow I may attain to the resurrection from the dead. Not that I have already obtained this, or already have been made perfect, but I press on hoping that I may lay hold of that for which Christ Jesus has laid hold of me. Brethren, I do not consider that I have laid hold of it already. But one thing I do: forgetting what is behind, I strain forward to what is before, I press on towards the goal, to the prize of God's heavenly call in Christ Jesus (Phil. 3:4–14).

This text, more deeply perhaps than any other, causes to be heard the call of life: to possess Christ, we must give up not only the goods of fortune, houses or fields, or even the dearest family relationships, brothers, sisters, mother, father, children, whose sacrifice Jesus asked of His apostles (Mk. 10:29); we must give up every personal gain of race, birth, and education, whose advantages the Pharisee loved to flaunt in the face of men, and even in the face of God. The sole ambition worthy of us is to gain Christ, and no carnal gain can raise us there; so divine a gift will always be infinitely above our natural grasp. The Precursor already said this to the Jews: "Do not think to say within yourselves, 'We have Abraham for our father'; for I say to you that God is able out of these stones to raise up children to Abraham" (Mt. 3:9; Lk. 3:8). God allows Himself to be grasped only because He gives Himself in His Son, whom He has handed over for our sakes to death, whom He reveals to us, towards whom He draws us, by whom He vivifies us and resuscitates us.

epilogue

❖❖❖❖❖❖❖❖❖

The Personal and the Social Life of the Christian in the Church, the Body of Christ

In the course of these studies, we have reread devoutly, attentively, the teachings of Our Lord and of His apostles. In the transparency of all these revelations, we have seen forming, bit by bit, under its manifold aspects, the divine and human ideal of a life surpassing our natural powers, but which alone fills our desires to overflowing and which alone responds to the countless benefits which God has bestowed on us through the Incarnation of His Son and through His redemptive death. In conclusion, I should like to consider, in this life which God offers us, the profound unity of the two ideal perfections which, in our short human experience, often enter into conflict: the personal life of the Christian and his social life.

The Son of God came down on earth to give His life for the world (Jn. 6:33): He offers it to each of us, He offers it to mankind in its entirety. And this life that He wills to give us is in the image of the divine life: it is for each a superabundant life (Jn. 10:10); it is for all a social life as closely united as the prayer of Jesus can accomplish: "That they may be one even as we are" (Jn. 17:11). Undoubtedly, this ideal model will never be adequately reproduced, but it will be the goal towards which the entire endeavor of Christians swept along by the grace of God will tend; it is by their incorporation in Christ that they will be able effectively to tend towards it.

At first sight, these two finalities, individual and social, seem opposed to each other: in our human outlook it seems to us impossible to tend always towards the good of the community without sacrificing ourselves at times for it, and without that sacrifice's diminishing our very selves. Thus it is, for example, that a son will sacrifice himself for the joy and the well-being of his parents, forgoing for their sakes the requirements of his career, a more complete but lengthier and more burdensome formation, which would assure him a more brilliant future, unwilling to leave his country, even temporarily, so that he might prolong their joy in his presence. These sacrifices might be morally absolutely necessary or simply reasonable or even unjustifiable; but he who accepts them is aware that he is, indeed, sacrificing himself and that, to be more fully a son, he will be a little less himself.

In the life of the Christian, it will not be thus: every sacrifice conceded to the social life will develop at the same time the personal life. To understand this, it is sufficient to recall the principle and the end of our Christian life: its principle is the Head, its end is the good of the Body; the members concur in it by the life they receive from the Head and which they pour out over the entire Body.

All appears to us in this powerful synthesis—the personal sanctity which each one of us ought to realize, the radiating influence he must exercise in the Church, the sanctity of the entire Body, which, thanks to the efforts of each of the members, grows and builds up in charity. All this, indeed, is one: there is no effective activity without sanctity; there is no sanctity which does not radiate in the Church; there is no grace which does not come from the Head, and there is none which does not flow from the member back over the entire Body.

If we shall consider individually each member, we see him laden with all the treasures of God:

Mine are the heavens and mine is the earth; mine are the people, the righteous are mine and mine are the sinners; the angels are mine and the Mother of God, and all things are mine; and God Himself is mine and for me, for Christ is mine and all for me.[1]

Tua mea sunt, O Domine Jesu! et mea omnia tua sunt. Alas! I ought really to say to Thee: *Tua mea sunt.* For it is only too true for the interest of Thy glory and Thy grandeur: Thy spirit belongs to me, and Thou givest it to me at baptism; Thy body is mine and Thou givest it to me in the Eucharist: Thy glory is mine and Thou givest it to me in Thy Paradise; Thy grandeur is mine and on earth it lowers itself in my miseries; Thy life is mine, and on the Cross I reduce it to death![2]

But all these treasures belong to him only in the measure that he himself has been given to Christ: "All are yours, and you are Christ's and Christ is God's" (1 Cor. 3:22–23). And, by being given to Christ, the Christian is given to all the members of Christ; he belongs to all and all belong to him. In this way there is applied to every Christian the law which God first applied to His divine Son on the day of the Incarnation: He is given to all, and all men are given to Him. It is the same with every Christian: "Having nothing, yet possessing all things" (2 Cor. 6:10). "None of us lives to himself, and none dies to himself; for if we live, we live to the Lord, or if we die, we die to the Lord. Therefore, whether we live or die, we are the Lord's" (Rom. 14:7–8). And this mutual gift defines our relations not only with Christ but with all His members. All the gifts which we receive from our Head, not only the gifts of exterior action, but the gifts of personal sanctification, of prayer, of contemplation, are given to us only for the building up of the Body of Christ: if we wish to enjoy them selfishly, we lose them; if we cast them into

[1] St. John of the Cross, *Avis,* pp. 190–192.
[2] Bérulle, *Grandeurs de Jésus, Discours,* IX, ed. Bourgoing, p. 319.

the common treasury, like the mite which the widow dropped into the Temple treasury, we save them for eternity.

And this is even better understood if one considers the particular vocation of each one. Apostle, prophet, evangelist, pastor, teacher—all those functions which the Head distributes to each of His members, not only sanctify him on whom they are conferred, but all tend, under various forms, to the sanctification of the Body as a whole. The more each of these organs is united to the Head, the more living, the more active it will be. If it wishes to fulfill its role worthily, it must first of all ensure the integrity of its health and of its life. The hand is not a stick; it can obey the head and serve the body only in the measure that it is living and flexible; if it becomes stiff, it will be good only for being carried in a sling. Here one can only repeat the urgent exhortation of St. Augustine:

He who wishes to live, knows where he can live, knows whence he can live. Let him draw near, let him believe, let him be incorporated in order to be vivified. Let him not destroy the harmonious union of the members, let him not be a decayed member, which must be amputated, nor a deformed member, of which one is ashamed. Let him be handsome, fit, healthy; let him cleave to the body, let him live for God, from God; let him work now on earth so as to reign later in heaven (*In Joann. P.L.,* XXXV, 1613).

We were saying a while ago that a member of Christ who wills to isolate himself, so as to develop his personal life, atrophies. We should add that a member of Christ who neglects his personal sanctity in order to intensify his activity, paralyzes it. There is for us no individual salvation, independent of the Body; but neither is there any fruitful activity for us without intimate union with Christ, the source, at one and the same time, of all sanctity and of all activity. We grasp, evidently, the inseparable union of these two tendencies which seem opposed: all for the social good of the Body, all for the personal development of each member; and here we recognize the fatherly will of God: it asks of us the total gift of ourselves, but at that price it guarantees to us the full blossoming of our lives. The God who has said to us, "That all may be one," is also He who has said, "All souls are mine." We are not a mass of men, but a body; we are not tools, but living members.

In the play of purely human activities, we can recognize some vestige of this divine plan, but it is barely an outline of it. Whoever devotes himself loyally and gladly to his profession, serves his country usefully: his work as farmer, craftsman, writer, professor or intellectual, is, at the same time, a good work as a citizen; but we will not say to him: You will be a better farmer, a better writer, in the measure that you are a better citizen. These two activities can rely on each other; but neither of them attains the very sources of life. By no means, then, do they depend necessarily on each other for the fruitfulness of their activity.

Here it is quite different: apostle, pastor, teacher, you will fulfill better your role in the measure that you are a better Christian. And if you let Christianity waste away in you, all your activity becomes fruitless: "Without me you can do nothing" (Jn. 15:5); you are no more than a tinkling cymbal (1 Cor. 13:1). Our activity is fed at the source of our Christian life, in our union with the Head. Other human activities utilize man and develop him; they do not grasp him in his entirety. Christ's work, on the contrary, can be fecundated only by Christ's life which at the same time transforms man. And, on the other hand, this life transforms man only in view of his activity in the Body of Christ: "Woe to me if I do not preach the gospel!" (1 Cor. 9:16). The edifice as a whole appears to us like a well-constructed arch: the thrust which it supports does not loosen it, but rather tightens it.

This remarkable conception was outlined already in the human family: the spouses are for each other; the parents for the children; then, as life advances, the children, after having been their hope and joy, become in turn their support. But here, the personal life tends to disengage them from the family setting; new homes are built; man leaves his father and mother to become attached to a woman; and even if he does not separate himself from his birthplace by new ties, he feels the bonds which sustained his childhood being loosened bit by bit. The close unity will have lasted as long as the rearing; the rearing does not last as long as life. For the Christian, it is not the same: until death he must tend towards "perfect manhood, to the mature measure of the fullness of Christ" (Eph. 4:13), and he can tend towards this effectively only in the Church: "My dear children, with whom I am in labor again, until Christ is formed in you!" (Gal. 4:19). Thus there is continued until death his personal growth and his social activity, both fed by the life-giving waters which flow from the breast of Christ.

If we wish to find, not deficient images, but the ideal model of this unity of life in the distinction of persons, we must gaze at the Holy Trinity: "That they may be one even as we are" (Jn. 17:11, 22). In God we see only one nature, one activity; and yet we confess the real distinction of Persons: Father, Son and Holy Spirit. The Persons are distinguished by their mutual relations, the Father begetting the Son, the Son receiving all from the Father, the Father and Son embracing each other in that mutual love which is the Holy Spirit. And these relations are by no means, as in human families, the origin of lives which will become, then, independent and develop in isolation. The divine eternity knows not this evolution, any more than the divine unity knows these separations: the generation of the Son and the procession of the Holy Spirit fill eternity.

In man, whose life is successive, perfection would not know how to be an eternal state; it is the ideal term of our whole existence. But, because this term cannot be attained here below, our life in its entirety tends towards it. It is not, as in the maturing of our physical life, a state we arrive at and go beyond; and, consequently, all the forces which are directed thereto continue, during the whole course of our lives, to carry us along. Until the end we must keep saying with St. Paul, "Not that I have already obtained this, or already have been made perfect, but I press on hoping that I may lay hold of that for which Christ Jesus has laid hold of me" (Phil. 3:12). As soon as we have been taken hold of by Christ, our life is raised by that yearning; the more faithful we are to it, the stronger it is. It is not a housing development whose different units we can erect as the money becomes available; it is a race we cannot give up without losing all; it is a mountain climb where we can find a rest station for a few hours' halt, but not a house where we can take up residence.

Our apostolic activity is sustained by the same force as our life: it is the attraction of Christ which continually repeats to us, *Sequere me!* He is in front of us as the goal we pursue; He is within us as the force drawing us along; He is also continually present to our memory as the Model we imitate. We see Him, the whole length of His mortal life, borne along towards the Father in an irresistible movement of His divine nature: *Quae placita sunt ei, facio semper* (Jn. 8:29). And we, His members, cannot be united to Him without being vivified by His life: *Vivo, jam non ego, vivit vero in me Christus* (Gal. 2:20). The member can have no other life than that of the Head. At the start, this life is not fully revealed to us; but the more intimate our union is with the Son of God, the more powerful is His action, and it tends to become irresistible: "As the living Father has sent me, and as I live because of the Father, so he who eats me, he also shall live because of me" (Jn. 6:58).

Here we attain the most profound aspect of this unfathomable mystery: we cannot understand the Body of Christ without understanding Christ Himself; and we cannot understand Christ except as wholly and completely orientated towards the Father. Thus this immense human family, scattered for so long a time like lost sheep, broken for so long a time into factions which rise up and confront each other, has found in Christ, its Head, the unity it dreams of. And this unity is not enclosed within itself; it is lifted up by the Son towards God, its Creator and Father, in order to be engulfed in Him. "I in them and thou in me; that they may be perfected in unity" (Jn. 17:23).

St. Paul, after expounding to the Corinthians the dogma of the Resurrection, continues with his vision of the last days up to the definitive establishment of the Kingdom of God. He describes it as follows:

As in Adam all die, so in Christ all will be made to live. But each in his own turn, Christ as first-fruits, then they who are Christ's, who have believed, at his coming. Then comes the end, when he delivers the kingdom to God the Father, when he does away with all sovereignty, authority and power. For he must reign, until "he has put all his enemies under his feet." And the last enemy to be destroyed will be death, for "he has put all things under his feet." But when he says all things are subject to him, undoubtedly he is excepted who has subjected all things to him. And when all things are made subject to him, then the Son himself will also be made subject to him, who subjected all things to him, that God may be all in all (1 Cor. 15:22–28).

God all in all—this is the final end; but it will not happen like a catastrophe falling on men and crushing them under its weight; it is the goal of the whole endeavor of the grace of Christ. In Jesus it is the yearning which continually impels Him: "I came forth from the Father and have come into the world. Again I leave the world and go to the Father" (Jn. 16:28), He said to His apostles; and in His supreme prayer: "I am no longer in the world, but these are in the world, and I am coming to thee . . . While I was with them, I kept them in thy name . . . Now I am coming to thee; and these things I speak in the world, in order that they may have my joy made full in themselves" (Jn. 17: 11–13).

The Head precedes the members, He goes to prepare a place for them; He does not abandon them: His call is more impelling ever since He has gone back to the Father. St. Ignatius of Antioch will soon write of it: "Nothing that is seen is good. Our God Jesus Christ certainly is the more clearly seen now that He is in the Father." [3] Hearing in the depths of his heart this continual call of his Head, the martyr is impatient to rejoin Him: "Him I seek who died for us; Him I love who rose again because of us. The birth pangs are upon me. Forgive me, brethren; do not obstruct my coming to life—do not wish me to die; do not make a gift to the world of one who wants to be God's. Beware of seduc-

[3] *To the Romans,* 3, in ACW 1, p. 81.

ing me with matter; suffer me to receive pure light. Once arrived there I shall be a man. Permit me to be an imitator of my suffering God." [4] But this voice of the supreme Head draws the saint still higher, beyond that holy humanity, up to the Father whither he tends: "There is in me a *Living Water,* which is eloquent and within me says, 'Come to the Father.' " [5] This living water is that which Jesus once promised to all those who would believe in Him: "If anyone thirst, let him come to me and drink. He who believes in me, as the Scripture says, 'From within him there shall flow rivers of living water' " (Jn. 7:37–38).

This grace is promised to all the faithful; all have received at baptism the Spirit of adoption; in all of them the Spirit causes to rise up towards the Father these prayers, these ineffable groanings: "Abba, Father" (Rom. 8:15). Here is the deepest principle of the unity of the Body of Christ; thereby the Christian is truly the brother of Jesus: "Whoever does the will of God, he is my brother and sister and mother" (Mk. 3:35); thereby he enters this divine family whose embrace will grow closer from day to day, if he is faithful. Surely this will by no means be the abolishment of his personal life, but, quite the contrary, that unexpected enrichment of a soul whom a boundless love dilates and fills. Here below Christ all in all; in heaven, for eternity, God all in all (Col. 3:11; 1 Cor. 15:28).

[4] *Ibid.,* 6; p. 83.
[5] *Ibid.,* 7; p. 83.